In Memoriam

CORNELIUS WALWORTH MIDDLETON
1893-1966

**Effective Advocate
Generous Benefactor
of Education**

Trustee

VIRGINIA FOUNDATION
FOR INDEPENDENT COLLEGES

1959-1966

Third Edition

OF THE
AMERICAN PEOPLE

Charles O. Lerche

Third Edition

FOREIGN POLICY OF THE AMERICAN PEOPLE
by Charles O. Lerche

© 1958, 1961, 1967 by Prentice-Hall, Inc.
Englewood Cliffs, New Jersey

All rights reserved. No part of this book may be reproduced in any form or by any means without permission in writing from the publisher.

Current printing (last digit):
10 9 8 7 6 5 4 3 2 1

PRENTICE-HALL INTERNATIONAL, INC., *London*
PRENTICE-HALL OF AUSTRALIA, PTY. LTD., *Sydney*
PRENTICE-HALL OF CANADA, LTD., *Toronto*
PRENTICE-HALL OF INDIA (PRIVATE) LTD., *New Delhi*
PRENTICE-HALL OF JAPAN, INC., *Tokyo*

Library of Congress Catalog Card No.: 67-10018

Printed in the United States of America

C

E
744
.L49
1967

TO MARGARET AND HERKY

106916

EMORY AND HENRY LIBRARY

The death of Charles O. Lerche in August 1966 was a great loss to his family, friends, and colleagues. Those who shared a little of each of these relationships with him, and thereby enjoyed the benefit of his articulate intelligence, most clearly recognize this loss. In behalf of the late Charles O. Lerche, I would like to thank Messrs. Lee S. Houchins, William F. Ahlstrom, Richard Fraenkel, and especially Abdul A. Said, for their devoted work in the final stages of the production of this book. It is our hope that this book will be a living testament to Charles O. Lerche as a scholar, teacher, and precise realist.

—Editor

Foreword

When his untimely death occurred late in the summer of 1966, Dean Lerche was about to complete the final reading of page proofs for the third edition of his highly regarded and widely used text, *Foreign Policy of the American People.*

The three editions of this excellent work encompass a decade in which momentous changes in the world position of the United States have taken place. It is a tribute to the keenness of insight of Dean Lerche that he was alert to these sometimes subtle developments as they were emerging, understood their significance long before some of his contemporaries did, and cogently explained them in this and his other writings in ways which have stood the dual tests of time and more recent analyses. This is why each new edition has a freshness all its own while retaining the essential viewpoint and methodology of the first.

In choosing the title of this book, Dean Lerche endeavored to emphasize the crucial place of the people in the process of determining the broad course of policy in a democracy during periods of crisis, but at the same time carefully defined why limitations are necessarily imposed upon public opinion in the conduct of diplomacy itself. This sense of balance between philosophical ideals and analytical reality manifests itself over and over again in these authoritative pages, as in the treatment of the United Nations with its hopes and its frustrations, as in the carefully reasoned explanation of the genuineness of American moral intention in extending foreign aid along with a sobering interpretation of its equally genuine grounding in pursuit of the national interest, and as in the appreciation of truth aligned against the distortions of propaganda at the heart of American information programs even as they have sometimes fallen short of these standards in the clash of national and ideological wills.

It has been said that a first-class textbook is one which starts with fundamentals and never forgets them. This is true of *Foreign Policy of the American People,* even in those sections which treat the most complex and difficult aspects of contemporary policy and prospective issues facing decision-makers. The fields of government and international relations overlap and merge in foreign policy analysis, and Dean Lerche never overlooked the basic principles of the one in his treatment of the other. This is the area in which the study of world problems becomes practical for the citizen as well as for the policy-maker, and it is for this reason that the analysis set forth by the head of the School of International Service is timely without being in any way transitory, lasting in value without being passé, and stimulating without being merely journalistic.

During the many lively conversations it was my pleasure to have with Charles Lerche at sessions of the Washington Institute of Foreign Affairs, two of his personal and professional qualities were most striking and most consistent. One was the seriousness of his concern for the purpose and direction his country had chosen in its foreign relations, and the other was the sheer enjoyment and satisfaction he had in pursuing his own scholarly and civic interest in this exciting field. Thus in a very real sense he at once exemplified both the privilege and the responsibility of one who believes that democratic foreign policy, with all its serious limitations and shortcomings, is a challenge worth accepting. His last book will help to make it a living reality for many students beyond his own time.

WILLIAM C. OLSON
Associate Dean
School of International Affairs
Columbia University

Preface

A decade ago, when the first edition of this book was in the planning stage, the author decided to base his analysis of the foreign policy of the United States upon the concept of the "American people" and to attempt to examine the responses of the mass democracy of the United States to the challenges of an unstable world environment. Now, two editions and countless crises later, he remains as persuaded as ever of the utility and the academic validity of this device. This edition, no less than its predecessors, seeks to analyze the interplay of the democratic process with the demands of a global foreign policy.

Otherwise, the book is considerably briefer in this edition, as the passage of longer spans of time has permitted more of an over-view of problems. One major difference in emphasis may be noted: Although the Soviet-American confrontation continues—as it must—to figure largely in the account, what might be termed the "expansion of the agenda" of American foreign policy has brought about something of a broader scope of consideration. The Sino-Soviet split, the erosion of the bipolar world, the rise of de Gaulle's France, the continuing instability and criticality of the non-Western world, and the ubiquity of scientific and technological questions receive at least a part of what the author feels is their contemporary due.

As the third edition was being prepared, the author was impressed—and, to a considerable degree, disconcerted—with how many of the analyses, criticisms, estimates, and recommendations he originally formulated in the mid-1950's remain (at least in his judgment) valid today. This is not to suggest a prescience or an insight beyond ordinary mortals on the part of the author, but rather that the problems of foreign policy have proved as intractable to the best efforts of the American government and the American people as was suspected a decade ago.

The author extends his profound gratitude to his many colleagues in colleges and universities in many parts of the United States for their generous and helpful comments, criticism, and suggestions during the life of this book. The fact that there is a third edition at all is due more to them than to any other factor.

In the preparation of this edition, the author is indebted to several of his graduate assistants, but especially to William F. Ahlstrom. His editorial skill and impeccable academic judgment have improved this volume in countless ways.

As usual, however, the author assumes full responsibility for all that follows.

C.O.L.

Washington, D.C., 1966

Contents

4

*The American Tradition
of Foreign Policy 106*

5

*American National
Interests 124*

PART FOUR

*CONTINUING ISSUES
IN AMERICAN POLICY
221*

9

*Continuing Political Issues
in American Policy 223*

10

*Continuing Military Issues
in American Policy 248*

PART 1

A CONCEPTUAL FRAMEWORK

CHAPTER 1

What Is Foreign Policy?

It is one of the truisms of political science that every state has a foreign policy. Each sovereign political unit, existing as it does in a world that contains approximately 120 other states, cannot escape having some kind of relations with them; common sense would seem to dictate that these relations should, if possible, be ordered and governed by some more or less rational plan. Foreign affairs, always one of the major fields of government action, has grown in importance under the conditions of modern technology so that today it is the principal concern of many states and is of primary significance to all.

Our major interest in this book will be the foreign policy conducted by the government of the United States in the name of the American people. We shall devote the bulk of our attention to a consideration of the ways in which government and people meet and attempt to solve the peculiar problems of international relations that fall to them. We shall be making our examination in terms of an analytical device that we may call our "conceptual scheme." We shall develop a number of general concepts and will then suggest some relationships among them. This will permit us to view our subject as more of a whole than it sometimes appears to be and will also provide a number of insights into both the strength and the weaknesses of American foreign policy. In this opening chapter, therefore, we shall attempt to lay most of these preliminary foundations.

The Concept of "Foreign Policy"

In this book, by "foreign policy" we mean the courses of action and the decisions relating to them that a state undertakes in its relations with other states in order to attain national objectives and to advance the national interest.[1] Such a definition contains several terms that themselves require definition, and it obviously stands in need of further analysis and refinement. We shall devote ourselves to this task in this chapter. This definition, as expanded, will incorporate the system by which we shall analyze American policy.

THE NATURE OF FOREIGN POLICY

Foreign policy, as an area of government action, shares many of the characteristics of any public policy; many of the generalizations about the conduct of public affairs developed by political scientists and other students of government are applicable to the study of the foreign relations of any state. We shall not attempt to enumerate these here nor to isolate the features that make the formulation and execution of foreign policy different from other forms of state action. Instead, in this chapter we shall discuss some of the considerations fundamental to an understanding of our subject without direct concern for their relevance to other problems of government.

THE COMPONENTS OF "POLICY." Foreign policy, as we analyze it here, has three major components. In the order of their appearance in the policy process, they are: (1) the state's criteria of judgment and evaluation, usually summed up in the phrase, "national interest": (2) the situational factors impinging on the state; and (3) the action taken by the state in the particular situation. Although the possible action patterns states may follow are so numerous that their classification and description fall outside our purpose in this book,[2] an analysis of the first two notions is necessary to our analytical method. In a moment we shall attempt to clarify both the notion of national interest and the typology of situational factors; later in the chapter we shall examine both subjects in some greater detail.

FOREIGN POLICY AS PROCESS. Before proceeding, however, we should emphasize that foreign policy is conceived here as a social and political

---

[1]For a more detailed analysis of the concept from a different but related point of view, see Charles O. Lerche, Jr. and Abdul A. Said, *Concepts of International Politics* (Englewood Cliffs, N.J.: Prentice-Hall, Inc., 1963), Chapter 1: "The Nature of Foreign Policy."

[2]For an analysis of patterns of state interaction, see Lerche and Said, *Concepts of International Politics*, Part II: "The Political System: States and Their Relations."

process. It is an on-going affair, not one that may be seized and studied in all its ramifications at a particular moment in time. Dynamism is the keynote of all international relationships, and our analysis should be so oriented as to take account of unceasing evolution and change. Only by devising techniques that encompass the notion of process can we develop a picture of foreign policy that is at all relevant to reality.

Of what does the foreign-policy process consist? If we define "process" as action consisting of a series of steps each of which leads to the next and all aimed at a predetermined end, we may put the matter this way: The foreign-policy process consists of the repeated application of a set of relatively constant criteria to an infinitely variable pattern of situational factors, and the subsequent adjustment of state action in response to the conclusions reached from such application. We can list the steps of the process as follows: (1) the establishment of the criteria; (2) the determination of the relevant variables in the situation: (3) the measurement of the variables by the criteria; (4) the selection of a goal; (5) the elaboration of a strategy to reach the goal; (6) the decision to act; (7) the action itself; and (8) the evaluation of the results of the action in terms of the original criteria.

We may further postulate that this process, since it goes on within every state and since all states function within a dynamic system, is for analytical purposes deemed to be unending. The criteria, as we shall see in a moment, tend to be less constant in practice than in theory; the ends of state action themselves are notoriously prone to revision in response to stimuli both rational and irrational; the system itself usually operates so as to frustrate the ultimate purposes of states. Though we can possibly conceive of an international order in which what we are calling "foreign policy" would no longer be present, the actual world in which we live is one in which the process not only goes on constantly but also shows no sign of diminishing either in importance or in complexity.

THE NOTION OF NATIONAL INTEREST.   National interest is the prime criterion (or criteria) in terms of which a state judges situational factors, determines the relative priorities to be given to different goals, establishes and evaluates courses of action, and makes decisions. It is the closest approximation to a fixed factor the policy process affords, but the nature of its components, its lack of absolute specificity, and the variety in the techniques by which it is formulated debar it from postulation as a true constant. Its rate of evolution and change, however, is much slower than is the case of the other raw materials of policy, and its role as the significant criterion gives such consistency as may be present in any foreign policy.

In most states, and certainly in the United States, national interest as a generalized concern arises from two sources. The first (and less specific) is what we call the "myth" of national purpose in international affairs: those mass-shared values in foreign policy whose maximization by government is demanded by a broad consensus. The ego-image a national group has of itself as it views the world cannot help but be basic to the specific foreign-policy steps it takes. The second source of national interest is the group of practitioners of foreign policy (the "decision-makers") themselves. Though forming part of the mass we call the nation and, as such, themselves partakers in the national myth, their insights, experience, and collective responsibility for action—as well as their peculiar bureaucratic point of view—often lead them to conceive the national interest differently than does the mass and to apply somewhat different criteria to its formulation. Occasionally such varying views of long-range public purpose are the cause of serious internal conflict.

CATEGORIES OF SITUATIONAL FACTORS. Situational factors that influence policy are infinite in both number and variety, but here we may subsume them under three general heads: (1) the international milieu in which the state is operating; (2) the specific actions taken by other states to which responses of one sort or another are appropriate; and (3) the state's own capabilities for action. Elements from each of these categories interact to create the situation to which the criterion of national interest is applied.

OBJECTIVES AND COURSES OF ACTION. When the national interest is applied to a situation that calls for decision and action, the outcome is the selection of an objective: a reasonably clearly defined state of affairs the accomplishment of which the decision-makers feel would be advantageous, at least under the controlling conditions. An objective is a target of state action: a goal the state wishes to reach. Its justification is the net gain to the state that its achievement would either bring about or make possible. The selection of an objective is followed by the development of a strategy to reach the goal and the subsequent execution of that plan; this last step is the purer (or at least narrower) referent to the term "policy."

THE "CHAIN" OF POLICY. We have now reached the point in this highly generalized survey of the concept of foreign policy at which we may suggest some causal relationship among the various steps. We can conveniently put this in the form of a "chain reaction."

Step 1. Popular traditions and official points of view, applied to (relatively long-range and fixed) conditions, interact to produce a formula of national interest.

Step 2. A formulation of national interest, applied to (middle-range and evolving) conditions, results in the selection of precise objectives.

Step 3. An objective, analyzed in terms of (short-range and immediate) conditions, leads to the selection of a course of action (a policy).

The energizing factor that moves the reaction from step to step is, of course, the varying impact of the situational factors impinging on the state. Foreign policy does not just happen; the state's decision to act is always the result of some change in the situation—internal or external—with which it is faced. Since we have agreed that the situational elements of international politics are in constant flux, it would be logical for us to conclude, as we suggested above, that the foreign-policy process is constantly operative, each step leading to the next and each new situational change touching off a new chain reaction of adjustment.

FOREIGN POLICY AND THE STATE SYSTEM

Although in our study we shall be interested primarily in the purposes and actions of one state—the United States—we shall be reminded at every turn that its foreign policy must be planned and executed within the confines of the state system. In many ways and at all times the requirements of the system affect the behavior of any of its members, and success most frequently comes to those states that best fit their policy into the peculiar demands of the society of which they are a part.

Although no purpose would be served by reviewing here a detailed theory of international politics, a summary of some fundamentals might throw a little light on our subsequent discussions. We shall briefly examine three notions: (1) the state's freedom of choice; (2) the channels of state action; and (3) the limiting controls on such action.

THE STATE'S FREEDOM OF CHOICE. The mystique of sovereignty confers one important area of freedom on all members of the state system: the freedom to choose. No external force can rightfully dictate to a state what its national interest should be; each state, in terms of its internal processes and dynamic, reaches and ratifies its own version of what is best for it. Each state is similarly free to make such situational analyses as suit its concerns and to select such objectives as it wishes. And finally, each state may adopt such policies as it sees fit, using such combination of techniques as to it seems expedient and wise. Interest, objectives, and policy are all—from the state's point of view—egocentric; each member of the state system may choose any policy at all and owe responsibility for its decision to no one outside itself. The basic motivations of foreign policy are therefore to be found within the state.[3]

THE CHANNELS OF STATE ACTION. State action in pursuit of an objective may assume any of a great variety of forms. Modern technology has added greatly to the supply of foreign-policy techniques available to the statesman. Despite their increased number, however, they all fall into one of the four traditional categories of tools and techniques, the four channels of state action. These four are: political action, through the mechanisms of diplomatic representation; economic action, through the productive and distributive system of the state; psychological action, through the techniques of mass

---

[3]One of the early developments of this point among American scholars was by Nicholas J. Spykman in *America's Strategy in World Politics* (New York: Harcourt, Brace & World, Inc., 1942), Chapter 1: "Power Politics and War."

persuasion; and military action, through armed force. From among these four types, a statesman chooses in such combination as seems to him to be best suited to the particular purpose he has in mind.[4]

THE LIMITS ON STATE ACTION.   There are both formal and informal limits on the possible action any state might take in pursuit of an objective. Their combined effect is largely to inhibit the state's real freedom.

The formal limits may be summed up as international law and international organization. International law incorporates a body of rules prescribing acceptable state conduct in a broad variety of situations. Although the system is incomplete and of uncertain enforcement, all states recognize its existence and admit it to be—to a substantial if imprecise extent—a limiting factor. International organization—most clearly epitomized in its major contemporary manifestation, the United Nations—limits state action both by its statutory competence to sit in judgment on state behavior and by its unique ability to form and express a mass international consensus. Although the formal limits on state action are yet rudimentary, and despite the fact that states occasionally succeed in evading their restraints, their overall limiting effect is perceptible and sometimes controlling.[5]

The informal limits on state action grow out of the dynamic of the state system itself. Each state, in pursuing its own policies, is confronted by all its fellows doing the same thing. Each therefore is faced with the ominous likelihood that any interstate relationship in which it becomes involved will be a competitive one and may well develop into open conflict. No state can afford to be engaged in disputes simultaneously with all other states; it must therefore seek to adjust its pattern of relations so as to maintain a satisfactory balance of support, sympathy, noninvolvement, and nonopposition from those states with which actual or potential conflicts are minimal or nonexistent. In this way it conserves its energy and power for use against those states with which it is involved over more important matters.[6]

In any such direct confrontation, another type of limit is operative. The principle of expediency that governs state action in a relativistic world demands that a state not press its cause against another beyond the point of its own capacity. The absence of effective institutional controls over state action tends to make each international dispute a clash of power, with victory going to the state better able to enforce its will. The point here is that prudent

---

[4]See E. H. Carr, *The Twenty Years Crisis, 1919–1939* (London: Macmillan & Co., Ltd., 1946), Chapter 8; for a "functional" approach to the subject, see Harold and Margaret Sprout, *Foundations of International Politics* (Princeton, N.J.: D. Van Nostrand Co., Inc., 1962), Chapter 4: "Power, Political Potential, and International Capabilities."

[5]For a thorough demonstration of this point, see Charles de Visscher, *Theory and Reality in Public International Law*, trans. P. E. Corbett (Princeton, N.J.: Princeton University Press, 1957).

[6]Henry A. Kissinger, in *The Troubled Partnership* (New York: McGraw-Hill Book Company, 1965), makes this point in the context of European-American relations. See especially Chapter 8: "What Kind of Atlantic Partnership?"

statesmanship allows for this condition and accepts as a limit on state action the general rule that a state should not voluntarily become involved in a controversy in which its position would be, on balance, weaker than that of its opponent.

National Interest

We have identified "national interest" as denoting the relatively constant criteria by which a state judges the evolving situation it faces and in terms of which operating decisions are made and policies undertaken. We have also pointed out that it arises, in somewhat different forms, from two sources: the controlling myth and value system of the nation as it contemplates the international scene, and the somewhat more sophisticated and operationally more precise notions that emanate from specialized official personnel. Each of these aspects merits some further examination.

THE MYTH OF NATIONAL MISSION

Within any nation of more than rudimentary political experience there exists a more or less well-formulated image of its national mission. This, indeed, is one of the characteristics of the modern nation-state. There may be some sovereignties in the world in which the population is so politically inert that such a myth does not exist, but such states would be few in number and of relatively minor importance in world affairs. Politically significant states all incorporate some such notion, and its role in articulating national interest and in determining the direction and frequently the methods of foreign policy is always large and sometimes dominant.

THE IMPORTANCE OF MASS ATTITUDES. It is axiomatic today that foreign affairs is no longer the exclusive plaything of a small group of political insiders, but that the mass of citizens—at least in democratic states—is deeply involved in the process. State objectives have become so broad and the effort demanded to attain them involves so many facets of national power that no statesman dares run the risk of alienating the support of any large portion of his people. This makes nationalism, the mass political emotion, a factor always to be taken into account in policy decisions.[7]

What this means for most policy-makers is that the actions they contemplate must be attuned to mass attitudes. If their projected action falls within the area permitted or demanded by the national myth, they can proceed confidently; if it does not comport with what the dominant attitude

---

[7]See Karl Deutsch, *Nationalism and Social Communication* (New York: John Wiley & Sons, Inc., 1953); for specific examples from Britain and France, see Arnold Wolfers, *Britain and France Between Two Wars* (New York: Harcourt, Brace & World, Inc., 1940), Chapters III, XIII.

feels is satisfactory, a preliminary problem in political leadership must first be solved. The mass must either be persuaded to expand or reorient its values by means of educational or propaganda techniques, or the policy must itself be altered or reinterpreted so as to bring it into conformity with the commands of the popular tradition.

Statesmen frequently chafe under the restraints imposed by such a myth, but contemporary political life affords few clues about how they may escape it. The mass may be manipulated, tricked, cajoled, temporarily evaded, or even tyrannized, but it cannot permanently be ignored. To the extent to which the mass tradition of international mission is clearly formulated and based on genuine value consensus, it is an absolutely controlling determinant of national interest. Statesmen must develop their own formulations within such freedom of action as it permits them.[8]

POPULAR PREFERENCES AND FOREIGN POLICY. In conceptualizing the myth of national mission, we must be wary not to draw overrigid inferences from our notion. Even in a tightly knit authoritarian society organized under a system of rigid social controls, voluntary unanimity on ultimate national purposes is usually impossible to achieve in any notable detail; in a fluid social structure, consensus seldom develops spontaneously except on extremely narrow issues and then only for limited periods. Such myth as exists in a democratic society usually finds expression either in broad value generalizations permitting great flexibility in official interpretation and application to specific situations or else in emotional slogans equally subject to manipulation by skilled leadership.

Popular preferences, therefore, as a source of national interest only rarely tie official hands completely. In a free society there is competition among individuals and groups who seek to express the controlling version of the myth; a variety of voices purport to speak the basic ("true") national interest. This situation often gives officialdom an opportunity to move shrewdly to cultivate the positions of which it approves and to play a constructive part in shaping the myth to dimensions appropriate to the action demanded at the moment.[9]

Even in this looser version of the concept of the national myth, however, we must nonetheless recognize its basic irrationality. Popular attitudes may

---

[8]Gabriel A. Almond, *The American People and Foreign Policy* (New York: Harcourt, Brace & World, Inc., 1950), deals extensively with this problem; see also James Rosenau, *Public Opinion and Foreign Policy* (New York: Random House, Inc., 1961).

[9]An almost classic example of this technique was the delicacy and skill with which President Lyndon B. Johnson identified his administration's policy in the war in Vietnam with the "honor," "prestige," and "good faith" of the United States in upholding "freedom" and "self-determination" for smaller states. At a time when criticism was widespread and fundamental in some circles (March-June, 1965), the President successfully won mass support and a vote of confidence from the public. The critics were substantially silenced for months thereafter.

seize upon an objective, a technique, or a condition and sanctify it as an integral part of basic national interest. Against such a move the statesman is helpess; as long as the myth is speaking, official discourse is powerless to be heard. Governments must cope with such commands as best they can.[10]

We may repeat, however, that ordinarily the "national interest," to the extent that it is imbedded in the culture as a prevailing myth and value system, finds expression only in the most general terms and is subject to most elastic interpretation. As a rule, officials responsible for government action find it a hurdle not impossible of clearance, although only rarely are they able to ignore it completely. An orderly analysis of the national interest of any particular state must recognize the peculiar role of mass value preferences and make its first task an estimate of their dimensions and effect.

NATIONAL INTEREST AS A POLICY DETERMINANT

When we turn from national interest as myth and consider it in its more material role as perhaps the prime determinant of government policy, we find ourselves capable of somewhat more precision, even though the literature of political science is replete with controversy over the exact meaning of the term. Although it has proved impossible to define it in a way satisfactory to everyone, we can discover sufficient agreement to permit clarification of the concept to a degree sufficient for our purposes. Certain notions reappear regularly in the discussions of scholars and the pronouncements of statesmen; the concrete formulations of interest made by states resemble one another relatively closely with reference to a handful of broad concerns. From these sources we may draw a few tentative conclusions.

THE IDEA OF NATIONAL INTEREST. As we analyze the role of interest in the foreign policy of actual states, we find that all of them seem to be perennially concerned to some important degree with the same three considerations. We may phrase these common desires of states as (1) self-preservation, (2) security, and (3) well-being. It is probable that for most states these three are listed here in their normal order of priority.

But these three areas of interest, as stated, are too generalized and abstract to be of much use, either for analysis or for policy-making. They must be given a more specific content. Each government makes such an elaboration with regard to the generalized situational context in which it is operating and to its long-range aspirations within that situation (the latter consideration is the peculiar province of the myth we discussed in the preceding section). This translation of abstract interest into relatively precise and long-lived

---

[10]For critical comment, see Walter Lippmann, *The Public Philosophy* (Boston: Little, Brown and Company, 1955), especially Chapter 2: "The Malady of Democratic States."

national wants and needs results in the working criterion by which the government measures the changing milieu. We need scarcely point out that, since no
two states face the same situation, no two formulations of national interest
are the same. For our purposes, therefore, the "national interest" as a determinant of policy consists of formulations of those (at least) semipermanent
ends, phrased at a high level of generalization, the pursuit of which the state
feels is necessary to its self-preservation, its security, and its well-being.

"INTEREST" VS. "INTERESTS."   We have come a little way in making the
notion of national interest more intelligible and useful, but our term is yet too
abstract to be used as an analytical tool. We will recall that our "chain of
policy" made situational factors the motivating element in policy; circumstances also play their part in translating the national interest into useable and
concrete terms. One attempt to formulate the process put the matter this
way:

> The *national interest* may be defined as the general and continuing end for which
> a state acts. . . . This is, of course, a highly generalized definition. But any lower
> level of generalization tends to lose substantive meaning, and the term becomes
> increasingly ambiguous. The reason for this is that the requirements of security and
> well-being not only change with circumstances but are, in addition, matters of
> judgment and calculation and hence open to varying interpretations. . . . [11]

To replace the general notion of "the national interest," the authors of this
selection suggest the plural term "interests," because such usage not only
reveals that interests "may conflict in any given set of circumstances," but also
that a choice must be made among them "in terms of priorities and values"
before specific objectives and policies can be selected. "Interests" are defined
as "what the decision-making group in a government determines is important
to the maintenance of the state."[12]

Such a substitution of "interests" for "the national interest" as an analytical tool has a good deal to recommend it on grounds of clarity and utility;
it makes a great deal more sense to say about a particular situation that "the
United States has an interest in . . ." than "the national interest of the United
States is . . . ." The use of "interests" makes it possible for the statesman or
analyst to proceed directly to concrete situations and speeds the process of
reaching a policy decision. But there seems to be some danger in relegating
the more general term to the discard and in concentrating entirely on
what "the decision-making group" in a state thinks is important. Conflicts
between competing interests within a state are frequent, and the quotation
above admitted that they are to be resolved by a choice made "in terms of

---

[11]William A. Reitzel, Morton A. Kaplan, and Constance G. Coblentz, *United States
Foreign Policy 1945–1955* (Washington, D. C.: The Brookings Institution, 1956), Appen-
dix A: "Definition of Terms," pp. 471–472. Italics in original. Reprinted by permission.

[12]Reitzel, Kaplan, and Coblentz, *United States Foreign Policy*, p. 472. Reprinted by
permission.

priorities and values." It does not seem illogical to suggest that such a choice might well be made in terms of a generalized version of interest rooted in mass tradition.[13]

"Ends" and "Means" in National Interest. Such an architectonic notion of national interest serves a very useful purpose in enabling a policy-maker initially to draw—and subsequently to keep in mind—the necessary distinction between "means" and "ends" in foreign policy. "Ends," being generalized goals largely rooted in the prevailing myth of national purpose, are postulated *a priori;* "means" are the rationally selected techniques selected in order to maximize a predetermined end. Ends, in other words, are internalized. There is no such thing as a "good" end except in terms of the unique value system of the society that establishes the end in the first place. No outsider can rationally criticize any ends-decision. Judgments regarding means, however, are amenable to analysis in terms of more or less objective criteria of efficacy and economy of effort.[14]

Ends may, in turn, be either proximate or ultimate. A proximate end is one the achievement of which will provide a springboard for a further advance toward an ultimate end. In this sense, a proximate end acquires some of the characteristics of a means and is open to critical analysis in those terms. But even so, proximate ends inexorably govern the means selected for their accomplishment; each ends-means relationship, whatever its level of generality, is symmetrical with all others. It is only when a means loses contact with its appropriate end that serious problems both of analysis and of statecraft arise. A successful foreign policy keeps ends and means in balance.[15]

National Interest: The Final Criterion. One final point needs to be made in this connection about national interest. It is more than the standard by which situational factors are given relevance and action inspired; it is also the ultimate criterion by which the state's "success" or "failure" is measured.

---

[13]Reitzel, Kaplan, and Coblentz use the term "principles" to refer to such a criterion: "*Principles* is used to mean the enduring modes of behavior or the relatively established guides to action that characterize nations.... The decision-making group, concretely concerned with *interests*, tends to think of *principles* as more-or-less subjective and to find them in occasional conflict with *interests*. Nevertheless, *principles* are deeply imbedded in the general culture and political philosophy of a society and are powerful, if intangible and subjective, guides to action.... They represent the underlying patterns of value that guide national action and to which determinations of *interests, objectives,* and *policies* over the long run tend to conform." *United States Foreign Policy,* pp. 472–473. Italics in original. Reprinted by permission. Such a definition seems to fit quite closely what we are calling the "myth" of national mission and may well be used as a definition for it.

[14]"[I think] of foreign policy as relating to means and ends and to the gap between them. ... Ends are concepts. Means are facts. Making foreign policy consists of meshing concepts and facts in the field of action." Charles B. Marshall, *Department of State Bulletin* (March 17, 1952), p. 416. See also the brief but powerful development of the same point in Walter Lippmann, *United States Foreign Policy: Shield of the Republic* (Boston: Little, Brown and Company, 1943), Chapter 2: "A Fundamental Principle of Foreign Policy."

[15]For a discussion of this problem as applied to American cold-war policy, see Charles O. Lerche, Jr., *The Cold War ... and After* (Englewood Cliffs, N.J.: Prentice-Hall, Inc., 1965), pp. 63–75.

A "good" foreign policy is one that advances the notion of interest that inspired the action in the first place; a "bad" one fails. Thus we might aphoristically say that the concept of interest is both the starting point and end of the foreign-policy process, and the entire sequence of action acquires a peculiarly circular character.

The permanence of national interest is, of course, only relative. Nothing stands still in international relations, and interest is no exception to this rule. But we must emphasize that a state's devotion to its self-preservation, its security, and its well-being (in other words, to its end-interests) remains constant, however different may be the forms in which problems present themselves. New political, economic, demographic, psychic, or technological facts may work great changes in the means-interests pursued by the state or even in the pattern of postulated end-interests. In this sense, interest unquestionably evolves in its detailed expression. But this mutability that we can see in the concept does not vitiate its key role in the policy process; some formulation of national interest provides the foundation for all subsequent steps in making and executing foreign policy.

Situational Factors

We indicated earlier that the situational factors in response to which policies are initiated fall into three categories: (1) the international milieu in which the state is operating; (2) the specific actions of other states; and (3) the state's own capabilities for action. Later in this book we shall examine each of these as they apply to the United States; here we need only clarify their content briefly to see how they fit into our conceptual system. Each, as we shall see, requires care and discretion in its analysis.

THE INTERNATIONAL MILIEU

The milieu of state action—including both the fixed factors confronting the state and the general "climate" of international affairs—is the source of a large share of what some call the "givens" of foreign policy. The setting in which policy is made and conducted itself influences the decisions states make and the actions they take.[16]

---

[16] A systematic survey and critique of the various interpretations of the milieu has been made by Harold and Margaret Sprout in *Man-Milieu Relationship Hypothesis in the Context of International Politics* (Princeton, N.J.: Center of International Studies, 1956); see also, by the same authors, "Geography and International Politics in an Era of Revolutionary Change," *Journal of Conflict Resolution*, IV, 1 (March, 1960), 145.

FIXED FACTORS IN THE MILIEU.   Each state is faced with a number of relatively fixed factors as it charts its course in international affairs. Some of these relate uniquely to itself, such as its size and location; these are generally considered as part of the tangible component of state capability. Others appertain more generally to the state system and its effect on the state concerned and must be fed into the policy calculations of a government. Examples might include the global distribution of power, the existing international institutions and their effectiveness, the stability or disorganization of international society, and so on.

THE CLIMATE OF INTERNATIONAL POLITICS.   But we have made the point several times already that no fixed scheme of relationships can convey an accurate impression of the international scene. Dynamic forces also form part of the milieu and tend to influence the interpretation and modify the impact of the fixed factors. The cumulative effect of the dynamic forces at work at any one time is to create the "climate" of international politics: the general atmosphere of state relationships. Some of the dynamisms that might contribute to the climate are a broad trend toward revolution or toward reaction, mass attitudes on war and peace (the "expectation of war"), the state of ideological disputation, and the level of nationalist identification among large groups of people.

THE ACTIONS OF OTHER STATES

What we really mean when we say that other states affect the course of policy-making by any government is that the state system itself constitutes a situational factor. What is there about this system that obliges a state to take into account the known and predictable responses of its associates when it is planning a policy move? Why is foreign policy such a mixture of action and reaction?

THE DUAL IMPACT OF OTHER STATES.   Each state impinges on any other in two ways. In the first place, as policy is executed, resistance by other states is often encountered. Such opposition may be overt and extensive; it may be covert and nominal; or it may even be passive. Each form of resistance must be anticipated as accurately as possible and measures devised for dealing with it. Second, each state must devote a large portion of its capability to coping with policy moves made by other states, resisting, cooperating, or accommodating as its own interest dictates. A surprisingly large share of each state's effort is thus spent in dealing with situations arising from action originating outside its own boundaries.[17]

---

[17]The points raised in this discussion are dealt with in more detail in Lerche and Said, *Concepts of International Politics*, Chapter 5: "Ideas and Patterns of International Politics."

COMPETITION IN THE STATE SYSTEM. The fictions of sovereignty—the independence and equality of all states—produce a system that in logic is absolutely competitive. States are free to select policies the implementation of which would require the attainment of absolute and ultimate ends. If all states are—at least in theory—committed to mutually exclusive purposes, satisfaction in a world of dispersed power lies beyond the capability of any of them.

The state system is thus inherently frustrating; every member is doomed to permanent dissatisfaction as it doggedly plods on in search of illusory Utopias. This frustration lends a certain peevish quality to interstate relations. It often seems as if states feel that as long as they cannot really accomplish their goals, they are determined to do the next best thing: to deny accomplishment of goals to others.

The international order is an intensely competitive one. Each state considers every other as its actual or potential rival; each assumes that its fellows would be perfectly willing under appropriate circumstances to deny it the fruits of any of its efforts.

This is a strong statement, and one often belied in practice. Absolute competition is often modified by the workings of national interest. For particular states and in special situations, cooperation in the pursuit of a shared objective may be more mutually profitable than competition. But if (or when) their interests—determined, we will recall, by each state for itself— again diverge, competition of almost any degree of intensity would immediately replace the earlier harmony.[18]

THE PURSUIT OF COMPENSATION. The actual working of the competitive principle usually takes the form of the pursuit of "compensation." Especially between states who are admitted rivals (in other words, between whom competition has come out into the open), an advantage gained by one state in its own policy effort usually touches off a search for offsetting compensation by the other (or, in a multilateral situation, by all others). They may attempt to offset the gain by resistance or by retaliatory action of their own; they may readjust their relations with each other to accommodate the change and restore something like the former relationship; or they may seek corresponding gains of their own.

International politics may be viewed as a complex series of initial moves followed by compensatory reactions. Statesmen contemplating policy moves must assume that any but the most minor steps will precipitate an attempt at compensation by some states.

THE EFFECT OF OTHER STATES. When a statesman makes his judgment

---

[18]The breakup of the two great cold-war coalitions, so obvious a feature of international politics during the 1960's, was due to nothing more complex than the operation of this principle. For the Western coalition, see Ronald Steel, *The End of Alliance* (New York: The Viking Press, Inc., 1964); for the Soviet bloc, see Edward Crankshaw, *The New Cold War: Moscow vs. Peking* (Baltimore: Penguin Books, Inc., 1963).

about the reactions his move will provoke, he knows that a broad range of action is open to the affected states. Some will agree with him, and perhaps will actively cooperate; others will be affected only slightly, and their moves in either direction will be minimal; still others will be in opposition and will initiate compensatory policies. The task of the policy-maker is to move through these permutations and combinations as deftly as he can and to extract from the situation such freedom of action—usually brought about by balancing favorable reactions off against opposing ones—as will permit him to make some contribution to the notion of interest he is serving.

STATE CAPABILITY

By "capability" we mean the ability of a state to achieve its objectives.[19] This definition, being almost perfectly circular, does not define. Perhaps it is more accurate to say that capability is the measure of the capacity of a state to have other states agree with it on matters in which it is interested. Among sovereignties the only way differences can be eventually terminated is by agreement, and it is immaterial whether such agreement is forced or free.

FORCE AND CONSENT. There are, as we have suggested, two different ways by which a state may secure agreement from other states. It may either compel agreement by force—the application of coercive or semicoercive techniques— or it may win agreement from them by free consent. Both force and consent, as devices for obtaining agreement, form parts of capability.[20]

Generally speaking, the more free consent a state can command in support of its policy, the less it needs force to reach its objective. Conversely, the less consent available, the greater the amount of force needed. Since under most circumstances agreement by consent is preferable to agreement by force (for reasons both of permanence and of economy of effort), states as a rule endeavor to maximize their area of consent.

There is, however, an inherent limit on this effort. No state would dare to depend entirely on the voluntary consent of other states in estimating its ability to fulfill its mission. Neither, for that matter, can a state trust itself entirely to force for any but the briefest of periods or the narrowest of objectives. "Capability" must, for each state, be a measure of the effective action open to it in the particular context, such effectiveness being composed variously of its coercive power and its command of the free consent of its associates.

---

[19]For systematic attempts to give content to the concept of capability (or "power"), see Stephen B. Jones, "The Power Inventory and National Strategy," *World Politics* (September, 1954); and Harold and Margaret Sprout, *Foundations of International Politics*, Chapter 4.

[20]This notion is extensively developed by Louis J. Halle in his *Civilization and Foreign Policy* (New York: Harper & Row, Publishers, 1955) and earlier in his "Force and Consent in International Affairs," *Department of State Bulletin* (September 21, 1953).

THE CONTENT OF CAPABILITY.   A state's ability to achieve its objectives is so much a function of time, place, and situation that we cannot ever attain anything like mathematical precision in its analysis.[21] We can, however, suggest here the broad areas of state life that bear directly on the concept; in a later chapter we shall fill in some of the details as they apply to the capability of the United States.

Capability involves both tangible and intangible factors. The former are to a great extent susceptible to measurement by objective criteria; the intangibles defy exact measurement—and often exact formulation as well—by statistical techniques. Students of international affairs—as well as statesmen —realize, however, that both sorts of concerns contribute to the total ability of the state to act constructively.

The tangible factors are usually listed under five heads: (1) geography; (2) population and manpower; (3) natural resources; (4) industrial and agricultural production; and (5) military organization and power-in-being. Each of these has been studied in detail; a wealth of information about their status in the majority of states is now available, and a host of revealing comparisons has been and is being made. Insofar as capability analyses can be made by the yardsticks represented by these five categories, we can do the job quite presentably.

Intangibles are nonquantifiable (as are indeed many of the aspects of the tangibles in the list above), but estimates must nevertheless be made of their effect if capability judgments are to have any utility at all.[22] Among the many ways of listing the nonmaterial components of capability, the one that follows is an attempt at synthesis; other lists might have more or fewer entries, but the general points included would be generally the same. We stipulate four categories: (1) the political, economic, and social structure of the state under consideration; (2) the educational and technological level; (3) the state of national morale; and (4) the international strategic situation of the state—its need for allies, its opponents, its general leader-follower status in international society, and the amount and kind of consent it can command.

THE RELATIVITY OF CAPABILITY.   Capability is a slippery concept, for it acquires meaning only in a relative sense. A state is not "capable" or "incapable" in any absolute way; instead, it is "capable" or "incapable" of doing some

---

[21]"Capability analysis proceeds from the tangible and easily measured factors to those which though still very tangible—indeed crucial—involve so many imponderables as to defy measurement." John S. Reshetar, Jr., *Problems of Analyzing and Predicting Soviet Behavior* (Garden City, N. Y.: Doubleday & Company, Inc., 1954), p. 33. Reprinted by permission.

[22]". . . the major dimension used in the analysis of the tangible factors is that of *quantity*. . . . The significant dimension in the intangibles is *quality*. . . . The analyst, in a word, *measures* the tangible factors but *evaluates* the intangibles; . . . ." Lerche and Said, *Concepts of International Politics*, p. 59.

particular thing. A capability judgment about a state is intelligible only when a decision is being reached about whether or not it can attain a particular objective. A state may be able to reach a goal when opposed by one state, but may be impotent when confronted by another; one objective may be within its capacity while another is completely out of reach.[23]

Thus each time a policy decision is under consideration, a capability judgment about the attainability of the various alternatives helps influence the choice of one of them. Capability is not a status to which states attain, but rather a device of measurement by means of which policy-makers can judge the relative feasibility of different courses of action.[24]

THE DYNAMISM OF CAPABILITY. Another controlling characteristic of the concept of capability is its dynamism. The several factors interact so subtly and in such a variety of ways that capability judgments must be made, so to speak, on the run.

We can almost say that it is impossible to reach any conclusion about the relative capabilities of states that is not at least partially obsolete at the time it is made. Many of the factors influencing such a judgment are moving so rapidly that even the latest information is out of date. This makes the detailed measurement and comparison of capabilities really a matter of isolating the significant trends of development within each relevant component, and then projecting each of these into the future. In this way, calculations of relative competences of states become the best possible guesses about conditions yet to arise.

THE TIME FACTOR. The relativism and dynamism of capability combine to suggest another qualitative element: the pervasive influence of time. Questions of "now" and "then" enter into every judgment. A state's capability to reach an objective may be inadequate at one moment, but ample a short while later (after conditions have changed). In like manner, time may work against a state. The components of capability change at an uneven rate, and the determination of the moment of maximum capacity for a particular course of action requires that the statesman carefully coordinate a number of factors moving at different speeds. The effect of time appears at every turn in international politics, and success in foreign policy rests to a great extent upon the ability of the policy-maker to calculate the optimum moment for action.

---

[23]This warning is even more apposite when the notion of "power" is under discussion in the same sense that "capability" is being used here. It is easier to visualize a "powerful" state than a "capable" one, and even more deceptive to do so. "Power" does not convey as clear an implication of the ability to perform a specific act as does "capability"; this is perhaps one of the more compelling reasons why the latter term has come generally to be regarded as both more accurate and more useful than the older one.

[24]For an elucidation of this point, see Feliks Gross, *Foreign Policy Analysis* (New York: Philosophical Library, Inc., 1954), p. 124.

Objectives and Policy

We turn now to two more concepts that play an important role in the foreign-policy process: objectives as goals of state action, and policy considered as a course of action designed to reach an objective.

OBJECTIVES

THE NATURE OF OBJECTIVES.   Foreign policy involves action in the national interest, but such action must be purposive. Each state organizes its purposes into a set of objectives that represent the goals it seeks to reach by deliberate action. We have defined an objective generally as a particular state of affairs that a state attempts to bring about. It may be positive in nature and demand affirmative action; it may be negative and demand only that a particular position be held against external pressure. Objectives are preferably verbalized in concrete terms that afford some criteria for determining when and if the objectives are attained and for devising strategies for their attainment.

FROM INTEREST TO OBJECTIVES.   In the policy process, the development of a situation to the point where it either requires or suggests action by the state calls for the application of the yardstick of national interest. Every government asks itself a question more or less as follows: "Considering the situation as of this momemt, what possible (that is, *attainable*) state of affairs would be most advantageous in terms of the national interest?" The answers it discovers to this question furnish the objectives it accepts and will seek to attain. Objectives, as we have seen, arise out of the situation as interpreted by a notion of interest.

THE MUTABILITY OF OBJECTIVES.   Realizing that any formulation of interest is subject to modification and that many situational factors themselves are inherently unstable, we are led to conclude that objectives (derived from these two elements) are themselves constantly liable to change along some minimum-maximum continuum. It is no wonder that states are continuously overhauling their patterns of objectives. Some goals are discarded as no longer valuable or as beyond attainment; some are modified in the light of situational change; some entirely new ones are adopted. No state can safely assume that the application of its version of interest to a general situation will produce the same result twice in succession; indeed, the contrary assumption is usually safer. Objectives provide targets at which to shoot and combine to indicate a direction in which policy moves, but only rarely does a state reach the exact goal after which it originally set out.

THE PATTERN OF OBJECTIVES.   Every state, of course, has a number of objectives. Each of the components of national interest normally gives rise to a more or less numerous family of specific concerns ("interests"), in responses to each of which some concrete objective is selected from the situational context. It is only seldom that these objectives fall neatly into a homogenous or harmonious relationship with each other; usually there is some degree of inner contradiction within the larger outline of interest and policy.

When this contradiction involves fundamentals, a real dilemma confronts the policy-maker; sometimes he may advance his state's interest in one area only by doing it serious or irreparable damage in another. Normally at this point major readjustments become necessary. More frequently, however, conflict among objectives is resolved in terms of time priority (Objective A, being urgent, must be achieved as soon as possible; Objective B, contradictory but less immediately critical, may be attacked at a later time) or some other rationalizing device.

If the controlling notion of interest is sufficiently clear, we would expect that all the specific objectives of a state could be comprehended within its terms, even if only at a very high level of generalization. Conversely, some approximation of what a state considers its interest may be reached by induction from an analysis of the motivations underlying its choice of objectives. In any case, a rationally conceived foreign policy, maintaining a working relationship with an understood and accepted notion of interest, would normally have more of harmony than of contradiction.

POLICY

Early in this chapter we defined foreign policy and warned that this definition would require further analysis. Between that point and this one we have examined the foreign-policy process and several of its components. We now return to the subject of "policy" itself, initially in a much narrower frame of reference than in our original definition, and later in its original broader sense. "Policy," as we are discussing it here, is not necessarily the same thing as "foreign policy."

THE MEANING OF POLICY. Our concern at this point is with "policy" considered in a strategic and tactical sense. Policy in these terms assumes an objective to have been already selected and refers to a method for its attainment. The term therefore has two connotations: It means either the actions actually taken to accomplish a purpose or the principles that govern such action. It may refer either to a series of overt moves made by a state in order to reach an objective or to the prepared plan under which such steps are taken. Both meanings are useful, and analytically the distinction between them is important; as we use the word in this discussion, however, the particular reference will usually be indicated by the context.

REACHING A POLICY DECISION. Making a policy decision to act in accomplishment of an objective is a power monopolized by the official decision-making personnel of a government. Action in international affairs takes place only by government mechanisms, and only those officials authorized in the name of the state to commit the government to act can make real decisions. Considerable study has been made of the process by which decision-makers, particularly in the United States, perform this task, and the nature of the operation is fairly well understood.[25]

Without going into the minutiae, however, we may say that as a rule governments follow some version of the generalized process we outlined on pages 4–5. Interests and situations are catalogued and analyzed, and the optimum possible state of affairs is determined. Particular emphasis is placed on canvassing all the possible alternatives of action. Each course that has any feasibility at all is spelled out, and each is evaluated rigorously in terms of the prevailing idea of national interest, the impact of the developing situation, and its possible success in attaining the objective. The final selection (at least in theory) is made of the one that seems to promise the maximum gain (or, on occasion, the minimum loss) in the fulfillment of the demands of national interest.

Various states formalize this process of developing alternatives to different degrees, and within any state it may vary from one situation to another. But some approximation of the technique is used by every government that takes foreign affairs seriously. No less detailed method would take enough of the variables into account.

THE FLEXIBILITY OF POLICY DECISIONS.   Policy decisions, being concerned more with "how" than with "what," are as often as possible taken with an eye to their possible revision as conditions evolve. This is one major reason for the elaborateness with which the open alternatives are frequently analyzed; if the strategy selected should prove unworkable, the state presumably can fall back on the policy line originally judged next best. States normally attempt to preserve the maximum room for maneuver; sometimes an objective will prove beyond reach by any possible policy technique, and then a new objective must be fixed and a new program accepted to reach it. Flexibility is sought in time, in quantity, in kind, and indeed in every dimension by which policy is measured.

The dynamism of the state system swiftly penalizes the state that fails to allow for change. A rigid policy—based on the (explicit or implicit) assumption that conditions will continue unchanged indefinitely—stands in constant

---

[25]Three useful, although very different, analyses of the foreign-policy process are Richard C. Snyder, H. W. Bruck, and Burton M. Sapin, eds., *Foreign Policy Decision-Making* (New York: Free Press of Glencoe, Inc., 1962); Philip W. Buck and Martin Travis, eds., *Control of Foreign Relations in Modern Nations* (New York: W. W. Norton & Company, Inc., 1957); and Joseph E. Black and Kenneth W. Thompson, *Foreign Policies in a World of Change* (New York: Harper & Row, Publishers, 1963).

danger of becoming irrelevant to new situational elements. If a policy supported by commitments of power faces the loss of effective rapport with its milieu, the state may well be forced into the expensive and hazardous effort of extemporizing to buy time while it adjusts to the new dimension of its problem. Prudent statesmen avoid this danger whenever possible by holding their commitments to the necessary minimum.

"POLICY" AND "FOREIGN POLICY." In this discussion we have been emphasizing that "policy" refers to the course of action a state follows in pursuing a single objective. A state thus has many policies—as many as it has objectives —and it follows each of them simultaneously. It is in this connection that we speak of a "policy decision": a decision to commit the government to act in a certain way in order to achieve an objective.

But, despite the built-in ambiguity that results, "policy" has another meaning. As used in the phrase "foreign policy," "policy" refers to the general pattern and direction revealed by the aggregate of a state's specific undertakings and the broad principles that undergird them. Thus we may say that Soviet foreign policy is expansionist, and we may also say that the Soviet pursues the policy of cultivating the friendship of the uncommitted states. There is no easy escape from this confusion of language; we may, however, suggest one possible clue. "Policy" as a generic concept is usually verbalized in general or abstract terms, whereas a particular policy of a state is (or, at any rate, should be) precise and concrete in its referents. Further than this we must fall back on the context to clarify the sense in which the term is being used.

PART II

A DEMOCRATIC
FOREIGN POLICY

CHAPTER **2**

The
Policy Process in
the United States

We have seen that foreign policy does not just "happen" but instead is the result of a long, difficult, and often painful process. We saw the conceptual ingredients of the policy process in Chapter 1; we now turn to an analysis of the way these ideas are translated into actual decisions and actions in the government of the United States.

Foreign-policy decision, in the strict sense, is of course a government monopoly; no private citizen can conduct his own policy toward other nations, and only responsible officials can speak in the name of the United States or commit its government to action.[1] It must also be kept very much in mind, however, that in this significant area of government action, as in all others, the impact of the democratic faith of the United States is powerful and often controlling.

A democratic government like that of the United States is ideologically committed to follow, as nearly as it can, the dictates of its constituents. This means that the policy-makers cannot confine

---

[1] Richard C. Snyder, H. W. Bruck, and Burton M. Sapin, *Decision-Making as an Approach to the Study of International Politics* (Princeton University: Foreign Policy Analysis Series No. 3, 1954) is devoted to an elaboration of this thesis and an inquiry into how decision-making may be most profitably analyzed; see also the 1960 Brookings Institution study, *The Formulation and Administration of United States Foreign Policy* (Washington, D.C.: Government Printing Office, 1960), especially Chapters 3 and 4.

their attention to the national interest as they perceive it themselves, but must always heed whatever they feel the voice of the people is saying. Popular influence on the decision-makers, present to some extent even in the most dictatorial of governments, is different in a democracy primarily in that it is thought to be normal, is constantly taken into account, and is accepted as controlling most of the time.

Officials in the United States, therefore, must cope with the forces of democratic consensus—and normally must operate within its bounds—as they seek to define and apply the national interest in a rapidly changing world. In subsequent chapters we shall often encounter the consequences of this relationship—consequences that assume the forms of chronic tension and occasional crisis. Here we shall only examine some of its major components before proceeding to a detailed examination of the government machinery for framing and implementing policy decisions.

A Democratic Foreign Policy

It was the French Revolution that democratized foreign policy by taking it out of the hands of absolute monarchs; modern nationalism conferred on the mass of the people of a state the right and the power to "make" foreign policy, at least in its broad outlines. In return, the populace acquired a reciprocal duty, that of executing the policy of which they were at least the partial architects. Compulsory military service was the first new civil responsibility; additional burdens of taxpaying, economic activity, intellectual pursuits, and other fields were added until today it is possible to speak of a "total" foreign policy in almost the same sense as we use the term "total war." Corresponding to the increase of mass responsibility for service in behalf of the national foreign policy came an increase in the degree of control popular attitudes exercise over foreign policy.

The more "democratic" foreign policy became, however, the more difficult became the foreign-policy process itself. The demands mass opinion made on government tended steadily to become less and less concrete, more and more absolute, and ultimately often verging on the unattainable. Caught between the pressures of emotionally involved and articulate public opinion on one side and the inexorabilities of the state system on the other, statesmen in many countries found themselves involved in an unhappy dilemma. They were obliged either to follow the whims of popular demand and undertake policies they thought unwise or to flout their people and run the risk of repudiation.

THE PUBLIC VS. THE POLICY-MAKER

There is no easy solution to the dilemma we have noted; each side has a persuasive case.

THE UNDEMOCRATIC NATURE OF FOREIGN POLICY. It is often said that foreign policy, by its history and by its nature, is inherently undemocratic. Of the many reasons advanced to support this generalization, we shall mention four of the most frequently encountered.

1. Foreign affairs is a government monopoly. The relations of states are carried on among governments, and in the exercise of this function officials must be free from close checking by irresponsible laymen.
2. Foreign policy requires, if it is to have any success, both speed and flexibility. Governments must be able to move quickly to meet unexpected contingencies; they must also be able to adapt their actions to meet whatever conditions prevail. Both these qualities collide with the practice of democratic states generally and the United States particularly.
3. Foreign affairs necessitates a constant concern with secrecy. Negotiations usually take considerable time to consummate; premature release of information often endangers the whole enterprise. Nothing more fundamentally opposed to American ideology can be imagined. The idea that the government is keeping secrets from the people immediately gives rise to powerful currents of resistance, resentment, and opposition.
4. A foreign policy must concern itself with what are often called "multiple constituencies." The American government is serving not only the American people. The clientele of American foreign-policy personnel also includes all the foreign supporters, opponents, and enemies of the United States. This means that the requirements of policy often demand that the State Department (for example) accede to the wishes of a foreign state rather than to those of the American people. This is also ideologically repugnant; a democratic government is popularly supposed to serve its people first and always.

We might add a fifth undemocratic requirement of foreign policy: the definition of the national interest. In later chapters we shall consider both the myth of American foreign policy and the working notion of interest that governs contemporary government action. In practice, however, the operating definition and formulation of interest are undertaken by the official elite.[2] This again suggests some conflict with democratic principles.

THE CLAIMS OF DEMOCRATIC IDEOLOGY. The democratic myth,[3] on the

---

[2]"Hence the national interest becomes defined in practice as what those in power declare it to be." Thomas I. Cook and Malcolm Moos, "The American Idea of International Interest," *American Political Science Review* (March, 1953), pp. 28–44. See p. 30. Reprinted by permission.

[3]This term is used in the sense in which it is employed by Gabriel Almond: "The democratic myth is that the people are inherently wise and just, and that they are the real rulers of the republic." *The American People and Foreign Policy* (New York: Harcourt, Brace & World, Inc., 1950), p. 4. Reprinted by permission.

other hand, has certain strong implications for foreign policy. They may be formulated as a series of propositions.

1. There is something called a "public interest," composed of the arithmetic total of individual interests. This is the "national interest" that the government should serve in foreign policy.
2. The "average citizen" knows and understands his own interests and those of his fellows; in other words, he knows where his private concerns fit into the total public interest.
3. The average citizen possesses the intellectual and moral resources to comprehend satisfactorily the issues of foriegn policy.
4. The average citizen can—and will—make meaningful decisions on those issues, and the total of individual decisions will constitute a clear directive to his servants in the government hierarchy.
5. The average citizen is a better (because disinterested) judge of basic alternatives than are special-interest groups or even highly specialized experts.

These propositions arise from the application of the individualist faith of traditional democracy to the questions of foreign policy. They incorporate a deep suspicion of special interests, government experts, institutional mechanisms, and indeed of any social structure that stands between "the citizen and his government." In their total impact they collide directly with the essentially undemocratic aspects of foreign policy we noted above.

THE ELITIST ARGUMENT. The defenders of an elitist approach to the making of foreign policy rely on an argument containing several elements. In the first place, they emphasize both the complexity of the task of foreign policy and the monoploy of competence in dealing with it possessed by a relatively small group of officials.[4] Furthermore, they make much of the professional ability of the specialists as compared with the inadequate training and insight of most amateurs in the field.[5] They constantly caution the public not to expect too much of even these dedicated professionals, since

---

[4]See Almond, *American People and Foreign Policy*, p. 143: ". . . foreign policy is a tapestry of infinite complexity, and even the expert can only hope to achieve familiarity with a part of its intricate design." However, Dorothy Fosdick, in *Common Sense and World Affairs* (New York: Harcourt, Brace & World, Inc., 1955), and Thomas K. Finletter, in *Foreign Policy: The Next Phase, The 1960's* (New York: Harper & Row, Publishers, 1960), disagree fundamentally with this thesis.

[5]". . . we could make much more effective use of the principle of professionalism in the conduct of foreign policy; that we could, if we wished, develop a corps of professional officers superior to anything that exists or ever has existed in this field. . . . However . . . we are probably condemned to continue relying almost exclusively on what we might call 'diplomacy by dilettantism.' " George F. Kennan, *American Diplomacy, 1900–1950* (Chicago: University of Chicago Press, 1951), pp. 93–94. Reprinted by permission. From among the more recent defenses of professionalism (most written by retired ambassadors), see Henry S. Villard, *Affairs at State* (New York: Thomas Y. Crowell Company, 1965).

even the most skilled experts suffer under rigid limits on their scope of action.[6]

Coupled with this defense of *expertise* is usually found a powerful attack on the mass public as totally incompetent to cope in any useful way with questions of foreign policy.[7] Admitting that even a totally professional policy-making "Establishment" must maintain some base in consensus, however, the elitists accept a small fraction of the total populace—the "elite public"[8]—into at least the antechamber of the deliberative edifice, where its members serve as "transmission belts" of semiofficial pronouncements and as conditioners of mass moods in desirable directions.[9]

THE ROLE OF THE MASS PUBLIC. In a very real sense, however, the argument of the elitists is largely beside the point; the American mass public is not prepared to accede to any verdict of inadequacy brought in against it. Mass participation in foreign-policy decision is, and will continue to be, a fact of political life in the United States.

Since this is so clearly the case, what does the mass public actually do? Is its effect always beneficent, as early democratic theory contended, or as pernicious as many contemporary elitists purport to discover?

The answer, as so often happens, lies between these extremes. The mass public in the United States performs—more or less knowledgeably—three important foreign-policy functions that are distinct but related. These are not only quite defensible in theoretical and ideological terms but also have proved to be operationally feasible. The three tasks mass opinion performs are: (1) the determination of the outermost limits of permissible government action; (2) the delineation of a general direction in which policy should move and the isolation of certain landmark objectives and techniques; and (3) the debate and decision of crucial issues so important in themselves that the govern-

---

[6]The most eloquent statement of the narrow range of choices faced by policy-makers is still Charles Burton Marshall, *The Limits of Foreign Policy* (New York: Holt, Rinehart & Winston, Inc., 1954).

[7]Almond says: "There are inherent limitations in modern society on the capacity of the public to understand the issues and grasp the significance of the most important problems of public policy. . . . The layman ordinarily cannot formulate alternatives so that he can see how and in what way his interests are engaged." *American People and Foreign Policy*, pp. 5, 8. Reprinted by permission. George Kennan speaks of "the erratic and subjective nature of public reaction to foreign-policy questions." *American Diplomacy*, p. 93. And no volume has more systematically destroyed the claims of mass opinion to foreign-policy relevance than Walter Lippmann, *The Public Philosophy* (Boston: Little, Brown and Company, 1955); see especially pp. 24–26.

[8]This is the term applied by Almond to "the articulate policy-bearing stratum of the population." *American People and Foreign Policy*, p. 138.

[9]"An effective approach to public information on foreign-policy questions will therefore be selective and qualitative. It will be directed toward enlarging the attentive public and training the elite cadres." Almond, *American People and Foreign Policy*, p. 233. Reprinted by permission.

ment elite dare not proceed until public sentiment has come to rest. In the aggregate, they make popular participation a reality.

THE ORGANIZATION OF PUBLIC OPINION IN THE UNITED STATES

"The public" does not function as an anthropomorphic entity in a democracy. Identifying the genuine *vox populi* from among the babble of voices that is always importuning government to act (or to refrain from acting) in a certain way is a constantly taxing task of the public official. One characteristic of opinion in the American system, however, simplifies this process to a major extent: "Public opinion" must, before it can be brought usefully to bear on a question, be "organized."

THE SEVERAL PUBLICS.   Students of public opinion agree that there are several "publics" that share in what is called public opinion. Gabriel Almond distinguishes three such within the American society:

One may speak of a "general public" if one keeps in mind that while it is characterized by a sense of identification and reacts to general stimuli, it also contains a variety of interests and groupings which are affected differentially by both general and specific stimuli. Second, there is an "attentive public" which is informed and interested in foreign policy problems, and which constitutes the audience for foreign policy discussions among the elites. Third, one may speak of the policy and opinion elites, the articulate policy-bearing stratum of the population which gives structure to the public, and which provides the effective means of access to the various groupings.[10]

Professor Almond feels that the "elite public" is the only portion of the whole that has policy relevance, since the competition among its various subsections (political, administrative, interest, and communications elites) is what really determines "public" opinion. "The 'masses,'" he contends, "participate in policy-making in indirect and primarily passive ways."[11] The attentive public listens to the discussions among the elites and, presumably, plays the most important role in making up the mass mind by telling it what to think.

Whether or not one accepts the whole of Professor Almond's rigorous analysis, it is difficult to question either its thoroughness or its fruitfulness. His major proposition remains beyond doubt; there are indeed several different publics, each with its peculiar characteristics, of which policy-makers must take account.

THE ORGANIZATION OF INTEREST.   An interest group scarcely needs elabo-

---

[10]Almond, *American People and Foreign Policy*, p. 138. Reprinted by permission.
[11]Almond, *American People and Foreign Policy*, p. 139. Reprinted by permission.

rate definition. It is a group of individuals organized on the basis of a single common interest or set of interests. The purpose of the group is to use any combination of a long list of techniques—all subsumed under the rubric of "pressure"—to persuade appropriate government officials, legislative or bureaucratic, to decide in its favor. Almost every conceivable interest in American life has been organized today; on major policy issues, both domestic and foreign, there are groups that represent almost every possible opinion.

Interest groups apply two kinds of pressure on government officials, usually termed "direct" and "indirect." Direct pressure is applied by the group leadership upon the officials personally. Techniques are varied: persuasion, threats of political reprisal (more effective on elected officeholders), technical information (even on foreign policy private groups may be better informed on special issues than are the responsible officials), promises of voting support for the official's party, and so on. The object of direct pressure is to impress the group's wishes forcibly on the decision-making official(s).

Indirect pressure concentrates on the creation of an active mass opinion that will in turn exert pressure on officials to take the desired steps. This usually involves disseminating propaganda aimed at the least common denominator of the public and stressing a simple action formula. The interest group's victory comes nearest to completion when it is able to stir up the public to the point where policy-makers face an opinion *fait accompli* to which they have no choice but to bow. Quantitatively, it is probable that the significant majority of interest-group effort is expended in this kind of indirect pressure.

But again we must note the competition among the groups for the public ear. When major policy questions are at issue, the "average citizen" is bombarded with appeals from every point of the compass. The battle of the propagandists is never ceasing. The individual chooses from among the various "messages" and takes his place on one side or the other of the question. One unexpected outcome of this group conflict is anathema to propagandists but increasingly evident to observers: There seems to be a growing tendency among members of the mass, when confronted with such a barrage of appeals for action, to express their confusion by a simple withdrawal and a refusal to take any stand at all. To a thoughtful person, this appears to be a perfect parody of democratic procedure.

THE PARTIES AND FOREIGN POLICY. Another source of influence on American decision-makers is the institution of the political party. American parties operate in a fashion almost diametrically opposed to pressure groups. Where the interest group is tightly identified with a specific program, the party by definition is decentralized and pluralistic. Where the interest group is largely concerned with policy, the party's focus is on government personnel. Where the interest group seeks to sharpen issues, the party attempts to blur them.

In the American two-party system, each party approaches foreign policy somewhat ambivalently. Foreign policy is a perfectly valid election issue, and party politicians see no fundamental difference between foreign issues and domestic ones; each type is important to them only to the extent to which it wins or loses votes. Consequently, we find professional politicians manipulating foreign-policy questions as expertly as those of domestic policy; party divisions on international issues run as deep as they do on any others.

Since 1945, however, it has become apparent that both major parties are split into two or more groups on major questions of foreign policy. American parties are not "responsible"; they owe no official allegiance to any central leadership, although the national conventions purport to exercise such authority through their party platforms. Much more revealing of party attitudes toward foreign affairs than any platform is the behavior of the party delegations in both houses of Congress, and here is where the sharp cleavages reveal themselves.

Both parties suffer from what may be called—somewhat inaccurately—an isolationist-internationalist division. There are not really two clear camps in each party, but rather a continuum covering the entire spectrum of foreign policy. On crucial foreign-affairs votes in Congress, however, something like definite points of concentration appear on either side of the boundary between these two popular terms.[12]

The Republican split is best known, taking roughly the form of a separation between the Middle West on the one hand and both coasts on the other. Under the leadership of President Eisenhower, the importance of the midwestern group declined both relatively and absolutely, but was never completely eliminated. Indeed, it dominated the party during the Goldwater campaign of 1964.

The Democratic cleavage was less obvious for a time but came into the open during the first years of the Eisenhower administration. Fundamentally it represents a split along North-South lines, with the South developing something that observers tended to identify with prewar Middle West isolationism.[13]

---

[12]The present author, in his *The Uncertain South: Its Changing Patterns of Politics in Foreign Policy* (Chicago: Quadrangle Books, Inc., 1964), argues the case that the real foreign-policy division in the United States is not along isolationist-interventionist lines but rather between "unilateralism" and "multilateralism." See pp. 18–22. This study identifies six different positions—three degrees of multilateralism and three of unilateralism—assumed by southern congressmen between 1952 and 1962 on important foreign-policy votes. See Chapter V: "The Range of Southern Attitudes."

[13]On at least one issue, the Mutual Security Program, southern opposition in Congress came to surpass that of the Middle West. In 1959, 48 per cent of the southern members of the House voted "nay" on the MSA renewal authorization, whereas only 41 per cent of the middle westerners accompanied them; in 1960, the respective percentages were 50 for the South and 40 for the Middle West. Oddly enough, nearly half of the Middle West's negative votes were cast by Democrats! See, for the figures, the present author's article, "Southern Congressmen and the 'New Isolationism,'" *Political Science Quarterly* (September, 1960); see also *The Uncertain South*, pp. 295–300, for additional roll-call data.

The upshot of the parallel divisions in both parties—at least in Congress—has been the development of informal foreign-policy coalitions that transcend party lines. Southern Democrats ally themselves with Republicans from the Middle West; northern and western Democrats make common cause on foreign policy with Republicans from the same regions. Like most generalizations about party politics, this conclusion cannot be elevated to the status of a hard and fast rule. It is sufficiently applicable, however, to qualify sharply any serious attempt to delineate party positions or party programs on foreign-policy matters. The illusory specificity of party platforms should not be permitted to obscure the fact of the actual lack of "party" foreign policies.

THE MASS MEDIA AND PUBLIC ATTITUDES. The media of mass communication—newspapers, radio, television, motion pictures, magazines, advertising, and, to a lesser extent, books—have become of tremendous importance in American culture as it has become more complex and dehumanized. Face-to-face contacts are of less significance in the transmission of ideas today than at any earlier time in the history of American culture. If mass media are indispensable and if foreign-policy ideas are the most important political concerns of our time, we would expect the media to play a large part in shaping foreign policy.

Being aimed at people in the mass, the messages brought by mass media are usually phrased in terms that will have a broad appeal: simple, brief, and striking. They must place no insuperable burden on the absorptive capacity or the tolerance of their consumers. Their content must be tailored to the sensed needs and desires of the audience; such changes as they bring about in audience attitudes are gradual, usually enlarging rather than breaching the existing bounds of acceptance.

What generalizations can we make about the impact of mass media and their manipulators on the foreign-policy process? We must first repeat our general conclusion that such effect as they have takes place generally within the preexisting preference pattern of the mass public. If any attitudinal change takes place among the mass, the media may well be in a position to capitalize on it,[14] but they have been so far unable to bring about any such change themselves.

Within these limits, however, we may identify at least three different effects of mass media on foreign-policy decision-making. (1) The media help focus issues during a period of readjustment and reassessment by means of constant and extensive discussion of various alternatives. (2) They do a nondiscred-

---

[14]The manner in which some more sensational American newspapers and magazines seized on the issue of Communist China when public attitudes crystallized after 1949 is an apt example of this adaptation to a new mood. See also Alfred O. Hero, *Mass Media and World Affairs* (Boston: World Peace Foundation, 1959). Other, more recent examples spring readily to mind: the Berlin wall (1961), the Cuban missile crisis (1962), and the war in Vietnam (1965).

itable job of mass education, informing the public of data and points of view that otherwise would not receive wide circulation. That this is done often for reasons other than public service should not detract from its value. (3) On the debit side, it must be admitted that the mass-media approach to foreign policy stresses its controversial and sensational aspects and minimizes its continuing, affirmative, and harmonizing functions. We are familiar with the cynical attitude of many newspaper employees that "nobody buys a newspaper to read good news"; this assumption underlies much of what all the mass media do in the foreign-policy area.

The Presidency

We now turn to the examination of the government mechanism for the making of foreign policy.[15] As we do so, however, we should always recall a point already made in this chapter: The officials of the United States operate within and under mass opinion; such freedom to act as they enjoy is less an inherent right than a provisional and temporary grant. This thought may not be entirely familiar to members of the general public, but even a casual acquaintance with a few decision-makers leads quickly to the conclusion that responsible public servants never forget for a moment their dependence upon public support.

EXECUTIVE LEADERSHIP

The executive branch of the federal government has a greater responsibility in making foreign policy than have its two fellows, the legislative and judicial branches. Logic, history, law, and necessity unite to confer on the President and his subordinates a peculiarly advantageous position in making the decisions that govern American action. From among the several reasons for such executive preeminence, we may select three that are especially pertinent.

First, the executive branch has access to, and possesses a great fund of, information without which action becomes impossible, useless, or dangerous.

---

[15]Detailed studies include: William Yandell Elliott *et al.*, *United States Foreign Policy, Its Organization and Control* (New York: Columbia University Press, 1952); Brookings Institution, *The Administration of Foreign Affairs and Overseas Operations* (Washington, D. C.: Government Printing Office, 1951); H. H. Bundy and J. G. Rogers, *The Organization of the Government for the Conduct of Foreign Affairs*, Task Force Report on Foreign Affairs, Hoover Commission (Washington, D. C.: Government Printing Office, 1949); and Arthur Macmahon, *Administration in Foreign Affairs* (University, Ala.: University of Alabama Press, 1953). A more recent study, emphasizing suggestions for improvement in both organization and procedure, is the Brookings Institution's Report to the Senate Foreign Relations Committee, *The Formulation and Administration of United States Foreign Policy*.

Second, the executive branch is the medium of official international contact; it deals directly with the other states of the world. This creates the intimate relationship between decision and execution that places the executive in the position of being prepared to act quickly. Third, the executive branch has the expertise, the competent agents who know the "how" and the "where" of policy and are thus able more effectively to suggest the "what" and the "why."

We must not assume, however, that executive leadership in foreign policy means executive monopoly. There are many important functions of policy-making that are shared with Congress; competition and frequent conflict between legislature and executive are as normal as is cooperation. Whether this is judged good or bad depends on one's point of view; it is, however, probably inevitable.

If we agree that the executive branch is central to policy formation, it follows that the President is at the heart of the process. It is often said that the Presidency is the most powerful political office in the world. Its great span of control over foreign affairs is one of the major ingredients in this judgment.

THE PRESIDENT'S ROLE

A combination of factors interact to make the President the key figure in policy-making, although the exact nature of his role is often difficult to define in detail. We know that his unique status as both head of state and head of government contributes largely to the possibilities of power and influence inherent in his office.[16]

THE POWERS OF THE PRESIDENT. We may say that the President's powers come from four separate sources, of unequal importance but each critical in appropriate situations. (1) The Constitution grants the President a limited number of foreign-affairs powers, including such important ones as command of the nation's armed forces and the power to negotiate and (with the consent of two-thirds of the Senate) to ratify treaties. (2) Congress has made literally dozens of grants of foreign-policy power to the President; some of the most significant policy moves of recent years have been implemented by the grant of discretionary powers to the President by act of Congress.[17] (3)

---

[16]See Edward S. Corwin, *The Presidency: Office and Powers*, 3d ed. (New York: New York University Press, 1948); more introspective studies include Clinton Rossiter, *The American Presidency* (New York: Harcourt, Brace & World, Inc., 1956), and Jack Bell, *The Splendid Misery* (Garden City, N.Y.: Doubleday & Company, Inc., 1960). The best study of a complex President is Theodore A. Sorenson, *Kennedy* (New York: Harper & Row, Publishers, 1965).

[17]The entire foreign-aid program of the United States has been handled in this way. See, for example, Title I of the Foreign Assistance Act of 1948 (the Marshall Plan), Public Law 472, 80th Congress.

The Presidency has also what can be safely called "inherent powers," at least in the field of foreign affairs; in the leading case on the subject, the United States Supreme Court admitted that the President has "a degree of discretion and freedom from statutory restriction which would not be admissible were domestic affairs alone involved."[18] (4) The President's unique role as national political leader gives him a special opportunity to grasp and hold the collective imagination of the American people.

This last point merits further elaboration. The President's power to act affirmatively has increased in direct relation to the augmentation of the public's image of the presidential office. If he maintains effective rapport with public attitudes, he has an almost ready-made consensus in support of whatever decisions he reaches. It is difficult for opposition to crystallize against a decision that a reasonably popular President has made and is actively defending before the public. No other executive official enjoys this advantage.[19]

THE FUNCTIONS OF THE PRESIDENT. The most important foreign-policy function of the President is that of assuming ultimate responsibility for all executive decision and action. As the only official voice of the United States in foreign relations, only he can make final policy decisions. He may and usually does delegate much of his operational authority to subordinates, but these latter officials can operate only because of their receipt of fiduciary presidential power and subject to his final (perhaps only implicit) ratification. The President cannot escape this responsibility; even in the case of policies virtually forced on him by Congress, his responsibility for execution and implementation cannot be shifted.

Within this general context, the President may make his role as large as his competence and inclinations dictate. He usually finds it congenial to confine himself to establishing a general line of action, formulating objectives, developing verbalizations of the national interest, and suggesting future emphases. These general charges are transmitted to subordinates for elaboration; from this point forward the President's task is largely one of administrative supervision.

Of course, he may make decisions at any level of detail he wishes. Ordi-

---

[18]United States v. Curtiss-Wright Export Company, 299 U.S. 304 (1936). For a later case limiting the inherent powers of the President, see Youngstown Sheet and Tube Co. v. Sawyer, 343 U.S. 579 (1952).

[19]Instructive examples of the application of this principle were provided—in very different ways—by President John F. Kennedy during the Cuban missile crisis in 1962 and by President Lyndon B. Johnson during the national uproar (or "debate") over the American escalation of the war in Vietnam during the spring of 1965. President Kennedy made his decision and communicated it to the public without warning or preparation; the shock effect solidified public support in astonishingly short order. President Johnson, on the other hand, waded into an on-going controversy and, by the skillful use of his power and his prestige, quickly reduced his seemingly formidable opposition to a forlorn fringe. Granted his immediate and total access to the mass media, the President today can go far in only a short time to win consensus for whatever policy he has chosen.

narily, administrative requirements confine him to the broad areas listed above, but he may intervene in the decisional process at any point. Various Presidents have exercised this function to different degrees, but it is a power open to any of them.

PRESIDENTIAL ASSISTANTS

An elaborate staff organization has been gathered about the Chief Executive. Its purpose is that of all staffs: to assist the President in performing his mission of initiating, coordinating, and bearing responsibility for action. Most of its members are grouped in an administrative holding company, the Executive Office of the President.[20]

THE NATIONAL SECURITY COUNCIL. The National Security Council is the most important single entity in the list of presidential assistants. It is a unique body, created by law in 1947 as part of the Excutive Office but operating clearly in its own sphere. It consists of the President as Chairman, the Vice-President, the Secretary of State, the Secretary of Defense, the Director of the Office of Emergency Planning, and such other figures as the President may choose to invite. These additional participants normally include the Chairman of the Joint Chiefs of Staff, the Secretary of the Treasury, and the United States Ambassador to the United Nations.

In practice, the Council has a dual function. First, it may make recommendations to the President on matters requiring presidential decision that bear on the security of the United States. Second, it brings together at the highest level critically important officials concerned with foreign policy and provides a setting for full and frank discussion.

Recent Presidents have differed significantly in the way in which they have used the NSC. President Eisenhower viewed it as a major staff agency, installing an extensive "Establishment" and meeting weekly in plenary session. President Kennedy used the NSC on a much more *ad hoc* basis, with irregular and relatively infrequent meetings and a sharp reduction in the number of formal "papers" and "studies." President Johnson—at least during the early years of his administration—fell between the two extremes: He has employed the Council more frequently than did President Kennedy, but he has not formalized its operation as did Mr. Eisenhower.[21]

---

[20]E. H. Hobbs, *Behind the President* (Washington, D.C.: Public Affairs Press, 1954), remains the most detailed study of the Executive Office of the President.

[21]The most elaborate analysis of the functioning of the National Security Council is found in Senator Henry M. Jackson's subcommittee report on the national establishment for security: Subcommittee on National Policy Machinery, Senator Henry M. Jackson, Chairman, for the Committee on Government Operations, U.S. Senate, *Organizing for National Security* (Washington, D.C.: Government Printing Office, 1961–64). The most relevant recent information has been gathered into one volume, Henry M. Jackson, ed., *The National Security Council* (New York: Frederick A. Praeger, Inc., 1965).

THE PRESIDENT'S PERSONAL STAFF. The White House Office contains the President's personal staff. It consists of a relatively small number of administrative and personal assistants, aides, and secretaries. It performs such duties as are set for each of the members by the President himself and, especially under President Eisenhower, has taken over a significant number of more or less routine executive functions. Included in this group, but of special importance, is a Special Assistant to the President, with a mission entirely in foreign or national security affairs and who, under Presidents Truman and Eisenhower, gained a relatively large degree of freedom in making policy decisions on his own.[22]

OTHER SPECIAL ADVISORY BODIES. The Executive Office of the President includes (in addition to the two foregoing bodies) the Bureau of the Budget, the Council of Economic Advisers, the Office of Civil and Defense Mobilization, the National Aeronautics and Space Council, and the President's Advisory Committee on Government Organization. Each of these exists for the purpose of advising the President in the special area of its interest and collectively includes the major problems facing the Chief Executive. Not included in the Executive Office, but as close to the President as if it were, is his top military advisory body, the Joint Chiefs of Staff.

THE CENTRAL INTELLIGENCE AGENCY. The Central Intelligence Agency, established by the National Security Act of 1947, can be most usefully conceived of as an intelligence clearinghouse, directly subordinate to the National Security Council. The United States has a number of other agencies engaged in gathering information upon which to base policy decisions; the CIA seeks to coordinate all of them and to serve as a central agency for the distribution of intelligence data, as a correlator of intelligence emanating from other sources, and as a synthesizer of "intelligence estimates." It performs a number of intelligence activities of its own, but (according to law) only those that are most efficiently performed centrally. Its detailed operations are one of the most security-cloaked—and controversy-ridden—activities of the government.[23]

---

[22]Two revealing studies of how the White House staff operated under different Presidents are Sherman Adams, *First Hand Account* (New York: Harper & Row, Publishers, 1961) and Theodore A. Sorenson, *Decision-Making in the White House* (New York: Columbia University Press, 1963).

[23]In recent years a number of volumes purporting to give the "truth" about the CIA have appeared. Best known among these are David Wise and Thomas B. Ross, *The Invisible Government* (New York: Random House, Inc., 1964); Paul W. Blackstock, *The Strategy of Subversion* (Chicago: Quadrangle Books, Inc., 1964); and Harry H. Ransom, *Central Intelligence and National Security* (Cambridge, Mass.: Harvard University Press, 1958).

The Executive Establishment

THE STATE DEPARTMENT

The Department of State, headed by the Secretary of State, constitutes the major single source of foreign-policy decisions in the entire government structure. Under the pressures of international problems that have forced American policy mechanisms to proliferate, the Department has been obliged to renounce its once-exclusive control over foreign policy, but yet retains a central position. Even when interdepartmental consultation and coordination are necessary, it is most often the Department of State that serves as the principal medium of cooperative action.

THE ROLE OF THE SECRETARY OF STATE. The Secretary himself is perhaps the most important decision-maker. As the President's major adviser on foreign policy, his exact role is largely dependent on his personality and that of his chief, on the problems that arise during his tenure, and on the specific issues that fall to him to decide.

The Secretary's relationship to the President is an elastic one. The law of 1789 that created the office did not give the Secretary any detailed responsibilities in foreign affairs, but directed him instead to assist the President in any way that the latter directed. This legal directive empowers the President to establish almost any kind of relationship he wishes.

He may give the Secretary his head and pointedly refrain from having any policy of his own; although fairly frequent during the nineteenth century, such a relationship would be suicidal today. He may go to the other extreme and become "his own Secretary of State." This practice also may be effective for a short time (President Roosevelt, for example, often simply ignored Secretary Hull during much of World War II), but in the long run the State Department is too important to be left out entirely. In practice, some form of teamwork based on an agreed division of labor seems to be the most effective form of rapport; the blueprint of presidential functions outlined above would leave the Secretary's role both well defined and critical. Within the broad limits thus laid down by the Chief Executive, the Secretary of State could move with some freedom in making decisions of his own.[24]

---

[24]Recent studies of the role of the Secretary of State include Alexander de Conde, *The American Secretary of State* (New York: Frederick A. Praeger, Inc., 1962); and Henry M. Jackson, ed., *The Secretary of State and the Ambassador* (New York: Frederick A. Praeger, Inc., 1964). For an "inside" look at the Department's relations with President John F. Kennedy, see Arthur M. Schlesinger, Jr., "How the State Department Baffled Him," *Life* (July 30, 1965), pp. 18ff.

ORGANIZATION OF THE DEPARTMENT OF STATE

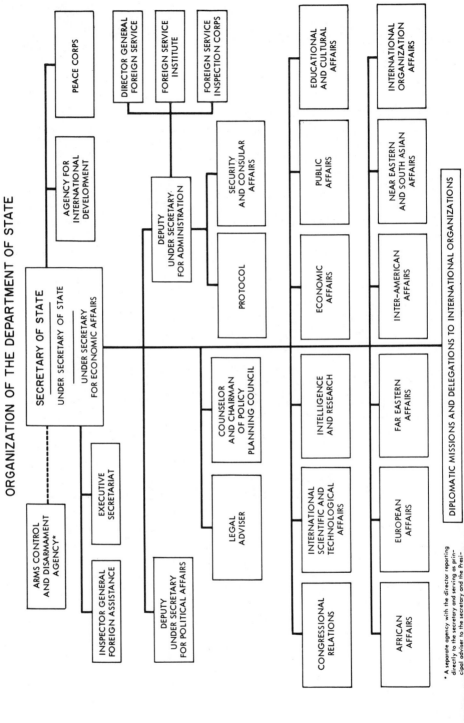

* A separate agency with the director reporting directly to the secretary and serving as principal adviser to the secretary and the Presi-

Today perhaps the most important policy-making role carried on by the Secretary is that of coordination. Whereas the Department's functions and staff have increased, its relative share in foreign policy has diminished. The military establishment, special agencies of all sorts, and Congress itself all play much larger parts than before 1941. As the key individual advising the President, however, and as the "senior" member of all varieties of coordinating bodies (such as the National Security Council), the Secretary is in a strategic position to exert major influence in determining decisions, whether or not he makes them himself.

THE ORGANIZATION OF THE DEPARTMENT. Although it is impossible to keep abreast of the Department of State's frequent (one is tempted to say "constant") reorganizations, the chart on page 42 is fairly recent and reveals its basic structure. It is doubtful that any future reorganization will make significant modifications.

As the chart indicates, the Department is organized at six levels. The highest is that of the Office of the Secretary; here are also found the Under Secretary and (at least in 1965) the Under Secretary for Economic Affairs. Also connected to the Department, through the Office of the Secretary, are the heads of the Agency for International Development, the Peace Corps, and the Arms Control and Disarmament Agency.

The next group consists of the two Deputy Under Secretaries, one for Political Affairs and the other for Administration. The third level is also sparsely populated at the present time: Here are found only two special-purpose staff members, the Legal Adviser and the Counselor (who directs the Policy Planning Council).

The fourth and fifth levels form the habitat of the Assistant Secretaries or their equivalent. The fourth consists of the "functional" bureaus, the fifth of the so-called "geographic" bureaus; in the latter are found the ubiquitous "desk officers," through whose hands flow so much of the raw material of policy. The sixth and final echelon includes all field representatives of the Department.

THE GEOGRAPHIC BUREAUS. Because of their central role in policy-making, the geographic bureaus are uniquely significant. There are, as the chart indicates, six such subdivisions. Each, in turn, is broken down into "offices," which are divided into "desks." The "desk officer" is usually known as "Officer in Charge of———Affairs," and is the specific point of contact the Department maintains with the country of his interest.

The Assistant Secretary in charge of a geographic bureau has a host of duties which vary literally with each turn of events. They may, however, be grouped under four main headings: (1) to communicate in all directions— upward to the Under Secretary and the Secretary on all matters needing their attention, downward to the subsections of his bureau and the "desk officers" within them, and laterally to his fellow Assistant Secretaries and others who may be interested parties; (2) to make decisions on questions falling within his scope on which he is empowered to decide and on which he has appropriate general directives for guidance; (3) to coordinate the offices within his bureau so that in his particular geographic area United States policy is both consistent within itself and also coordinated with American efforts in other parts of the world; and (4) to make recommendations on policy to the higher levels of the Department.

The geographic breakdown among the bureaus reflects the changing international environment. Illustrative of the manner in which change affects organization is the recent (1959) creation of the Bureau of African Affairs; elevation of that region to Assistant Secretary status indicates the increasing importance of Africa to the United States. Also revealing is the classification of relations with international organizations equally as important as Europe, the Far East, and Latin America.[25]

We should not be deceived by the illusory clarity with which functions are divided in the Department. Organization charts can do no more than suggest relationships; human beings persist in developing their own channels of communication and operation. The neat distinction between "functional" and "geographic" bureaus—with the former being in principle "nonoperational" and the latter charged with exclusive responsibility for operations—does not obtain in practice. Nor does every observer agree that they should remain mutually insulated.[26]

THE PROBLEM OF PERSONNEL. The Department of State is vexed by a constant personnel problem. The United States Foreign Service—a career service of professionals—was created by the Rogers Act of 1924 for the purpose of representing the United States abroad. Always small in number and high in quality, the career Foreign Service performed very creditably until World War II.[27] Under the pressure developed by the vast increase in functions, however, the career officers were joined by large numbers of noncareer civil service personnel. A serious cleavage developed within the Department between the elite group of FSO's and the much larger group of civilians. The latter, moreover, tended to monopolize lower- and middle-level policy-making

---

[25]We should note also that reorganization in response to new needs also occurs in the functional bureaus. For example, the Bureau of International Cultural Relations was also created in 1959.

[26]See the discussion in the Brookings Institution's report to the Senate Foreign Relations Committee in 1960: *The Formulation and Administration of United States Foreign Policy*, No. 9 in the Compilation of Studies, Committee on Foreign Relations, U. S. Senate, *United States Foreign Policy* (Washington, D.C.: Government Printing Office, 1960), Chapter 4.

[27]A valuable sketch of the history and the problems of the American Foreign Service is contained in J. Rives Childs, *American Foreign Service* (New York: Holt, Rinehart & Winston, Inc., 1948); an eloquent defense of the career service is made by former Ambassador Henry S. Villard in *Affairs at State*.

positions in the Department, with the predictable effect of further intensifying disagreement.

The obvious solution had long been known. In a permanent large-scale operation such as that in which the Department was engaged, there was no rational reason to continue a bifurcated personnel system. It made no sense to deny the United States the policy-making wisdom accumulated by long overseas service by the career personnel; it was equally nonsensical to require that policy be made by men who usually had no personal experience in the areas for which they were responsible. Amalgamation of the two services would solve both these operating difficulties at once.

Between 1948 and 1953 several attempts had been made to put some such plan into operation, but without success. The Foreign Service wished to keep its exclusive status; many of the civil-service group had no interest in overseas service. It was not until 1954, under the direction of Secretary Dulles, that amalgamation was accomplished. It came about as the result of recommendations by the Secretary's Public Committee on Personnel, known as the "Wriston Committee" after its chairman, Dr. Henry Merritt Wriston, the former president of Brown University.[28]

"Integration"—a word that became common currency in the Department for several years—involved the classification of virtually all the nonclerical posts of the Department, both overseas and home, as "dual": that is, capable of being filled either by career FSO's or civil-service personnel. A directive from the Secretary then ordered the gradual integration of the two services, not to be accomplished by the creation of an entirely new hierarchy but by the absorption of the great bulk of the civil-service policy personnel into the Foreign Service by "lateral entry." Civil-service employees not wishing to become liable for overseas service were to be separated without prejudice. The upshot was to be the creation of a vastly augmented Foreign Service.

There were many administrative difficulties involved in lateral entry and not a small amount of hard feelings; by and large, however, there was general satisfaction that the Foreign Service under the new scheme was destined to retain a sizeable amount of its old esprit de corps and at the same time to benefit from the large infusion of new blood.[29]

THE NEW FOREIGN SERVICE. The Wriston Report also dealt with another difficulty of the old Foreign Service. A combination of a peculiar philosophy of selection and restricted personnel budgets had made the FSO's an over-homogenous group. The Committee argued that recruitment policies should

---

[28]The Committee's report, *Toward a Stronger Foreign Service* (Washington, D. C.: Government Printing Office, 1954), was submitted to the Secretary on May 18, 1954. See also Dr. Wriston's *Diplomacy in a Democracy* (New York: Harper & Row, Publishers, 1956).

[29]See the three-part study by George F. Kennan, "World Problems and America's Administrative Response," *Foreign Service Journal*, XL, Nos. 8, 9, 10 (August, September, October, 1963).

be amended to attract candidates from a broader social, economic, educational, and geographical base. Its assumption, though never made explicit, was that the Service should be "democratized."[30]

Beginning in 1955 the recruitment recommendations were put into effect. An entirely new examination procedure was instituted, stressing general education and innate intelligence rather than specialized knowledge. Emphasis was placed on obtaining young men and women whose training encompassed such diverse fields as agriculture, accounting, and law. Appointments under the new system revealed some greater diversity than under the old, and there seemed to be grounds for hoping that the Committee's ideal of a "more representative" Foreign Service would be, to some extent, realized.

THE DEPARTMENTAL POINT OF VIEW. As the result of its own history, traditions, and place in the government hierarchy, the Department of State has developed a distinct point of view toward the problems with which it is called upon to deal. Although this attitude has elements of real strength— such as its emphasis on professionalism, its concern with the concrete and the practical, and its insistence on the service of its notion of the national interest —it also has a number of shortcomings that affect its role in modern American society and government.

Some of the deficiencies in the departmental point of view are not peculiar to it but grow instead out of its status as a major government department. Many of the familiar bureaucratic vices are present in the State Department, some of them in excessive amounts. The Department often seems obsessed with procedure and routine; many of its members are hypersensitive to considerations of career, prestige, and power.

More peculiar to the State Department itself is the sharp sense of cleavage between departmental personnel (domestic or foreign) and the American public at large. This may be explained to some extent by the unique relationship the Department has with the American people; after all, the argument sometimes runs, the Department's clientele is not the American public at all. "State" deals with foreign governments rather than with American citizens. In whatever way one may defend or explain it, however, the fact remains that a sense of nonidentification with the American mass public has led to two clear consequences of great importance. On the part of the Department, it has helped foster the growth of elitism: a self-generated impression that only the Department knows fully the real problems confronting the United States and what should be done about them. Large segments of the public have reciprocated by developing disdain, contempt, and distrust for departmental personnel. On both sides this is a disquieting outcome.

Operationally, the Department's point of view stresses caution, a faith in precedents (substantive and procedural) proved by time, and a preference for

---

[30]*Toward a Stronger Foreign Service*, pp. 39–44.

"making policy on the cables." Despite the lessons learned during the period since 1945 and many reorganizations of structure, and also despite uncounted high-level directives stressing the need for prevision and an adequate operational plan, the Department retains much of its pre-1941 disinclination to plan in advance. The obvious misuse of the Policy Planning Council as a high-strategy board instead of as a group freed from day-by-day operations underscores this tendency. The usual desk officer refuses to deal with "hypothetical questions" and seems to extract much satisfaction out of making the "brush fire" approach to policy a normal operating procedure. This tends to make the Department swing between routinized administration during periods of calm and frenzied extemporization during crises, neither of which seems to the casual observer the ideal way to conduct American foreign policy.

THE MILITARY

One of the significant changes in the making of American foreign policy since 1945 has been the systematic inclusion of the military point of view. This, as we shall see later, is not part of the traditional image of how American foreign policy is made; military and foreign affairs were usually thought to be two separate worlds, to be kept apart at all costs. Today, however, the picture is completely reversed; most of the controversy over the point deals with whether or not the views of the armed forces receive too much consideration rather than too little.[31]

MILITARY CALCULATIONS IN AMERICAN POLICY. What sort of military considerations are appropriate to American policy decisions, and why has it become so important since World War II that they be included? The answer lies in certain basic relationships between ends and means in any state's foreign policy.

The ends of policy—the objectives of the state—must be served by such means as are available and appropriate. Military power is one of these possible means open—at least to some limited extent—to every state. Any policy-maker, therefore, should take account of his state's ability to apply military pressure and, conversely, of its ability to withstand any probable similar pressure applied by other states. As long as international politics goes

---

[31]The general subject of military influence on foreign policy is analyzed critically in Samuel P. Huntington, *Changing Patterns of Military Politics* (New York: Free Press of Glencoe, Inc., 1962), and in Burton M. Sapin and Richard C. Snyder, *The Role of the Military in American Foreign Policy* (Garden City, N.Y.: Doubleday & Company, Inc., 1954); see also Raymond Aron, *The Great Debate* (Garden City, N.Y.: Doubleday & Company, Inc., 1965), and F. W. Mulley, *The Politics of Western Defense* (New York: Frederick A. Praeger, Inc., 1962).

on within the state system as we know it today, such judgments will continue to be necessary.

American policy, therefore, must in part be based on two kinds of military judgments: the calculation of the affirmative employment of military measures and the provision of defensive measures against hostile (or potentially hostile) measures taken by others.

One final statement seems in point. Means-ends analysis is a very tricky subject. In practice, means often look disconcertingly like ends, and vice versa. This is particularly true in American military policy. Weapons supremacy, such as in strategic bombardment aircraft or in thermonuclear bombs, in theory is significant primarily as a means to some other policy objective, such as superiority over a potential enemy. As actually carried out, however, weapons leadership over all comers (or, as sometimes among air-power enthusiasts, over any combination of comers) becomes a policy end of the first priority. This point has led to more controversy over the military contribution to American foreign policy than perhaps any other.[32]

THE PENTAGON AND FOREIGN AFFAIRS. The Department of Defense and the three service departments under its direction share directly in the foreign-policy process at all levels. The Secretary of Defense is, of course, a member of the Cabinet where his views have been regularly solicited by the President. He is also a permanent member of the National Security Council where his special concerns are even more directly in point.

The Secretary of Defense and the three service secretaries each have special foreign-policy assistance in the form of an assistant secretary or other high-ranking civilian official who is charged with direct responsibility for making the Department's contribution to all interagency or joint decisions. Since so many operational decisions are taken on a multidepartmental basis via the National Security Council or lower-level joint bodies, it can be seen that great care is taken to have the "military point of view" represented in almost every sort of decision-making body of more than routine importance.

THE JOINT CHIEFS OF STAFF. The preceding paragraphs considered the Secretary of Defense as the spokesman for the military, even though most of the top leadership of the Defense Department is civilian. It is via the Joint Chiefs of Staff that the viewpoint of the uniformed services is expressed.

The Joint Chiefs are the principal military advisers to the President, the

---

[32]One of the most influential discussions of the military contribution to American policy is Samuel P. Huntington, *The Common Defense: Strategic Programs in National Politics* (New York: Columbia University Press, 1961). The problems of conventional war are discussed in Morton H. Halperin, *Limited War in the Nuclear Age* (New York: John Wiley & Sons, Inc., 1963). The various facets of the problem of security are discussed in Ralph E. Lapp, *Kill and Overkill* (New York: Basic Books, Inc., Publishers, 1962), and in Gordon B. Turner and Richard D. Challener, eds., *National Security in the Nuclear Age* (New York: Frederick A. Praeger, Inc., 1960).

National Security Council, and the Secretary of Defense. Their approach is professional and technical; they personify the "means" role of the military. Their advice in theory does not concern itself with any aspect of policy other than its military feasibility and/or its military consequences. Much of the dispute over the role of the Joint Chiefs (such as the heated battle that developed as the aftermath of the Indochina crisis of 1954) stems from the widely shared suspicion that they often slip out of their purely instrumental role into an advocacy of substantive policy.[33] To the extent that this charge can be substantiated, there is some basis for arguing that civilian supremacy is being undermined and that the always-unclear distinction between substantive policy ends and purely military means is also being eroded.

OTHER EXECUTIVE AGENCIES

The power to make foreign policy is widely shared in the executive branch.[34] To make a catalogue of the exact part played by each of the hundred-odd agencies that participate in one way or another would exhaust both compiler and reader. All we can do is to sketch some of the broader outlines and to indicate one or two bodies of special importance.

THE TREASURY DEPARTMENT. The Treasury Department constitutes the third in the foreign-policy "big three" Cabinet departments. In part, this stems from the central proposition that foreign affairs consumes the great bulk of the annual budget of the United States; with so much money involved, the Cabinet's fiscal expert naturally becomes a key figure. The requirements of a budget in balance, or at least in near-balance, in time of peace often could have great controlling and directing effect on American policy.[35]

The Treasury Department has operating responsibilities as well, however; a good share of American policy deals with financial and monetary matters

---

[33]Admiral Arthur B. Radford, the then Chairman of the Joint Chiefs, presented his notion of the role of the group in an interview in *United States News and World Report* (February 25, 1955) entitled "We Give Military Advice Only."

[34]A famous chart appearing in the Hoover Commission's Task Force Report on Foreign Affairs indicated the "Organization Units of the Executive Branch Participating in the Conduct of U. S. Foreign Affairs." What was striking was the small number—less than twenty—of executive agencies that did not in some way share in foreign policy; even some of these were open to debate. Among the few that the Task Force felt did not qualify were the National Archives, the Office of the Housing Expediter, the Indian Claims Commission, the National Labor Relations Board, the National Capitol Park and Planning Commission, the Railroad Retirement Board, and the Commission on Fine Arts. Also in this group was the Selective Service System; many a recent draftee might argue that this agency plays a great—if indirect—part in American foreign policy!

[35]Under President Eisenhower, Treasury Secretaries Humphrey and Anderson were generally supposed to be peculiarly influential in holding down government expenditures on military and international programs.

and the Treasury makes basic decisions in this area. There is in the Department an Office of International Finance concerned entirely with this general problem; perhaps its major concern is with American membership in the International Monetary Fund, the International Finance Corporation, and the International Bank for Reconstruction and Development. Tariff administration, direct international loans, and other aspects of economic foreign policy are other areas in which Treasury recommendations carry great weight. Its importance is underscored by President Eisenhower's decision to include the Secretary as a regular member of the National Security Council.

OTHER CABINET DEPARTMENTS. All the other Cabinet departments share in policy-making, although in unequal amounts. All their administrative heads participate in Cabinet meetings and thus have access to the President when international issues are being discussed. All of them, in addition, enter the foreign-policy field to some extent in performing their statutory duties.

Perhaps the most significant of this group are the Departments of Commerce and Agriculture, for reasons that are largely self-evident. Commerce is responsible for the whole matter of foreign trade; Agriculture enters such fields as the international movement of food products and the procurement of agricultural experts for American technical assistance programs. The rest of the Cabinet Departments—Labor, Post Office, Justice, Interior, Health-Education-Welfare, and Housing-Urban Development—have roles that, although equally as direct as those of Agriculture and Commerce, are not as extensive. Labor, for example, functions through the International Labor Organization; the Post Office represents the United States in the Universal Postal Union; the Justice Department controls immigration and resident aliens; Interior administers American overseas possessions.

NON-CABINET AGENCIES. One of the administrative problems of American government—a perennial concern of all attempts at reorganization—is the large number of administrative bodies that lie outside the Cabinet department structure and are responsible only to the President. This condition applies in foreign affairs as well as in any other area; some of the most significant policy decisions are made and implemented by non-Cabinet bodies.

Perhaps the most important of these, now that foreign aid has once again been taken directly into the Department of State, is the Atomic Energy Commission. It is responsible for dealing with all aspects, domestic and international, of the development of atomic energy.

Other independent agencies with foreign-affairs functions include the Maritime Commission, the Civil Aeronautics Board, the Federal Communications Commission, the Export-Import Bank, and the United States Tariff Commission. Each of these to some extent makes policy in its own area and influences decisions—often by representation on interdepartmental bodies—on questions in which it is interested.

COORDINATION IN THE EXECUTIVE BRANCH

THE DECENTRALIZATION OF POLICY. It has become clear in the foregoing discussion that policy-making is highly decentralized in the executive branch. The power to commit the United States to action has been widely diffused. It is true that total responsibility for all executive action lies on the President, but it would not be humanly possible, or even desirable, to force him actually to make all the decisions for which he is responsible. He must, in some way, delegate authority so as to reduce his own task to manageable proportions.

Administrative theory and the needs of foreign policy agree, however, that delegating decision-making power is not in itself a sufficient answer. Guidance and control must be exercised by the delegating authority; a general policy line must be stipulated and mechanisms developed to guarantee that the action taken by subordinates agrees with the overall orientation. One index of the efficiency and effectiveness of American foreign policy is the extent to which detailed decisions made by operating personnel are consistent with the broader policy directives issued by higher ranking officials.

THE NEED FOR COORDINATION. Since policy-making is so extensively decentralized, some apparatus for coordination becomes necessary. This task has dimensions both horizontal and vertical. Horizontally, there must be agreement at any level among the various agencies making policy so that their cumulative effort is exerted to a common end; this basic harmony must be both intradepartmental and interdepartmental. Vertically, units lower in the hierarchy must coordinate with those higher up (even though in a different department). Only if this is done successfully can excessive confusion, contradiction, and frustration be avoided and something like a single American foreign policy be forged.

THE FORMS OF COORDINATION. In the attempt to devise a sufficiently high working level of coordination, four sorts of devices have been developed and are used individually or in conjunction.

1. The first, dealing mainly with vertical coordination, involves the President himself and the White House Office. The prestige and position of the Chief Excutive make it possible for him to demand—and usually to receive— a considerable amount of effective harmony in making and executing policy. The National Security Council is the archetype of this kind of coordinating body; the Bureau of the Budget, in a different way, performs the same task.[36]

2. A second coordinating device consists of assigning coordinating authority over a particular policy area to a single department. Such an agency is

---

[36]Hobbs, *Behind the President*, Chapter 2: "Bureau of the Budget."

directed to provide general guidance to all other interested agencies and to see to it that their various efforts mesh into a coherent whole. The Department of State has been most frequently given this sort of directive. The Treasury has something of a similar role with regard to a number of multi-agency financial programs.

3. Most commonly, coordination is attempted by means of the interdepartmental (or interagency) committee. On these bodies—of which there are dozens—all "interested" units are represented and are supposed to achieve a happy harmony, both in reaching decisions and in seeing to their execution. Although hallowed by much use, and despite the very considerable success that some of them have enjoyed, the interagency committee remains a technique of only limited utility. Their numbers have multiplied to the point where membership on any of them is apt to be conferred on such low-ranking members of the department that none may authoritatively speak for their own agencies. If the appropriate committee cannot do its job of providing coodination, this leaves the department that has the inside track on the policy area in question to enjoy virtually a clear field.

4. Finally, a "supercoordinator" was created in 1955 when the Operations Coordinating Board came into existence by executive order. This body consists of the Under Secretary of State as chairman, the Deputy Secretary of Defense, the Director of the CIA, the Director of the United States Information Agency, a representative of the President, and a representative of any other agency the President selects. Its efforts were clouded in controversy, and President Kennedy decided upon its dissolution in February, 1961. Mr. Kennedy's rationale in dispensing with the OCB was based on the principle that high-level coordination was primarily a task for the White House. Here the matter has since rested, as Presidents Kennedy and Johnson have attempted (with uneven success) to exert their personal influence in the direction of better coordination.

Congress and Foreign Policy

Although it has become commonplace to point out that the part played by Congress in foreign policy has increased, both relatively and absolutely, during the decade since the end of World War II, we must nevertheless admit that even this augmented role has remained secondary to that of the executive. From the very beginning of the Republic, Congress has chafed at the logic that has made the Presidency the chief inspiration for foreign policy; the history of legislative-executive relations over international issues is one of recurrent dispute. In recent years the legislative branch has made some progress in defining its own place in the foreign-policy process; today Congress has a role that is of major importance.[37]

But this is not to say that the national legislature has achieved equality in policy-making, or that it is desirable that it should. Law and logic agree that the initiative and the lion's share of the decisions naturally reside "at the other end of the [Pennsylvania] avenue." This would lead us to suppose that Congress's role in the process is essentially a reacting one; we would expect its function to be that of modifying, amplifying, and expediting decisions already taken by the President or his assistants. Recognizing the operation of checks and balances in the American system, we would further assume that Congress would be peculiarly prone to exercise some form of negative control on executive decisions, either by refusing to accept them or by changing their substance, direction, or timing. These indeed seem to represent the nature and extent of congressional power over foreign policy.[38]

We should make one further qualification before briefly examining the ways in which Congress affects the course of policy-making. Although congressional *power* itself has definite and measurable limits, the same cannot be said for congressional *influence*. Being generally more sensitive to the tides of electoral politics than is the President (this is especially true of the House, whose members must face the voters every two years), Congress is prone to reflect shifts of public opinion that its members detect (or think they detect). This gives congressional opinion great weight in the executive branch whenever the responsible bureaucrats believe that the legislators are convinced that they are expressing a popular consensus. This matter of congressional influence, so difficult to measure, often goes further to explain the legislative impact on foreign policy than does any detailed consideration of the legal powers of Congress.

CONGRESSIONAL FUNCTIONS

How does Congress enter into the policy-making process? One very interesting answer was made in a study generally favorable to the legislature's aspirations to a major role, and listed six specific functions:

1. It has a responsibility to identify and inquire into problems that may call for legislative action.

---

[37]The leading study is James A. Robinson, *Congress and Foreign Policy-Making* (Homewood, Ill.: Richard D. Irwin, Inc., 1962). See also Robert A. Dahl, *Congress and Foreign Policy* (New York: Harcourt, Brace & World, Inc., 1950), and Ernest S. Griffith, *Congress: Its Contemporary Role*, 3d ed. (New York: New York University Press, 1960).

[38]See especially Daniel Cheever and H. Field Haviland, *American Foreign Policy and the Separation of Powers* (Cambridge, Mass.: Harvard University Press, 1952).

2. It shares with the Executive the function of framing broad national objectives.
3. It can help to estimate the relative merits of alternative approaches to dealing with various problems.
4. It may give attention, on a selective basis, to questions of detail related to broader issues.
5. It has the exclusive responsibility for enacting authorization and appropriation legislation.
6. It can help, as part of its investigatory function, to evaluate the performance of the Executive, again on a selective basis.[39]

Without seeming captious, we may point out that these six functions, although phrased generally in favorable terms and aimed at portraying Congress's role at its largest, are all essentially reactive in nature. Congress may question, evaluate, investigate, and often must authorize; it plays an indispensable role in assaying the climate of politics in which decisions must be taken. Important as this role is, however, even the most sympathetic students of Congress cannot elevate the legislative function to as critical a place as is occupied by the executive.

In carrying out its function, Congress has a significant array of powers. Most of these partake of the general legislative role and are of special relevance to foreign affairs only because of the expanded place international relations now occupies in the concerns of congressmen.

THE SENATE: TREATIES AND APPOINTMENTS.   Of the two houses, the Senate enjoys superior power and prestige in foreign affairs.[40] Part of this primacy arises from the popular notion of the Senate as the "upper house"; part from the greater age, average length of service, and freedom of discussion that characterize senators. But the bulk of senatorial leadership comes from two specific constitutional provisions: the power to approve treaties and the power to confirm appointments.

The Constitution gives the President the power to make treaties with the "advice and consent" of two-thirds of the Senate. As students well know, the "advice" part of this provision is a dead letter except as the President chooses to consult with individual senators during the negotiation phase of a treaty. "Consent" involves a two-thirds vote of the Senate in favor of a treaty, the effect of which is to open the document to ratification of the President.

The Senate thus enjoys, as one author puts it, a "treaty veto";[41] it may simply refuse to approve the treaty. Such action voids the entire enterprise.

---

[39]Brookings Institution, *The Formulation and Administration of United States Foreign Policy*, p. 24.

[40]For a sympathetic study of the lower house, however, see Holbert N. Carroll, *The House of Representatives and Foreign Affairs* (Pittsburgh: University of Pittsburgh Press, 1958).

[41]D. F. Fleming, *The Treaty Veto of the American Senate* (New York: G. P. Putnam's Sons, 1930).

The Senate, however, may not change the treaty in any way. It may suggest amendments which, if made, would make the document acceptable; what happens to these proposed amendments, however, depends on the President. He may choose to renegotiate the treaty and seek to have the amendments written into the agreement; on the other hand, he may find them unacceptable and simply drop the whole affair. The treaty veto has been a favorite subject for discussion by critics of the American constitutional system ever since the defeat of the Treaty of Versailles in 1919; the historical record indicates, however, that only a small minority of all treaties have been defeated. Nor should we overlook the fact that executive agreements are free from any necessary congressional control, although some congressional opinion feels that a legislative veto should be placed on these agreements as well.

Appointments of ambassadors, ministers, and consuls—the entire foreign service—must receive senatorial approval. Occasionally, as in the struggles over the confirmation of Mr. Charles Bohlen as Ambassador to the Soviet Union in 1953 and Mrs. Claire Booth Luce as Ambassador to Brazil in 1959, this power has great significance for foreign policy. It has been generally felt in the Senate, however, that the President should have a free hand in selecting his foreign-policy personnel, and it is seldom that confirmation of a diplomatic appointment becomes an important issue.

LEGISLATION. It is in the general function of legislation that the whole Congress comes squarely to grips with foreign policy. There are only a few areas of foreign policy in which the President can move freely without the necessity of any legislation; usually some implementing law must be passed before policies can be effectively carried out. This means that most major programs must be submitted to Congress in the form of bills. Here is where the legislature may exercise its amending or negating authority, and it is rare for an executive suggestion to pass through the congressional mill without being reshaped in some way.

So important is the potential impact of Congress on any project that the executive tends to consult with congressional leaders in advance so as to tailor his requests to what Congress will accept; sometimes—as in the case of the Marshall Plan—Congress will run away and develop its own program anyway.[42] To the extent that policy declarations come to be formalized into specific programs of action—and this is a great extent indeed today—Congress has great power to alter the executive designs; at the very least, such a constant possibility requires that the President and his advisers always take congressional opinion into account.

APPROPRIATIONS. What is true of legislation applies even more sharply to one special manifestation of legislative power: the appropriation of funds.

---

[42]John C. Campbell, *The United States in World Affairs, 1947–48* (New York: Harper & Row, Publishers, 1948), p. 503.

American foreign policy demands money in great amounts, and no funds at all are forthcoming from the Treasury of the United States except as a result of congressional appropriation. Congress tends to be more generous in authorizing appropriations than in actually making them; the appropriations committees of Congress (particularly in the House) are more wary of granting funds than are the substantive committees.

INVESTIGATIONS. We must also recognize the importance to foreign policy of investigations by congressional committees. This is a case of influence rather than of power; the net effect of committee investigations is frequently to create powerful currents of public opinion for or against particular policy emphases. On occasion these have had great impact on the executive by affecting mass opinion and forcing department heads to conform to the wishes of the particular committee. Obviously the extent to which an investigation succeeds in this regard depends on public reaction; what direction is taken usually depends on the orientation of the committee's efforts.

RESOLUTIONS. Also in the category of functions of influence is the device of the congressional resolution, either by one house or—more effectively—by both. A resolution, expressing the "sense of the house(s)" but without legal effect, serves notice to all concerned that the congressional mind has been made up on the particular point. Such resolutions are most effective (1) when they represent accurately the state of public opinion on the questions and (2) when they are passed prior to the making of a firm commitment by the executive. Examples of important resolutions include the so-called "Vandenburg" resolution in 1949 that was in effect an advance acceptance of the North Atlantic Treaty and the several resolutions of the House between 1953 and 1956 opposing Communist China's admission to the United Nations.[43]

CONGRESSIONAL CHARACTERISTICS ON FOREIGN POLICY

Recognizing that generalizations about 535 legislators are hazardous, we may nevertheless suggest a few common characteristics revealed by Congress as it copes with the issues of foreign policy. Perhaps the safest and broadest

---

[43]Mention should be made of the less than totally wise resolution passed (with fewer than 60 dissenting votes) by the House in September 1965 expressing the "sense of the House" that it was the right of any western hemisphere state unilaterally to intervene in another if, in the opinion of the intervening state, there was a danger of a communist takeover. This move was generally regarded as an attempt to vindicate President Johnson's intervention into the Dominican Republic the preceding April, a move widely criticized at the time and attacked only a few days previous to the House resolution by Senator J. William Fulbright, Chairman of the Senate Foreign Relations Committee, in a speech on the Senate floor. The resolution was not opposed overtly by either the White House or the Department of State, although their displeasure was obvious at the time.

statement we can make is that the legislative branch is quite well equipped to perform its checking and amending function and does so with reasonable success; when it turns from this, however, and attempts to make policy on its own, the outcome is usually unfortunate.

NEGATIVISM. One reason for this limitation on the effectiveness of Congress is that body's fundamentally negative orientation to foreign policy. Because of the nature of the problem and its place in the scheme of government, Congress is best fitted for saying "no." It usually cannot take the initiative efficiently; its function is commonly confined to reacting to proposals emanating from the executive offices. Only in special and infrequent cases is it possible for Congress to play a positive role. The frequent pleas for Congress "to seize the initiative" in foreign policy have uniformly failed to mark out any clear procedure whereby the legislature could make its will effective in opposition to the President.

CONFLICT WITH THE EXECUTIVE. A second characteristic grows out of the first. Under the checks and balances system of American government, competition and conflict between legislature and executive is to be expected; this is the reason that Congress is made to share in so many executive powers. On purely domestic policy, Congress may and often does take the initiative, and the resulting relationship with the executive is more nearly an equal one. But on foreign policy, certain advantages inhere in the President, and Congress's exercise of its checking role gives rise to much controversy. Many congressional moves in foreign policy defy rational explanation on any other ground than its simple determination to differ with the executive and to make its disagreement effective.

It should be emphasized in this connection, however, that both the amount and the kinds of legislative-executive conflict in foreign policy are in a state of constant evolution. Today there is much more partnership than open disagreement between the branches on fundamentals; Congress (or, more frequently, its committees) cooperates with the executive both in identifying objectives and in exploring basic approaches.[44] In exact relationship to the extent to which agreement has increased on fundamentals, the tendency of Congress to quarrel about details has grown stronger.[45]

POLITICAL ORIENTATION. We have already alluded to the all-too-obvious

---

[44]An interesting example of this relationship is furnished by the series of fifteen studies on particular problem areas of United States policy undertaken during 1958 and 1959 by private and university research organizations under contract for the Senate Foreign Relations Committee. These reports in the aggregate constituted a major mobilization of the nation's intellectual resources on foreign policy issues, and evidence multiplied that the recommendations they contained were being taken seriously by the executive.

[45]Even the first session of the 89th Congress that convened in January, 1965—a Congress more responsive to presidential leadership than any since the first term of Franklin D. Roosevelt—found a number of occasions on which to disagree with President Johnson on minor details of foreign policy.

fact that Congress in general, and the House of Representatives in particular, tends to be more responsive than the President to short-range voter (or interest-group) pressure. Repeatedly the executive has recommended programs that, although open to question on their merits, at least were devised in all seriousness as an attempt to advance the prevailing idea of national interest. When the Congress seized upon them and attacked the problem of their implementation, far too often for comfort the dominant concern of many members was not whether the programs would be advantageous to the nation. Rather their preoccupation was with the effect of such policy implementation on their individual political fortunes. Foreign-aid and military appropriations have been especially obvious political footballs in this respect; an articulate and powerful bloc in Congress has consistently felt that voters in the grip of a cold war would never object to large military expenditures but that they would resent "giveaway" of which foreigners were the beneficiaries.

Although a major indictment can be made of Congress on the grounds of a shortsighted truckling to vociferous and self-serving elements of public opinion, it would not do for us blithely to dismiss the political approach of Congress as being entirely without justification. There is always an "ivory-tower" tendency in any government bureaucracy, and particularly in a foreign-affairs bureaucracy; it is all too easy to dismiss mass opinion as beneath serious consideration. To the extent that the top echelon of decision-makers becomes divorced from the tides of popular attitudes, it is thoroughly salutary for Congress continually to remind them that there is an American public and that its wishes must be taken into account.

DELIBERATENESS AND LACK OF INFORMATION. Two final characteristics of congressional activity in foreign policy remain to be noted. Congress tends to operate slowly, and it almost always acts upon incomplete and inaccurate information. The first stems from its function as a deliberative body; it would be violative of the congressional responsibility in American democracy for it to be expected to reach its decisions with great speed and in total silence. Yet, even after granting this, we may still contend that much of Congress's slowness is unnecessary; it seems evident that it could work more rapidly without sacrificing anything essential to the legislative process.

The poverty of congressional information is a much more serious problem. In the past ten or fifteen years, Congress has made great efforts, and with some success, to improve the amount and the reliability of the information on which it must base its decisions. Yet the question is still unsolved, and may even prove insoluble. How can Congress play its part in shaping American policy if it simply does not have available enough data to make the right kind of decisions? The information that is necessary is often by definition a secret; to open the executive files to congressional investigation would make extremely delicate matters subject to heated, partisan, and very public debate.

Alongside this we must place the lack of mutual trust and confidence between Congress and the executive department.

If Congress must depend on the executive for all its information, there is a real danger that the data fed it will be—in the delicate bureaucratic word— "selective": that is, deliberately chosen and slanted so as to influence Congress in the direction the bureaucracy desires. The most the legislative branch has been able to do up to this point is to staff its specialized committees on foreign affairs and related subjects with experts of its own and to try to develop such liaison with the executive as is possible and effective.

LEGISLATIVE-EXECUTIVE COOPERATION

There is little purpose in our reiterating the need for legislative-executive cooperation in foreign affairs. Everyone realizes that the United States cannot afford to have its President and its Congress always at swords points over foreign policy. There is likewise no advantage in wishing more or less plaintively (as many scholars have done)[46] that the United States had a parliamentary system such as that of Great Britain, in which the problem would simply never come up. The United States has separation of powers and checks and balances, and there is no possibility of their abandonment in the foreseeable future. Within their context Americans must devise a workable mechanism of foreign policy.[47]

CONSULTATION. The most frequently relied-upon device for achieving some such sustainable level of agreement is that of formal or informal consultation. The President frequently calls meetings of congressional leaders (not necessarily limited to foreign-policy experts) and briefs them, sometimes submitting to questioning. Less often, similar sessions are held by department heads. Informally, legislative-executive contacts are extensive and frequently quite productive. There is no doubt that consultation has been at least a qualified success in reducing the chasm between Congress and the executive; how effective it is in any particular case depends on both the political climate and the personalities involved.[48]

LIAISON. Recently executive departments have begun to add to their

---

[46]See, for example, the argument advanced in James MacGregor Burns, *Congress on Trial* (New York: Harper & Row, Publishers, 1949).

[47]This problem, and some recommended solutions, are dealt with in Cheever and Haviland, *American Foreign Policy and the Separation of Powers.*

[48]No President ever consulted as often, as intimately, or as effectively on an informal basis with Congress as Lyndon B. Johnson. His well-known affinity for the telephone and his wide acquaintanceship on Capitol Hill led to frequent—almost constant—consultation with both friendly and hostile members of Congress as important questions of foreign policy were being discussed.

staffs specialists on congressional liaison. The State Department has an Assistant Secretary for Congressional Relations whose mission is, as one department official put it privately, "to keep Congress happy." President Eisenhower added a liaison specialist to his personal staff; other agencies have done the same. In this way the executive, needing the support of Congress, has sought to establish a favorable relationship. We may perhaps regret that no reciprocal effort may be remarked on the part of Congress.

COMMISSIONS.   Less widespread than the first two, and by nature perhaps destined to remain so, are the mixed legislative-executive investigating commissions. Part of their membership is appointed by the President, and the remainder consists of members of Congress; the congressional representation is usually drawn from both parties in both houses. Such a body, once it deals with an issue and makes a recommendation, represents a fusion of opinion that cannot help being reflected in some way in subsequent policy. Outstanding examples of recent years are the two Hoover Commissions on administrative reorganization and the Randall Commission on foreign economic policy.[49]

THE PERMANENCE OF THE NEED.   None of these devices has solved the problem, however; legislative-executive relationships on foreign affairs are always uncertain and, as we know, often hostile. It is probable that the issue can never be thoroughly resolved as long as the United States retains its peculiar political system. No one would deny, however, that the importance of maintaining enough cooperation to ensure the adoption and implementation of adequate policies is great enough to justify continuing effort, however much we may despair of final perfection.

The Execution of American Policy

Although any oversharp distinction between the formulation and the execution of American foreign policy would give rise to serious misunderstanding (since each impinges upon and affects the other), it is nevertheless true that there is specialization of function between those who make decisions and those who execute them. Generally, this division follows a home office-field service breakdown. As might be expected, most of American foreign policy is executed beyond the boundaries of the United States.

---

[49]The Randall Commission's report: *Report to the President and Congress, January 23, 1954*, Commission on Foreign Economic Policy (Washington, D.C.: Government Printing Office, 1954).

DIPLOMACY

The State Department is the instrument of American diplomacy, operating through the United States Foreign Service and the overseas missions. Because of the multiplication of overseas programs and the discovery and exploitation of new channels of power, the diplomatic specialists today must share responsibility with other executive agencies. Yet it is true that the diplomatic instrument of policy, personified by the resident American ambassador, still occupies the paramount position in executing American foreign policy.

MULTIAGENCY REPRESENTATION. The non-State Department representatives abroad can be grouped in three categories: military, foreign-aid, and informational. Between 1947 and 1954 each of the three types of representation grew to the point where in many states it rivaled the American diplomatic mission in prestige and in importance.

Military representation occurred through the various service attachés in the embassies, through the military-aid missions, and through the training groups. Foreign-aid representation was at its height under the Economic Cooperation Administration, where the various "country chiefs" of ECA had more money to dole out and consequently were in a position to maneuver the resident American ambassador off the stage and into the wings. A few of them, it might be noted, did exactly that. The Mutual Security Administration, since it simplified the administration of American aid, somewhat improved this situation. Informational activities were never the threat to regular diplomats that the first two types were, largely because State carried on so many itself.

In line with the general doctrine now governing the execution of American policy that State is the single agency *primarily* responsible for foreign *policy* and that coordination is to be brought about under State Department *leadership*, the moves taken in the past decade have all been aimed at strengthening the position of the senior foreign-affairs agency. The theory behind the attack on multiagency representation abroad can be summed up in President Eisenhower's language when he sent the foreign-affairs reorganization plans to Congress in 1953: "[It shall be the duty of] each Chief of Diplomatic Mission in each foreign country [to] provide effective coordination of, and foreign policy direction with respect to, all United States Government activities in the country."[50]

THE AMBASSADOR. As the quotation above indicates, the United States Ambassador is responsible for the orderly and coordinated execution of all United States policy in the country to which he is assigned. Because of the

---

[50]*Congressional Record* (June, 1953), p. 5849.

sheer size of the operation, American ambassadors are to a surprising extent primarily administrators. They operate their own embassies (in some states no small task in itself) and supervise the activities of a congeries of other American operating groups. Administrative talent is an only-recently recognized requirement for a successful ambassador.

The "traditional" diplomatic functions of representation, communication, and negotiation are still performed, but in terms more appropriate to contemporary technological conditions. Communication with the home office is nearly instantaneous, negotiation tends to be back-seat driven from Washington, and representation is much more ceremonial than heretofore. The changed circumstances under which an ambassador operates have given rise to the frequent accusation that the ambassador has become a mere messenger boy for the Secretary of State. This judgment is overdrawn; there remains a great reservoir of power in the ambassadorial role.[51]

One factor underscoring the new significance of the ambassador's function is the evolving concept of what constitutes representation. In the eighteenth century, "Citizen" Genet, French Ambassador to the United States, was declared to be *persona non grata* because of his attempt to "go over the heads of the government" and apeal directly to the American people for support of his government's policy. This era has passed. Today the American ambassador to any country is—as much as he is anything else—a specialist in public relations. He is expected to make himself available to the public as the visible embodiment of the United States and to do whatever he can to create an image favorable to the United States. Difficult to specify, this new form of representation is an important part of the ambassador's task.

THE OVERSEAS MISSION.   The American mission to a foreign country (known in bureaucratic circles as the "country team") varies in size according to the volume of business and the intrinsic importance of the relationship. The organizational structure is likewise flexible. Generally speaking, the ambassador, as chief of mission, has as his principal assistant a counselor of embassy. The latter usually succeeds to leadership (as *chargé d'affaires*) when his chief is absent. Below the counselor the mission splits into operating sections according to the nature of the work load; political and economic sections are universal, and consular and administrative sections are increasingly common. Outside the normal hierarchy of the mission, but full parts of it, are the various special attachés. In addition to the familiar military, naval, and air attachés, commercial, agricultural, legal, labor, cultural, and several other types of attachés exist. The attachés have a peculiar status. Although they are full-fledged members of the ambassador's staff, they remain employees of agencies other than the State Department. They are nominated by the Depart-

---

[51]For a memoir developing the role of the modern ambassador, see (former Ambassador) Charles M. Thayer, *Diplomat* (New York: Harper & Row, Publishers, 1959).

ments of Commerce, Agriculture, Army, Navy, Air Force, Justice, and so on; they remain administratively under their home department's control.

MILITARY FOREIGN POLICY

One index of the growing maturity of American foreign policy has been the gradual, although yet incomplete, meshing of military policy with foreign affairs. There is little disagreement today that foreign policy has a military dimension and that armed might is both an end in itself and a means to the accomplishment of other American objectives. A good deal of what the United States does in international affairs today is oriented to military calculations. The execution of what we call military foreign policy therefore becomes a separate problem.[52]

Generally speaking, operational responsibility for the military aspects of foreign policy—with the principal exception being the negotiation of treaties of alliance, agreements on bases, and so on—rests with the Department of Defense, acting usually through the Secretary or his principal assistant for these matters, the Assistant Secretary for International Security Affairs. The three service departments have roughly similar arrangements in their respective heirarchies for the accomplishment of the same general purposes.

WAR. Perhaps the most obvious, but also the most basic, military operation with a foreign-policy implication is the conduct of war. We shall remark in a later chapter on the time-honored American tendency to regard war as an interruption in the orderly course of international affairs, and to conceive the spheres of diplomacy and warfare as occupying different universes. This idea has virtually disappeared among policy-making officials; there is also some reason to believe that its acceptance is declining among the general public.

There is no more important foreign-policy mission than the prosecution of a war. This is the supreme test of a nation's ability to achieve its objectives; to exert the enormous effort required for modern warfare without having a concrete political objective in mind is today a waste that not even the United States can afford. The Korean conflict—despite General Mac-Arthur's valedictory to the effect that "in war there is no substitute for victory"—is an example of a military struggle that was kept always at the service of a reasonably clear set of political objectives. It did not involve expending more effort than necessary to meet the limited political goals and did not result in a conclusive military victory.

Today, with hydrogen bombs, intercontinental ballistic missiles, biological warfare, and the other horrors of modern total war, there is considerable

---

[52]See Sapin and Snyder, *The Role of the Military in American Foreign Policy.*

doubt about the long-range utility of large-scale warfare as an effective instrument of national policy. The time may come when a military establishment will lose all utility in executing policy and become instead merely an example of national conspicuous consumption; mankind, however, is not yet at that point. As long as total war remains a possibility, the United States must be prepared if necessary to implement at least the bare minimum of its objectives —continued survival—by military means.

OCCUPATION OF DEFEATED STATES. Following World War II another example of the execution of foreign policy by military means was provided by the American occupation of the defeated enemy nations.[53] Occupation had a political purpose; to occupy Germany and Japan merely for the sake of revenge would have been childish. The military outcome of the war required physical occupation of the terrain as the only way the Allies could make any beginning on their ambitious plans for postwar reconstruction. The Allied plan called for the reasonably early replacement of military by civilian control over the Axis; the cold war, however, intervened and the whole project was drastically remodeled. It is generally agreed, however, that the military branches performed their share of the mission creditably.

MILITARY AID. In the contemporary period, one of the major preoccupations of the military establishment of the United States is the administration of the American military-aid program. Since the end of the 1940's, furnishing military assistance to growing numbers of foreign states has been a major element of American policy. The execution of these programs has been entrusted to the Department of Defense.

Control over military aid, under the terms of the various statutes, is vested in the Secretary of Defense and exercised by the Assistant Secretary for International Security Affairs. To supervise the general assistance program by coordinating requests from the various states, there was created the Joint United States Military Advisory Group (JSMAG) that works in close harmony with the Assistant Secretary. In each foreign state receiving American military aid there is a Military Assistance Advisory Group (MAAG) that cooperates with its host government in developing recommendations for aid. Both JSMAG and MAAG are composed of representatives of the three uniformed services.

Another form of international military assistance, often coupled with the supply of materiel, is a training mission. The Department of Defense and the service departments have sent a sizable number of training missions to states

---

[53]For Germany, see E. H. Litchfield, *et al.*, *Governing Postwar Germany* (Ithaca, N. Y.: Cornell University Press, 1953); for Japan, see Kazuo Kawai, *Japan's American Interlude* (Chicago: University of Chicago Press, 1960) and (former Ambassador) William Sebald, *With MacArthur in Japan* (New York: W. W. Norton & Company, Inc., 1965). See also Hajo Halborn, *American Military Government* (Washington, D. C.: Infantry Journal Press, 1947).

in Europe, the Middle East, the Far East, and Latin America. Obviously the military establishment of a nonindustrialized nation that receives large shipments of American equipment—Turkey, for example—needs considerable instruction in its employment. Even if formal assistance in "military end-items" is not involved, it is in the interest of the United States to see to it that its allies have as efficient a military force as possible.

ALLIANCES.   One final form of policy executed by the military is the fulfillment of continuing American responsibilities in the various mutual-security pacts to which the United States is a party: NATO, SEATO, ANZUS, OAS, CENTO, and a number of bilateral agreements. Since the primary military mission today is deterrence, it would seem that this elaborate alliance structure plays a major part in discouraging communist attack.

Of all the alliances, NATO is both the most elaborate and the neatest example; military planning and military action in the others are not nearly so advanced. NATO is, of course, under civilian control at the highest level, the North Atlantic Council. From there on, however, it is a military matter organized into a Supreme Headquarters various subordinate commands, and elaborate logistical arrangements. Throughout all of these, American military personnel may be found; the post of SACEUR—Supreme Allied Commander, Europe—has never been filled except by an American.[54]

FOREIGN AID

One of the most dramatic departures in American policy after World War II was the popular acceptance of responsibility to extend large-scale assistance of all sorts—economic, military, and technical—to friendly foreign states. With the details of that program we shall be concerned later; at the moment we are interested only in the organizational pattern for administering this aid as it has developed since 1947.

THE STATE DEPARTMENT AND FOREIGN AID.   From the very beginning of the aid program there was serious disagreement about the most efficient and expeditious method of its administration, and now, after nearly two decades, the issue is in no way settled. The central problem has always been the relationship of the Department of State to the overall aid program. Obviously, if the Department is the principal agency for policy recommendation, and if foreign assistance is to be at or near the center of American policy, there are good reasons for the State Department to exercise some manner of control over the whole operation. On the other hand, the serious diminution of the Department's prestige with Congress and the public, and the formidable

---

[54]Between 1951 and 1965, the several commanders were Generals Eisenhower, Ridgeway, Gruenther, Norstad, and Lemnitzer.

arguments against loading the Department down with extensive operating responsibilities, raised doubts about the value of giving it direct responsibility for the program. Various solutions have been attempted, involving virtually every possible form of relationship between the Department and the aid program, but no clear verdict has yet been rendered.[55]

CHANGING ADMINISTRATIVE PATTERNS. The various administrative arrangements made for the foreign-aid program over the years illustrate both the changing fortunes of bureaucratic war and the evolution of the program itself. Five separate stages can be distinguished.

The first "aid agency" to be created was the Economic Cooperation Administration, set up in 1948 to administer the Marshall Plan for Europe. ECA was under an administrator of Cabinet status who was not under the control of the Department of State but whose exact relationship with the Secretary was never precisely defined.

In 1951 ECA was replaced by the Mutual Security Administration, charged with all aid operations in the field except for technical cooperation and—by explicit directive of Congress—completely independent of the Department of State. MSA's only rival was the Department of Defense which was obviously central to the rapidly evolving military aid program.

The inauguration of President Eisenhower brought about the next change. MSA was abolished in 1953 and replaced by the Foreign Operations Administration. FOA took over everything except direct military aid but lost the independence enjoyed by MSA; the Secretary and the Department of State were given "policy direction" over FOA at all levels.

The Department of State won its greatest victory in 1955. In that year FOA was abolished in its turn and succeeded by the International Cooperation Administration. This new body was significant in two ways: First, its name suggested the growing emphasis on economic development within the aid program; second, ICA was brought entirely within the Department of State. ICA was, it is true, defined as "autonomous," but its administrator was a direct subordinate of the Secretary and its activities were under the day-by-day policy control of the Department.

The final (at least up to the present time) stage began with the arrival of President John F. Kennedy's New Frontier. In 1961 the name of the aid agency became the Agency for International Development (AID—a fortunate but not accidental acronym). Otherwise, except for the constant increase in the economic-development aspect of the effort and a corresponding reduction in direct aid programs, AID's responsibility and status are the same as were those of ICA.

---

[55]The various alternatives are discussed in the 1951 Brookings report, *The Administration of Foreign Affairs*, pp. 90–101. See also two later Brookings studies: *Administrative Aspects of U. S. Foreign Assistance Programs* (Washington, D. C.: Government Printing Office, 1957) and *The Formulation and Administration of United States Foreign Policy*, pp. 65–71.

INTERNATIONAL INFORMATION

Another policy area of great significance is "international information," a delicate euphemism for the somewhat more blunt words "propaganda" and "public relations." Like military foreign policy and foreign aid, the development of large-scale information programs was an event of the postwar period. Propaganda for political purposes is a pursuit in which Americans do not yet thoroughly feel at home (although why this should be so is somewhat difficult to understand; in the United States advertising is a fine art), and the record compiled by the various information programs is not breathtaking.

THE PROPAGANDA PROGRAM. The pressures of the cold war forced the United States to develop an elaborate, if somewhat helter-skelter, propaganda program. The State Department was central to the process from the beginning, with its own activities being conducted by the International Information Administration. The two major areas of the Department's work in this field prior to 1953 were the Voice of America, a global network of radio stations beaming propaganda at hostile and neutral nations, and the United States Information Service, under whose auspices hundreds of American "information centers" were set up throughout the world. These last provided outlets for American publications of all sorts and gave thousands of foreigners their first insights into what the United States was really like.

The Department of State was not alone in the field, however. It is a characteristic of American government today that every operating agency in the executive branch is acutely sensitive to the need for good public relations, and nearly every one of the many agencies with responsibilities in foreign policy began to handle the propaganda aspects of its own mission. The State Department's principal competitor in this field was the series of foreign-aid agencies, notably ECA and MSA. Rapid turnover in personnel, persistent attacks from all directions by a variety of opponents, discontinuity in policy, and a failure in its own public relations made the International Information Administration a somewhat less than popular agency. Its critics pointed it out as a glaring example of the inadvisability of conferring program responsibility on the Department of State.

PSYCHOLOGICAL WARFARE. Further complicating American information policy was the concept, born apparently some time in the early stages of the Korean war, of "psychological warfare." This phrase implied something new in foreign policy, aimed at undercutting the strength of opposing regimes by destroying the bonds of loyalty between the people and their governments. It was argued that, if the United States were to use the resources of modern techniques of persuasion in a coordinated attack on the stability of opposition governments, it might be possible to solve all the problems of the cold war at one blow, with great economy in manpower, resources, and money. It was indeed an attractive prospect.

Interagency committees of various sorts were created to develop an overall strategy of psychological warfare and to coordinate its execution by the appropriate departments. Between 1951 and 1953 a great deal of effort was expended with little perceptible change in the pattern of propaganda being put forth by the United States overseas.[56] President Eisenhower, shortly after taking office, instituted an entirely new survey of the entire field of psychological warfare by the so-called Jackson Committee. The committee's report, made in mid-1953, exploded the entire concept of psychological warfare as a specialized technique, susceptible of manipulation by specialists in persuasion and capable of ending the cold war speedily and economically. The committee contended that all policy had its psychological aspects, that they could not be separated from other facets, and that everyone engaged in policy implementation was in effect carrying on psychological warfare.

THE UNITED STATES INFORMATION AGENCY. The United States Information Agency (USIA) was created in 1953 by executive reorganization directive. This body was the counterpart in its field of the Foreign Operations Administration; it took over all information programs from whatever agencies had been carrying them on. In particular, it absorbed the International Information Administration and the Voice of America. Again like the FOA, its operational monopoly was not matched by equal freedom in policy. Instead it was ordered to follow the policy direction of the Secretary of State; the material it distributed (whether by broadcast or by printing) was subject to censorship by the Department.

Even more illustrative of the status of the Agency was the relation of its overseas representatives, known as Public Affairs Officers (following the delicate nomenclature of the Division of Public Affairs [relations] in the Department of State). These propaganda chiefs were to be part of the American diplomatic mission in the country to which they were assigned and, although under the general administrative direction of the Director of USIA, were also under the operational control of the resident American chief of mission. Both in Washington and in the field, the propaganda arm of American policy is now under the day-by-day control of the State Department. This development is part of the broader plan of clarifying the status of the Department as chief policy-maker for the entire government.

---

[56]An interesting view of the early stages of the American "sykewar" effort is presented by Edward W. Barrett, former Assistant Secretary of State for Public Affairs, in his valedictory, *Truth Is Our Weapon* (New York: Funk and Wagnalls Co., Inc., 1953).

CHAPTER **3**

The
Heritage of
the Past

For many Americans, "foreign policy" as something about which the citizen should concern himself dates from some point in the period between 1940 and 1946. Prior to the crisis that brought about World War II, American disinterest in international affairs was endemic; popular ignorance and unconcern about international relations was a dominant cultural trait in the United States between 1920 and 1939. Foreigners have often remarked about the nonhistorical outlook of American culture. In no area is it more true that Americans are unaware of the record of their own past than it is in foreign affairs.

But American foreign policy has a history, and a long and complicated one at that. Present-day Americans are in large measure the heirs of the record, good and bad, made by their ancestors. That the statesmen of an earlier day are today often without honor or even any particular recognition by their descendants in no way minimizes the importance of their work.

This chapter will attempt to characterize the course of American foreign policy up to the end of World War II. We shall not attempt to detail, or even to summarize, the continuous story in a strict chronological sense; excellent studies of superb scholarship and considerable literary value have already performed this task for us.[1] Our task will rather be to extract from the whole of the history of American foreign policy those particular elements, whether broad trends or uniquely important events, that have special pertinence to contemporary American foreign relations.

The Formative Century

The nineteenth century—by which we mean the period of somewhat more than a hundred years between the Treaty of Paris (1783) and the Open Door notes (1899 and 1900)—may be called the "formative era" in American foreign policy. During this time two sorts of things happened that have had consequences far beyond their historical setting. First, a number of relatively firm policy lines aimed at particular objectives were developed by the American government and came to acquire the semi-sacrosanct character of fixed commitments. The United States is still struggling with the more unfortunate consequences of some of these undertakings. Second, and related to the first by the normal processes of democratic government, a rather clear popular tradition of American participation in foreign affairs became an article of faith with the bulk of the politically articulate and active population.

CONTINENTAL EXPANSION: "MANIFEST DESTINY"

Certainly the most obvious foreign-policy trend of the nineteenth century was the process of continental expansion that began almost as soon as the new United States set itself up in business as an independent sovereignty. We should recapitulate briefly the series of moves that brought the United States to its present continental boundaries within a short fifty-year period of active expansion.

THE LOUISIANA PURCHASE. The first great acquisition—and the largest single one—was the purchase of the Louisiana Territory from France in 1803.

In 1800 Napoleon of France had persuaded Spain to cede him the Louisiana Territory. The United States became uneasy at the thought of having

---

[1]The leading diplomatic histories are those by Samuel Flagg Bemis, *A Diplomatic History of the United States*, 5th ed. (New York: Holt, Rinehart & Winston, Inc., 1965); Richard W. Leopold, *The Growth of American Foreign Policy* (New York: Alfred A. Knopf, Inc., 1962); Thomas A. Bailey, *Diplomatic History of the American People*, 7th ed. (New York: Appleton-Century-Crofts, 1958); and Julius W. Pratt, *A History of United States Foreign Policy* (Englewood Cliffs, N. J.: Prentice-Hall, Inc., 1955). Among the many collections of documents, one of the most useful is Daniel M. Smith, ed., *Major Problems in American Diplomatic History* (Boston: D.C. Heath & Company, 1964).

powerful France as its neighbor to the west instead of weak Spain as well as at the possibility of being forever barred from access to the port of New Orleans. Napoleon, on his part, soon lost interest in Louisiana in the light of his pressing need for funds to continue his European conquests. Jefferson, supported by Britain, offered to purchase Louisiana for $15 million. Napoleon agreed, and in one stroke of a pen the United States had more than doubled its area.

THE FLORIDAS. The next step took the United States southward. "The Floridas," comprising today all the state of Florida and the Gulf coast of Alabama and Mississippi, were under Spanish sovereignty at the time of the Louisiana Purchase. For fifteen years after 1803, American expansionism clashed with weak Spanish rule. Finally, in 1818 Secretary of State John Quincy Adams presented Spain with a virtual ultimatum. The Bourbons surrendered; in 1819 Spain ceded the United States all her lands east of the Mississippi in return for some token concessions from the United States.

TEXAS. In 1845 the independent republic of Texas was annexed to the United States by joint resolution of Congress. Texas had seceded from Mexico in 1836 after a successful war of independence and had thereupon sought admission to the Union. Political pressures, generated largely by the slavery issue, made it impossible to secure the necessary two-thirds majority in the Senate in favor of a treaty of annexation. A bare majority could be scraped up in both houses for a joint resolution, and this somewhat questionable device was used to approve the annexation of the first independent sovereignty to become one of the United States.[2]

OREGON. The Oregon Territory, including most of the northwestern corner of the United States and part of present-day British Columbia, had long been claimed by both Great Britain and the United States. President James K. Polk took a strong diplomatic line with the British in 1845; by mid-1846 a relatively favorable compromise was reached. The boundary, running along the 49th parallel, added a rich and large territory to the existing United States.

THE MEXICAN CESSION. By the terms of the Treaty of Guadalupe Hidalgo that terminated the war with Mexico, in 1848 the United States gained another enormous bloc of territory. The area ceded included present-day California, Nevada, Utah, and parts of Arizona, Colorado, New Mexico, and Wyoming. Vast as this new acquisition was, it almost failed to satisfy the expansionist elements in the United States. The "all-Mexico" movement gained such momentum that total annexation was seriously discussed in high government circles.[3]

---

[2]Pratt, *A History of United States Foreign Policy*, pp. 231–233, discusses the political maneuvering. Hawaii also was an independent republic at the time of its annexation by the United States.

[3]Bailey, *Diplomatic History of the American People*, pp. 263–265.

THE GADSDEN PURCHASE. The territory won in the Mexican War filled in the outlines of the continental United States of today with a single exception: the Gila River Valley in southern Arizona and New Mexico. In 1853 (a half-century after the Louisiana Purchase) the American minister to Mexico, James Gadsden, successfully negotiated the purchase of this area from Mexico for $10 million. Subject to some minor frontier rectification, the limits of the United States on the North American continent had been reached.

HEMISPHERE HEGEMONY: THE MONROE DOCTRINE

To many Americans, the phrase "Monroe Doctrine" has a familiar ring. Depending on their historical knowledge, their political sophistication, and their educational background, they know a variety of things about it. Most people suspect that it has something important to do with Latin America; a smaller number understands that it also has implications for the "Old World" in general and Europe in particular. Its more subtle ramifications tend to be overlooked in its contemporary relevance as a symbol of the "good old days" in American foreign policy.

THE ORIGINAL DECLARATION (1823). The "Monroe Doctrine" proper refers to certain paragraphs in President James Monroe's annual message to Congress on December 2, 1823. In these sections he dealt with the problem of the newly independent republics of Latin America and the growing possibility that the European powers might intervene to return them to the European colonial powers. On the basis of this specific issue a doctrine was formulated that went far beyond the crisis at hand.

Monroe's message first declared that the "American continents" were "henceforth not to be considered as subjects for future colonization by any European power." Any attempt on the part of the European states "to extend their system to any portion of this Hemisphere" would be considered as "dangerous to our peace and safety." In return for forbidding European penetration in the Americas, Monroe then restated the intention of the United States to refrain from interfering in exclusively European matters.[4] This latter point, often thought of as one of the doctrinal roots of isolationism, we shall discuss later in this chapter.

THE POLK RESTATEMENT (1845). The doctrine, so bravely enunciated, lapsed without application until the Oregon crisis in 1845. As a part of the vigorous diplomacy he was conducting with Great Britain, President Polk's message to Congress in December, 1845, averred flatly that "no future

---

[4]The relevant portions of Monroe's message are quoted in Smith, *Major Problems in American Diplomatic History*, pp. 167–169.

European colony or dominion shall with our consent be planted or established on any part of the North American continent."[5] This carried Monroe's original doctrine a step further. The original doctrine had been intended to inhibit European colonization or armed intervention; Polk's reformulation was expanded to include even diplomatic action as falling within the forbidden area.[6]

THE MEXICAN CRISIS. The first real test of the Monroe Doctrine came during the American Civil War when Napoleon III of France established his puppet, Maximilian of Austria, as Emperor of Mexico. This was an open defiance of the doctrine; once the American decks had been cleared by the end of internal conflict, however, American pressure on the increasingly uncomfortable Napoleon induced him to withdraw his troops, and the native Mexican forces destroyed Maximilian's *papier-mâché* empire. The Monroe Doctrine had been vindicated; an open European attempt to penetrate an American preserve had been turned back.

THE ESTABLISHMENT OF AMERICAN DOMINANCE. After the Civil War, the United States turned to Central and South America as a matter of right. The United States came to interpret the Monroe Doctrine as meaning something more than just the defense of the hemisphere against European penetration. Little by little, beginning in the Caribbean and working gradually southward, an increasing measure of American control over Latin America became apparent under the cloak of the Monroe Doctrine. So far had this gone by 1885 that Secretary of State Olney could claim that "the United States is practically sovereign on this continent, and its fiat is law upon the subjects to which it confines its interposition."[7] The development of this trend into what was known as "dollar diplomacy" did not occur until after 1900, but the principle was well established long before the turn of the century.

ANGLO-AMERICAN COOPERATION:
THE UNADMITTED ALLIANCE

What is remarkable about the long record of Anglo-American relations during the nineteenth century is that neither party would openly admit the fact of cooperation. The burden of responsibility for this condition rests mainly on the Americans; the popular image of Britain as the ancient enemy of American independence made open and admitted coordination of effort

---

[5]Dexter Perkins, *Hands Off: A History of the Monroe Doctrine* (Boston: Little, Brown and Company, 1941), p. 62.

[6]Perkins, *Hands Off*, p. 90.

[7]*Foreign Relations of the United States, 1895* (Washington, D.C.: Government Printing Office, 1896), Vol. I, p. 558.

a political near-impossibility. "The redcoats are coming" had too strong a hold on American ideology for any formalization of what was for many years a real—if tacit—working agreement.

It was not until the crisis of the Spanish-American colonies that cooperation became real. Although the United States rejected Prime Minister Canning's proposal for joint action because of Secretary of State Adams' disinclination "to come in as a cock-boat in the wake of the British man-of-war,"[8] the American government's decision for a unilateral declaration was clearly founded on an assumption of Britain's approval.[9] Canning himself gloated that he had "called in the New World to redress the balance of the Old."

THE SHIELD OF SEA POWER. It was British sea power that made the Monroe Doctrine effective; it was British sea power that made American continental expansion possible. Continental Europe could not break through the wall of ships thrown up by Britain and strike at the United States; neither, for that matter, could the United States easily exert much influence on European affairs. This whole situation pleased London immensely. At least until the United States entered into the Pacific and came into direct contact with the states of Europe there, most American dealings with continental states were conducted, either directly or at one remove, via the British Foreign Office. Though Americans would have bitterly resented being told so, the facts are that the United States was, during most of the nineteenth century, the protégé of British sea power.

THE LATTER HALF OF THE CENTURY. After the Civil War the nature of the Anglo-American relationship changed, at first subtly and then radically.[10] In the western hemisphere itself, the burgeoning American feeling of competence encouraged the United States to act vigorously on its own, even—as in the Venezuelan boundary dispute of 1895—to the point of defying Britain itself. Britain found that the young American republic was no longer a protégé in Latin America but a rival.

Meanwhile, the United States and Britain were both expanding into the Pacific. Here the old relationship was untenable; American sea power was, at least in the central and eastern Pacific, superior to the British. By the time of the rise of Japan, Britain found itself obliged to accept the United States

---

[8]John Quincy Adams, *Memoirs*, C. F. Adams, ed. (Philadelphia: J. B. Lippincott Co., 1875), Vol. VI, p. 179.

[9]Walter Lippmann, *United States Foreign Policy: Shield of the Republic* (New York: Pocket Books, Inc., 1943), p. 14.

[10]For this general point, see Crane Brinton, *The United States and Britain* (Cambridge, Mass.: Harvard University Press, 1945), pp. 122–132; for a graphic elucidation of the necessity of Anglo-American cooperation in sea power, see Eugene Staley, "The Myth of the Continents," in H. F. Armstrong, ed., *The Foreign Affairs Reader* (New York: Harper & Row, Publishers, 1947), pp. 317–333.

as an equal power in many Pacific ventures and in some cases to defer to American leadership.

Even Britain's European position deteriorated so sharply in the face of German dynamism that Canning's idea of the "new world redressing the balance of the old" came to take on a new meaning. Instead of hoping to keep the United States out of Europe, Britain began to think wistfully of the advantages of having it as a full participant in the system.[11] Active American entry into European affairs was to wait until after 1900 and the Presidency of Theodore Roosevelt, but long before that time Britain was planning to extend Anglo-American cooperation into the area of European great-power relationships.

NONINVOLVEMENT IN EUROPE: "ISOLATIONISM"

We come now to what is one of the most misunderstood elements in nineteenth-century American foreign policy as well as perhaps the most abused term in the entire language of discourse about the external relations of the United States: isolation. No other single idea has had such an influence on the shaping of American attitudes toward the outside world, nor has any had a more complicating effect on the American task of coming to terms with the twentieth century.

EUROPE AND THE YOUNG UNITED STATES. Americans sometimes forget that the accomplishment of American independence was only partially due to the valor and the patriotism of the Revolutionary generation in the United States. The war of American independence was only one part—and a relatively minor part at that—of the long series of great-power struggles that persisted in Europe for nearly two centuries. The Treaty of Paris that ended the American war marked a phase in this Europe-wide conflict; the next era opened with the wars against revolutionary France only a few years later. The birth of the United States was a direct outcome of a convulsion in the society of European states, and several of its members naturally looked on the new state as a creature of their system.

THE POST-REVOLUTIONARY INVOLVEMENT. During the thirty-one years between the Treaties of Paris and Ghent, the young United States was buffeted by the tides of great-power politics. American policy was tossed back and forth by the three great powers of the period: Britain, France, and Spain. With Britain the United States fought the War of 1812. Relations with France included an undeclared war and twenty-five years of bickering over navigation, commercial regulation, and so on. With Spain was opened the

---

[11]See L. M. Gelber, *The Rise of Anglo-American Friendship* (New York: Oxford University Press, Inc., 1938).

tedious and ill-tempered maneuvering that continued until the cession of the Floridas in 1819.

The early experience of the United States with the states of Europe was an unhappy one. Young, weak, inexperienced, and sensitive, the American government found its abrupt introduction to the ways of great-power politics an event not to be celebrated and if possible to be avoided in the future.

THE MONROE DOCTRINE. The Congress of Vienna, in 1815, ended the long period of general European war and ushered in the peaceful century of what is sometimes called the *Pax Brittanica*. This left the way open for the brave pronouncement of the Monroe Doctrine. President Monroe's statement not only denied the western hemisphere to future European colonization but also foreswore any American interest, present or future, in "the wars of the European powers, in matters relating to themselves. . . ." "The political system of the allied powers [in Europe] is essentially different in this respect from that of America," he went on. This was the genesis of formal American isolation.

UP TO 1900. The principle of noninvolvement, thus promulgated at a moment when the times were most propitious to its success, endured throughout the rest of the nineteenth century as the basis of American attitudes toward Europe.[12] It was never intended that isolation should be complete to the point of nonintercourse. Indeed, the very word "isolation" did more to confuse than to illuminate. Perhaps the more accurate term to characterize American policy toward Europe would be "independency."[13] This word carried a double connotation. In the first place, it suggested that the United States would intervene in European affairs only when and to the extent that American national interest demanded. It also implied clearly that such intervention would never create a precedent but would always be a matter of circumstance.

OPERATIONAL BASES OF NONINVOLVEMENT. Why did noninvolvement work so well for so long? What were its working bases? What happened to make it irrelevant after 1900? There are three explanations for the effectiveness of the policy and its eventual obsolescence.

The first reason is geographic. The United States was separated from

---

[12]One of the most famous later expressions of the principle was that of Secretary of State Seward in 1862: "The American people must be content to recommend the cause of human progress by the wisdom with which they should exercise the powers of self-government, forbearing alliances, intervention, and interference." Quoted in John Bassett Moore, *Digest of International Law* (Washington, D.C.: Government Printing Office, 1906), Vol. VI, p. 23.

[13]The word was popularized by the late Charles A. Beard, who developed his ideas in detail in several works including *The Idea of National Interest* (New York: The Macmillan Company, 1934); *The Open Door at Home* (New York: The Macmillan Company, 1935); and *The Devil Theory of War* (New York: Vanguard Press, Inc., 1936).

Europe by an ocean, and this fact does more to explain isolationism than do many more complex exegeses. The three thousand miles separating Europe from the Atlantic coast of the United States might as well have been three million; they made America as remote from European concerns as if it had been on the moon.

The second explanation has a political root. British success in keeping the European states pinned down on the Continent during all but the last quarter of the century left the United States with only one possible enemy: Britain itself. We have seen that the harmony of interest between Britain and the United States prevented any fundamental clash from developing. Thus the United States again had Britain to thank, this time for making the reality of isolationism some approximation of the ideal.

Finally, we must mention technology. In 1823 all the great powers were European and played their major roles on that continent. As long as the technology of warfare and statecraft enabled Europe to maintain its global dominance, the principle of American noninvolvement squared with the facts of international life. When the great British effort collapsed in the face of the new technology, the bases of American policy were washed away. The extension of the European state system to non-European areas, the breakout of Germany into rivalry with Britain, and the rise of Japan all spelled the end of *Pax Brittanica* and of American isolation.

BEGINNINGS OF A PACIFIC POLICY

American interests in the Pacific grew bit by bit during the nineteenth century. The original base of American entry into the affairs of Asia and the Pacific rested on nonpolitical foundations. It was a combination of economic and missionary activities, plus the urge to abolish the humiliating status ceremonies that all Westerners endured before Oriental courts, that brought the United States into the Pacific in the first place. American Far Eastern policy was already a reality before the outcome of the war with Spain made the United States a full-fledged Pacific power.

CHINA. Although the United States was one of the leaders in the commercial penetration of China, it refused to follow Britain and France into the practice of extracting economic concessions by strong diplomacy and, occasionally, by force. Candor compels us to admit, however, that American insistence on the most-favored-nation clause in dealings with China usually resulted in any new concessions won by Britain and France being extended to the United States in turn. This technique was later formalized as the "Open Door."

JAPAN. In 1854 the famous expedition of Commodore Matthew C. Perry succeeded in forcing Japan to open its gates to the outside world. Throughout most of the rest of the century a succession of able American diplomats played a large part in Japan's transformation. So important was their work that one scholar has said that Japan at the turn of the century "was largely a child of American diplomacy."[14]

ALASKA, SAMOA, AND HAWAII.   In 1867, the United States acquired Alaska by purchase from Russia,[15] thus giving the nation a strategic position over-looking the entire north Pacific and bringing it within a few miles of Asia. Only after 1941 did Americans realize the critical importance of this northern outpost. Much less well known are the circumstances surrounding the acquisition of Samoa during a confused period between the first treaty in 1878 and the German-American agreement of 1899 that divided the archi-pelago between the two states. In the South Pacific the United States found itself directly involved in European great-power politics.

Then in 1898 the United States annexed Hawaii—an independent republic at the time. This action was the culmination of a half-century of American religious and economic penetration into the native government of the islands. Pressure from American sugar interests for annexation, the overthrow of the native government, and the expansionist fervor generated by the war with Spain combined to persuade Washington to undertake the annexation, but only after long and partisan debate.

SUMMARY ON AMERICAN PACIFIC POLICY.   This brief recital of American penetration into the Pacific and the Far East suggests one or two conclusions. First, isolation, or noninvolvement, was never a reality in the Orient. Ameri-can expansion in that region had a long history, and the United States was perfectly willing to come to grips with the great powers of Europe in an Asiatic setting. Second, there is little evidence that most Americans—or their government—were self-consciously pursuing a crystallized idea of national interest in the Orient. Each step in United States policy in the Far East was either accidental, prompted by a special-interest group, or brought on by a vague nationalist expansionist urge. By the time the war with Spain made the United States a major power, the nation already had large Pacific commitments without being overly sure of what it was supposed to do with them.

The Birth of Great-Power Status

Historians often divide their time periods into centuries, with each hun-dred years characterized in a different way. This device is sometimes artificial;

---

[14]Bailey, *Diplomatic History of the American People*, p. 314.

[15]A brief survey of the negotiations leading to the purchase of Alaska is found in W. A. Williams, *American-Russian Relations, 1781–1947* (New York: Holt, Rinehart & Winston, Inc., 1952), pp. 21–22; see also Pratt, *A History of United States Foreign Policy*, pp. 324–328.

very seldom does human history move from one era to another just as a century ends. In the case of United States foreign policy, however, this method comes close to the actual facts. During the last two years of the nineteenth century the United States passed through a major change in status; it entered the twentieth century with a new set of problems and a new orientation to them.

THE WAR WITH SPAIN

It was the American victory over the decaying monarchy of Spain that signaled the arrival of the United States at international maturity. Out of this brief and in many ways sordid conflict came the new posture that has so radically altered the foreign policy of the United States.

THE COMING OF THE WAR. There is no need for us to analyze the complex and unedifying train of events that led up to the American decision to go to war.[16] Perhaps most important was the Cuban insurrection that was so bloody on both sides and so close to the territory of the United States. But there were other factors at work as well. The expansionist urge, fortified by the Samoa and Hawaii incidents and by American truculence in the Venezuelan dispute with Great Britain, was frankly searching for someone upon whom to test America's newly realized national strength.

It was also during this era that "yellow journalism" began to have a major influence on mass attitudes on foreign policy. In the Spanish crisis, such newspapers as the New York *Journal* and the New York *World* took credit for forcing the government's hand. Just as it seemed as if diplomacy had succeeded in adjusting American claims against Spain, public opinion— whipped up by the press—shook off all restraint. Popular clamor for war and a belligerent Congress forced a reluctant President McKinley to accept battle.

MILITARY VICTORY. Although marred by stupidity and ineptitude, the Spanish-American War resulted in an American victory in an *opera bouffe* atmosphere. The Spanish fleet was destroyed at Santiago, Cuba, and Admiral Dewey sank the Spanish naval force in Manila harbor in the Philippines—a long way, we may note, from the Cuba the United States was allegedly fighting to liberate. On land, the fighting in Cuba was fitful and inconclusive, although admittedly sanguinary. The Americans won a few small victories in Cuba, occupied Puerto Rico, and looked around for more worlds to conquer. But Spain had had enough.

Legal war with Spain had begun on April 21, 1898; on August 12, hostilities were ended by a protocol signed (on behalf of Spain) by the French

---

[16]For a highly critical study of the preliminaries of the war, see Walter Millis, *The Martial Spirit* (Boston: Houghton Mifflin Company, 1931).

Ambassador to the United States. The peace conference convened in October in Paris. Negotiations continued until the peace treaty was signed in December; the treaty was approved by the United States Senate in February, 1899. By the terms of this agreement the United States served notice on the world that a new great power had been born, with augmented interests in both oceans.[17]

THE EXPANDED FRONTIER

The most visible result of the war was the acquisition of a vast (or, at least, far-flung) empire. The American security frontier had been thereby tremendously expanded. In the two areas where American naval power could be expected to exploit the new bases most effectively, the Caribbean and the Pacific, the outcome of the war presented the United States with entirely new situations.

THE NEW EMPIRE. By the terms of the peace treaty, the United States succeeded to what was left of Spain's world position: a colonial empire in the western hemisphere and a position as a major power in the Pacific. There were two major territorial acquisitions and several smaller ones to serve as booty for the "splendid little war."

Cuba, the ostensible pretext for the war, achieved independence—but only of a sort. In a compromise between the "no-annexation" Democrats and the expansionists, Cuba became a protectorate of the United States under the terms of the "Platt Amendment" of 1901. The island republic continued in this status until the wholesale revision of the Latin American policy of the United States that took place during the 1930's.

The Philippines, on the other hand, were openly annexed, but only after a bitter debate. The "anti-imperialists," led by William Jennings Bryan, seemed to be winning the argument in favor of early independence for the Philippines, but they were routed by the Filipino insurrection of 1899. By the time the islands were pacified, annexation was a *fait accompli;* World War II intervened before the Philippines were freed.

Of the rest of the new empire, Puerto Rico was the most important segment. Annexed outright—there having been no indigenous independence movement to complicate matters—Puerto Rico rapidly become an essential American base for Caribbean operations. Guam, also won from Spain, was transformed into a naval base; Wake Island became, in its turn, an outpost of American power in the Pacific.

THE CARIBBEAN. We have noted that American hegemony over the Caribbean and northern Latin America had been claimed before the Spanish-

---

[17]For an interesting analysis of the peace negotiations, see A. L. P. Dennis, *Adventures in American Diplomacy, 1896–1906* (New York: E. P. Dutton & Co., Inc., 1928).

American War, most explicitly by Secretary Olney during the Venezuelan boundary dispute. After 1898, with the acquisition and occupation of advanced offshore bases in Cuba and Puerto Rico, American influence in the Caribbean became paramount beyond any doubt. Operating from Cuba and Puerto Rico, President Roosevelt was to find it relatively simple to maneuver the winning of the Panama Canal Zone; the maintenance of a force-in-being made the later evolution of the Monroe Doctrine much easier to formulate and implement.

A natural outgrowth of the new bases was the southward extension of the area of Latin America in which the United States was able to exercise primacy. Before 1898, Mexico, the West Indies, and Central America had marked the effective limits of American power; after the war American control extended to all South America north of the "bulge" of Brazil.

THE PACIFIC. The principal result of the war, however, was a drastically changed American status in the Pacific. It is doubtful that Americans realized fully just how deeply they had put themselves into Asia; even after the Japanese attack on Pearl Harbor in 1941 it came as a shock to many Americans to realize that to go from Tokyo to Manila required a compass setting to the southwest. The other Pacific acquisitions of this era—Guam, Wake, Samoa, and Hawaii—formed a series of stepping-stones that made it possible for the United States to sustain its advanced base in the Philippines.

The United States arrived in the far Pacific just as the late phase of European imperialism in Asia was reaching its height. The European powers were at work trying to carve up and divide the last rich imperial prize, an apparently prostrate China. Japan had just come on the scene as an imperial power; the Sino-Japanese War had just ended, and the Russo-Japanese War was just a few years away. The "Open Door" policy of the United States, enunciated almost at the very moment that Washington was settling uneasily into its new seat among the mighty, marked the new departure in American policy. The expanded security frontier of the United States had brought Americans into the thick of what was probably the most important theater of great-power controversy at the turn of the century, the ticklish question of Asiatic imperialism.

THE NEW IMPERIALISM

At various points in the preceding pages we have noted the growing expansionist spirit that seized Americans during the last fifteen or twenty years of the nineteenth century. We have suggested that in some ways the war with Spain and its consequences were the logical aftereffects of this new spirit. If being tagged with the opprobrious term "imperialist" was an outcome of achieving the new version of American manifest destiny, most Americans were willing to bear that burden.

Most, but not all. The ratification of the peace treaty with Spain provoked a bitter fight in the Senate, and the two-thirds vote that finally passed it was a bare minimum. The Senate battle was only a pale reflection of a deep division among the public, one that was never to heal fully.[18]

ANTI-IMPERIALIST ATTITUDES. Anti-imperialism drew its justification from ideological, historical, and logical bases. Ideologically, the opponents of empire alleged a fundamental disharmony between professions of democracy and the possession of an overseas empire of subject peoples. Historically, they raised the issue of isolationism, the negative aspects of the Monroe Doctrine, and the wisdom of the American record of staying out of great-power embroilments. Logically, they pointed to the folly of undertaking a war to free Cuba and then becoming a Pacific power on the opposite side of the globe from the Caribbean.

Underlying anti-imperialist sentiment was a combination of what our era would call guilt feelings and insecurity. Imperialism as a too familiar manifestation of power politics seemed to many people to be something that the American political genius was constitutionally incapable of carrying off successfully. The prospects of imperial rule were admittedly intoxicating, but many well-meaning people wondered if, in gaining the renown of the world, Americans were not running the danger of losing their own souls.

IMPERIALIST ATTITUDES. The imperialists, if they felt such scruples, kept them well under cover. We need not recite the catalogue of imperialist arguments in detail; they are all familiar to students of modern history. Economic advantage, strategic gain, the siren call of prestige, the iron law of history, the beckoning finger of destiny, and the requirements of Christianity were all pressed into service in the fight—as indeed they had been in every state that felt the call to imperial greatness. Perhaps the rationalization that played the largest part in carrying the day for the imperialists—in addition to popular resentment at the Filipino insurrection—was the seductive idea of the "white man's burden."[19] Today a term of derision, in 1898 and 1899 it provided the ideological escape hatch through which many worried citizens could make their way to the acceptance of imperialism.

---

[18]For the American debate over imperialism, see Julius W. Pratt, *Expansionists of 1898* (Baltimore: Johns Hopkins University Press, 1936).

[19]Rudyard Kipling's poem, "The White Man's Burden" (1899), helped persuade Americans where their duty lay. The most impressive of the poem's seven stanzas is the fifth:

> Take up the White Man's Burden—
>   And reap his old reward:
> The blame of those ye better,
>   The hate of those ye guard—
> The cry of hosts ye humour
>   (Ah, slowly!) toward the light:—
> "Why brought ye us from bondage,
>   Our loved Egyptian night?"

Quoted from *McClure's Magazine* (February, 1899).

THE UNITED STATES AMONG THE GREAT POWERS

THE NEW AMERICAN ATTITUDE. The more informed and sophisticated among the Americans of 1900 had a fairly clear understanding that the United States had come to the end of an era. The new overseas territories of the United States meant a good deal more than just a vast augmentation in prestige, however satisfying to nationalist appetites that might be in itself. They required the United States to walk a new path in foreign affairs, to concern itself with new problems, and to solve them in new ways.

But even though informed opinion grasped the implications of the new role of the United States, if only imperfectly, not even that much can be said about the general content of public opinion. It seems probable that the mass of the American people in 1900 did not realize what had happened to them. There was great pride in the victory over Spain; there was a good deal of self-congratulation at being an imperial people; there was considerable missionary zeal for spreading the message of the American way to backward peoples. Except for a few belligerent and quasi-chauvinist voices, however, there seems to have been little inclination to recognize the fact that, for good or ill, the United States had left the past behind. The oceans still existed and the British navy still sailed upon them; Europe and the great powers still seemed as far away as they had a hundred years before. Most Americans simply assumed that, now that the war with Spain was over and the predictable result had taken place, things would somehow readjust themselves and the United States could again rock along in its pleasant insularity.

THE ATTITUDE OF THE OTHER POWERS. If the United States was ignorant of what had happened to it, this happy state was not shared by the other great powers. As much earlier as the time of the American Civil War, the European states, contemplating the awful military might that the United States had mobilized on both sides, realized that America was ready then to join the circle of the internationally elect. By 1900, as the European state system analyzed the American victory over Spain, each of its major members thought through what the entry of the United States into their councils might mean.

Great Britain, alone among the major powers, welcomed the United States as a potential ally; the others were to some extent disturbed by being obliged to expand their closed system to accommodate a new member. France and Russia were perhaps the least inconvenienced: France was pointedly neutral, whereas Czarist Russia was solicitous to preserve its long-standing (if not overly impressive) history of friendship with America. Germany was discomfited at this new obstacle to its project of undermining British control of the seas, and anti-German sentiment in the United States was already a reality. Japan, itself a new member of the great-power group, was the most immediately affected of all the states: The United States arrived in the Far East just as Nippon was beginning its own program of expansion there. From this almost accidental historical coincidence was to grow the rivalry that was to culminate in open war in 1941.

World War I

The first major consequence of American great-power status was the historical process that drew the United States into World War I. The United States owed its birth to a general European war, and until it successfully disentangled itself from the European state system in 1820, the United States was part of the general society of states. Between 1820 and 1900, however, the United States stood outside the mainstream of world affairs and escaped all the wars that occurred within it. When Americans rejoined the family of nations, there was no way for them to avoid being caught up in the next major upheaval. What makes the 1914–1918 period important for us is the extent to which this—the war's major lesson to the United States—was missed by Americans.

THE PREWAR ERA, 1900–1914.   During the period between the war with Spain and the onset of world war in 1914, the United States made an attempt to capitalize on its new power. In several parts of the world, American action demonstrated an unusual forcefulness and vigor. The United States was following the advice of its favorite contemporary political leader, Theodore Roosevelt, and was undertaking to live "the strenuous life."

In the Caribbean, President Roosevelt obtained the Panama Canal Zone in 1903 by direct and effective—if questionable—action.[20] He laid down the "Roosevelt Corollary" to the Monroe Doctrine, giving the United States the self-proclaimed right to intervene into the domestic affairs of the Latin American countries.[21] Spurred by the protection thus guaranteed, American investments flowed into the Caribbean; American government action in promotion and support of this effort rapidly gained the unpopular name of "dollar diplomacy" and contributed to the lasting discredit of the United States in Latin America.[22]

China was the second great arena of American action during this period.[23]

---

[20]See H. C. Hill, *Roosevelt and the Caribbean* (Chicago: University of Chicago Press, 1927), Chapter 3.

[21]On the corollaries of the Monroe Doctrine, see Perkins, *Hands Off*, Chapter 7: "The Policeman of the West."

[22]See the criticism in Scott Nearing and Joseph Freeman, *Dollar Diplomacy* (New York: The Viking Press, Inc., 1925).

[23]A. Whitney Griswold, *The Far Eastern Policy of the United States* (New York: Harcourt, Brace & World, Inc., 1938), Chapters 2, 3.

Involved as the United States was with all the major states in the problem of China, it was imperative that an American position be developed quickly. This took the form of the "Open Door" policy of 1900—long regarded as a landmark of American diplomacy. Put at its simplest, it called for equality among imperialist states as they went about their economic penetration of China and for the preservation of "Chinese territorial and administrative entity." Neither high-minded philanthrophy nor realistic power politics, the Open Door had one great merit: It was based solidly on the American interest in a Far Eastern balance of power and the consequent need for the continued existence of a free China. It suffered, as later events were to show, from a lack of follow-up: The United States was unwilling either to support it with power or to bargain realistically with the states that were willing to do so.[24]

The new American posture as the defender of China did not escape the attention of Japan; Tokyo was already eyeing China with anticipation. The United States rapidly drifted into a series of disagreements with Japan over the Russo-Japanese War in 1905 and over Japanese immigration into the United States during 1906. Tension seemed to be rising and, although the disputes were resolved by the Root-Takahira Agreement of 1908, the old relationship was never resumed. The era of American sponsorship of Japan was over; both states had major interests in the Pacific that were irreconcilable. Rivalry had replaced friendship, and the United States had acquired an enemy in the Pacific.

The Moroccan crisis of 1905, involving Germany and France directly and the other European powers indirectly, seemed for a time to threaten general war. President Roosevelt offered his good offices to help settle the crisis, and it was largely due to this effort that the Algeciras Conference was called. At this conference the United States had official delegates; there was no pretence of isolation. Americans negotiated, composed differences, and played a large part in the proceedings.

There was some soul-searching in the United States over this adventure, for it was in clear violation of the noninvolvement policy of hallowed memory. Nobody was particularly pleased about it, but its apologists justified American intervention on grounds of sheer necessity. The Moroccan intervention foreshadowed the eventual total irrelevance of noninvolvement in Europe to the working interests of the United States.

THE EFFECT OF WILSONIANISM. American policy during the era of the First World War was materially affected, if not actually governed, by the fact that its major architect was President Woodrow Wilson. Mr. Wilson

---

[24]George F. Kennan has a wryly humorous and heavily critical interpretation of the Open Door in *American Diplomacy, 1900–1950*, Chapter 2: "Mr. Hippisley and the Open Door."

brought a distinct philosophy of foreign affairs to the Presidency and sought
to order the behavior of the United States according to its principles. Both
his great successes and his ultimate repudiation grew out of this preoccupation.

Wilson adopted a "democratic" theory of international relations entirely
in harmony with what Walter Lippmann has called the "great illusion" of the
nineteenth century.[25] He submitted the behavior of states to the measurement of moral criteria, derived from the democratic ideology of the United
States and a strict puritanical conscience. He accepted a set of morally
desirable values: peace, self-determination, the rights of small states, the
superiority of public opinion to the calculations of diplomats, and the
abolition of self-seeking national interest. He attempted to circumvent the
apparatus of traditional power politics and to substitute therefor a new
methodology in world affairs stressing the implementation of the democratic
dogma. In so doing he was giving forceful and very literate expression to
long-standing and basic popular attitudes in the United States.

NEUTRALITY AND ITS FAILURE

The coming of the European war in August 1914 at first had little impact
on Americans. Here, mass attitudes seemed to imply, was another European
struggle of the old type, growing out of certain inherent flaws in the political
structure of Europe and the states within it. In this kind of conflict the
United States had no interest. The proper role of Americans was to remain
on the sidelines and to capitalize on their advantage by dealing with problems
nearer home. With this popular attitude President Wilson and his advisers,
principally Secretary of State William Jennings Bryan, were in general
agreement.

NEUTRALITY VS. UNNEUTRALISM. At the onset of the war, therefore, the
United States issued proclamations of neutrality almost as a matter of
routine.[26] As Americans watched the course of the fighting, however, they
discovered that noninvolvement could not and did not mean impartiality.
The sympathies of the bulk of the people were unquestionably on the side
of the Allies, in spite of the fact that some ethnic groups in the United States
were either pro-German or anti-British. Here again the government, although better informed and somewhat more sophisticated than mass opinion,
shared its predilections; Mr. Wilson himself was tortured by the conflict
between his pro-British leanings and his insistence on a policy of noninvolve-

---

[25]In Lippmann, *United States Foreign Policy* (Boston: Little, Brown and Company,
1943), p. 30.
[26]The standard work is Charles Seymour, *American Neutrality, 1914–1917* (New Haven:
Yale University Press, 1935).

ment. Only Secretary Bryan, by now almost a confirmed pacifist, was relatively untroubled by any bias in favor of Britain.

THE VIOLATION OF AMERICAN RIGHTS. The unneutral attitude of Americans was strained by the studied violation of American "neutral rights" by both sides from almost the very beginning of the war. During the first part of the war, Britain seemed to be the more persistent violator of American rights. The United States grew restive under the constant diet of harassment, and the considerable agitation for forthright action was barely offset by the persistent anglophilia of the government and the people.

The British, however, enjoyed another natural advantage in the struggle for American sympathy. Germany, without enough of a surface navy to challenge British supremacy, turned to the submarine as its preferred weapon against seaborne commerce. Submarine warfare, by definition, made mincemeat out of the ordinary rules of neutral shipping—rules that the British had retained in principle however drastically they might have interpreted them in practice. The crowning blow, and the one event that tipped American sympathies irrevocably in favor of the Allies, was the sinking of the *Lusitania* in 1915.

THE GERMAN CHOICE FORCES WAR. The United States responded quickly to the German challenge. Secretary Bryan resigned rather than approve a stronger American policy, and President Wilson took over active direction of American strategy. He sought by vigorous diplomacy to persuade Germany to limit its submarine warfare and, for a time, seemed to have won his point as Germany promised to restrain itself.

By early 1917, however, Berlin made a deliberate calculation of what was involved and elected to resume unrestricted submarine warfare. The imperial government realized that this might bring about American belligerency; it reasoned, however, that it could win the war before American participation could tip the scales. The United States immediately broke off diplomatic relations; in April, after the revolution in Russia and the revelation of German plots in Mexico, the United States declared war.[27]

THE UNITED STATES AND THE WAR

American participation in the war furnished almost a laboratory example of the traditional American attitude toward war in general. The war, as popular opinion saw it, had been forced upon the United States by vicious and depraved men. The American government had been patient; it had

---

[27]For critical studies of American entry into the war, see Walter Millis, *Road to War* (Boston: Houghton Mifflin Company, 1935), and Charles C. Tansill, *America Goes to War* (Boston: Little, Brown and Company, 1938).

reasoned with the aggressors; it had sought to stave off battle as long as possible. Finally, given no choice, the United States went to war. America had no sordid objectives of material gain or the satisfaction of national interest; its concern was with principle. After the war was won, Americans were prepared to help straighten out the world before they went back to their own concerns.

AMERICAN IDEALISM.   Put as baldly as we have stated them above, these propositions might seem almost fatuous and puerile to a more skeptical generation of Americans. Later scholars (and some contemporary ones) have argued that President Wilson was as sensitive to the requirements of the European balance of power as were his associates in Britain and that American entry into the war was a natural and realistic decision to attempt to forestall German hegemony on the Continent.[28] And yet—and this is a danger peculiar to our time—we must not overlook an historical fact: Most Americans believed that these abstractions were what they were actually fighting for—and so did most foreigners, enemy and Allied alike. We must never forget that Germany surrendered on the basis of the Fourteen Points, Wilson's most ambitious effort to translate his own idealism into practical terms.

WILSON'S WAR AIMS.   President Wilson thought he was fighting the war for a single objective: peace—durable, honorable, and satisfying. To him, the only kind of peace settlement that stood any chance of enduring was one that incorporated his own (and his country's) philosophy of international relations and applied it to the settlement of concrete issues.

As Wilson saw it, peace for the world required the simultaneous application of a handful of general principles. These were self-determination, political democracy, untrammeled intercourse between peoples, and international organization (the last of Wilson's Fourteen Points—the crucial one for Americans in dealing with the Treaty of Versailles—dealt with a "general association of nations" to guarantee "political independence and territorial integrity" to all states). He wrapped all of these up into a single operating hypothesis that was in turn dependent on a basic article of faith: that the spontaneous common opinion of mankind, if given the chance to speak freely, would always declare for peace, justice, and freedom. He dedicated the United States to the cause of creating mechanisms for the expression of that mass will.[29]

---

[28]See Edward Buehrig, *Woodrow Wilson and the Balance of Power* (Bloomington: University of Indiana Press, 1956). Compare this study, however, with another that takes the opposite position: John M. Blum, *Woodrow Wilson and the Politics of Morality* (Boston: Little, Brown and Company, 1956), especially Chapter 8.

[29]Wilson's war message (April 2, 1917) put this proposition at its simplest: "Our object . . . is to vindicate the principles of peace and justice in the life of the world as against selfish and autocratic power and to set up amongst the really free and self-governed peoples

THE UNITED STATES AND THE ALLIES. The fundamental distinction that Americans drew between their own war and that being fought by the rest of the Allies is shown by the amorphous relations between them. The United States never became an "Ally" but remained only an "Associated Power" to the end. At the Paris Peace Conference itself, Wilson (although the popular idol of the European masses) ran into constant opposition from his opposite numbers around the table and finally fell between the two stools. He failed to get the kind of peace settlement he wanted at Versailles, but what he did get was too much for the United States Senate. Neither Europe nor the American people were ready for a Wilsonian peace in 1919.

The Renaissance of Isolationism

Looking back to the 1920's, we can suggest several explanations for the renaissance of isolationism that flowered after the end of the war. It was perhaps inevitable that a people who could not grasp the meaning of great-power status, who had fought their greatest war with emotional slogans and crusading zeal and without any rational understanding of how to approach their idealistic goal, and who thought of war as a matter of punishing sinners, would lapse into disillusionment when Heaven proved difficult to locate. Party politics, always a factor in American political decision, played its part as well in bringing back isolationist prejudice; President Wilson's unbending insistence on his own particular way alienated many otherwise sympathetic internationally minded people. But it serves no purpose to analyze the motives of 1920. For good or ill, Americans once again turned their backs on the world. Their action had a perceptible effect on the course of events during the next twenty years, called by E. H. Carr "the twenty years crisis."[30]

THE REJECTION OF THE LEAGUE

The genesis of neo-isolationism is found in the struggle over the ratification of the Treaty of Versailles and American entry into the League of

---

of the world such a concert of purpose and of action as will henceforth insure the observance of those principles. . . .

"We are glad . . . to fight thus for the ultimate peace of the world and for the liberation of its peoples . . .: for the rights of nations great and small and the privilege of men everywhere to choose their way of life and of obedience." *Congressional Record*, LV, No. 103 (April 2, 1917), 104.

[30]E. H. Carr, *The Twenty Years Crisis, 1919–1939* (London: Macmillan & Co., Ltd., 1940).

Nations. Once this battle was over and the concept of "normalcy" had captured American political life, the emotional drive for noncommitment had taken charge of American policy. The issues raised during the 1919–1921 period were not to be settled until after V-J Day.

WILSON'S TACTICS. To a considerable, although immeasurable, extent, the rejection of the League of Nations was the outcome of the political tactics of President Wilson. Never noted as a compromiser and prone to insist on his way if he felt a moral issue was involved, he laid a political trap for himself by the manner in which he handled the issue of international cooperation.

His first error was made prior to the congressional election of 1918: He urged the election of a Democratic Congress as the surest way to guarantee a successful peace settlement. Such an identification of either party with superior virtue or patriotism is never especially good politics in the United States and, under the circumstances, practically guaranteed the eventual Republican victory. The election meant that Wilson went to Paris after what amounted to a popular repudiation—an outcome he could possibly have avoided. What was worse, the delegation he chose to accompany him included no Senators and only one Republican—and a lukewarm one at that. It would seem that Wilson had omitted doing nothing that might antagonize the majority party in the Senate.

After the treaty had been submitted, the President made his lot even more difficult. He rejected the Lodge reservations which, had he accepted them, would have permitted American membership in the League on a slightly different basis (Britain and France were both prepared to accept the Lodge reservations). Instead, he insisted on his own version of the League and expressed his determination to stand or fall on it. Even after all of this (and the President's physical collapse that further complicated an already tangled situation), there was enough Republican support for the Treaty that it fell only eight votes short of the required two-thirds.[31]

THE ELECTION OF 1920. The presidential election of 1920, coming after the long and bitter battle over the League, sealed the fate of the United States. Although the victorious Harding was, as a candidate, vaguely in favor of "an association of nations," the Democratic defeat was correctly interpreted as a mandate. The American people were turning away, not only from the League, but from the broader idea of systematized and institutionalized action to preserve peace. During the Republican era of the 1920's—and even during Franklin D. Roosevelt's first term—it was axiomatic in American politics and in American foreign affairs that the United States

---

[31]See Denna F. Fleming, *The United States and the League of Nations, 1918–1920* (New York: G.P. Putnam's Sons, 1932).

was not to become involved in any permanent international arrangements requiring political commitments. The interwar isolationism was much more a state of mind—popular and official—than it was a matter of practical policy. The people had spoken and, this done, turned to other matters.

DISARMAMENT

Perhaps the most conspicuous and well-meaning effort of the United States toward the establishment of a peaceful order during the interwar period was the long attempt at "disarmament." The word is put in quotation marks here, although in the minds of Americans of the day it was taken literally to mean the ultimate abolition of all weapons of war.

The disarmament movement suited American predilections exactly: By stripping nations of their capacity to fight a war, the desire to fight would be eliminated; by making a commitment for peace, peaceful process would by guaranteed. Foreign policy for the United States would then consist only of trade relations with the outside world and the exploitation of America's natural hegemony, principally in the western hemisphere.

THE WASHINGTON CONFERENCE.   In 1922 the United States led the way in moving toward disarmament. The Washington Conference, called on the initiative of the United States, attempted to arrest the postwar naval race among the United States, Britain, and Japan. Although the United States had a construction program under way that would have made it the world's greatest naval power in a few years, America agreed to the suspension of the building effort and to the stabilization of the three greatest navies on a capital-ship ratio of 5-5-3. France and Italy were added to the ratio at 1.75 each, and it seemed as if a great stride had been taken for peace.[32]

THE GENEVA CONFERENCE.   The Washington Conference had provided a ratio by which to control capital ships, but left the door open to a new naval race in smaller vessels. President Coolidge therefore called for a new naval disarmament conference in 1927, to meet at Geneva. Here the United States sought to extend the 5-5-3 ratio to all classes of warships, but it proved impossible to reach any agreement. The conference ended in a total fiasco.

---

[32]The Conference also dealt with the problems of the Pacific. The Four-Power Treaty abrogated the Anglo-Japanese alliance and engaged the United States, Britain, Japan, and France to respect each other's rights in the Pacific; the Nine-Power Treaty reaffirmed the Open Door, pledging the signatories (the Pacific powers) to respect the "sovereignty, the independence, and the territorial and administrative integrity of China." See Raymond Leslie Buell, *The Washington Conference* (New York: Appleton-Century-Crofts, 1922). A more recent study is John Chalmers Vinson, *The Parchment Peace* (Athens, Ga.: University of Georgia Press, 1955).

THE KELLOGG-BRIAND PACT.   In this connection we should mention the ill-starred Pact of Paris, the Kellogg-Briand Pact for outlawing war. This document, once thought of as one of the major diplomatic triumphs of the United States, renounced war "as an instrument of national policy" and promised that the settlement of international disputes would not be attempted "except by pacific means." Almost all the states of the world finally ratified it, but many (including the United States) added significant reservations that permitted "defensive" war. Signed in 1928, the Pact became politically irrelevant in 1931, when Japan's invasion of Manchuria ended the myth of achieving a warless world by proclamation.

THE LONDON CONFERENCE.   The next disarmament effort was made in 1930. After long preliminary negotiations between Britain and the United States, the five major naval powers met at London. Here some concrete results were achieved, although the total reduction in naval strength was negligible. The major result of the conference was to stabilize the relative strength of the three largest navies: The United States and Britain agreed to complete parity in all types of vessels; Japan accepted smaller ratios than the other two in every category except submarines; and a ceiling was placed on the construction of all types of ships. The naval race seemed halted, except for the famous "escalator clause." This provided that the ratios were to be null and void in case a nonsignatory power entered into a naval race with any of the parties to the treaty.

THE WORLD DISARMAMENT CONFERENCE.   In 1932, after over a decade of preparation, the League of Nations "World Disarmament Conference" finally convened. The great goal of this gathering was the creation of some limits for land armaments analogous to those hammered out for naval vessels. The United States participated and tried its admittedly feeble best to promote something concrete; President Hoover even went so far as to propose an immediate one-third cut in all existing armaments. The politics of security in Europe and Japan's Manchurian adventure cast a pall over the conference, however, and it broke up without any progress. The next year Hitler came to power in Germany and the entire discussion became pointless as the world began its downhill march to World War II.

THE UNITED STATES AND DISARMAMENT.   It is impossible to find fault with American intentions during the whole long and ultimately tragic history of the attempt at disarmament. The difficulty with the American conception was its general irrelevance to the actual problems with which it was designed to deal. It was no use to dismiss French concern with security as frivolous and stubborn; it was pointless to shrug off Japanese insistence on naval parity as presumptuous. The political problems of the interwar period were real and pressing, regardless of the fact that they may have seemed slightly indecent to Americans. The way to peace was not to be found—at least in the 1920's—by voluntary acts of self-abnegation by sovereign states.

THE DEPRESSION

During the period we have been considering, European relations had changed swiftly from crisis in 1924 (marked by French occupation of the Ruhr) to a remarkable degree of reconciliation after 1925 (the year of the signature of the Pact of Locarno). Between 1925 and 1930, the climate of international relations in Europe raised hopes for permanently improved relations. This was the era of the Pact of Paris and the heyday of the League of Nations. This more or less halcyon phase came to a close with the Depression of 1929.

Even before the stock-market collapse that touched off the worldwide economic distress, economic relations between the United States and Europe had been complicated by the question of the so-called "war debts."[33] The coming of the Depression elevated what had been an annoyance to the level of a major crisis. The economic tensions remained strong until the war began in 1939.

THE DEBT QUESTION. About two-thirds of the debt owed the United States by its European allies had orginally been contracted during the war; the remainder had taken the form of a post-Armistice loan. The end of the war found the Allies at first arguing for cancellation of the entire debt; this the United States rejected as being both a matter of bad faith and of bad business. The next European contention was to assert that there was a connection between the inter-Allied debt and the collection of reparations from Germany. This the United States found equally unacceptable, since there was already (by 1922) a suspicion that the reparations bill would prove uncollectible. Throughout the 1920's, payments trickled in from the European debtors accompanied by a rising tide of ill will. To millions of Europeans, the United States became "Uncle Shylock," intent on getting his pound of flesh at whatever cost. American attitudes, already sensitive toward European criticism, retaliated by becoming more belligerently nationalistic and isolationist.

THE MORATORIUM AND DEFAULT. In 1931, President Hoover attempted to reverse the disastrous trend of international economic relations by proposing a one-year moratorium on the payment of Allied debts. During the year, the European powers substantially cancelled the reparations due from Germany (by the terms of the Lausanne Agreement, 1932) and then looked expectantly to the United States for the cancellation of their own debt. President Hoover refused; his example was followed early in 1933 by Franklin D. Roosevelt. Despairing of obtaining relief from the United States,

---

[33]See Harold Moulton and Leo Pasvolsky, *War Debts and World Prosperity* (New York: Appleton-Century-Crofts, 1932).

almost all the debtors defaulted by June 1934. The single exception was Finland, whose debt was miniscule and who reaped a harvest in favorable publicity over the years worth far more than its negligible payments.

ECONOMIC ISOLATIONISM. By 1933 the European states realized that only an international solution could be found for an international depression. Accordingly, an International Economic Conference convened in London in June to consider some form of joint international action to restore prosperity. After some encouraging progress, the discussion turned to the gold standard and currency stabilization. Here was the rock on which the conference foundered.

The Roosevelt New Deal, it must never be forgotten, was in the grand tradition of American reform movements; as such, it emphasized domestic policy and was profoundly and quaintly isolationist in spirit.[34] Currency manipulation was part of its program for fighting the Depression at home; it had no intention of sacrificing any part of its control over the American economy on behalf of any illusory scheme of international cooperation. As a result, President Roosevelt intervened in the Conference, rebuking the membership for considering joint currency stabilization and cutting the ground out from under the American delegates. The United States had joined the major states of Europe in a policy of economic nationalism that was to endure until World War II.

One break in the otherwise solid front of economic nationalism was the Reciprocal Trade Agreements Program, originally enacted in 1934. This program authorized the negotiation of bilateral executive agreements covering tariff reductions. By means of the most-favored-nation clause, reductions brought about in American duties under the terms of one of these agreements were given application to many other nations. By 1941 the Reciprocal Trade Agreements Program had brought about an overall reduction in American tariff barriers that, although encouraging, was never any more than moderate.[35]

THE LIQUIDATION OF DOLLAR DIPLOMACY

One credit mark in the record of American foreign policy prior to World War II was the liquidation of dollar diplomacy in Latin America and the adoption of the Good Neighbor Policy. Credit for this movement in the direction of the abandonment of imperialism must be divided between the administrations of Hoover and Roosevelt.

---

[34]Eric F. Goldman, *Rendezvous with Destiny: A History of Modern American Reform* (New York: Alfred A. Knopf, Inc., 1953), pp. 374–379.

[35]For further discussion of the program and its more recent history, see Chapter 11.

THE REINTERPRETATION OF THE MONROE DOCTRINE. From its beginning, the Hoover administration made clear that it was abandoning the more extreme interpretations of the Monroe Doctrine popular under Theodore Roosevelt, Taft, and Wilson. In 1930 there was published a long and detailed *Memorandum on the Monroe Doctrine*, written in 1928 by Undersecretary of State J. Reuben Clark.[36] This document returned to the original conception of the doctrine as a policy vis-à-vis Europe rather than Latin America. During the Hoover administration the government remained generally faithful to its new principles, recognizing *de facto* governments in the western hemisphere without concerning itself with their legitimacy and withdrawing American forces from Haiti and Nicaragua.

THE GOOD NEIGHBOR. The New Deal followed up the initial advantage. The Montevideo Inter-American Conference (1933) resulted in a pact, supported by the United States, that denied any right of intervention. Later the President specifically underscored the end of intervention and dollar diplomacy by a studied policy toward recurrent Latin American crises which was a good deal different from former American tactics. The United States entered World War II with the hemisphere more united and less hostile toward the "Colossus of the North" than at any time in sixty years, although provisions for multilateral action in enforcement of the Monroe Doctrine— hemisphere cooperation against outside threats—were not to be worked out until later.

The Rise of the Dictators

The rise of Hitler, Mussolini, and Imperial Japan to the point where the United States finally recognized them as menaces marks one of the major turning points in the history of American foreign policy. Before a rational course of action could be decided on, however, the last full measure of noninvolvement was to be tried and found wanting.

THE NEW THREAT OF TOTALITARIANISM

THE TOTALITARIAN MENACE. In the policies of Nazi Germany, Fascist Italy, and a newly intransigent Japan the United States found something for which it was unprepared. The initial American reaction to their irrational behavior was simply one of shocked incredulity; the United States could not take seriously the threats uttered by the Axis. When Americans finally

---

[36]J. Reuben Clark, *Memorandum on the Monroe Doctrine* (Washington, D.C.: Government Printing Office, 1930).

realized that these governments meant exactly what they were saying, something like panic replaced the earlier bemusement. The democracies appeared to be almost hypnotized by the speed and precision with which the dictators won victory after victory. After a quasi-hysterical attempt at total withdrawal, the United States came at last to realize that there was only one way to deal with the sort of menace it faced: to meet force with greater force.

FIRST STEP: MANCHURIA.   Japan opened the dictatorial drive for world power by invading Manchuria in 1931. The United States, both because of its interest in the Open Door and its concern with peace, opposed the move and ultimately gave voice to the "Stimson Doctrine": The United States would not recognize any territorial changes brought about in violation of treaty obligations.[37] This was a weak move at best, and when Britain and France refused to follow the American lead the attempt collapsed.

The Japanese invasion of Shanghai in 1932 produced a stronger reaction in the United States. Public opinion at last grew seriously concerned and urged strong action against Japan. The government of the United States, however, contented itself with strong protests. Japan finally withdrew, but the damage had been done; Tokyo had broken the peace and had been permitted, not only to escape punishment, but to retain most of the fruits of its aggression.

ETHIOPIA AND SPAIN.   There then ensued a pause of some three years while Hitler came to power in Germany and Mussolini poised to strike. In 1935 Italy invaded the African kingdom of Ethiopia and succeeded in making good its conquest in the face of an abortive attempt to impose sanctions by the League of Nations. In 1936 civil war broke out in Spain, with the rebels receiving open support from Hitler and Mussolini. Once again the best efforts of the European democracies were weak and futile; the dictators scored another victory.

ISOLATION BY LAW

How was the United States reacting to the rise of totalitarian power? In the first place, there was the Depression to combat at home; this absorbed the bulk of official and popular attention. When foreign affairs finally forced themselves on American attention, the reaction was all too predictable. The United States attempted to legislate isolation.

THE NEUTRALITY ACTS.   The only way war could come to the United States, Americans felt, was by deceit. The United States would fight only if

---

[37]For the "Doctrine" itself and for a picture of the crisis from the point of view of a major participant, see Henry L. Stimson and McGeorge Bundy, *On Active Service in Peace and War* (New York: Harper & Row, Publishers, 1948), pp. 266–239.

tricked into it by the wiles of European diplomats or by the selfish manipulation of war profiteers—the "merchants of death," who became famous through the activities of investigating committees of Congress. So the United States sought to protect itself from these twin dangers by passing laws: the Neutrality Acts of 1935, 1936, and 1937.

The 1935 act made it illegal to sell or ship munitions to belligerents. In 1936 loans to belligerents were prohibited. In 1937 the law was extended to include such civil wars as were proclaimed by the President. One concession was written into the 1937 law: the "cash-and-carry" rule that raw materials could be sold to belligerents only if they paid cash and took them away in their own ships. This provision had only a two-year life; this turned out to be important because World War II was to begin within a few weeks after this provision expired.

The Neutrality Acts were misnomers; they represented the complete abandonment of neutrality rather than any protection of it. Their effectiveness, of course, would depend in practice on an intangible: Would the United States remain sufficiently impartial in a major war so that both sets of belligerents could be treated alike, particularly if the prospective victor had interests inimical to the United States? This question, to be answered during the 1939–41 period, was not raised while the acts were being passed.

THE NAVAL RACE. But American policy during this era was not all a matter of head-in-the-sand. The 1935 London Naval Disarmament Conference failed because of Japan's withdrawal and Italy's nonadherence to the draft treaty. Recognizing finally that disarmament was a futile effort during the 1930's, President Roosevelt moved to build up the United States Navy to treaty strength. By 1938 the United States was active again in the naval race.

"QUARANTINE" AND MUNICH

By 1937 the Roosevelt administration had at last learned that the dictators were actual dangers rather than mere annoyances and that the United States could not afford any longer to ignore them without seriously undermining American security. In Europe and in the Far East American policy began to grapple with the threat of totalitarianism, at first hesitantly and then later with more determination (if with but little more effectiveness).[38]

---

[38]For American policy beginning with the "quarantine" speech and leading up to American entry into the war, the literature is already enormous. Worthy of special note are the two volumes by William L. Langer and S. Everett Gleason, *The Challenge to Isolation* (New York: Harper & Row, Publishers, 1952) and *The Undeclared War* (New York: Harper & Row, Publishers, 1953). A more recent work on the period is Robert A. Divine,

THE "QUARANTINE" SPEECH. The first clear sign that a new American policy was in the making was the famous "quarantine the aggressors" speech of President Roosevelt in October 1937. Attacking what he called "international lawlessness," he emphasized the American interest in peace and suggested that aggressors should be "quarantined." The President declared that 90 per cent of the world wanted to live in "peace under law" and according to accepted moral standards and that the 10 per cent who were lawless should be restrained. "There must be," he said, "positive endeavors to preserve peace."

Though forcefully stated, Roosevelt's speech represented only the line of official thinking rather than any clear action program. Public opinion, though probably inclined toward his position, was nevertheless divided; the American people had not gone as far as had their government in awakening to the changed situation.

TROUBLES WITH JAPAN. Meanwhile, troubles were multiplying in the Pacific where, earlier in 1937, Japan had initiated the "China incident," a euphemism for a general war of aggression against China. It was inevitable that episodes would occur involving Americans; the most serious event was the sinking of the United States gunboat *Panay* in December, 1937.

In the diplomatic dispute that then ensued, Japan announced a "New Order in East Asia," the end of the Open Door and the establishment of Japanese hegemony. This the United States was obviously unprepared to accept and, in mid-1939, the government abrogated its commercial treaty with Japan preparatory to the establishment of a munitions embargo.

MUNICH AND THE THREAT OF HITLER. Up to this point Japan and Italy had been the most conspicuous dictatorships; Germany's Hitler was a semi-comic figure with many apologists in the United States. During 1938, however, Hitler moved to the front as the leader of the new Axis of fascist states and became the most ominous threat to American security.

After destroying the Versailles Treaty in 1935 by rearming and by reoccupying the Rhineland, Hitler struck next in 1938. Early in the year he annexed Austria by a superlatively efficient coup; in the autumn came the great crisis over the Sudetenland area of Czechoslovakia. In this critical moment the United States moved quickly and, in contrast to some of its earlier efforts, to some effect. President Roosevelt personally urged Hitler and Mussolini to accept a peaceful solution to the crisis and, when the fateful

---

The Illusion of Neutrality (Chicago: University of Chicago Press, 1962). Bitterly critical of United States policy during this period are Charles A. Beard, *President Roosevelt and the Coming of the War* (New Haven: Yale University Press, 1948) and Charles C. Tansill, *Back Door to War* (Chicago: Henry Regnery Co., 1952). A less partisan viewpoint is expressed in Donald F. Drummond, *The Passing of American Neutrality, 1937–1941* (Ann Arbor, Mich.: University of Michigan Press, 1955).

Munich conference was convened, felt relieved that war had been averted.[39] American policy was by this act deeply involved in the tangled course of European affairs.

But the United States swiftly learned the folly of what was already being called "appeasement." Peace—of a sort—had been sustained at Munich, but only at the price of giving the dictators what they demanded. When, in the spring of 1939, Hitler tore up the Munich agreement and annexed all Czechoslovakia, to be followed shortly by Mussolini's rape of Albania, the United States placed itself in support of Britain and France in their attempts to prepare for what now seemed to be an inevitable open clash. During the last six months of peace, American policy sought to mobilize world opinion against the dictators and to give what help it could to the democracies who were struggling to get ready for the war they had hoped they would not have to fight.[40]

THE COMING OF THE WAR

Hitler, who seemed to be timing his moves to coincide with the equinoxes, began his next aggression during the late summer of 1939. His target this time was Poland. Warsaw, backed by the now-spirited Allies, Britain and France, resisted Nazi pressure; the western democracies were busy negotiating a pact with the Soviet that, they hoped, would prevent Hitler from going to war. These plans evaporated late in August when the famous Nazi-Soviet nonaggression pact was announced. Hitler had won the diplomatic battle.

WAR AND NEUTRALITY. President Roosevelt made one more attempt to head off the conflict, personally urging Hitler, the President of Poland, and the King of Italy to submit the dispute to peaceful settlement. Hitler, however, was ready for the battle and saw no reason to defer either to public opinion or to any adjusting agency. On September 1, the Nazi forces invaded Poland. On September 3, Britain and France declared war on Germany after the Nazis had ignored their ultimatums; on September 5, the United States issued its proclamations of neutrality. The Neutrality Acts were invoked, and President Roosevelt said: "As long as it remains within my power to prevent it, there will be no blackout of peace in the United States."[41]

---

[39]Arthur S. Link, *American Epoch* (New York: Alfred A. Knopf, Inc., 1955), pp. 473–474; see also Jules Davids, *America and the World of Our Time* (New York: Random House, Inc., 1960), pp. 167–175.

[40]For Roosevelt's policy in this period, see Link, *American Epoch*, pp. 472–475; and Langer and Gleason, *The Challenge to Isolation*, pp. 75–90.

[41]*The New York Times* (September 4, 1939).

106916   EMORY AND HENRY LIBRARY

The War Years

With the course of battle during World War II, we have little to do; what is important from our point of view is the basic reorientation in American foreign policy that took place during the fighting. During the second great war Americans finally learned a good deal of what they should have known before the first.

COOPERATION BEFORE PEARL HARBOR

The United States, though sympathetic toward the Allies, was determined to remain out of the war. Up to the fall of France in June, 1940, American policy sought more and more ways of making explicit its policy of noninvolvement. Hitler's sensational victories in the West in 1940 overturned this illusion; once the Allied foothold in Europe had been reduced to the British Isles, American statesmen were forced into a frenzied recalculation of the entire situation. Never before had it been so clear that American success in remaining uninvolved in Europe depended on the British navy; if Britain fell, there would be nothing to protect the United States from the full wrath of the dictators.[42]

THE END OF NEUTRALITY. The American government immediately began giving extensive "aid short of war" to the Allies. Arms shipments were made under strained interpretations of the law—or even in defiance of it; British warships were repaired in American shipyards; the United States provided sites and personnel for the training of British flying crews. The most spectacular of these moves, made in September, 1940, was the famous transfer of fifty overage destroyers to Britain in return for a series of sites for American naval bases in a number of British possessions in the western hemisphere. The United States had scrapped any notion of neutrality; America was becoming a nonbelligerent ally.

LEND-LEASE AND CONVOYING. But more was to come. Early in 1941, the United States adopted the Lend-Lease Act that converted America into the "arsenal of democracy." Under this law, the United States pledged itself to "lend" or "lease" defense commodities of every sort to any government that the President saw fit to support in this way.[43] Since everyone knew that all such aid was to be given to those states fighting the Axis, the distinction

---

[42]On this period, see especially Langer and Gleason, *The Undeclared War*.

[43]E. R. Stettinius, *Lend-Lease: Weapon of Victory* (New York: The Macmillan Company, 1944).

between lend-lease and outright war was a very slender one; this, however, was about as far as American opinion cared to go at the time.

During the spring and summer of 1941. German submarine sinkings of Allied convoys reached the point of real danger, capped by open Nazi attacks on American shipping. By July the United States Navy was convoying merchant vessels and defending them against submarine attacks; in September Roosevelt ordered American ships to "shoot on sight" at submarines; in October the Neutrality Acts were repealed and American merchant ships began to be armed. Most Americans by this time regarded the United States as virtually at war.

THE ATLANTIC CHARTER. In the purely political area the most sensational single event of the pre-Pearl Harbor era took place: the "Atlantic Charter" issued by Roosevelt and Churchill in August 1941. This eight-point program was a joint declaration of peace terms (they could not be called "war aims," since the United States was not officially a belligerent) and was widely discussed at the time, during the war, and afterward. The particulars were not novel; one author calls them a "mixture of the Rooseveltian New Deal and the Wilsonian Fourteen Points."[44] It is significant, however, because it tied the United States to Britain in working for a common peace—an enterprise that could be accomplished only by fighting a common war.

THE JAPANESE EXPLOSION. World War II came to the United States via the Pacific. Japan had capitalized on the Nazi victory in Europe to launch a strong diplomatic offensive aimed at establishing its "New Order" in Asia. American opposition grew in turn more rigid, and throughout the latter half of 1941 the respective positions hardened. Japan insisted on American recognition of Japanese economic and political preeminence in Asia; the United States demanded nothing less than the abandonment of Japan's foreign-policy line after 1931 and Tokyo's retreat to its pre-Manchuria position. It seems obvious today (and, as a matter of fact, it was obvious at the time) that there was no way to reconcile these two positions.

The Tojo Cabinet that took office in Japan in October 1941 was pledged to no retreat, and during the last phases of Japanese-American negotiation Tokyo was making secret military preparations. President Roosevelt made one last try on December 6, personally appealing to Emperor Hirohito to keep the peace. It was too late; the Japanese task force was already at sea. Early in the morning of December 7, Japan attacked Pearl Harbor, and war had come to the United States.[45]

---

[44]Bailey, *Diplomatic History of the American People*, p. 729.

[45]The most dramatic of the many accounts of the events leading to the attack is that by Walter Millis, *This Is Pearl!* (New York: William Morrow & Co., Inc., 1947); more sober and factual is Herbert Feis, *The Road to Pearl Harbor* (Princeton, N. J.: Princeton University Press, 1950). See also Robert J. C. Butow, *Tojo and the Coming of the War* (Princeton, N. J.· Princeton University Press, 1961).

THE UNITED NATIONS

Unlike American experience in 1917–18, almost from the very beginning the United States was part of a massive international body for fighting the war. The United Nations Organization—the wartime fighting alliance—was not only the closest and most intimate arrangement ever created among so many states for such a large object, but it also provided the basis for the establishment of permanent cooperation and organization for postwar unity. The United States received its baptism of fire in the troubled arena of joint action during the war; the lessons learned were to be applied later.

THE UNITED NATIONS DECLARATION. On January 1, 1942, the formal structure of cooperation was set up by the signature of the Declaration by the United Nations, adhered to orginally by twenty-six anti-Axis states and finally by over forty. This document bound all the signatories to the principles of the Atlantic Charter and pledged no separate peace. Thus the specific provisions of the Roosevelt-Churchill agreement acquired a policy significance as official war aims that they had not previously had and involved the United States—at the very beginning of its part in the conflict—in the accomplishment of a set of specific objectives.

RUSSIAN RELATIONS. One consequence of the war was to throw the United States into intimate contact with the Soviet Union, an experience for which Americans were not emotionally or politically prepared. Once the two nations became allies, each was forced to learn how to deal with the other—a task complicated by the fact that it had to go on in the midst of a frustrating, expensive, and total war.

Moscow had its share of objections to American policy. Many were petty, but some had a good deal of substance. The Russians never felt that they were receiving an adequate share of lend-lease equipment. They objected to some of the more questionable features of American wartime diplomacy. They found fault with the Allied policy toward the governments-in-exile in London, particularly the openly anti-Russian Polish regime. Most specific was their constant cry for a second front in Europe to relieve the pressure on the Red Army and to speed the defeat of the Axis.

American criticism of the Soviet proceeded generally from an ideological root of anticommunism. In terms of policy, the United States never understood Russia's refusal to go to war against Japan until victory was already assured; there was also considerable official resentment at Moscow's reserved and suspicious attitude toward its western allies.[46]

---

[46]See John A. Deane, *The Strange Alliance* (New York: The Viking Press, Inc., 1947), and W. A. Williams, *American-Russian Relations, 1781–1947* (New York: Holt, Rinehart & Winston, Inc., 1952), pp. 258–282.

Even so, after 1943 American-Russian (or—more accurately—Allied-Russian) cooperation proceeded adequately. By means of top-level conferences and an elaborate hierarchy of coordinating committees, liaison officers, and so on, the governments kept each other passably well informed. There was a considerable degree of consultation on major strategy and a lesser amount of tactical coordination.

THE CONFERENCES. The new dimensions of American foreign policy were demonstrated for all to see by something that, although not entirely new, was completely novel in its scope. This was the policy-making device of the top-level conference permitting the heads of the allied governments to meet face-to-face and informally to reach basic decisions. The "Big Three" of World War II were a familiar group to newspaper readers during the war, as they met in several different parts of the world: Washington, Casablanca, Quebec, Cairo, Teheran, and—best remembered of all—Yalta.

In all of these President Roosevelt participated personally; yet probably the most important single conference of the war years was the Foreign Ministers' Conference at Moscow in October, 1943. Here the logjam in Russo-American relations was broken, and it was on this occasion that Britain, the USSR, and the United States (joined by China) pledged themselves to the establishment of a new international organization to preserve the peace.

The conferences were large-scale diplomacy with a vengeance. It seemed shocking to many Americans, even in the midst of a global war, that their President should sit in a room with the Prime Minister of Great Britain and the dictator of Communist Russia and jointly remake the map of the world. When, at the end of the war, the information about the "secret protocols" of the Yalta agreement leaked out, public opinion was strong. The mass revulsion against strong executive action in foreign affairs, originally set in motion by the wartime conferences, continued into the postwar period in the form of proposals (such as the so-called Bricker Amendment) to inhibit the treaty power and to give Congress and state legislatures a suspensive veto over international engagements entered into by the United States. None of these attempts to inhibit the international role of the United States, however, succeeded in winning acceptance.

PLANNING FOR THE POSTWAR WORLD

On one account the United States in World War II clearly improved over its record during the earlier conflict—planning for the peace. Indeed, the postwar difficulties into which the United States drifted were not a result of the want of a plan but rather of having too many plans. Perhaps the most accurate way to put the point is this: The deficiency was not in the plans themselves but in the fact that the plans were drawn to cope with a situation that never arose, whereas the actual problems that appeared were foreign to the blueprints under which the United States was trying to operate.

THE MOSCOW DECLARATION.   The Atlantic Charter, in words of studied vagueness, had pledged Britain and the United States to work for the creation of some new kind of world organization. This idea languished during the early years of the war. It was only with the Moscow Conference of foreign ministers, in October, 1943, that the promise was made specific. This, the original germ of the United Nations, merits quotation. In the communiqué the following statement was made:

4. That they [the United States, the United Kingdom, the Soviet Union, and China] recognize the necessity of establishing at the earliest practicable date a general international organization, based on the principle of the sovereign equality of all peace-loving states, and open to membership by all such states, large and small, for the maintenance of international peace and security.[47]

DUMBARTON OAKS AND YALTA.   The major effort in direct implementation of the Moscow Declaration was the Dumbarton Oaks Conference of August –October, 1944. Here representatives of the four major allied powers worked out a draft of a world organization. Despite general agreement that the new structure was to have "teeth" as contrasted with the powerless League of Nations, the thorny question of the voting formula to be used in controlling the enforcement action of the organization could not be finally decided. Without such a decision, there could be no United Nations.

This was solved—after a fashion—at the Yalta Conference. It was at this meeting that the much-discussed "veto" provision, requiring the unanimous vote of all permanent members for the Security Council to take any action on a nonprocedural matter, was decided upon by Roosevelt and Stalin. With this out of the way, the call was issued at Yalta for the United Nations Conference to draw up the Charter of the proposed organization.[48]

THE SAN FRANCISCO CONFERENCE.   Based on dates of its meeting (April 21–June 25, 1945) the San Francisco Conference belongs in a discussion of the war years, but it may also be thought of as the beginning of the postwar era. Before the Conference adjourned, Germany had surrendered and the final blows were being prepared for the destruction of Japan. Another reason for considering it a postwar development was the appearance at San Francisco of what were to become some of the most ominous lines of cleavage

---

[47] *Department of State Bulletin* (October 16, 1943), p. 254.

[48] See E. R. Stettinius, *Roosevelt and the Russians*) Garden City, N. Y.: Doubleday & Company, Inc., 1949), Chapters 7, 10; also John N. Snell, Forrest C. Pogue, Charles F. Delzell, and George A. Lensen, *The Meaning of Yalta* (Baton Rouge, La.: Louisiana State University Press, 1956).

in postwar politics: the East-West split and the great-power–small-state controversy.

The Charter of the United Nations emerged from the Conference much as it had come from Dumbarton Oaks and Yalta. The smaller states made a few significant amendments, mainly in the direction of increased emphasis in structure and function on "nonpolitical" questions—economic, social, and technical. They also succeeded in reducing slightly the almost complete monopoly over security issues that the Big Five had originally hoped for. But in the main the Charter was close to what its original sponsors had planned.

Unlike the Covenant of the League, the Charter had no difficulty winning ratification. The quick action taken by the United States Senate marked something of the distance the United States had come since 1919. The Foreign Relations Committee held only brief hearings, Senate debate lasted only six days, the final vote was eighty-nine to two, and the United States was the first state to ratify. Americans, having come out of one war into attempted isolation and almost complete frustration, were determined to try a different tack as they emerged from the second.

CHAPTER **4**

The
American Tradition
of Foreign Policy

Each nation has a more or less formalized ego-image: a psychic picture of itself as it performs its mission in the world. Such generalized impressions often largely determine much of its behavior. In this chapter we shall analyze the "tradition" of American policy: those ideas, impressions, and feelings about the external relations of the United States that have their roots deep in history and are widely shared among, deeply felt by, and virtually self-evident to the mass of the American people today.

Being imbedded so firmly in popular political consciousness, this tradition represents a relatively constant and fixed factor that must be taken into account by both American and foreign policymakers. Any tradition changes only slowly and reluctantly; the fast-moving world of today has done violence to many of the most cherished presuppositions and preferences of Americans. Although modified to some extent by the impact of circumstances, the tradition endures to this day, alternately strengthening and stultifying the government's attacks on international problems.

The Tradition of American Foreign Policy

The American people have approached foreign policy in general agreement on certain basic assumptions. These have grown out of native American history and culture and have reflected certain basic characteristics of the whole of American life. This was indeed inevitable; a nation's foreign policy may perhaps be less than its overall *Weltanschauung*, but it can never be more.[1]

THE SECONDARY NATURE OF FOREIGN AFFAIRS

We may lay down a basic postulate at the outset. Foreign affairs, however exciting they may have become during particular crises, in the long run have been of only secondary importance to Americans. They have felt that their ultimate salvation was to be found within the United States and, although agreeing that they must accept the world, they have argued that they dare not trust themselves entirely to it.

THE IMPORTANCE OF DOMESTIC AFFAIRS.   Initially, this notion grew out of a very natural preoccupation with domestic affairs. Americans have tended to be most interested in those things that were either close to them in space or that affected them directly, and for most citizens the rest of the world was far away. Today it is less far away than it used to be, perhaps; yet the immediacy of international problems is seldom as great for most Americans as that of local, municipal, state, or national ones—except in moments of great crisis.[2]

Nowhere has this been more clearly indicated than in the dominant popular attitude toward domestic politics. Presidential elections are traditionally fought out essentially on national issues, and Americans have had some difficulty in grasping the supranational significance of their political struggles. "Foreign policy" has been an election issue to be dealt with by both parties in such a way as to harvest the greatest number of votes; it has been no different —and of no more importance—than agriculture, labor relations, tax policy, or any of a dozen other perennial problems that help decide elections.

DISTRUST OF THE OUTSIDE WORLD.   A second explanation for the relatively low place occupied by foreign policy in the American attitude has been a genuine distrust of the outside world. This is by no means to say that

---

[1]For somewhat different approaches to the problem discussed in this section, see, among other works, the following: Dexter Perkins, *The American Approach to Foreign Policy* (Cambridge, Mass.: Harvard University Press, 1952); Robert E. Osgood, *Ideals and Self-Interest in America's Foreign Relations* (Chicago: University of Chicago Press, 1953); Frank Tannenbaum, *The American Tradition in Foreign Policy* (Norman, Okla.: University of Oklahoma Press, 1955); Walt W. Rostow, *The United States in the World Arena* (New York: Harper & Row, Publishers, 1960); and Erich Fromm, *May Man Prevail?* (Garden City, N.Y.: Doubleday & Company, Inc., 1961).

[2]For an explicit example of this attitude, emphasizing the minor importance and essentially amoral character of foreign affairs in general, see Felix Morley, *The Foreign Policy of the United States* (New York: Alfred A. Knopf, Inc., 1951).

Americans have been totally uninterested in what goes on abroad; indeed, American curiosity about alien cultures is famous everywhere in the world. But the political overtones of this curiosity have been suspicion, reserve, and mistrust.

Since Americans have had to make their way in a world peopled by men who, if not actually doing evil, were always capable of it, their tradition has tended to place a low estimate on what they could achieve in dealing with them. The rewards of foreign policy were thought to be by their very nature limited in extent and of only an inferior order of worth. For what good the United States could achieve in the world Americans felt they must count ultimately only on themselves.[3]

CULTURAL ISOLATIONISM.   A final explanation of the basic popular skepticism about foreign policy grows out of the first two. Culturally Americans have been in the past—and to a considerable extent still are—isolated from many of the main streams of social development. Most adult Americans— and their forebears—grew to maturity in a climate relatively unsullied by alien influences and free from direct concern about the size or the complexities of other societies.

Thus unaware of the cultural diversity of men, or—more accurately— aware of the diversity but insensitive to the difference such cultural variation made, Americans have tended to judge the world by their own standards. Their self-identification was epitomized in the famous phrase from Washington's Farewell Address: "Why quit our own to stand on foreign ground?" "Why, indeed?" have echoed generations of Americans; foreign policy thus came inevitably to reflect a dominant cultural particularism.

THE UNIQUENESS OF THE UNITED STATES

Despite the secondary place of foreign policy in the American attitude, Americans nonetheless recognized early in their history that they must deal with the rest of the world. Into their contacts with other states they carried the second element of their evolving tradition: a profound conviction that they were a unique people, unlike any other and therefore subject to different standards of behavior and judgment.

THE SENSE OF "DIFFERENCE."   American history led to the conclusion that Americans are different from any other people. Nobody was quite like Americans, and it was unfair to expect them to behave quite like anyone else.

---

[3]This idea was the foundation of the later foreign-policy thinking of the late Professor Charles A. Beard. See especially his *Open Door at Home* and *The Devil Theory of War* as well as his polemics on American entry into World War II, *American Foreign Policy in the Making* and *President Roosevelt and the Coming of the War.*

The international role of the United States, therefore, came to be conceived as different from that of any other state.

Americans claimed to be uninterested in the ordinary goals pursued by ordinary governments; they felt that they were engaged in a (regrettably) necessary but ultimately loftier enterprise than the common run of nations. The United States was in the world—this much Americans would admit—but it was emphatically not of it. The nation contended that it would not make any compromises with its principles in order to gain advantages that, at best, could never be more than temporary.[4]

MORAL SUPERIORITY. This sense of detachment from the world rapidly led to a manifestation of what anthropologists call "ethnocentrism." The differences between other peoples and Americans came to be regarded as measures of the extent to which outsiders fell short of America's high moral standards. Morality became the index of uniqueness; Americans were simply "better" people than the ordinary run of mortals whose shortcomings Americans would endure but never emulate.

One of the unspoken but ubiquitous premises of American foreign policy has been that the United States was always dealing with its moral inferiors. Particular states, of course, varied in the degree to which they fell short of the American standard; generally, the more closely they resembled the United States the greater amount of moral conviction they were admitted to have. Generally, Great Britain was agreed to rank the highest. But since no one could ever be quite like Americans, no one could really come up to their moral level.[5]

AN INTERNATIONAL DOUBLE STANDARD. Being different, and this difference being epitomized and most clearly demonstrated by moral preeminence, Americans had only a short step to take before arguing that should be judged by a different set of standards than those applied to lesser states. In this way deeds wrong in themselves when done by other peoples became perfectly permissible when done by the United States; other forms of state action, regarded as normal by the international community, were barred to Americans. It was not "imperialistic," for example, for the United States to annex overseas territories, since American purposes were high-minded and philanthropic; the United States was to rule colonial peoples for their own good.

---

[4]For example, Washington's Farewell Address pointed out: "Our detached and distant position invites us and enables us to pursue a different course [from that of the states of Europe]." James D. Richardson, ed. and compiler, *A Compilation of the Messages and Papers of the Presidents* (New York: Bureau of National Literature, 1897), Vol. I, p. 214.

[5]For a sharp critique of American moralism in international affairs, see George F. Kennan, *American Diplomacy, 1900–1950*, pp. 95–103; for an indignant demand that Americans return to the historic moral base of their foreign policy, see Morley, *Foreign Policy*, pp. 154–156. See also Hughes, *America the Vincible*, Kenneth W. Thompson, *Political Realism and the Crisis of World Order* (Princeton, N.J.: Princeton University Press, 1960), and Rostow, *the United States in the World Arena*.

According to the converse of the same principle, "power politics" was "un-American" and immoral; Americans would not indulge in it, no matter how widespread the practice might be among other states.

For a long time Americans overlooked the ethical trap they were laying for themselves by the advocacy of this double standard. Today many Americans are wrestling with the issue, but without reaching any answer that satisfies both the requirements of effective policy and the insistent promptings of their consciences.[6]

AMERICAN UTOPIANISM

Finally, the American approach to foreign policy has been essentially Utopian. This term has been used variously as an anathema or as an accolade, but its substantive import has been fairly consistent. The Utopian assumption has been one of the more durable and versatile components of the American tradition.

A SENSE OF MISSION. In the first place, Americans have been called Utopian because they have recognized and have accepted a sense of mission. The popular attitude toward foreign policy, once the United States has actively entered the international arena, has usually been an urge to "set things right." Americans disapprove of purposeless action; they have sought an affirmative goal of improvement, of rectification, or of organization.

Remembering their unique orientation to the world, we would expect that the missions accepted by the American people would be thought of as being of a higher and more moral nature than would ordinarily be expected of a state. There has been a strong popular preference for objectives expressed as moral absolutes. National missions have only infrequently gained popular expression in either concrete or egocentric terms.[7]

---

[6]A most dramatic instance of the application of the double standard was the massive intervention of United States armed forces into the Dominican Republic in April and early May, 1965. Acting completely unilaterally in order to prevent an outcome (victory of communist elements in the on-going revolution) judged contrary to national interest, the United States was somewhat taken aback by the storm of foreign criticism engendered by the move. The step, so amply justified to Americans by the overriding need to prevent "any more Cubas" in the hemisphere, proved in the eyes of many countries to be uncomfortably reminiscent of Soviet intervention in Hungary in 1956—an aggression the United States had roundly condemned at the time. The difference was perfectly clear to Americans but agonizingly obscure to many foreigners.

[7]Although hackneyed by much quotation, Woodrow Wilson's speech on the Fourteen Points merits one more repetition because of its admirable evocation of the idea of "the American mission": "We entered this war because violations of right had occurred which touched us to the quick and made the life of our own people impossible unless they were corrected and the world secured once for all against their recurrence. . . . The program of the world's peace, therefore, is our program. . . ." *Congressional Record*, Vol. LVI (January 8, 1918), p. 691.

THE GOAL OF PERFECTION. Utopianism has also been apparent in the deliberate pursuit of the goal of perfection. Implicitly Americans have seemed to assume that all international problems have a "right" answer, discoverable by men if only they put all their resources of reason and goodwill to work on it. The right answer usually was one that forever settled the problem and removed it to the category of the not-to-be-thought-about-again. Not only were single issues attacked in terms of finding the correct solution for each of them, but the long-range target was frequently formulated as a world organized into a single, self-regulating system. Such perfection, Americans thought, would obliterate forever the irrational scourges of war, crisis, and turmoil.

LEADERSHIP BY EXAMPLE. But we must not infer that Utopianism led Americans into active commitment to the cause of the perfect order they desired. On the contrary, the dominant popular conception of the role of the United States was one of leadership by example rather than of direct participation in concrete cooperative projects. The best way to bring about a world of law and justice, Americans felt, was for them to act always as the United States wished everyone else to act, to be prompt to point out the failures of other peoples, and to be willing to give advice as to how to behave. In this way the sheer force of example would do more to bring about a better day than would self-defeating involvement in the imperfect and frustrating process of day-by-day international politics.

TRADITIONAL FORMULATIONS OF THE NATIONAL INTEREST

Within the developed tradition of foreign policy, the American people developed a number of concrete formulations of interest that reflected the national sense of mission. Many of these traditional interests have been carried virtually untouched into the contemporary era; others have been abandoned in favor of newer formulas. As we saw in Chapter 1, however, whatever specific forms the myth of national purpose may take, it remains a major factor influencing the decisions made by the American government on concrete issues. In times of stress or sudden crisis the spontaneous tendency of much of public opinion is to revert to traditional concepts of interests; to accept some new formulation usually demands an effort of mass will spurred by self-conscious leaders.

THE MYTH OF ISOLATIONISM. We should first dispose of a pernicious but remarkably tenacious component of the American myth: the notion of isolationism. We have already seen that the word itself was more a tool of political manipulation and a component of the mystique of democratic politics in the nineteenth century than it was descriptive of the actual content of American foreign policy. There is little evidence that the working notion of American national interest was ever based on any purely isolationist premise.[8] Total nonintercourse with the outside world has never been seriously attempted by the United States. The record indicates that the American tradition of national interest has been too many-sided to be successfully fitted into any slogan as rigid as "isolationism." It has taken a different turn in each major region of the world, and we must consider it in terms of its principal specific manifestations.

HEMISPHERE HEGEMONY. No element of American foreign policy received such unanimous acceptance by the public or a more solid place in tradition than the principle that the United States should be absolutely dominant in the western hemisphere. The Monroe Doctrine is, as we have pointed out, a phrase with which almost all Americans are familiar, and the package of emotional reactions that it evokes has had a powerful impact on the actual policy of the United States.[9]

As worked out by the interaction of doctrine and practice, the American interest in the western hemisphere consisted of three related concerns: (1) The United States insisted on the exclusion of non-American power from the hemisphere except for the minor colonial holdings of Britain, France, and the Netherlands. (2) The United States was to brook no real rivals in the region; America was to regard the hemisphere as a United States preserve in which Washington reigned unchallenged. (3) The Americas were to be organized into a single more or less cohesive entity under United States leadership.

EUROPEAN NONINVOLVEMENT. We have already pointed out that the principle of "isolationism" was relevant only to Europe, and then only in a rather special sense. Tradition energetically foreswore any entanglement in intra-European politics, a game which Americans felt themselves unequipped to play; many Americans are still uncomfortable at the thought that they may be caught in a political web in the capitals of Europe from which they can never escape.[10] Such participation in European affairs as the United

---

[8]See the elaborate synthesis made by Albert K. Weinberg in "The Historical Meaning of the American Doctrine of Isolation," *American Political Science Review* (June, 1940).

[9]This story is well told in Perkins, *Hands Off*, and in Samuel F. Bemis, *The Latin American Policy of the United States* (New York: Harcourt, Brace & World, Inc., 1943). A more recent example of the capacity of the symbolism of the Doctrine to evoke powerful responses in the United States took place in 1960. In the midst of some heated Soviet-American exchanges over American "threats" to Cuba, Premier Khrushchev committed the indiscretion of claiming that "the Monroe Doctrine is dead." The Department of State responded immediately (with the approval of the public) that "the principles of the Monroe Doctrine are as valid today as they were in 1823 when the Doctrine was proclaimed." Khrushchev's statement may be found in *Soviet News*, No. 4304 (July 11, 1960); the Department of State's reply is in the *Department of State Bulletin* (August 1, 1960), pp. 170–171.

[10]Typical—although somewhat extreme—examples of this attitude can be found throughout Harry Elmer Barnes, ed., *Perpetual War for Perpetual Peace* (Caldwell, Idaho: The Caxton Printers, Ltd., 1953).

States could not avoid was reluctant and broken off as soon as possible. We should also note again, however, that noninvolvement was more a matter of geography than of an antipathy to the European states as such. The traditional interests of the United States have always permitted extensive relations and even binding commitments with the powers of Europe on questions that were non-European in nature. It was only at European problems, narrowly defined, that the United States drew the line; in Latin America and in the Pacific, American tradition approved of intimate dealings with the world of Europe.

BALANCE OF POWER IN ASIA. "Intervention" characterizes American traditions in Asia—or, more properly, the Far East—as much as "noninvolvement" does the American outlook toward Europe. In the Pacific and on Asia's eastern face, crystallized interests called for the United States to follow an active policy and to enter into the thick of affairs.[11]

Simplifying drastically, traditional American interests in the Far East can be reduced to three interdependent propositions, whose application with varying degrees of skill to changing circumstances can tell the story of American policy in the region since 1900. These three propositions are:

1. The overriding concern of the United States is with the internal and international stability of the Far East.
2. Stability in the region can best be achieved by ensuring a balance of power on the Far Eastern littoral; that is, the area must not be permitted to fall under the domination of any single power.
3. Stability and the balance of power, in turn, depend upon the fate of China; only if China were guaranteed "territorial integrity and political independence" could Asia be structured according to American interests.[12]

IMPERIALISM: AMERICAN STYLE. Most Americans would reject the bald statement that imperialism is any part of their traditional version of national interest. The word and the idea both run counter to what has been expressed as the "different" international role of the United States. Yet Americans, although late starters, did get caught up in the international race for overseas colonial possessions, and a rationale for such a policy became incorporated into the American tradition.

The American empire was not particularly large, though it was admittedly widespread. In its acquisition and exploitation Americans revealed the common characteristics of an imperial people, primarily that of rationalizing their colonizing mission into one of philanthropy.[13] The United States

---

[11]See Griswold, *The Far Eastern Policy of the United States.*

[12]See the Open Door note of 1899 and the circular telegram of 1900, quoted in Smith, *Major Problems in American Diplomatic History*, pp. 318–320, 321–322.

[13]For a general discussion of this point, see J. A. Hobson, *Imperialism: A Study*, 3d ed. (London: George Allen & Unwin, 1938), pp. 196–198.

purported to be interested primarily in the betterment of the unfortunate peoples for whose destinies the American government had made itself responsible.

What made the imperial tradition of the United States unusual, however, was the fact that Americans took their own professions quite seriously. The record reveals a constant—although unevenly effective—attempt to live up to the repeated claims of goodwill. The more "civilized" colonies—Puerto Rico, Hawaii, and the Philippines—were prepared for self-government; the backward peoples became the objects of a host of programs of betterment. In this effort the United States government was responding to a genuine and deep-seated urge growing naturally from the self-image of the American people.

Traditional Techniques of Foreign Policy

Corresponding to their traditional formulations of the national interest, Americans developed what we might call a traditional methodology of foreign policy. The mass of Americans have accepted this tradition as the way foreign policy *should* be conducted and as the way it *will* be conducted when the world is finally arranged the way it should be. Part of the problem of managing American foreign affairs in the contemporary world arises from the necessity felt by officials to meet concrete problems effectively without at the same time doing irreparable violence to the nation's procedural tradition.

THE DISTRUST OF POWER POLITICS

Traditionally, for reasons both too well known and too complex to develop fully here, Americans have distrusted power politics. The United States has practiced it only under duress, and then with acute embarrassment and no great skill. Power politics, the amoral and opportunistic pursuit of national interest by all expedient means, is historically repugnant to Americans. They have preferred instead to prosecute their policy by other—and morally more defensible—methods.

THE IMMORALITY OF POWER POLITICS. As a nation whose history has been called "the vindication of Puritan morality," it was strictly in character for the American people to reject power politics on grounds of immorality. The cynicism of many statesmen about human motives and their crass calculations of expedient alternatives have repelled the conscience of Americans and driven them to search for some "finer" principle upon which to base their international conduct.

It has seemed to Americans that power politics as carried on by the courts and chancelleries of the "Old World" (Europe) was a pastime of men whose intellect had overwhelmed their moral sense. The United States, by playing the game by the same rules, would dirty its own hands with the same pitch. To attempt an American version of power politics would be to sully the national ideals and to cheapen the very truths the United States was seeking to universalize.[14]

AMERICAN INADEQUACIES. To be honest, however, we must also admit that popular disgust with power politics had another root. Not only were Americans outraged by its immorality, but they also entertained shrewd doubts about their ability to hold their own in it.

Americans seem to have had a difficult time escaping some of the aftermaths of their long-ago colonial status. One heritage from this era and the struggle for independence with which it closed was a chronic fear of American political inadequacy. Not so strong as to be called a national inferiority complex, it has taken the more restrained form of a reluctance to put the United States to the test of active entry into open diplomatic competition with other states. As the late Will Rogers put it, "The United States never lost a war or won a peace."

We will find in the historical record very few overt admissions of concern by Americans of their nation's possible ineptitude; by and large, the public and its spokesmen have preferred to find moral bases for eschewing power politics. Yet the obvious discomfort many Americans feel with diplomatic bargaining (at least with states that are in the category of major powers and of whose "friendship" there may be some doubt, such as the Soviet Union or Gaullist France) is evident even today. Even the Armageddon of a "showdown" seems preferable to many citizens to the possibility of being bested in a negotiation.[15]

ARMED FORCE IN THE AMERICAN TRADITION

A logical outgrowth of this strong opinion about politics is the traditional American view of armed force as an element in foreign policy. Not sharing the prevailing assumptions about the nature of interstate life, the American people developed some indigenous ideas about the role of military power in it.

---

[14]From among the many criticisms of this position, see Thompson, *Political Realism and the Crisis of World Politics*, Chap. 4: " The Limits of Principle in International Politics."

[15]This raises the related point of the great fear Americans have of being deceived and cheated. Saul Bellow, in a review-article dealing with Theodore A. Sorenson's *Kennedy*, argues the point that the "fear of being gulled" is probably the most powerful factor shaping public attitudes. *Book Week* (*The Washington Post*) (October 3, 1965).

THE NATURE AND PURPOSES OF WAR. According to the traditional American idea, war can be either of two things: It may be the outcome of the diabolical schemes of cynical and depraved aggressors; it may, on the other hand, be merely the result of the diseased outlook of unsound rulers. Whether rational but unprincipled or the end product of sheer insanity, war is always considered an abnormal event. It is never deliberately selected as a technique by worthy statesmen; organized hostility is a departure from the rational norm of international affairs.[16] Americans have based much of their approach to international affairs on the assumption that the ideal of a world without war could some day be achieved.

Once the United States was involved in a military struggle, the tradition also provided a guide to the conduct of the conflict. Americans have felt a strong compulsion to fight only for some "higher" purpose than mere selfish interest. Usually American war aims were phrased as lofty abstractions. Americans tended to see their foes as needing chastisement for their antisocial behavior and for their temerity in disturbing the peace. The object of war was to inflict a military defeat with no regard for the political consequences of the victory.[17]

THE ARMED FORCES IN PEACETIME. The American conception of armed force has been of a piece with this theory of warfare. Until recently the United States did not see the necessity of having a peacetime armed force of more than token size. Americans clung to the myth of the invincibility of the "embattled farmer" of the Revolution and trusted in the native fighting ability of the ordinary American citizen who, armed with the products of American industrial ingenuity and the reinforcement of a just cause, could withstand any possible combination of enemies.

The American people have been far more willing to support a large navy than a large army; in recent years air power has moved to the top of the list in public acceptance, even ahead of the navy. Two factors might help explain this traditional preference for sea and air power: Both are less greedy of manpower than is a land army, and both tend to exert their influence beyond the limits of the United States and are less obvious to an affluent American society.

---

[16]Robert E. Osgood, *Limited War: The Challenge to American Strategy* (Chicago: University of Chicago Press, 1957), Chap. 2: "The American Approach to War."

[17]George F. Kennan puts the point this way in *American Diplomacy, 1900–1950*, pp. 65–66: "Democracy fights in anger—it fights for the reason that it was forced to go to war. It fights to punish the power that was rash enough and hostile enough to provoke it—to teach that power a lesson it will not forget, to prevent the thing from happening again. Such a war must be carried to the bitter end.

"This is true enough, and, if nations could afford to operate in the moral climate of individual ethics, it would be understandable and acceptable. But I sometimes wonder whether in this respect a democracy is not uncomfortably similar to one of those prehistoric monsters with a body as long as this room and a brain the size of a pin. . . ." Reprinted by permission. See also Gordon R. Turner, "Classical and Modern Strategic Concepts," in Turner and Challener, *National Security in the Nuclear Age*, pp. 3–30.

AMERICAN POLICY AND THE MILITARY.   Seeing no necessary connection between armed might and an orderly foreign policy and distrustful of a major military establishment in peacetime, it is no wonder that Americans traditionally have given little thought to overt military calculations in foreign policy. The popular image of foreign policy made it the province of diplomats; only when negotiations failed completely was the matter supposed to be turned over to the military. This has meant that the advice of military men was not sought when policy moves were being considered. The military function was thought to be limited to two tasks: (1) to guard the security of the United States and (2) to fight—and win—a war at the command of the civilian authorities. With the circumstances leading up to that war, they were not to be concerned; nor did they have any interest in its political outcome.

THE AMERICAN METHOD IN FOREIGN POLICY

Since tradition rejected the usual basis of international affairs—power politics—and its necessary motive force—armed strength—Americans were forced to develop a foreign-policy method of their own. Its dominant characteristic was its great reliance upon persuasive and nonviolent techniques; starting from its assumptions, it could scarcely have done otherwise. We must note, however, that the American version of persuasion did not take the form that it did in other conceptions of foreign policy, that of diplomacy. Diplomatic haggling and adjustment smacked too strongly of the immorality of power politics; Americans tended instead to prefer persuasive procedures more in harmony with their own predispositions.

THE APPEAL TO REASON AND MORALITY.   Perhaps most characteristic of the United States and most consonant with its general position was the technique of appealing to the good sense and the goodwill of the states with which it was in contact. Democratic ideology taught that men were possessed of reason and morality and that they would respond to appeals made in those terms. Americans therefore attempted to stake out positions that were justifiable in rational and ethical terms and to apply these norms in relations with other states.[18]

This approach often had two practical advantages. First, when the United States espoused the cause of abstract reason and morality, it frequently put

---

[18]For a provocative treatment of this point—and the American preference for rational and moral techniques generally—see the article by Hans J. Morgenthau, "The Mainsprings of American Foreign Policy: The National Interest *vs.* Moral Abstractions," *American Political Science Review* (December, 1950), pp. 833–854. See also Senator J. William Fulbright's devastating critique of American moralism in the context of Soviet-American relations, as developed at length in his *Old Myths and New Realities* (New York: Random House, Inc., 1964), esp. pp. 7–16.

its opponents in an uncomfortable position. To disagree with truth and right as defined by Americans often meant favoring or apologizing for irrational and immoral conduct. Many instances could be cited in which this device left the United States in an unassailable position. Second, anyone who opposed the United States was—according to Americans—*per se* a "bad" (irrational and/or immoral) person, and Americans were thus in a better frame of mind to prosecute the ensuing struggle.[19]

THE INVOCATION OF PUBLIC OPINION.   In complete harmony with democratic ideology was a great faith in the wisdom and the omnipotence of "public opinion." The policy of the United States has long been to attempt systematically to influence mass attitudes everywhere and to identify American policy with what were taken to be the commands of popular opinion. American political ideas have always assumed a disharmony between the people of any "autocratic" or "dictatorial" state and their government, and Americans felt that it would not be difficult to win the masses of men to the American side in any dispute. Men, the argument ran, are inherently reasonable and just; American policy is reasonable and just; all rational and moral men will automatically support the United States if only they know the truth; the ultimate vindication of the American position is therefore certain.

The operational problem of United States policy therefore resolved itself primarily into one of communication. All the United States need do was to make its own position clear beyond misunderstanding (being sure to orient it on objective truth and moral right) and then to discover mechanisms for bringing its message to the world. Public opinion everywhere would recognize the justice of American policy, and all wise and good men would demand that their respective governments immediately accede to the wishes of the United States. No regime, however inimical it might otherwise be, could resist this pressure.

THE DEVELOPMENT AND USE OF "LAW."   Another traditional nonviolent technique much favored by Americans has been a heavy reliance on law, legal reasoning, and legal rules. In international relations the United States has been sensitive to the existence of legal rules and has usually attempted to shape its policy in accordance with them. Not only has the United States attempted to "have the law on its side," but it has also sought to foster the continual elaboration of international legal rules. To Americans, social

---

[19]In the two great crises of the 1960's—Cuba in 1962 and Vietnam in 1965—the United States went to great effort to brand its respective adversaries with the tag of immorality. The task was complicated in the case of Cuba by the fact that the very same act judged "immoral" when done by the Soviet Union—the placement of missiles menacing the United States—had been previously undertaken by the United States in Turkey and elsewhere; in Vietnam, the Viet Cong had to be classified as "aggressors" before American policy became clear, in spite of the Viet Cong's being composed entirely of Vietnamese who were fighting (as they thought) on their own homeland. In both cases, however, the moral base of American policy was firmly and officially asserted as self-evident.

relations sanctioned by juristic norms are always preferable to extralegal ones; a "world of law" would be better on all counts than a "lawless" one. The United States has pioneered in the extension of the international legal frontier so as to encompass more and more of interstate life.

ECONOMICS: THE PUNITIVE SANCTION. But what if reason, justice, law, and public opinion were to prove inadequate; what was the United States to do if the forces of evil did not yield to these rational techniques? The American tradition, although repudiating armed force except in extremes, nevertheless made allowances for a punitive sanction. Such open coercion as was necessary was to be accomplished by economic means.

This again was only to be expected. In a highly materialistic culture in which major emphasis is placed on the rewards of economic activity, the promise of economic reward or the threat of economic deprivation has come to have a distinctly coercive character. What could be more natural for Americans than to conclude that this weapon would prove as efficacious in international relations as it was in their private lives?

And so the United States came to feel that its productive power made it really unnecessary for it to fight wars or to play the more ordinary forms of power politics. All America really needed to do was to use its immense economic strength coercively, and any possible opponent would be, if not stopped, as least handicapped to the point where it would yield to American techniques of persuasion.[20]

Public Opinion and American Foreign Policy

The first two sections of this chapter have dealt with the popular image of foreign policy as it was formed during earlier periods of history. We have considered the mass attitudes and preferences that are still alive today in the subtle and complex phenomenon we call "public opinion." This concluding section will deal with American public opinion as it bears upon specific issues of foreign policy, using the version of its role that we sketched out on page 31.

THE CHARACTERISTICS OF PUBLIC OPINION. We shall be enumerating certain common characteristics of mass attitudes in the United States. It

---

[20]Throughout the cold-war era, influential segments of American opinion have continued to argue the economic weakness of communist society and to call for the systematic application of American economic pressure as a quick, cheap, and safe way to win the final victory. None of the American efforts to use economics as a punitive sanction, either unilaterally or by means of the free-world alliance, has had any significant success, and the hostility of the allies of the United States to this enterprise has long been obvious. See Fulbright, *Old Myths and New Realities*, pp. 13–16, for an analysis and critique.

seems scarcely necessary to remind outselves that any such list contains certain inherent shortcomings: (1) No single person demonstrates all the following characteristics, either of strength or of weakness, in his own attitudes; (2) the general public seldom exhibits all the characteristics simultaneously; and (3) no single characteristic is present in the public all the time.

If these limitations are kept in mind, it is possible to construct two almost parallel lists, one including the major weaknesses of American mass opinion and the other its significant strengths, as both apply to questions of international affairs.

WEAKNESSES OF AMERICAN PUBLIC OPINION

It has been fashionable for a number of years for scholars to find ample fault with the American mass mind as it comes to grips with international problems.[21] Either because of an admiration for the "superior" efficiency of dictatorial or aristocratic governments or because of a deep and sincere faith in the greater wisdom of professional officialdom, many writers have made very detailed and thoughtful criticisms of the way Americans think about foreign affairs. We may find their conclusions unpalatable and their recommendations controversial, but we must admit that they have made a very sizable indictment of American public opinion .

LACK OF INFORMATION. Perhaps the most far-reaching, and the most difficult to contradict, of the asserted weaknesses of American opinion is its uninformed character. Americans have access to a greater amount of information than does any other people in the world; newspapers, magazines, radio, television, and every other mass medium pour forth data in a great flood. The stark fact remains, however, that mass audiences do not take advantage of the available data to the extent that one might expect and hope.

No one expects laymen to have complete information about all the problems facing the nation. But the "ordinary citizen" does not seem to have enough information at his command to play even his limited public part with full efficiency. Public-opinion polls reveal a startling lack of knowledge about such important matters as the United Nations, NATO, the nature of communism, and so on. Without basic data, it is a near-impossibility for individuals to make intelligent decisions—or even any decisions at all.

IMPATIENCE. Americans are an impatient people. Their culture emphasizes direct social action with speedy results; they tend to prefer immediate solutions to problems, with no excuses accepted for delay. When applied to

---

[21]A leading example is Lippmann, *The Public Philosophy*.

foreign affairs, in which progress is often tortuous and usually slow, this cultural trait can cause serious conflict.

Impatience makes Americans fretful under the tedious and delicate course of most diplomacy; it frequently leads to the advocacy of showdown or all-out techniques when less extreme measures might be preferable. It makes continued crisis difficult to endure, eroding national self-control and perspective. It generates tremendous pressures for action that officials find very difficult to withstand.

EMOTIONALISM. Emotion bulks large in American international attitudes. Americans go to greater lengths in indulging their international loves and hates than do the people of any other major state. It is difficult to maintain mass enthusiasm for the controlling constant of national interest; the public most commonly follows the course dictated by current likes and dislikes. This gives American opinion toward major issues a peculiar wavelike quality arising from its tendency to great emotional swings from one extreme to the other.

THE PREFERENCE FOR DICHOTOMIES. Finally, we must mention the American preference for dichotomies. Americans generally have an all-or-nothing attitude in international affairs; the dominant national assumption is that the only alternative outcomes of a situation are extreme ones. Public attitudes think only of total peace or total war, total love or total hatred, Russian friendship or Russian enmity. This simple black-or-white formulation of problems grows out of the first three points we have made above and, in turn, influences each of them.

STRENGTHS OF AMERICAN PUBLIC OPINION

Less frequently discussed, at least in any objective fashion, are the positive strengths of American public opinion. It is somewhat surprising that this is so; in a democracy in which public opinion is given a significant role to play we would expect that considerable effort would be expended in analyzing the positive contributions made by mass attitudes. Yet it is relatively rare to find a systematic study of the sources of strength provided by the public.[22]

We may nevertheless prepare a list suggesting some of the favorable or advantageous characteristics of American public opinion. We must keep these in mind in reaching any overall judgment on the democratic process as it applies to international affairs. Concentrating only on popular shortcomings

---

[22]Probably the most ambitious attempt in this direction was made by Dorothy Fosdick, in *Common Sense and World Affairs.* See also Hughes, *America the Vincible,* and Rosenau, *Public Opinion and Foreign Policy.*

prepares the way for the possible acceptance of some doctrine of elitism and might ultimately lead to at least a partial rejection of the entire democratic idea. The strengths of American opinion at least help balance the most glaring of its weaknesses.

THE DEBATING OF MAJOR ISSUES. One of the chief strengths of American public opinion is a popular insistence on thorough public airing and debate of major international issues. On any important question nearly every possible point of view has at least an organization or two to express its views. As each prosecutes its case, the basic alternatives often receive a thorough airing. Pressure groups and political parties also share in keeping debate and disagreement alive, with the party in control of the White House (and therefore presumably responsible for policy) usually defending its record and the opposition engaged in attacking and criticizing.

COMMON SENSE. The next characteristic we mention might at first seem contradictory when set alongside our ealier indictment of American emotionalism. There is in American public opinion a strong strain of common sense that historically has often come to the rescue just as it seemed as if emotional excesses were to sweep the United States away.

Americans seem to need their periodic emotional indulgences; perhaps they provide an outlet for pent-up frustrations and tensions. But after each of these outbursts of love or hate, there comes a reaction. Often it goes too far in the opposite direction, and the new attitude is actually as emotional as the old. But ultimately the pendulum tends to come to rest, and most Americans —emotionally purged—take a stand on the dead center of common sense.

If this model is accurate, and if we may assume that such common-sense judgments are usually satisfactory, we may regret that the American people seemingly must go through their initial emotional sprees. But, at least up to this point in history, the American people have not been able to dispense with their preliminary reliance on pure sentiment; and it would be a brave man indeed who would argue that American public opinion would always be of a higher type if all emotional preferences were abandoned and all judgments made on the basis of cold common-sense calculation. A good case can be made in defense of at least some feeling in American mass attitudes.

ALTRUISM. American public opinion, finally, is genuinely altruistic. We commented earlier on American Utopianism and tried to suggest some of its failings. No one, however, can question its sincerity. Americans do generally wish everyone well and devote an unusually large share of their efforts to trying to improve the lot of man.

It is easy—and, in some circles, fashionable as well—to deride the simple good-heartedness of Americans as reflecting naiveté and immaturity. Yet such sophistication frequently misses an important point: America's genuine concern for other peoples is widely recognized abroad. The reputation for altruism that Americans enjoy is itself a source of great strength; when they depart from it and instead seek to play the role of pure power, they are usually the losers. The American government has been struggling to learn to reconcile the conflicting demands of moral and physical power, and it could do worse than to trust to the innate altruism of Americans.

PRELIMINARY VERDICT ON PUBLIC OPINION

Balancing strengths against weaknesses, what can we say at this point about American public opinion on foreign-policy issues, particularly in the light of America's international ego-image as we developed it in the first part of this chapter? In one sense, to answer this question is the purpose of this book, and an attempt to do so is made in the final chapters. Even at this early stage of our inquiry, however, certain points can safely be made.

It would be inaccurate to condemn American attitudes as inherently unsound but equally as erroneous is the assumption that public opinion is an infallible guide to policy. The weaknesses of American opinion are all dangerous to intelligent planning; no policy-maker could safely trust himself and the national interest to the whims of a rapidly shifting, stereotype-ridden, impatient, and highly emotional body politic. Coping with this phenomenon raises problems of political leadership of a grave difficulty. On the other hand, the advantages we saw in American attitudes strengthen the hand of American statesmen and give them a freedom of action (once opinion has come to rest) that makes it possible for the government to act in accordance with the major outlines of a preconceived strategy.

Both the strengths and the weaknesses of American opinion, therefore, have an impact on American policy. The concern of both the statesman and the public would seem to be one of curbing the excesses and capitalizing on the advantages of this situation so as to produce a workable relationship between the demands of mass opinion and the concrete purposes of official leadership.

CHAPTER **5**

American
National Interests

In Chapter 4 we considered the American tradition of foreign policy as a major contributing factor to the operative climate of decision in the government of the United States. At this point, we shall take the next forward step: We shall attempt to stipulate the basic ingredients of the actual (or at least the predominant) concept of national interest accepted and implemented by the corps of official decision-makers. Applying this notion to the prevailing environmental factors affecting the United States, we shall then formulate a pattern of generalized goals and objectives.

This is a difficult task for anyone not of the governmental hierarchy, but it is by no means an impossible one. The American outlook on the world and the imperatives of international life combine to exert a powerful influence on the contemporary foreign policy of the United States. Certain lines of action are virtually closed to the United States, others are almost ineluctably demanded of it, between these extreme compulsions we can find a broad complex of choices. Even in this less well-defined area, however, we may suggest a set of reasonably well-clarified wants and needs—what we can call interests—that go far to govern the rational choices made by American policy-makers. An understanding of these preoccupations will throw a good deal of light on what has been done and will be done in the future by the government of the United States.

THE CLASSIFICATION OF FOREIGN POLICIES

We should first undertake a preliminary exercise in political taxonomy. We shall be fitting American policy and the concept of national interest that undergirds it into a rough system of classification. From such a scheme, we may draw certain inferences from the general category into which United States policy falls. Our first task, therefore, should be to delimit our classifications.

THE DICHOTOMY OF STATE ATTITUDE.   Despite the obvious fact that no two states have the same foreign policy, and the equally self-evident conclusion that there are many subtle shades of difference among even very similar ones, in the most general sense some type of either-or proposition underlies everything that any state does. There seems to be a single choice that every government initially makes, consciously or unconsciously; once made, its subsequent action flows naturally and almost inevitably from it. Major change in its foreign policy is difficult and unlikely unless this original decision is reversed.

This crucial determinant, the major criterion of our system of classification, is the state's attitude toward the general world situation in which it finds itself. Any state must somehow determine which of two possible alternatives it will choose: it may either accept—at least in general—the combination of advantages and disadvantages that together give it a status relative to all other states and to the system at large, or it may be dissatisfied with its role and determined to improve its place. Which decision it makes, and how and by what means that decision is reached, is determined by forces within the particular state, although external factors must be taken into account. The choice of a fundamental outlook determines the form and the direction of the greater part of all its later action. The two groups of states, divided by this watershed of attitude, provide the two categories of our system of classification.

STATUS QUO VS. REVISIONISM.   Scholars have given names to the two halves of our dichotomy. The first group of states, satisfied with what they have and interested in preserving it, is most commonly called the "status-quo" states. The other group, interested in overturning the prevailing distribution of rewards and power to their own advantage, is usually called "revisionist." Oppositions other than "status-quo"–"revisionist" are open to serious question because the classificatory words tend to carry policy implications that are not really necessary. In our discussion we shall confine ourselves to the simple status-quo–revisionist antinomy.[1] We may draw

---

[1]For an extended discussion of the classification of foreign policies, see Hans J. Morgenthau, *Politics Among Nations*, 3d ed. (New York: Alfred A. Knopf, Inc., 1960), Chapters 4, 5, and 6. Professor Morgenthau finds three types of policies: status quo, imperialist, and

certain limited but basic conclusions about the general foreign-policy lines of these two types.

A status-quo state normally pursues policies aimed at preserving its status: policies of limited objectives that are in the broadest sense defensive in concept and inspiration. Generally such a state is more concerned with devising responses to problems that arise from external sources than with initiating positive long-range programs of its own. It usually has a major interest in peaceful international intercourse, particularly in the process of peaceful change. Switzerland is perhaps the archetype of the status quo.

A revisionist state, on the contrary, is actually or potentially always on the offensive. Revisionist policy assumes the strategic initiative, actively exploring any situation that promises advantage. We cannot generalize that such an outlook must be one that looks forward to or plans war, but we can safely stipulate that the choice between war and peace made by a revisionist state is governed only by considerations of operational expediency and utility rather than by any basic demand of national interest; it is a "means" rather than an "ends" decision. Nazi Germany in its heyday, dedicated as it was to incessant attack, is a classic example of revisionism in action.

THE LIMITS OF CLASSIFICATION. We shall be using the status-quo–revisionist dichotomy as an analytical device throughout our discussion of American foreign policy. Its usefulness will perhaps be demonstrated as we progress, but at the outset we must enter a large caveat. The "science of international politics," of which taxonomy is such a fundamental part, is still rudimentary and imprecise. Our system of classification can do no more than to suggest certain rough categories divided by a line often difficult to discover and frequently violated in practice, and the inferences we draw from the status-quo or revisionist status of any state can never be any more than tentative.

One additional warning seems in point. Any objective analysis of foreign policies must proceed on the assumption that the choices that states make are rationally determined. No one would be so foolhardy as to insist that all states (or, for that matter, any state) will follow policies dictated only by the calculations of pure reason. We are constantly confronted by examples of status-quo states undertaking moves that would seem logical only within a revisionist context; less frequently, we see the opposite. Here is the province of the inescapable irrational factor,[2] and to the extent that it controls the behavior of states the usefulness of our classification is seriously impaired.

---

prestige. We include the latter two under the more general rubric of "revisionism." For a more detailed analysis of the dichotomy discussed here, see Lerche and Said, *Concepts of International Politics*, pp. 17–22.

[2]Feliks Gross calls this "factor *x*," to be allowed for in all policy analyses. *Foreign Policy Analysis* (New York: Philosophical Library, Inc., 1954), pp. 124–125.

The United States and the Status Quo

The United States is, by our criteria, assumed to be a status-quo state whose major interest is in the preservation of its present advantageous position. We shall modify this generalization as we examine American interest more closely, but in its essentials it will remain as the fundamental consideration of our analysis of the basic American motivations in foreign policy.

THE UNITED STATES AS A "HAVE" POWER

THE SATIATION OF THE UNITED STATES. What sort of things make a state a "have" power? Why does a state become a defender of the status quo, at least as it perceives it? By answering these questions with particular reference to the United States we may examine the broader issue.

Generally speaking, a state accepts a status-quo position for either of two reasons. In the first place, it may lack the capability to achieve any more of its objectives; it therefore settles for the most it can get from the given situation. Sweden's open renunciation of its ambitions after 1721 resulted in such a posture. On the other hand, the status quo may be accepted simply because the state concerned has reached all the objectives it deems important, and such as remain unattained would require more trouble than they would be worth. Although capable of getting more, the state elects to content itself with what it has.

It seems clear that if the United States is a status-quo power, it arrived at this position by the second route. It has only been since 1945 that the status quo as a policy channel has become fully rationalized to American policy-makers and has served as a base for calculated strategic and tactical decisions. At the moment that the more or less deliberate choice was made to defend the status quo, the United States possessed ample capability—both of force and of consent—to reach an entirely new set of goals. American statesmen, acting in harmony with popular attitudes as they understood them, instead chose to concentrate on the defense of the postwar situation of the United States.

In 1945 there was little disagreement among either officials or citizens that the United States had reached virtual satiation. The nation no longer had any obsessive objectives; there were no major international adventures upon which Americans were determined to embark. Left alone, Americans would bother no one, conquer no new territory, overthrow no governments, start no wars. They wished only to be free to enjoy the advantages of their civilization and—within reason—were willing to permit everyone else the same right to enjoy their own.

THE NINETEENTH CENTURY. As we have seen, American preoccupation with the status quo is a relatively recent development. During much of the nineteenth century the United States had a dynamic, expanding foreign policy that was an accurate reflection of the dominant American revisionism.[3] Until the United States achieved continental expanse, hemisphere hegemony, and economic maturity, it had long-standing purposes to whose accomplishment successive administrations devoted themselves. During the first century and a quarter of its history as a sovereign state, therefore, the United States became involved in a series of major disputes with most of the great powers and fought three large-scale international wars: with Great Britain in 1812, with Mexico in 1846, and with Spain in 1898. With the achievement of American "manifest destiny" by 1900 the approach of the United States changed. During the twentieth century the United States has been concerned mainly with holding on to its winnings rather than with adding to them, although full realization of this role did not come until after 1945.

SELF-PRESERVATION, SECURITY, AND WELL-BEING. In Chapter 1 we postulated that the basic concerns of every state are self-preservation, security, and well-being. As Americans faced the world in 1945 and attempted to apply these general terms to their own situation, the condition of the United States was revealed as one of high satiation. Although there was room for some improvements, the nation was considered to be so well-off on all three counts that most Americans concluded that to seek major alterations in an already happy situation might jeopardize the foundations of America's enviable status. Indeed, any extreme policy was felt to be dangerous. The decision was reached and ratified that no adventuresome expansion would be undertaken and that henceforth the major American effort would be in defense of already established positions.

THE AMERICAN ATTITUDE TOWARD CHANGE

"Status quo" as a policy orientation has a reasonably precise meaning that derives from a state's attitude toward the overall world situation as it sees it. It is dangerously easy, however, to take the next step and to conceive a status-quo policy as one of merely holding a particular position and of resisting and attempting to prevent any and all change. This conclusion does not necessarily follow from a status-quo assumption; one of the distinguish-

---

[3]See, for example, Julius Pratt's two studies, *Expansionists of 1812* (New York: The Macmillan Company, 1925), and *Expansionists of 1898* (Baltimore: Johns Hopkins University Press, 1936).

ing marks of the American approach to world affairs is the activist implication that is built into the defensive posture the United States assumes on most substantive questions.

THE AVOIDANCE OF STAND-PATTISM. It is a serious misjudgment to assume (and it has been done often, by Americans and foreigners alike) that because the United States considers itself a status-quo state, it is committed to rigidly opposing either evolutionary or revolutionary change. The kind of world in which Americans want to live is one that cannot be achieved by simply holding fast and letting everyone else take care of himself. The United States cannot stand pat. This would be impossible under the conditions of modern technology and national self-consciousness; what is more, even if it were feasible it would be unwise and possibly disastrous.

CHANGE IN THE AMERICAN INTEREST. Let anyone attempt to visualize the kind of international society in which he would feel personally secure, and then let him ask himself if this kind of order can ever be created without first making significant change in the world as it is at present. The answer, at least as given by most rational and well-intentioned people, would in most cases call for action and change on a broad front; the world of today is not one that will permit the United States the luxury of ignoring it.

The basic interests of the United States and the American people demand, not stagnation and immobility, but fundamental change in many parts of the world. It would be fatuous for Americans to prate solemnly of "order" or "stability" in the world while at the same time their government neglected or inhibited efforts to remove the conditions that breed war. The final guarantee of the American concept of the status quo demands action; the United States cannot retain its preeminence by denying improvement to everyone else or by neglecting action to create the conditions conducive to peace. In this sense the United States violates the stereotype of the status-quo state; Americans are instead—on this point—truly revisionist.

THE REQUIREMENT OF AFFIRMATIVE ACTION. Nor does the American identification with the status quo confine the United States indefinitely to a passive, negative policy of doing nothing until some kind of threat arises and then of confining its action to mere countermeasures. Defense—military, political, ideological, and economic—has a real place in American strategy, but it is by no means the only or even the most important concern of policy. The kind of peaceful order that Americans seek—to speak metaphorically— is not the peace of the cabbage patch, but rather the peace of the beehive.

The notion of interest that we are developing here demands, therefore, that the heart of the foreign policy of the United States consist of vigorous, positive action to create the kind of world that Americans want. This means an international order in which the United States and its citizens will be free to enjoy their advantages in the maximum possible security. This means

—and this is as good a formulation of American national interest as any—
a world of peace, order, and stability.

THE PROCEDURAL STATUS QUO

Thus far we have argued that the United States is basically a status-quo
power with a major concern with the defense of its own situation, but with
the additional qualification that to a very real extent the United States is also
committed to at least some of the principles of what we have called revisionism. Can we now reconcile these two positions and, in doing so, clarify
the content of the American adherence to the status quo?

THE SCOPE OF AMERICAN REVISIONISM. We may put the matter in this
way: As regards the bulk of the substantive questions of international
politics, the American attitude is either actually or potentially revisionist.
The United States excepts from its general tolerance of change only a few
substantive issues that bear adversely and immediately upon American
interests. Although insisting on the continued maintenance of those factors
that contribute to the security and prosperity of the United States, American
policy-makers generally retain an open mind on the prospects of material
change elsewhere.

We are not claiming here that the American attitude of substantive
revisionism makes the United States always favor change for its own sake.
The American government is not committed to a principle of constant
dynamism any more than it is to simple stagnation. Some forms of substantive change contribute to the advancement of American interest, and
these the United States approves, urges, and seeks to bring about; others
are potentially or actually inimical, and these the United States disapproves
and seeks to prevent. In between these extremes are many developments
and evolutions that do not permit of such ready categorization. American
interest demands that each of these be scrutinized, measured against the
yardstick of relevance to American concerns, and then favored or opposed
in its terms.

THE AMERICAN CONCERN WITH PROCEDURE. Where the American
identification with the status quo is complete, however, is the general area
of international procedure. The United States insists that the mechanisms
of international contact, adjustment, and necessary change must be peaceful
and orderly. On this point the United States cannot make any concession.
Peaceful process—the mark of an orderly society—is the central ingredient
of the status quo Americans seek to preserve in their own interest.[4]

---

[4]No more graphic demonstration of this premise could be made than American reaction
to the Anglo-French-Israeli invasion of the Suez Canal Zone in 1956. The basic ingredient
in American policy was the principle that no provocation, however extreme, justified the

This was the major operational decision involved in the post-World War II policy choice made by the United States. Americans recognized, as we shall see below, that the situation in 1945 demanded extensive long-range planning and action by their government if the full results of victory were to be achieved. There was little of the traditional status quo in that decision, except for a basic dedication to the ideal of an orderly world. To this commitment the American government and (to a large extent) the American people have remained generally faithful.[5]

Peace, Order, and Stability

We summarized American national interest above as a continuing concern with permanent peace, order, and stability in the international society as the best way to guarantee American independence, security, and well-being. We turn now to a more detailed analysis of this generalization.

THE UNITED STATES AND INTERNATIONAL CONTROLS. The United States is seeking a flexible and adaptable international order with only one drastic modification in the traditional patterns of state behavior: the introduction of a set of fixed outer limits on permissible state action. One of the long-run objectives of American policy, therefore, is the development and application of a set of controls on the freedom of action of all states and the creation of self-activating mechanisms of adjustment in the international order.

What we mean by "controls" and "self-activating mechanisms of adjustment" can be simply stated. We are referring to procedures and institutions that will (1) prevent states from resorting to war at their own decision and (2) provide satisfactory solutions to problems so as to make war unnecessary. War, therefore, is the focus of the entire enterprise. If state action

---

adoption of force as a technique. See President Eisenhower's speeches on October 31, 1956 (*Department of State Bulletin*, November 12, 1956, p. 743), and February 20, 1957 (*Department of State Bulletin*, March 11, 1957, pp. 387–390). In the latter speech, he said: "If we agree that armed attack can properly achieve the purposes of the assailant, then I fear we shall have turned back the clock of international order. We will, in effect, have countenanced the use of force as a means of settling international differences and through this gaining national advantages. . . . We cannot consider that the armed invasion and occupation of another country are 'peaceful means' or proper means to achieve justice and conformity with international laws." The intervention of American forces in the Dominican Republic in April 1965 was widely attacked, at home and abroad, as a violation of this principle and therefore as not really in the interest of the United States. Tacit admission of the partial validity of these charges by the United States was shown by the compromising policy the government subsequently pursued in dealing with the several Dominican factions.

[5]Hans J. Morgenthau, in *The Purpose of American Politics* (New York: Alfred A. Knopf, Inc., 1960), delivers a devastating attack on the lack of purpose and initiative on the part of American policy-makers. Thomas K. Finletter, in *Foreign Policy: The Next Phase, The 1960's*, argues for the renewal of substantial dynamism in American policy.

could be confined to nonviolent procedures, the worst dangers of the state system would be eliminated.

This notion, of course, underlies the idea of collective security, and its applicability to the United Nations explains a large part of American support of that organization. The attempt to place controls on state action by United Nations action squares exactly with American interest, and it is only to be expected that the United States would approve most such moves. But the realization that the United Nations, by itself, is not enough has kept the American government active in other areas, attempting in many ways to bring new forms of control mechanisms into existence.

THE AMERICAN INTEREST IN PEACE

We have already dealt briefly with two matters bearing directly on the American interest in peace. We have suggested that the status-quo identification of the United States necessarily implies peaceful process as the preferred vehicle of international adjustment, and we have also noted American concern with the development of a system of international controls that incorporates peace as a way of life.

ARE AMERICANS A PEACE-LOVING PEOPLE? We should first recognize an old issue. In Chapter 4 we saw that the American ego-image is one of uniqueness: Americans generally think of themselves not only as inherently peace-loving but as superior to other peoples in this regard. The national self-image is of a people tolerant to a fault, slow to anger, but mighty in its wrath when aroused. The United States has never gone to war, Americans normally argue, except to administer just punishment to vicious and un-principled aggressors.

It comes as a blow to many Americans to be told that this picture is not shared by most foreign peoples, either in Europe or Asia. The United States is frequently thought of instead as being impatient, trigger-tempered, and liable to explosion at any moment. American history, foreigners point out, is speckled with big and little wars, many of them (including the War of 1812, the Mexican War, the Spanish-American War, and countless campaigns against the Indians) suspiciously similar to acts of aggression. Today many of the allies of the United States are frequently concerned about American bellicosity and the danger to peace that it represents. Americans are not likely to become a nation of pacifists. Certainly the serious crises of the 1960's—the Berlin wall in 1961, the Cuban missile crisis in 1962, the Dominican intervention of 1965, and the Vietnam war of the middle years of the decade—have done little to reinforce the image of a United States whose interest in peace was paramount, however justifiable American policy may have been on other grounds.

THE DISAPPEARING UTILITY OF WAR.   War, as an instrument of national policy, is neither inevitable nor accidental. Wars do not simply happen; they come about as the result of a deliberate policy decision by some state (though it is true that external conditions play a major part in making such a decision probable). The technology of warfare in the twentieth century has made war less and less useful to the foreign policy of major states. The costs of large-scale conflict today are so prohibitively high that there is only a tiny handful of objectives—most of them intimately connected with self-preservation—whose worth would justify a state's coolly electing to initiate a total war. With the possible rewards of war so nearly balanced (or actually outweighed) by its predictable costs, American national interest has embraced wholeheartedly the desirability of permanent peace.[6]

What is applicable to offensive war applies, with some modification, to defensive warfare as well. The United States will not accept a military challenge thrown out by a potential aggressor without first exhausting all alternative methods of coping with the threat. Defensive war is a rational alternative for Americans only if they are convinced that there is literally no other endurable way out of the crisis. Accordingly, since 1945 the United States has ignored numerous provocations and threats that, under other circumstances or at some earlier time, might have resulted in a decision to retaliate with force.[7] The American government will wage defensive war only when it feels itself forced to do so.[8]

THE AMERICAN INTEREST IN A PEACEFUL WORLD.   But America's interest in peace is more extensive than the mere urge to stay out of war itself. It demands a constant American effort toward the progressive elimination of war as a practice in the state system and the working objective of a warless world.

War anywhere is a threat, either direct or—occasionally—remote, to the interest of the United States. It is not enough for the American govern-

---

[6]President Johnson, throughout the escalation of the Vietnam crisis in 1965, continually emphasized that "The peace of mankind must not, and will not, be lost again." "The Peace of Mankind," *Department of State Bulletin*, LII, No. 1356 (June 21, 1965), 986–989.

[7]This conviction is apparently shared at least to some degree behind the Iron Curtain as the Kremlin and Washington have both come to the conclusion that it is impossible to meet provocation with force. This has resulted in a great increase in the severity and frequency of provocative mŏves made by both sides. The U-2 incident and the tongue-lashing that President Eisenhower received at the hands of Premier Khruschev in 1960 would have brought war very close indeed in earlier times. This conviction was also operative in 1962 when President Kennedy and Premier Khruschev both realized that the Soviet Union had gone too far in Cuba but that it must have a graceful exit from a most embarrassing position. A sort of tacit cooperation resulted in a retreat from the brink.

[8]There is a school of thought in the United States, however, that professes to be very concerned lest the country lapse into pacifism. For examples, see Henry A. Kissinger, *Nuclear Weapons and Foreign Policy* (New York: Harper & Row, Publishers, 1957), and *The Necessity for Choice* (New York: Harper & Row, Publishers, 1961); see also Dean Acheson, *Power and Diplomacy* (Cambridge, Mass.: Harvard University Press, 1958).

ment to meet threats to the peace, from whatever source, as they arise. American interest demands a continuing effort, both from the United States and from such other states as can be mobilized in this effort,[9] to broaden the area in which peaceful process is the controlling technique of international relations. A peaceful world obviously requires that each state limit its policy objectives to those that can be gained peacefully; part of the American concern with peace is a continuing insistence that other states make this kind of self-denying commitment in response to similar action by the United States.

ORDER AND STABILITY

The remaining two components of broad-gauge American interest are order and stability in international society. As used here, "order" refers to the existence of peaceful and regular *methods* of conducting international affairs, and "stability" is the *condition* that will prevail when these orderly techniques are so widely used that state behavior will be, in great measure, predictable. Together, the two terms fill in the outline of the general concept of "peace" and make it a more comprehensive guide to American policy.

THE ROLE OF LAW AND LEGAL RULES. In Chapter 4 we noted the traditional American preference for social relationships that are regulated by legal rules. Here is one of the many instances in which a popular, nonrationalized impression is also very good practical policy for the United States. Despite the chronic overestimation of the potentialities of legalisms as control factors in international relations, it is undeniable that order and stability, as we have defined them, can be permanently realized in international life only when they rest on a substructure of legal principles.[10] Law and its practitioners go far to stabilize any society in which they are operative.

It is therefore quite apparent that American national interest should include an appreciation of and concern with the extension of the scope of international law. This may be implemented in two ways capable of being undertaken simultaneously. On the one hand, the United States may seek to assist in the development of new legal rules to formalize evolving inter-

---

[9]From the many official statements of this position, we may cite three presidential speeches, one almost immediately after World War II and the others more recent: Mr. Truman's Navy Day speech, October 27, 1945 (*The New York Times*, October 28, 1945), Mr. Eisenhower's campaign speech of September 27, 1956 (*The New York Times*, September 28, 1956), and Mr. Johnson's 1965 State of the Union Message (*Department of State Bulletin*, LII, No. 1335 (January 25, 1965), 94–100).

[10]Ralph Linton, in *A Study of Man* (New York: Appleton-Century-Crofts, 1936), points out: "The only cases in which new forms of society have been established successfully have been those in which the plan for the new society has included a large body of concrete rules for behavior" (p. 97). Reprinted by permission of Appleton-Century-Crofts.

national relationships that have reached or are reaching stability; one contemporary example is the question of international civil aviation.[11] The other area in which the United States could take the lead is in the formulation of principles of law incorporating the verb "ought" and in the attempt to bring the actual conduct of states into conformity with these humanitarian rules. Perhaps the best-known recent example of this is the United Nations Convention on Human Rights, a document in whose drafting the United States played a leading part.

THE NECESSITY OF ORGANIZATION. But order and stability require more than just a system of legal rules. The effective operation of the kind of world order the United States is seeking necessitates a more elaborate structure of institutions, a more detailed organization.

International society is distinguished by a relative scarcity of agencies of joint action. Although the institutional structure of interstate life is not entirely lacking, we must admit that it is no more than rudimentary. There is a lack both of control mechanisms and of instruments for positive cooperation. In times of crisis, both types must be extemporized.[12] Many scholars have noted that this shortcoming of the state system is responsible for the tendency of international problems to fail to reach complete resolution except by violence.[13] The converse of this proposition is self-evident: If an adequate institutional structure were to be created, much of the strain and crisis of international politics would be eliminated. This principle leads the United States to its interest in the progressive elaboration of international institutions and to the maximum possible participation in them.

We are not saying that, as of any particular moment, the more organization the better. No institution can be created until the social setting is prepared; men must be aware both of the social need and of the suitability of the proposed organization for satisfying the need before they will permit its creation and participate in it.[14] The most we can say is that the United States has an interest in seeing to it that the level of international organization—both in terms of extent and of effectiveness—is at its practical maximum. As the acceptance threshold of the society of states lowers, more and more organization can be introduced.

---

[11]See the International Air Services Transport Agreement, drawn up at the Chicago conference on air transport in 1944. *Proceedings of the International Civil Aviation Conference* (Washington, D. C.: Department of State, 1948–49).

[12]For example, the United Nations Emergency Force recruited to enforce the Middle East cease-fire in 1956 was created in great haste in the midst of an extremely dangerous situation.

[13]Clyde Eagleton, *International Government*, rev. ed. (New York: The Ronald Press Co., 1948), p. 19; J. L. Brierly, *The Law of Nations*, 4th ed. (Oxford: Clarendon Press, 1949), pp. 42–46.

[14]Marion Levy, *The Structure of Society* (Princeton, N. J.: Princeton University Press, 1952), pp. 102 ff; Ralph Linton, *The Tree of Culture* (New York: Alfred A. Knopf, Inc., 1955), p. 31.

Where will it end? Are we saying that the national interest of the United States demands that ultimately the organization principle should be carried to its logical extreme in the form of a world government? We are not going so far, at least at the present stage of our discussion. We are generalizing only to state that order and stability in international relations demand organization and that the more that international politics is fitted into an effective organizational scheme, the more orderly and stable it will be. Since 1945 the United States has accepted this idea and has been more or less consistently acting upon it.

PEACEFUL CHANGE.   One final aspect of order and stability, implicit in the preceding discussion of law and organization, merits some consideration in itself. This is the discovery, acceptance, and utilization of the techniques of peaceful change. It is possible to argue—as many students have—that this is the central political problem of our time.[15] Man seems to have tacitly agreed that war can no longer be used for the settlement of disagreements among great states; the question that perplexes everyone is: What shall be used as a substitute for violence in international affairs? If men could develop an acceptable method of coping with this issue, most of the other political dilemmas of contemporary life might prove to be less fearsome than they seemed when confronted in the face of the specter of war.

Change, as we have seen, is of the very essence of international relations. The abandonment of war will not eliminate the need for allowing for constant evolution. A stable world order must contain procedures that will make change possible, feasible, and acceptable, all the while limiting state action to something short of war.

The national interest of the United States naturally leads to American acceptance of the doctrine and—to a lesser extent—the practice of peaceful change. Despite the degree to which its necessity has been obscured by the exigencies of the cold-war era, a backward look today will reveal that the United States has made real, if limited, progress in promoting the principle. How this has taken place we shall see in later chapters.

Action Principles: The Constant Interests

From the highly generalized concept of American national interest that we have been developing—summarized as a continuing concern with the creation of a world of peace, order, and stability—there flows a small number of what we might call "action principles." These are the relatively

---

[15]For a survey of the rationale of peaceful change and the pacific settlement of international disputes, see Inis L. Claude, *Swords into Plowshares*, rev. ed. (New York: Random House, Inc., 1959), pp. 219–234.

permanent enterprises that are so fundamental to the American design that their inclusion in actual American foreign policy is axiomatic. These principles constitute an initial step in translating the idea of interest into the concrete courses of action that we call policy. We shall discuss three such constant interests.

SELF-DEFENSE

It might seem almost redundant to make the detailed point that the United States has a great interest in its own self-defense, but the concept of "defense" and the mythology that surrounds it today require us to examine the point systematically.

THE STATUS QUO IN PRACTICE. We must always remind ourselves that the new world of peace, order, and stability that the United States is seeking to create does not yet exist. The society of states in which the United States fits is one still dominated by the doctrine of sovereignty and the egoistic promptings of national interest. So long as this condition persists—and for safety's sake we must assume its indefinite existence, no matter how the United States attempts to modify it—American national interest must depend for its satisfaction primarily on the acts of the American people and the government of the United States.[16]

Our starting point in this analysis of American interest was the postulate that the United States is a status-quo state. From our previous review of the American concept of national interest, we can see the fundamental place occupied by the requirement of self-defense. Americans wish to preserve their advantages; in the long run the best way to accomplish this is by helping to develop a world in which all states and all people can feel secure. But, if the long-range plan fails, or at least during the period before it is consummated, the defense of the status quo as it affects Americans must rest on the United States itself.

MULTIPLE DEFENSE. "Self-defense" has a different connotation in the middle of the twentieth century than it has had in any earlier epoch. Traditionally, "defense" has meant the development of the capacity to resist armed attack; this is the classic idea of "security" as a state objective. But

---

[16]This is an elementary example of what is called the "minimax" theory of strategy, drawn from the mathematical theory of games. It is based on the construction of a plan of action that assumes that the worst possible outcome will be the result of the game; by planning in this way the player's losses are held to a minimum, and yet he remains in a position to maximize his gains if events are more favorable than he had assumed. See Kenneth E. Boulding, *Conflict and Defense: A General Theory* (New York: Harper & Row, Publishers, 1962), and Thomas C. Schelling, *The Strategy of Conflict* (Cambridge, Mass.: Harvard University Press, 1960); see also the discussion in Morton Kaplan, *System and Process in International Politics* (New York: John Wiley & Sons, Inc., 1957).

one of the paradoxes of modern world politics is the increasingly clear fact that technology, as applied to warfare, is a sword that cuts two ways.[17] It has vastly increased the destructive power of weapons and has made it operationally feasible to destroy an entire civilization. But the events of the cold-war era suggest that just to the extent to which weapons have grown more fearsome and efficient, the likelihood of their use in all-out conflict has decreased. And so military defense—as we shall see in detail in a later chapter—has assumed a new dimension today; deterrence of war, rather than victory on the battlefield, has become the dominant military concern of the United States.

But the decline in the centrality of the purely military component of self-defense has been matched by a corresponding increase in its other forms. The military danger to the United States may be less today than heretofore, as many experts believe; other sorts of threats, however, pose problems each as acute in its way as a military one would be. "Political warfare," economic conflict, ideological and propaganda war, and the frequently overemphasized but always real danger of subversion are only a few of the areas in which the United States is called upon to defend itself.[18]

There is very little inclination in the United States today to argue that unilateral self-defense is the route to ultimate salvation for Americans. Most Americans realize that, in seeking some approximation of the late Senator Robert A. Taft's "fortress America,"[19] the United States would be voluntarily sacrificing many of the happy domestic circumstances that American foreign policy is pledged to preserve. It would be stupid for the United States to seek to build a better world without first paying due attention to its own defense, but it would be catastrophic for it to make self-defense, narrowly defined, its only principle of action.[20]

---

[17]W. F. Ogburn, ed., *Technology and International Relations* (Chicago: University of Chicago Press, 1949); Bernard Brodie, ed., *The Absolute Weapon* (New York: Harcourt, Brace & World, Inc., 1946); Kissinger, *Nuclear Weapons and Foreign Policy*.

[18]For an excellent early summary of the multidimensional problem of American defense, see Hanson W. Baldwin, *The Price of Power* (New York: Harper & Row, Publishers, 1948); see also W. W. Kaufman, ed., *Military Policy and National Security* (Princeton, N. J.: Princeton University Press, 1956), and Oskar Morgenstern, *The Question of National Defense* (New York: Random House, Inc., 1959).

[19]In *A Foreign Policy for Americans* (Garden City, N.Y.: Doubleday & Company, Inc., 1951).

[20]An illustration of such a conflict in emphasis has been the long controversy within government circles over the form and direction to be assumed by the space effort of the United States. A considerable body of opinion, led by military spokesmen, has contended throughout that the significance of space was primarily military and that official policy should be directed toward gaining strategic advantages and avoiding threats from space to American security. In 1959 President Eisenhower placed the space program under the National Aeronautics and Space Administration, a civilian body. Military circles have never been completely reconciled to this decision; although unable to secure its reversal (at least as of this writing), the United States Air Force has won at least a limited approval of some of its projects for the military utilization of space. Its effort to broaden its role can be expected to continue.

COOPERATION FOR PEACE

If self-defense alone is not enough, and if positive action toward a world of peace and order is demanded in the American interest, we come next to the major question of how the United States is to proceed in this task. Here we consider a much-debated question: the necessity for, and the most desirable extent of, "international cooperation."

THE LIMITS ON UNILATERAL ACTION. We may take it as axiomatic that the United States cannot build the new world alone. The detailed framework of a peaceful order will be so many-sided, so complex, and so extensive that even the tremendous strength of the United States would be insufficient to construct it without help from outside. The United States cannot enforce peace by its own unaided efforts; it cannot order all the relationships of men, groups, and states; it cannot alone require that all forms of state action everywhere should be confined within the limits declared to be acceptable. The American interest in a new basis for international society is of such dimensions that assistance from other states is a *sine qua non* of success. The United States must have partners if its long-range plans are to bear fruit.

HARMONY OF INTEREST WITHIN THE STATUS QUO. What makes American national interest, as we are formulating it, a viable basis for policy is the fact that there is a sizable group of states that share the general idea of the status quo as defined by the United States and that have no major disagreement with its particular American version. There are at least several dozen fundamentally status-quo states; that is, they are not revisionist and are willing indefinitely to sustain the present distribution of rewards as it affects them.[21] Though most have some quarrel with the United States on points of detail, none makes its abasement a matter of primary concern. Thus a genuine harmony of interest obtains within this group on the commitment to the principle of a world of order; further, all are generally willing to accept American advantages as part of the world system they are interested in preserving.

THE STRUCTURE OF COOPERATION. Granted a harmony of interest in the maintenance of the procedural status quo and the absence of fundamental disagreement on the minimal substantive status quo that Americans demand, the discovery and application of methods of cooperation become a matter of operational technique. Cooperation between states is always possible— and usually practical—if it is based on a genuine, unforced, harmony of interest.

States, however, do not cooperate just for the sheer joy of cooperating.

---

[21]See, for example, Barbara Ward, *Policy for the West* (New York: W. W. Norton & Company, Inc., 1951).

Joint action, if it is to serve a useful purpose, is purposive: it is aimed at specific goals and involves the exchange of definite commitments to do particular things. American interest demands, therefore, that any cooperative enterprise have a predetermined objective in mind, that the participants be limited to those states that share the particular purpose, that the mutual obligations be precisely stipulated, and that each such venture be evaluated rigorously in terms of its contribution toward the long-range purposes of the United States. Under these assumptions the United States has associated itself with many states in a broad variety of cooperative enterprises. Some, like NATO, have had relatively productive histories; others, like the abortive Suez Canal User's Association of 1956, have failed. Such failures have generally been due to the nonapplicability of one of the above criteria to the project.

HOSTILITY TO NONPEACEFUL STATES

If we agree that cooperation with like-minded status-quo states is demanded by the national interest of the United States, is the converse of the proposition true? Does American national interest demand hostility toward all revisionist states? If we remember the American version of the status quo, if we confine revisionism to procedural matters, and if we define revisionism sharply, this proposition can be defended.

THE DEFENSE OF PEACEFUL PROCESS.   The logic of American national interest leads the United States to oppose any state that seems willing to violate the structure of peaceful process in international relations. This is the procedural status quo, pure and simple. American hostility to procedural revisionism is independent of the specific objectives the state is seeking; it is conceivable that the United States might approve or even support an identical program if it were to be prosecuted peacefully.[22] If it is an order of permanent peace that is the goal of American policy, simple logic and common sense would seem to demand that the United States offer immediate and total opposition to any state openly defiant of this end. This principle, as we shall see, underlies the entire anti-Soviet line that has bulked so large in postwar American policy; the United States has been hostile to the USSR primarily because of the Kremlin's demonstrated willingness to advance its interests by means of perpetuated disorder, frequent crisis, and threatened war.

---

[22]This point may be made with regard to the American attitude toward Israel following the 1956 Middle East crisis. The American position, as developed during the long controversy precipitated by Israel's refusal to evacuate the Gaza strip and the Gulf of Aqaba area, was that the United States opposed Israel's use of force while generally supporting the specific objectives Israel claimed to be seeking. See the speech of President Eisenhower, February 20, 1957, *Department of State Bulletin* (March 13, 1957).

THE INDIVISIBILITY OF PEACE. Peace, as the United States defines the term, is indivisible. It is not sufficient for the United States to oppose only those disturbers of the peace that directly threaten purely American interests; any state anywhere that is willing to rupture peaceful international relationships runs equally afoul of American concerns. We can argue that Communist China represents a direct and immediate threat to the United States and that American hostility to Mao Tse-tung can be explained on that basis; no such claim could be made, however, for United States insistence upon peaceful settlements in such faraway and relatively noncritical trouble spots as the Congo, Yemen, Israel, or Kashmir. The most spectacular application of the principle during the entire postwar period, however, occurred a decade ago when, in 1956, the United States blocked the Franco-British intervention in the Suez Canal Zone.

It is worth emphasizing, however, that American opposition to procedural revisionism does not manifest itself lightly, being confined to overt acts and overlooking empty threats and even ideological hostility. Only when tensions boil over into action does the United States initiate retaliatory and opposing action. No problem illustrates this point more clearly than does the ticklish question of Communist China. Ever since the victory of Mao Tse-tung in 1949, Peking has made no secret of either its total rejection of the American concept of peace, order, and stability or its determination to pursue an active and aggressive revisionist line. For more than a decade and a half, Chinese spokesmen have made merry with a chorus of anti-American diatribes, seemingly calculated to tempt the United States into reckless action. Yet China's excesses of language have been coupled with great caution and restraint in action (with the single exception of the war in Korea, in which case it is clear that China saw itself acting under great provocation), and Peking has been scrupulous not to transgress America's threshold of tolerance. The result has been that the United States has taken very few overtly anti-Chinese moves, even though public opinion has long been restive in the face of China's strong (and infuriating) professions of ideological and political animosity.

It is the principle of peaceful process to which the United States is committed as a matter of national interest. Affirmative action in its behalf is naturally to be expected, but so is the policy of resistance to any state that would go to war. Peace, order, and stability require not only that the United States build a new institutional edifice, but also that it protect its work against those who would destroy it.

AMERICAN POLICY
IN ACTION

CHAPTER **6**

The World Arena of American Policy

Up to this point, we have been concentrating our attention upon the intellectual ("theoretical") components of the foreign-policy process. Now, as we turn to the real world as the arena within which the United States must act, we must remind ourselves that implementation is the only true test of success or failure in foreign policy. No matter how impeccable a decision may be in abstract terms, it must submit itself to the test of execution. In these terms, it follows that an appreciation of the operational environment of policy is prerequisite to an understanding and an evaluation of the quality of the decisions themselves.

In Chapter 1 we dealt briefly with the "situational factors" that influence decisions. At that time we classified them under three heads: the nature of the international milieu, the actions of other states, and the action capability of the individual state in question. In this chapter we shall deal with the first two as they affect the United States, and in the next we shall discuss American capabilities for action. No discussion as inclusive as that in these two chapters can hope to be exhaustive. What we attempt here is no more than an outline of the various concerns with which responsible policy-makers must deal in decisional situations.

The Political World since 1945

All wars of any importance rearrange the political relationships of nations. World War II, however, set a new mark in this respect, even surpassing the overturns that resulted from the first general war of the century. No quarter of the globe escaped major effects, and every state in the world has been in some significant manner influenced by the aftermath of the struggle. The arena of international politics after 1945 has resembled only in small measure that of 1939.

THE REDISTRIBUTION OF POWER

World War II, as perhaps its most widespread effect, produced a wholesale redistribution of power on the grandest scale in history. The pre-1939 classification of states into "great powers," "middle powers," and "small powers" was completely invalidated; in its place the postwar world offered the strange spectacle of the overwhelming bulk of the available power concentrated in two states, whereas at the other end of the scale huddled all the rest, differing from one another only in the degree of their weakness relative to the two giants.

THE DISAPPEARANCE OF THE FORMER LEADERS. Of the seven generally accepted "great powers" of 1939,[1] five were summarily removed from the circles of world leadership. Three—Germany, Japan, and Italy—were defeated, humbled, occupied, and were to be remade in a fair way by the victors. Britain and France, although among the "victors," had been so drained by the war that neither could present a valid claim to dominance.[2] International affairs presented a strange appearance with these erstwhile leading participants playing a secondary role.

Opinions differed in 1945 as to the permance of the reduced role of the former great powers. There was general agreement that Italy would never again be a serious contender for top rank. There was much the same opinion about France, although later events were to prove the unsoundness of this judgment. Germany presented a different problem; even in 1945 the victorious Allies agreed that their former enemies could not be kept in permanent

---

[1]See Frank L. Simonds and Brooks Emeny, *The Great Powers in World Politics* (New York: American Book Company, 1939), p. 154.

[2]Writing in 1944, William T. R. Fox, in *The Super-Powers* (New York: Harcourt, Brace & World, Inc., 1944), conceived of Britain (and the Commonwealth-Empire) as one of the three peacekeeping "superpowers" of the postwar world.

subjugation but would require reintegration into the community of nations on some mutually satisfactory basis. Japan also presented a ticklish issue; no one seriously hoped to keep in secondary status a nation of 100 million proud and vigorous people with a powerful tradition and a solid industrial and political base.

Britain's status as well was uncertain in 1945—as it has indeed remained throughout the postwar era. Although badly battered by the war, Britain saw itself as destined for an early return to leadership. Installed as the key ally of the United States, Britain has sought to exploit its remaining advantages. Its continuing dilemmas, however, have kept London in constant difficulty; the future role of Britain in the latter third of the century remains unclear.

THE RISE OF THE NEW LEADERS. Of the old great powers, only two survived the war intact. The United States and the Soviet Union had not only come through the war without serious debilitation; their power positions had improved as well, both relatively and absolutely. The gap between them and the rest of the world has continued to widen, but not only because the weak have become weaker; the strong have become stronger as well.

The USSR, although injured by having been an active theater of combat, had nevertheless become the second military power of the world in 1945. The war had also ended what was left of its pariah status;[3] Stalin had been a close collaborator in the planning of high strategy during the war and in the framing of the United Nations.[4] The United States, on its part, had dazzled the world with its incredible productivity and, by the end of the war, with its massive military power as well. Economically and militarily, the United States was the most powerful state in the world and, with the Soviet, controlled all but a small fraction of the total available global power.[5]

It seemed in 1945 as if Moscow and Washington, simply by virtue of their enormous power, were destined to rule the world indefinitely. It is all the more surprising, therefore, that we can see today that the entire postwar period has been one of relative decline in the capacity of the bipolar giants to dominate world affairs. The Soviet Union and the United States still "lead" today, but they can no longer be said to "control" the course of international politics.

---

[3]Frederick L. Schuman, *International Politics*, 6th ed. (New York: McGraw-Hill Book Company, 1958), pp. 498–503; see also his *Soviet Politics at Home and Abroad* (New York: Alfred A. Knopf, Inc., 1946).

[4]For an early postwar estimate of the Soviet position, see *Major Problems of United States Foreign Policy, 1948–49* (Washington, D. C.: Brookings Institution, 1948), pp. 16–17, 22–26.

[5]For the former President's version of America's situation at the end of the war, see Harry S. Truman, *Year of Decisions* (Garden City, N. Y.: Doubleday & Company, Inc., 1955), Chapters 30–34.

THE MIGRATION OF POWER.   What we are saying here is that the verdict of World War II was not final, at least in terms of the distribution of power. Although the total capability of the United States and the Soviet Union has increased in an absolute sense, other political units—old and new—have gained enormously in their own power. The dispossessed of 1945 have regained a considerable degree of their prewar eminence; Germany, France, and Japan are all factors to be reckoned with today. Many of the new states born in the breakup of imperialism have likewise shown an impressive ability to frame and execute policy, most notably India and China. Furthermore, so rapidly is the migration of power progressing today that no one can be certain that any slowing down of the process is on the horizon.

THE ECLIPSE AND REBIRTH OF EUROPE

The end of the war saw the eclipse of the "European system." After 1945 the world was no longer ruled from half a dozen capitals in Europe. Just as the political world was adjusting to this devastating new development, a contrary and unexpected trend asserted itself: Europe suddenly reversed its downward spiral and began a new rise. This down-and-up course of western Europe is one of the most interesting aspects of world politics since World War II.

THE CAUSES OF EUROPE'S DECLINE.   Why, after surviving so many wars, did Europe suffer a "political collapse"[6] after 1945? What were the causes of Europe's decline?

Two reasons suggest themselves. First, the two wars of the twentieth century brought the states of Europe to the point of mutual exhaustion. Ruling the world demanded that the states of western Europe maintain high morale and adequate power-in-being; World War II had sapped their interest in world dominion as well as their ability to maintain it. Second, by 1945 technology had progressed to the point that Europe could be said to be suffering from political obsolescence. The end of the war ushered in the age of the giants: the United States (170 million people, over 3 million square miles, continental expanse) and the USSR (210 million people, 8.5 million square miles, continental expanse). The states of Europe, much smaller and much less populous, no longer could compete with them on any basis of even near-equality.

TARGET EUROPE. The end of the European era was signaled by a complete reversal of that continent's historic role. Europe was transformed from an area in which power was wielded and out from which power flowed all over the globe, into the principal target of power originating outside itself. Europeans, who had traditionally used non-European peoples as pawns in their

---

[6]Hajo Holbron, *The Political Collapse of Europe* (New York: Alfred A. Knopf, Inc., 1951).

own games of power politics, found themselves becoming counters in a competition on an even more massive scale. This was most clearly revealed in the struggle for the political heart of the new Europe, Germany. Its remarkable revival was at least partially due to the strategic advantage arising from its position as an object of courtship by both sides.

But the rest of Europe was not afforded the same opportunity to play off East and West against each other. As the primary target of the policies of the two super-powers, the bulk of the European states found themselves forced to join one side or the other in the cold war; target Europe was divided down the middle by the Churchill-described "Iron Curtain." It was not for a decade, until the cold war changed character in 1955 and 1956 and the forces of European integration gained the upper hand, that Europeans again won some little freedom of maneuver.

EUROPE'S REVIVAL. Once freed, at least partially, from the pressures of bipolarity, however, Europeans began to move swiftly. Inspired by the economic revival of West Germany and the political initiatives (after 1958) of the Fifth Republic of France, Europe began actively to seek and to play a role in world politics obviously different yet in reality derived from its erstwhile world hegemony. Today the cold-war adversaries and the nonaligned world alike take full acount of European ideas and European political energy.

ASIAN INSTABILITY

One of the "war aims" of the United States between 1941 and 1945 was "the restoration of the balance of power in Asia." This turned out to mean largely that the United States was hoping to restore the Asian status quo of about 1937, with the single exception that Japan was to be deprived of all her gains and forced to retire to her home islands. Otherwise the map of Asia was to remain substantially unchanged.

Insofar as this was a real aim of the United States, the war was a failure. Asia after Japan's surrender refused to return to its prewar configuration. Instead of the (perhaps illusory) stability of Asian politics between 1920 and 1931, the entire enormous land mass seethed with powerful and upsetting new forces after V-J Day. All the way from India to Japan instability has been endemic even since 1945.[7]

THE DISAPPEARANCE OF HISTORIC POWER. Perhaps the principal reason for the great instability of Asia, at least in the early postwar period, was the disappearance of historic power from the region. Dutch, Chinese, and Japanese power were removed from the scene after 1945; Britain and France found

---

[7]For general discussions of the factors involved in postwar Asian instability and of Western attempts to meet it, see Edwin O. Reischauer, *Wanted: An Asian Policy* (New York: Alfred A. Knopf, Inc., 1955); François d'Harcourt, *Asia: Awakening of a World* (New York: Harcourt, Brace & World, Inc., 1964); and Hugh Tinker, *Ballot Box and Bayonet: People and Government in Emergent Asian Countries* (New York: Oxford University Press, Inc., 1964).

their roles drastically diminished. The Soviet Union, at least up to the rise of Communist China, was the dominant land power in Asia; the United States, operating at the end of a 6000-mile supply line and tied to the sea, has long been reluctant to bring adequate force to bear in the region. Thus indigenous Asian forces have been left substantially to their own devices, and Western (and Soviet) remonstrances have not been notably effective.

THE RISE OF ANTICOLONIALISM. Thanks largely to the impact of Japan's early victories during 1942, the myth of white supremacy as the base for imperial rule in Asia was destroyed during the war. Anticolonialism as both an ideology and an action platform stirred Asian nationalisms into action. Ever since 1945 the once-quiescent Asian masses have been politically self-conscious and increasingly self-assertive, both toward the Western world from which they see themselves as escaping and increasingly toward each other.

THE SOCIOECONOMIC REVOLUTION. A second aspect of Asia's awakening is social and economic instead of political. The war had brought the twentieth century to Asia as the masses began to awake to some of the possibilities of self-improvement. Closely linked with the burgeoning nationalisms ever since 1945 has been a broadly based (if often only half-articulate) demand for social and economic betterment. This "revolution of rising expectations," matched as it is in all the other so-called "emerging areas" in Africa, Latin America, and the Middle East, has been one of the controlling phenomena of world politics for more than two decades.

THE RISE OF AFRICA

Almost equal in magnitude to Asia's upheaval, and far surpassing it in complexity and unfamiliarity (at least in the United States), has been the rise of the new Africa. Breaking so suddenly out of its context of imperial rule, economic backwardness, and political anonymity, the Dark Continent has in recent years provided raw material for endless analysis and much controversy.

THE END OF IMPERIALISM IN AFRICA. Africa lay almost quiescent for a decade after 1945—at least as far as a world gripped by the cold war could determine. Almost without warning, however, the imperial structure of Africa fell to pieces within a few short years as British, French, and Belgian colonies were (willingly or grudgingly) granted independence. In 1954, for example, there were only four sovereignties on the continent: Egypt, Ethiopia, Liberia, and South Africa; ten years later there were more than thirty. Never before in history had so many new political units been born in so short a time.[8]

---

[8]Since 1960 there has been a flood of chronologies of the African independence movements and the history of the new governments. Among the most useful are Immanuel Wallerstein, *Africa: The Politics of Independence* (New York: Vintage Books, Inc., 1961); Gwendolen Carter, *Independence for Africa* (New York: Frederick A. Praeger, Inc., 1960); George W. Shepherd, *The Politics of African Nationalism* (New York: Frederick A. Praeger, Inc., 1962); and John C. Hatch, *A History of Post-War Africa* (New York: Frederick A. Praeger, Inc., 1965).

THE AFRICAN STATES IN WORLD AFFAIRS. Generalizing about so many new states is obviously unsafe, but we nevertheless characterize the new Africa as playing an assertive—almost belligerent—role upon the world stage. These states have been unwilling to assume the subordinate role that their youth, military weakness, political instability, and economic backwardness would seem to demand; instead they have exploited their freedom of action to the fullest extent and have been vociferous in their demands for "justice" and "freedom" from their quondam rulers. The established states have found Africa extremely difficult either to comprehend or to cope with.[9]

THE UNITED NATIONS

The final item in this brief list of the new situational elements in the political world since 1945 is the existence of the United Nations. Although the world organization has not institutionalized perfection or even realized the hopes of the more optimistic of its original architects, there is no doubt that the United Nations has had a profound—if often indirect—impact on world affairs ever since its birth.

THE FAILURE OF THE ORIGINAL CONCEPT. As drawn up at the San Francisco Conference in 1945, the Charter of the United Nations was designed to provide a vehicle for great-power cooperation in the Security Council in maintaining "international peace and security," whereas the role of the small states was expected to be played out in the broader—but less meaningful—arena of the General Assembly. The basic premise of the original concept of the United Nations, great-power unanimity, was invalidated by the rise of the Soviet-American conflict even before the organization settled down to work. Through the history of the United Nations, therefore, the Security Council has functioned only fitfully and unpredictably as the eccentricities of cold-war politics have from time to time led Moscow and Washington to pursue parallel courses toward a shared objective.[10]

THE RISE OF THE GENERAL ASSEMBLY. The failure of the Security Council to assume its primary role, however, has not halted the evolution and growth of the United Nations. Thanks to a series of American-inspired decisions in 1950, the General Assembly has assumed (critics would say "usurped") the power to deal directly with political and security issues if the Security Council

[9]For analyses of the world role of African states, see especially Thomas Hovet, *Africa in the United Nations* (Evanston, Ill.: Northwestern University Press, 1963), and Vernon McKay, *Africa in World Politics* (New York: Harper & Row, Publishers, 1963).

[10]Two useful works that analyze the roles of the superpowers in the United Nations and international organization generally are Richard N. Gardner, *In Pursuit of World Order: U.S. Foreign Policy and International Organizations* (New York: Frederick A. Praeger, Inc., 1964), and Alexander Dallin, *The Soviet Union at the United Nations* (New York: Frederick A. Praeger, Inc., 1962). A more detailed analysis of American involvement in the United Nations is found in Franz B. Gross, ed., *The United States and the United Nations* (Norman, Okla.: University of Oklahoma Press, 1964).

could not. From this has grown the notion of "peacekeeping"; the entry of international armed forces (provided by national states but operating under the command of the United Nations) into critical situations. The technique was first used at the time of the Suez crisis in 1956 and has been applied on a number of subsequent occasions. In almost all cases of peacekeeping it has been the General Assembly that has served as the organ of action, although some signs can be seen that Soviet-American cooperation might lead to a more peacekeeping role for the Security Council.[11]

ECONOMIC AND SOCIAL ACTIVITIES. Although still a minor portion of the total work of the organization, the economic and social functions of the United Nations cannot be dismissed as irrelevant. Especially since the vast increase in membership took place, there has been great and continuing concern with issues of anticolonialism, economic development, health, human rights, and so on. Optimists are prone to overestimate the immediate effects of such activities, especially since these seem so often to be above the crass calculations of politics; we should not fall into this trap, but neither should we assume that we may safely ignore them. Their true effect—if any—will be discoverable only in the future; in the meantime we should exercise due caution in estimating their place.[12]

New Forces in World Politics since 1945

We have just examined the major modifications in the postwar international scene; we turn now to consider some of the new dynamisms that have been operative since 1945.

ECONOMIC AND POLITICAL INSTABILITY

The second great war of the twentieth century far surpassed World War I in the costs it charged mankind. The wealth destroyed by the actual fighting and by the upheavals that accompany total war was enormous and amounted to a huge setback to the world. Even more disrupting, however, was the heritage of instability it left behind. Almost nowhere outside the United States were there peoples whose economies were normal and healthy and

---

[11]For an overview of the evolving role of the General Assembly over twenty years, see Sydney D. Bailey, *The General Assembly of the United Nations* (New York: Frederick A. Praeger, Inc., 1964); see also Herbert G. Nicholas, *The United Nations as a Political Institution* (New York: Oxford University Press, Inc., 1963).

[12]A very good overall survey of the economic and social activities of the United Nations is found in Robert E. Asher *et al.*, *The United Nations and Economic and Social Cooperation* (Washington, D.C.: The Brookings Institution, 1957).

whose political systems were secure. During the years since 1945, the solution of one problem of economic or political instability has tended to give rise to a family of others; Americans are still grappling with the unpalatable fact that, although themselves committed to order and stability, they will be forced to cope with chronic instability and change for an indefinite period.

ECONOMIC CONSEQUENCES OF THE WAR. The war dealt most of the industrial areas of the world a shattering blow. Industrial plants were destroyed or obsolete; manpower pools were dissolved. Financial resources were exhausted, and life for the industrialized masses of Europe and Asia seemed to have deteriorated to a grim struggle against poverty or actual starvation. Transportation and trade were paralyzed as well. Agricultural production was upset by the devastation of the land, the dispersal of labor, the loss of markets, and the dislocation of distribution. Economic life in the immediate postwar period, in a word, verged upon stagnation.

THE REVOLUTION OF RISING EXPECTATIONS. The problem of the industrial areas of the world—especially those open to American assistance—was not insoluble. The various assistance programs of the United States combined to restore healthy and prosperous production in most of the free world by approximately 1950. But no such success can be claimed for the second major factor of economic instability: the awakening of the underdeveloped areas and their demand for economic improvement. Here completely unprecedented plans and procedures were unmistakably called for.

The "revolution of rising expectations" in the entire non-Western world is a product of World War II. We have become familiar with the concept of "underdeveloped area" and realize that such a region is in need of technical and financial assistance in order to realize its economic potential. What is somewhat less well understood is the fact that non-Western peoples are determined to obtain what it takes to bring up their economic and social levels to a point nearer that of the industrialized West. Nor are they especially interested in the source of the assistance, insisting only that it be given in sufficient quantity and soon enough to bring about the transformation they wish. This constant pressure has been a powerful factor of continuing instability, not only in the underdeveloped areas of the world but also in the West itself.

POLITICAL FLUX. The economic pressures that have contributed to constant shifts in the international climate have been matched by equivalent mutability in political forms and relationships. The war had been fought by the United States to establish democratic values once and for all against the threats of totalitarianism, but victory brought no such security.

We have already taken note of Europe's revival since the war. Impressive though it may be in economic and power-political terms, however, no one can see in Europe's rebirth any vindication of Western-style democracy. The two most powerful European statesmen in the two decades after the war were

Konrad Adenauer in West Germany and Charles de Gaulle in France. Neither can be classified as a dedicated paladin of democratic thought and process. Although the commitment of Italy and Great Britain to democracy is beyond question, both have found it impossible to solve their pressing problems by free government. Only in Scandinavia, the Low Countries, and Switzerland can the postwar experience be interpreted as a vindication of stability through democratic procedures.

Throughout Asia and Africa, change and crisis marked the new political climate. The historic Afro-Asian political structures—imperialism, feudalism, despotism—were challenged everywhere by a variety of new forces. In some places, old orders were swept away almost without a trace; in others the outer appearances of prewar society were retained despite enormous inner modifications.

Such a massive development could not be expected to proceed smoothly. After the war, Asia erupted. At one extremity was Japan, whose entire semi-feudal structure was shaken by the deliberate American policy of unleashing new social and economic forces; in far southwest Asia the Arab world was being transformed by nationalism, independence, and petroleum. Everywhere in between new elements were added to the political pattern whose combined effect was to transform a once-static situation into a highly dynamic one. Africa's shift, although a little later in developing, was even more spectacular. The first state of "black Africa" to gain independence after the war, Ghana (1957), opened a new era. By 1966 only a handful of European colonies remained in all of Africa. It was not surprising that such a rapid transformation produced the wave of tensions that made many observers feel that Africa was to be the next crucial battleground of world affairs.

It is significant that political forms in the postwar world have been widely regarded as being susceptible to rapid and drastic change. This has meant that no permanent shape could be given to international relationships, no coherent pattern of interstate alignments could emerge, until domestic political life had first been stabilized. Consistent foreign policy can rest only on consensus, and in dozens of states there has been no such broad agreement on fundamentals. The arrangements made in international society could not escape being tentative and exploratory, subject to sudden revision in the light of the rapid pace of political change in most of the world.

THE IMPACT OF COMMUNISM

For many Americans the most important—and the most baleful—of the new forces abroad since 1945 has been communism; for some, indeed, it is the only important one. We shall see later how the popular tendency in the United States to blame all America's difficulties on the official Soviet ideology has resulted in serious policy distortion; we can thoroughly understand the impact of communism only in relation to other dynamisms of the postwar period. At this point, however, we shall consider communism only in terms of its general impact on the pattern of world politics.

THE RISE OF COMMUNISM. Communism, as doctrine, was nothing new to students of ideas. Marx had written the *Communist Manifesto* in 1848, nearly a century before; Marxist and Communist parties had long been part of the European political scene. Since 1917 Russia had been under communist rule, and its agents had been active in every part of the world. The world knew communism and thought it understood it. Yet, at the end of the war, this dogmatic ideology broke out as one of the controlling forces of world affairs. How did this sudden rise take place?[13]

The primary reason is of course the revolution in the status of the Soviet Union. Courted instead of shunned, powerful instead of weak, one of the arbiters of the world, Bolshevik Russia had become a global giant. Nothing succeeds like success, and Moscow had undoubtedly succeeded in its greatest test. Communism received much of the credit.

In the resistance movements against the Axis occupations between 1940 and 1945, communists everywhere had set examples of courage, organization, ingenuity, and devotion. In Europe they earned—and received payment on— a great debt of gratitude for their wartime services. In Asia they sought positions of leadership in native nationalist movements and used their new respectability to consolidate themselves against the day of peace. In both Europe and Asia, peace found communists either in or near the seats of power in many states, and in all they had improved their positions. From none, furthermore, have they been voluntarily or easily removed.

COMMUNISM AND THE DISCONTENTED. We have seen that political and economic instability were widespread at the end of the war. The prevailing mood throughout much of the world was one of discontent, whether sullen and passive in Europe or active and revolutionary in Asia. This presented the communists with a tempting opportunity.

Communism, as its students can testify, is a very elastic ideology; it can be given almost any turn appropriate to circumstances. This gives its manipulators a tactical advantage in that they can shape their appeal to attract supporters in a great variety of situations. During the postwar era communism, modified to meet differing situations, has been aimed squarely at discontented masses everywhere. The communists have preached only one message with infinite variations: hope for a better world.

---

[13]The two best surveys of the rise of Russian communism to world power are found in Hugh Seton-Watson, *From Lenin to Khrushchev: The History of World Communism* (New York: Frederick A. Praeger, Inc., 1960), and Cyril E. Black and Thomas P. Thornton, eds., *Communism and Revolution* (Princeton, N.J.: Princeton University Press, 1964).

The communist appeal to the discontented has been all the stronger because of the seemingly reactionary character of much of its opposition. Democracy in Europe seemed to look backward to 1939 for its ideal; imperialism and authoritarianism in Asia likewise sought to turn back the clock. It seemed to many as if only communism held promise for the future, as if only the communists were advancing any new ideas.

COMMUNISM AND CHANGE. Perhaps one more comment might further clarify what we are saying. Communists, whose stock in trade (at least outside the Soviet bloc) is the constant advocacy of change, have been quite successful in tuning in on the controlling wavelength of the contemporary world. Since 1945 it has frequently seemed as if only the communists of all men were preaching change in economics, in politics, and in social structure. The unsophisticated American tendency to identify communism with the other revolutionary forces of the age—nationalism, anticolonialism, and so on—has played into communist hands. Americans were bound to be frustrated so long as any overdue change in relationships was fought as being either communist-inspired or at least in harmony with what communists were demanding.

THE AFRO-ASIAN REVOLUTION

By 1900 Africa and Asia had become the football of European politics. Although the stirrings of national and regional self-consciousness had been felt in Afro-Asia prior to 1939, it was not until after the end of the war that the peoples of these continents asserted themselves firmly. They set in motion the enormous mass movement whose consequences are now shaking the world and that may yet prove to be the most significant outcome of World War II.

There is of course no such thing as "Afro-Asia," only a number of separate peoples, cultures, and states coexisting upon the two largest continents of the world. Furthermore, there is no single "Afro-Asian revolution," but rather several dozen individual revolutions scattered through the two continents, each following its own course and each seeking its own fulfillment.

But each of these mass movements resembles all of the others in some common features; there is, in other words, a model of an Afro-Asian revolution, if not of the Afro-Asian revolution. The forces, groups, and trends are analogous if not similar. It is in these general terms that we now speak.

A REVOLUTION OF MULTIPLE DIMENSIONS. In the first place, revolution in contemporary Africa and Asia is multidimensional. It is neither exclusively political, entirely economic, nor purely psychic, but instead partakes of all three characteristics. Particular groups may emphasize one element or another, but success in no single one would satisfy any revolutionary movement; the goal each of them seeks is nothing less than a new posture toward the outside world. Nor is it feasible for the West (or for the communists either, for that matter) to devise a single formula for satiating all revolts individually or the Afro-Asian revolution in general. Despite their general similarity, each movement is rooted in indigenous factors, and the technique for coping with them must be conspicuously flexible and capable of infinite adaption.

ROOTS OF THE REVOLUTION.   To analyze fully the roots of revolution in Africa and Asia—if any Occidental could do it successfully—would require an extensive and detailed history of the impact of the West on the East. We may at least suggest, however, a very general cause: Africa and Asia are now determined to receive their just due in their relations with the rest of the world.[14]

That Western imperialism—political, economic, and cultural—was a technique for the perpetuation of inferior status was long known to the intellectual and political leaders of Afro-Asia. As long as this insight was confined to a tiny and impotent section of the population, however, effective resistance to the West was impossible. It required the catalyzing action of the war to make the masses aware of this situation and to inspire them to end it. Once political self-consciousness had been born, leaders in each country were able to capture the mass movements and to provide them with both platforms and programs for action. The Afro-Asian revolution represents a reaction against the past and a hope for the future.

POSITIVE AND NEGATIVE ASPECTS.   Not the least of the confusing aspects of the revolution is that it has both a positive and a negative side. Affirmatively, the common demands of the various mass movements stress the necessity of developing an equitable basis of relationships with the rest of the world. The most common components of the positive creed are political self-determination, economic independence, and cultural and social equality; none of these, we will note, is unfamiliar to Americans. Afro-Asians demand the same deference values as do other peoples. Negatively—and frequently overlooked even by Western sympathizers—there is a significant element of revenge involved. At last free from the more humiliating aspects of tutelage by the West, many Afro-Asians are deeply committed to demonstrating their new freedom, often in a most flamboyant way. All the old scores are being settled; they are determined to balance their psychic accounts.

No one can yet foretell the direction that revolutionary Afro-Asia will eventually take. Communism early moved to take advantage of it, and many of the nationalist movements acquired a distinct pro-Soviet tinge. But as long as communist ideology requires subservience to Moscow or Peking, there is

---

[14]For an interesting development of this theme, see Arnold J. Toynbee, *The World and the West* (New York: Oxford University Press, Inc., 1953), Chapter 5: "The Psychology of Encounters."

little prospect of a permanent communist victory in Africa and Asia; these peoples did not liberate themselves from Western imperialism in order to offer themselves to Red hegemony. The problem facing both the West and the communists is not how to control the revolution (it is too massive for "control" in any ordinary sense) but rather how to come to terms with it.

THE TECHNOLOGICAL EXPLOSION

The twentieth century is the era of technology. It is often pointed out that there have been more changes in man's way of life since 1900 than in the entire span of recorded history up to that year. This process of technological change and advance has, if anything, accelerated in the years since 1945. It is natural, therefore, that an international political system born in the seventeenth century should suffer great shocks from rapid and thoroughgoing technological development.

TRANSPORTATION AND COMMUNICATION. The most immediately obvious effect of the new technology on world politics was in the areas of transportation and communication. The jet aircraft put Europe six hours away from the United States; research looking toward a supersonic transport airplane promised a two-hour transoceanic voyage.[15] Other developments in air transportation opened the entire world to relatively easy penetration from almost any direction. This produced a great breakthrough in mobility of individuals with a consequent broadening of horizons.

Communication—instantaneous, worldwide, and accurate—has also exploded. Politically, communication facilities have made it possible for governments to control their representatives abroad on a day-by-day (or hour-by-hour) basis, thus drastically modifying the conduct of diplomacy. Techniques of mass communication progressed to the point, on the other hand, where manipulation of domestic consensus or massive campaigns of foreign propaganda were both much simpler than heretofore. As a counterpoint, however, the new communications also made it more feasible for individuals to maintain international contact and thus to offset to some extent their government's monopoly over information and message flow.

A final aspect of transportation and communication should be mentioned briefly: its effect on problems of defense and security. Missiles now can fly six thousand miles with great accuracy and hit a target; the "lead time" the United States now has in the event of a major attack has been reduced to as little as fifteen minutes. Obviously the problems of maintaining an adequate

---

[15]Since the early 1960's, the United States Government had been cooperating with aviation companies in the development of a supersonic transport (SST) which would carry between 150 and 200 passengers at speeds in excess of 1500 m.p.h. In the spring of 1965, the program was accelerated to keep up with British and French competition.

defense posture have been incredibly complicated by this special development in transportation and communication systems.

MEDICINE. It would require a long list compiled by a specialist to cover all the revolutionary medical advances since the beginning of World War II. Never before has the profession of medicine had so much knowledge and so many weapons to use in the fight against disease.

Medical advance may be divided into two somewhat overlapping areas: those techniques particularly suited to curing illness in individual patients and those especially oriented toward preventive medicine in a context of public health. The combination of the two has led during the postwar period to a marked reduction of death rates (particularly infant mortality) in many parts of the world. In the West, gratification has been general at this success in the highly commendable enterprise of preserving human life; the actual effect on both the economic and political structures of the underdeveloped world was slow in gaining appreciation.

Today demographers, ecologists, and agronomists warn of the "population explosion" and the danger that the world will lose its ability to feed its people.[16] This has led to a drastically new political issue's gaining a place on the agenda of international discussion: population control by means of deliberate contraception.

ATOMIC ENERGY. Best known of the technological feats of the war was the American success in harnessing nuclear energy. The overpowering implication of nuclear fission was of course military; we shall discuss this aspect below. But scientists and technologists realized that atomic energy had a signficance that far surpassed its use in bombs; it carried profoundly revolutionary overtones for the whole of international society.

ATOMIC ENERGY AND INDUSTRIALIZATION. Atomic energy, despite its spectacular nature, is merely another kind of energy; atoms produce heat as do other kinds of fuel. As such, it is capable of being put to the uses to which other energy sources are put; this means, most commonly, turning the wheels of industry. The principal industrial energy sources today are coal, petroleum, and, less importantly, hydroelectric power. Atomic fuels produce fantastic amounts of energy in proportion to their weight and volume and thus would seem to be ideal for industrial purposes.

This meant that, if the time were to come when men would be free to use atomic power for industrial purposes, the modernization or extension of a

---

[16]Among the most outspoken of these arguments are William Vogt, *Road to Survival* (New York: William Sloane Associates, Inc., 1948), Fairfield Osborn, *Our Plundered Planet* (Boston: Little, Brown and Company, 1948), and Harrison Brown, *The Challenge of Man's Future* (New York: The Viking Press, Inc., 1954); see also Harrison Brown, "The Prospective Environment for Policymaking and Administration," *Formulation and Administration of United States Foreign Policy* (Washington, D.C.: The Brookings Institution), pp. 139–161.

mature industrial structure would be no very complicated matter, and the creation of an entirely new one would be very much simplified. As the long-range aspect of atomic energy was pondered, many discussions began to be heard about a "new industrial revolution."[17]

THE EQUALIZATION FACTOR. But if a new industrial revolution were indeed coming, it was destined to be a very different one. The coal-iron technology of the industrial age that began in the eighteenth century tied industry to its energy base; nations without extensive endowments of coal were seriously handicapped in the race for industrial power. Italy and Japan, for example, suffered chronically in this respect.

The introduction of nuclear fuels, however, would change this picture greatly. Relatively inexpensive and needed only in small volume, their procurement and exploitation are beyond the reach of only the smallest and weakest of states. If a new industrial race were to begin, most states would start approximately evenly; the advantages enjoyed by the handful of presently dominant economies might disappear quickly. This point was understood by both the industrialized and the nonindustrialized states, and the ultimate implications of atomic power have remained one of the unknowns of the postwar era.

THE NEW WARFARE

One of the most pervasive of the new forces in world politics after 1945 has been the effect of the new warfare. The new techniques and doctrines of the military art, developed during the war and refined in the era of constant tension that followed it, found no real place in the day-by-day course of international affairs. The state system, on the other hand, found itself unable to adjust to the changed patterns imposed by military requirements; obvious frustration was the predictable result.

TOTAL WEAPONS. The apex of military ingenuity up to the end of the war was the atomic bomb, but it was by no means the only new development of total techniques of war. Dozens of others, less horrible to contemplate but no less effective, were perfected; weaponry was at its highest point of elaboration in history when peace came. Under the impetus of cold-war tensions even newer horizons in weapons development have been opened.

Most awesome of these was, of course, the hydrogen bomb. There were those after 1954 who argued that with it had been born the true "absolute weapon"[18] capable of wiping man off the planet. Equally great effort has been

---

[17]Fritz Sternberg, *The Military and Industrial Revolution of Our Time* (New York: Frederick A. Praeger, Inc., 1959).

[18]This term was originally applied to the atomic bomb. See Bernard Brodie, ed., *The Absolute Weapon* (New York: Harcourt, Brace & World, Inc., 1946).

lavished on perfecting vehicles for the delivery of nuclear bombs to their targets. From the supersonic jet aircraft to the ICBM (intercontinental ballistic missile) was an easy step. Both the United States and the USSR have test-fired missiles more than nine thousand miles—over one-third of the distance around the earth. Truly no one was any longer out of range of the new weapons.

On top of the missile and H-bomb programs came the assault on space. Obviously, the conquest of space had military significance—for reconnaisance, for manned "space stations," or for bases for space-to-earth missiles. It seemed to many, as they watched the pyramiding of the new weapons, as if warfare had indeed reached the point of mutual saturation.

TOTAL WAR. The new weapons required a new theory of war. Classically, the object of warfare was to "destroy the enemy's will to resist" and to have him bend to your will. This concept entailed the prosecution of combat by uniformed armed forces fighting according to a generally understood code. The new weapons, however, had only limited utility under tactical conditions; their most effective targets were the productive centers of the enemy, where they could exert maximum effectiveness on the concentration of facilities and the congregations of people. Total weapons thus led to a theory of total war.

Total war is total in every respect: total in weapons, total in targets, total in strategy, total in mobilization, and, finally, total in objectives. Total war is war for annihilation. Its alternative objectives are the abject surrender of the enemy or his total obliteration. Negotiated peace becomes a thing of the past; all peace terms are to be either dictated after surrender or else are irrelevant because the enemy no longer exists. If total effort be required for total victory, objectives become absolute as well; nothing less than absolute hegemony over the defeated is a sufficient enticement to make the effort and risks worthwhile.[19]

THE INEXPEDIENCY OF MILITARY POWER. However consistent the new theory of war may have been with its premises and its techniques, it broke sharply with the traditional theory of international politics. War is usually conceived as an instrument of national policy, as the only ultimately efficacious technique available to a state for the enforcement of its will on others. Total war, however, is an efficient instrument only for the accomplishment of total objectives; if total war is the only kind of war that a state is in a position to fight, its less extreme policies are seriously handicapped. It lacks the means of applying force in amounts graduated according to the objective sought and the resistance encountered and thus is brought to face a hard choice. Objectives less

---

[19]See B. H. Liddell Hart, *The Revolution in Warfare* (New Haven: Yale University Press, 1947); and W. W. Kaufmann, ed., *Military Policy and National Security* (Princeton, N.J.: Princeton University Press, 1956); see also Lapp, *Kill and Overkill*.

than total must either be prosecuted without any real reliance on military techniques—a frustrating and often futile enterprise—or expanded so that they become important enough to justify the new warfare.

THE BALANCE OF TERROR. By the mid-1950's the world had begun to grasp the meaning of total war. Although the United States and the USSR possessed military striking power unmatched in any earlier peacetime era (and probably in any earlier period of war), neither felt any more secure for it.[20] What was worse, neither had any illusions about its ability to use force against the other to win political victories; retaliatory capability so effectively neutralized striking force that both found themselves caught in a "balance of terror." To complete the cycle of frustration, so frightened were both sides by the prospect of war that they acted in unadmitted concert to prevent any smaller states from using war to reach a political decision. Warfare had largely canceled itself out[21]—and the state of international relations testified to the vacuum it had left behind.

Political Trends since 1945

It has been within the general context outlined in the preceding pages that the course of international politics has proceeded in the years since the end of the war. Certain trends stand out as being more important, and this brief comment on the international scene as the United States surveys it should include some mention of them.

GREAT-POWER RIVALRIES

Central to the course of world affairs during this period—as they have been in every era—are the rivalries and disagreements among the handful of major states. Our catalogue of trends must begin with at least the most significant of these.

THE COLD WAR. The history of American foreign policy since 1945 is largely the history of the cold war. It is also true that the Soviet-American conflict has been the largest single factor in world politics. We shall be considering the cold war in detail later, so there is no need to elaborate at this

---

[20]See, for example, Jerome B. Wiesner and Herbert F. York, "National Security and the Nuclear-Test Ban," *Scientific American*, CCXI, No. 4 (October, 1964), 27–35, in which the nuclear arms race is seen as reaching a point of diminishing returns with a decline in the absolute security of both Russia and the United States as a result of the systematic exploitation of technological advances.

[21]We shall be discussing this question in more detail, particularly with reference to the so-called doctrine of "limited war," in Chapter 11.

point. In our immediate terms of "rivalries," however, we should point out that there are least at three dimensions of great-power disagreement built into the contemporary structure of the cold war.

First, and best known, is the Soviet-American confrontation itself, modified but not fundamentally changed by the fact that associated with the United States are several other major states.[22] Second, there is the much newer Chinese-American controversy, with the full implications of which Americans are not yet acquainted; this battle, furthermore, is one that the United States must prosecute largely by itself, since its Western allies are not involved to the same extent with the communist regime in China. Third, there is the Chinese-Soviet rivalry both for ideological preeminence and for concrete advantages that each feels it may win from the other.[23]

NEW RIVALRIES AND OLD. Sometimes within, but more frequently without, the cold-war structure other major-power rivalries have given color and tone to international relations. Some are of ancient vintage, others much newer. Most of them have developed since 1954, after the rigidity of the earlier bipolar era had relaxed. We may mention three, each of which will appear in our later discussions: (1) the revolt of Europe against American dominance that took form both in the movement for European integration and in the increasing independence of American wishes shown by Britain and France after 1956; (2) the revival of the classic balance of power in Britain's European policy, most clearly expressed in London's counterattack on the rise of de Gaulle in France and the whole movement of European economic integration; and (3) the sudden eruption of rivalry betweeen China and India, in which the ultimate stakes were no less than the leadership of the new Asia.

THE RISE OF NEW POWER CENTERS

In 1945 there were only two centers of power in the world, Moscow and Washington. Many Americans in the postwar era succumbed to the easy assumption that this was all there ever would be and that all questions would ultimately be decided by the relations between the Soviet and the United States. Both the great powers have had difficulty in adjusting to the fact that

---

[22]The concept of the cold war as a "great-power rivalry" is developed in detail in the present author's study, *The Cold War . . . and After*. See esp. Chaps. 7, 8.

[23]Since Donald S. Zagoria coined the phrase in *The Sino-Soviet Conflict, 1956–1961* (Princeton, N.J.: Princeton University Press, 1962), there have been many works purporting to deal decisively with the increasing rift between the communist giants. The best of these are Edward Crankshaw, *The New Cold War: Moscow vs. Pekin;* William E. Griffith, *The Sino-Soviet Rift* (Cambridge, Mass.: Massachusetts Institute of Technology Press, 1964); and Geoffrey F. Hudson, ed., *The Sino-Soviet Dispute* (New York: Frederick A. Praeger, Inc., 1961).

several new power centers have risen and now exert a major influence on world affairs.[24]

CHINA.   The communist conquest of China, followed so swiftly by Chinese participation in the Korean war, signaled the end of the era when China could safely be written off as an independent power center. Peking is now a major world capital, whose opinion on any question is listened to and whose intentions are a matter of major concern.

INDIA.   Although playing a radically different role than China, India has also become a power center of major relevance to world concerns. For many years, India was skillful in mobilizing a pool of international consensus in support of its positions, and the international image projected by New Delhi is one that has made India bulk increasingly large. No more eloquent testimony to its critical role could be adduced than the great attention both the Soviet and the United States have lavished on it.

EUROPE.   The revival of Europe, spearheaded by the "German miracle," also gave birth to still another center of independent power. Not only did West Germany, France, and Britain undertake larger roles, but the evolution of the European Community on the continent gave promise that some day a new entity known simply as "Europe" would be a member of the group of great powers. Americans generally welcomed this prospect, for most expectations were that an independent and unified Europe would act in a way favorable to American long-range interest.[25]

THE MIDDLE EAST.   It is not yet accurate to call the Middle East a power center, at least in the singular; the remarkable rise in influence of the Middle Eastern states on world affairs has not yet been matched by an equivalent consolidation of the region's potential. But it remains true that there is today a great deal of indigenous power within the region and that eventually it will coalesce—at least for international purposes. Until that day, however, the present situation will generally obtain: There will be several Middle Eastern states with supraregional capacity, and the tendency toward the settlement of Middle Eastern questions by the direct action of the states of the region themselves will increase. Nonregional powers will for a time, however, continue to affect regional affairs.

AFRICA.   The same sort of comment may be made about Africa. No real center of political power now exists in Africa south of the Sahara, but when

---

[24]The trends toward polycentrism in both the West and the East are discussed in Ronald Steel, *The End of Alliance: America and the Future of Europe* (New York: Viking Press, 1964), and Walter Laqueur and Leopold Labedz, *Polycentrism* (New York: Frederick A. Praeger, Inc., 1962).

[25]Discussions of American attitudes toward an emergent Europe are found in Steel, *The End of Alliance*, Max Beloff, *The United States and the Unity of Europe* (Washington, D.C.: The Brookings Institution, 1963), Robert Kleiman, *Atlantic Crisis: American Diplomacy Confronts a Resurgent Europe* (New York: W. W. Norton & Company, Inc., 1964), and Kissinger, *The Troubled Partnership*.

the numerous small and young states there come together on an issue, Africa's voice is heard. The trend toward some form of integration or consolidation in Africa is only beginning, but it seems certain to go much further. Future statecraft will have to reckon with African participation in world affairs as a major factor.

THE CHALLENGE OF THE NON-WESTERN WORLD

We have already alluded to the Afro-Asian revolution and have attempted to suggest that it is a much more complex phenomenon than might appear at first glance. Indeed, the longer the revolt of the non-Western world continues, the more the impression gains currency that it is one of the really significant forces in contemporary world politics. We shall be returning to this problem frequently in later chapters.

THE END OF IMPERIALISM. The most obvious immediate result of the birth of political consciousness in the non-West was a fundamental change in the map of the world. By 1965, over forty new states had been born in the aftermath of the war, almost all by conversion from colonial status. Throughout Asia and Africa there remained only a relative handful of colonial possessions, most of them small and undeveloped. Granted the breakneck speed with which independence movements were being born and the inability of any colonial power to hold them off, it seems likely that imperialism as the world has known it for centuries is dead.

Accompanying political independence was the determined and fairly successful effort of the former colonial states, new and old, to rid themselves of "economic imperialism." Making full use of their new freedom of action, many deliberately sought to break their old economic ties with their former mother country and to create new ones. For several this involved the risky but potentially profitable enterprise of turning to the communist bloc and then enjoying the consternation they caused and the better bargains they then received from both sides.[26] This maneuver, however, called for statesmanship of the highest order.

THE VOICE OF THE NON-WEST. The new states of the non-Western world brought a surprising amount of consensus into world politics. For obvious reasons, by and large the non-Western world (with a few conspicuous excep-

---

[26]The early dearth of works on the newly independent states and their role in world affairs has been overcome by a torrent of volumes, among the best of which are Cecil V. Crabb, Jr., *The Elephants and the Grass: A Study of Nonalignment* (New York: Frederick A. Praeger, Inc., 1965), Richard Harris, *Independence and After: Revolution in Underdeveloped Countries* (New York: Oxford University Press, Inc., 1962), John H. Kautsky, ed., *Political Change in the Underdeveloped Countries: Nationalism and Communism* (New York: John Wiley & Sons, Inc., 1962), and Kurt London, *New Nations in a Divided World* (New York: Frederick A. Praeger, Inc., 1963).

tions) argued for peace, disarmament, a stronger United Nations, technical and capital assistance from the West, and full equality of deference and status from their erstwhile masters.

Their chosen instrument was the General Assembly of the United Nations. Here (as well as in regional "Afro-Asian" conferences) they gave expression to their fears of great-power tensions and their demands for satisfaction in both tangible and intangible ways. Although physically weak, even when united, the military frustration of the great powers gave them surprising effectiveness, especially on the questions they made peculiarly their own: the liquidation of colonialism, technical assistance, and human rights.[27]

NEW TECHNIQUES IN WORLD POLITICS

Earlier in this chapter we pointed to the decreasing utility of military power in solving international problems. Since world affairs do not stand still, the international order has been obliged to develop a battery of new techniques in order to perform at least the indispensable tasks of reaching decisions and normalizing relationships.

ECONOMIC ASSISTANCE. Inaugurated by the United States in 1947 with the Greek-Turkish aid program and elaborated by all major participants in international politics since that time, economic assistance has become a standardized technique. Applicable in a great variety of circumstances and available in some measure to almost any state with a productive surplus it wishes to put to a political purpose, it has proved to be a method peculiarly suited to the requirements of contemporary international life.[28]

The major unsolved question about economic assistance as a technique of policy lay in the realm of the conditions to be placed on such aid. The instinctive reaction of the United States Congress to put "strings" on aid, whether in the form of controls over the expenditure of funds or of political commitments, had very uneven success: Several recipients refused aid programs entirely or seriously compromised them by developing extreme (if largely unfounded) suspicions of American purposes. On the other hand, the Soviet meticulously avoided apparent political conditions and contented itself largely with negotiating clearly restrictive trade agreements with the recipients

---

[27]See Vera Micheles Dean and Harry D. Harootunian, *West and Non-West* (New York: Holt, Rinehart & Winston, Inc., 1963), Gabriel A. Almond and James S. Coleman, eds., *The Politics of Developing Areas* (Princeton, N.J.: Princeton University Press, 1960), and Eugene Staley, *The Future of Underdeveloped Countries: Political Implications of Economic Development* (New York: Harper & Row, Publishers, 1961).

[28]For discussions of American economic and technical assistance programs, see Herbert Feis, *Foreign Aid and Foreign Policy* (New York: St. Martin's Press, Inc., 1964) and George Liska, *The New Statecraft: Foreign Aid in American Foreign Policy* (Chicago: University of Chicago Press, 1960).

of its aid. It must be admitted, however, that Moscow had little more success in evoking direct responses to its aid program than did the United States.[29] The whole "foreign aid" technique, while of admitted usefulness, clearly was unsuited to any sort of coercive purpose.

TECHNICAL ASSISTANCE. The same general observation can be made with regard to the general area of technical and development assistance. Although all major powers made some effort in this direction, a decade of experience with it indicated that its usefulness was primarily long-range. There was no effective way to use technical or development aid as a tool of short-run policy. So sensitive were the underdeveloped countries to this sort of danger that they made every effort they could to put as much as possible of the whole program under the aegis of the United Nations, where it could not be used as a tool of national policy by any large state and where the recipients could have some control over general policy.

CONSENSUS AS A TOOL OF POLICY. Woodrow Wilson would have been pleased to see the extent to which his dream of an international consensus was realized in the postwar world. The United States, the USSR, and the Afro-Asian states all at one time or another were able to mobilize and capitalize upon a mass consensus as an efficacious tool of policy. The major instrument for verbalizing such broad-gauge agreement was the General Assembly of the United Nations. Among its most convincing statements were the 73–1 vote in 1957 condemning Israel's continued occupation of the Gaza Strip in Egypt and the 70–0 vote in 1960 in support of Secretary-General Hammarskjöld's Congo policy; almost as impressive was the steady decline in the majority by which the United States annually prevented any discussion of the admission of Communist China. No one state had control of this consensus, no one state could turn it on at will in support of its own policy; when it did crystallize on a particular issue, however, it was clear that no countervailing power existed in the international order.

SCIENCE AND CULTURE AS TECHNIQUES. A final word should be said about the use of science and culture as tools of policy. The more recent postwar era is a time when science and culture are truly international again, in reaction to the crude nationalism of the interwar and early postwar period. Cultural and scientific delegations crisscrossed the map in almost every direction: across the Iron Curtain, between West and non-West, to and from the new Africa. There was a major internationalizing of these areas after the decline in the militancy of the cold war.

Candor forces the admission, however, that there was at least a duality of motivation behind these scientific and cultural explorations. On the one hand, most (perhaps all) had a healthy curiosity about other peoples and wished to know more about them; the newly shrunk world made it imperative to acquire

---

[29]See Victor Lasky, *The Ugly Russian* (New York: Trident Press Bk., 1965).

a greater cross-cultural sophistication. But there was a distinct element of "one-upmanship" present in all these exchanges as well. Nations were alert to put their best feet forward and to score such prestige victories as were for the taking in what came unfortunately to be thought of as a cultural competition.

This was of course most painfully obvious in the "science race" between the Soviet and the United States that followed the initial breakthrough into space in 1957. What started as a cooperative scientific venture in the International Geophysical Year soon deteriorated into a contest to determine which nation could send up the most, the biggest, or the most spectacular satellites.[30] But even so, most observers felt that this was a safer way to compete than in military power or diplomatic *faits accomplis.*

---

[30]Following the early Russian successes, most Americans succumbed to a "let's catch up" philosophy of the space race. In spite of American successes in communications and manned satellites, this attitude continued into the mid-1960's. When Astronaut Edward White took his "walk in space" during the four-day Gemini 4 flight in June 1965, a public controversy arose and accusations were hurled at NASA for "prematurely" trying to match a similar Russian feat. The public and the news media still thought of the United States as "closing the gap" in the space race with the Russians.

CHAPTER 7

American
Capabilities

In Chapter 1 we noted that the concept of state capability refers to the tools and techniques that a state has available to use in accomplishing its objectives and advancing its interests. Now that we have laid some of the groundwork for our consideration of American foreign policy and have examined both the operating concept of interest and the major external factors affecting American policy since 1945, the next step in our analysis is a somewhat more detailed study of the capabilities of the United States.

Formulating the Problem

The techniques of capability analysis, as we pointed out earlier, do not yield results of mathematical precision. We can discuss American capability intelligibly only after carefully recognizing the limits on what we are attempting and stating the assumptions upon which we are proceeding. We shall attempt to formulate our problem in terms that will permit us enough leeway to reach helpful (if only tentative) conclusions and at the same time will prevent us from attempting overmuch.

THE LIMITS OF CAPABILITY ANALYSIS

RELATIVITY, DYNAMISM, AND TIME.   At the outset we should restate the three most important qualitative factors in the notion of capability. (1) State capability is highly relative, as to other states, as to objectives, and as to time; no state is "capable" in a vacuum. (2) Capability is a dynamic condition whose contributory elements are always changing. A state's capability to accomplish an objective is always either rising or falling; it cannot remain static. (3) Finally, time has a major impact on capability. Comparative analyses may be made either on the basis of existing information (and by that token are always obsolete) or on the basis of the projection of trends, and thus must involve a large element of guesswork.

THE CONCRETE CONTEXT.   One other limit on capability analysis seems to be even more fundamental. No study of a state's capability can be made without some reference to what it is that the state is capable of doing. In other words, a concrete context is a prerequisite to an intelligible capability study; the more detailed the context, the more valid the analysis.[1] Capability analysis is always undertaken with reference to a set of (implicit or explicit) assumptions regarding objectives and strategy, both of the state itself and of the other states involved. Comparative capabilities, therefore, are most usefully analyzed with regard to a particular problem situation.

This problem will reappear throughout this chapter. The context of our analysis must be total, and the objectives of the United States must be postulated in the broadest possible terms. We shall, therefore, remain at a high level of generalization; there will be all too obvious limits on the precision with which we can draw conclusions from the raw data we discover. Our later estimates of American capability in narrower situations will attempt to build upon the less specific conclusions we shall reach in this chapter.

ASSUMPTIONS OF THIS ANALYSIS

In this chapter we shall be assuming the analytical role of the "nonparticipating observer"; that is, we shall make our judgments independently of the

---

[1]Harold Sprout, a pioneer in the development and refinement of the concept of state capability, emphasizes the contextual element in his treatment of the term, particularly with reference to the role of the estimator: ". . . capability analysis, by which the military, diplomatic, industrial, or other capacities [sic] of states are described, evaluated, and compared, consists mainly of estimating the opportunities and limitations which the estimator judges to be significant with reference to various hypothetical contingencies." Harold and Margaret Sprout, *Man-Milieu Relationship Hypotheses in the Context of International Politics* (Princeton, N.J.: Center of International Studies, 1956), p. 47; reprinted by permission. See the refinement and expansion of these concepts in a more recent work by the same authors: *The Ecological Perspective on Human Affairs* (Princeton, N. J.: Princeton University Press, 1965), pp. 211ff. The present author is indebted to Professor Sprout for much of the theoretical structure upon which the analysis in this chapter rests.

strategic requirements of contemporary and continuing American policy. This will give us great breadth in analysis but at the same time will deprive us of the special point of view of the official decision-maker. We suggested earlier some of the substantive assumptions of our approach; we may list them here serially:

1. American capability will be considered in relation to the overall foreign-policy problem of the United States rather than to any particular issues within it.

2. The objectives of American policy to the attainment of which the capability of the United States is put are those stemming naturally from the concept of American national interest discussed in Chapter 5.

3. The situational context in which American capability will be analyzed is the broadest possible one: the world as it emerged from World War II and as it has evolved since that time.

4. The major operational problem of American policy calling the nation's capability into question has been the communist threat; the most frequent comparisons with other states have been with the Soviet Union and Communist China.

Tangible Elements in American Capability

We listed the tangible elements of state capability in Chapter 1; there we found that they include geography, population and manpower, natural resources, industrial and agricultural production, and military organization and power-in-being. On each of these we may comment briefly as they appertain to the situation of the United States as it confronts its present and future problems.

GEOGRAPHIC FACTORS IN THE AMERICAN POSITION

We shall assume that the fundamentals of American geography are common knowledge and do not require reiteration. What we shall consider here are some of the specific ways in which American geography confers strength or weakness (actual or potential) on the United States.[2]

GEOGRAPHIC ADVANTAGES OF THE UNITED STATES. In the light of the conditions of world politics in the twentieth century, we may conclude that the United States has been fortunate in the geographic material with which it has been obliged to work. In terms of the more common criteria by which states are measured geographically, the United States ranks consistently high.

---

[2]A handy discussion of geographic influences in general and analyses of great-power geographic positions is J. P. Cole, *Geography of World Affairs* (Baltimore: Penguin Books, Inc., 1960).

No strong neighbors menace American security. The eastern, the western, and a large part of the southern frontiers of the United States are formed by the open sea; its common boundaries with Canada and Mexico do not constitute security problems. The coastlines furnish many excellent ports; the United States has easy access to the high seas and to the rest of the world. In general we may say that, except for a few points noted below, the effect of geography is to make a near-maximum contribution to American capability.

SHORTCOMINGS OF AMERICAN GEOGRAPHY. The major geographic handicaps of the United States are functions of distance. In the first place, for Americans both internal and external distances are usually great. The longest east-west dimension in the United States is 2,807 miles; from north to south it is 1,598 miles. Airline distances to points abroad are similarly great: New York-Paris is 3,630 miles; Seattle-Tokyo, 4,700; New York-Rio de Janiero, 4,840.

We should emphasize, however, that sheer distance is not automatically a shortcoming and might well actually be a source of advantage. To the extent that American policy emphasizes defense, distance from hostile centers is still an advantage, even under conditions of modern aircraft and missiles. But if—as is the case—the major preoccupation of the United States is to extend its influence outward from its own shores, the greater the distance to be traversed the greater the difficulties of doing so. Internally, distance also has a complicating effect, stemming primarily from the pattern of population distribution. The clusters of people along the east and west coasts are separated by the vast underpopulated area of the Great Plains, the Rockies, and the intermountain basin.

Internal distance becomes even more significant when another geographic handicap is considered: the concentration of population and industry in relatively few areas. One of the often-alleged advantages of size to a state is the facility of dispersal. The fact remains, however, that important portions of American activity cluster within certain confined geographical areas, particularly in southern California and in the so-called "Boston-Chicago-Washington" triangle. Such uneven human and economic spacing raises questions both of vulnerability to modern weapons and of the efficient distribution of goods throughout the entire area of the United States.[3]

POPULATION AND MANPOWER

The human base of American capability is a population of approximately two hundred million. The more sophisticated analysis of population figures requires us to consider factors additional to sheer numbers; these demographic ponderables throw more light on the present and future importance of American manpower.

---

[3]See Seymour Melman, *Our Depleted Society* (New York: Holt, Rinehart & Winston, Inc., 1965).

DEMOGRAPHIC PATTERN OF THE AMERICAN PEOPLE. There are approximately one and one-half million more females in the United States than there are males. After several decades of increase, the median age of the population has dropped slightly from a high of 30.6 years to its present level of 29.5. Nearly 40 per cent of the population is under 21 years of age, and some 10 per cent is over 65. The bulk of the American people clusters between 21 and 65, the age bracket of maximum effectiveness for public service. In this age group is found a manpower pool (male and female) for military and industrial service of nearly one hundred million people.

Population density varies widely. According to the 1960 census, the national figure was 50.5 persons per square mile; the state that most closely approximated this figure was Iowa (49.2), followed by Mississippi (46.1). In contrast to these average figures, however, were such concentrations as those in Rhode Island (812.4), New Jersey (806.7), and Massachusetts (654.5), as well as those in such underpopulated states as Alaska (0.4), Nevada (2.6), and Wyoming (3.4).

Two additional distributional factors are of some significance. As of the 1960 census, almost 70 per cent of the American people lived in urban areas. The Northeast, with 80.2 per cent of its people urbanized, led the nation; the West and the North Central States ranked next with 77.7 and 68.7 per cent respectively. The South has made the greatest shift of all the regions of the country; long the last stronghold of rural life, in 1960 it saw its urban percentage leap almost ten points to a figure of 58.5. The other datum is that of racial distribution. In 1960 there were some twenty million nonwhite people living in the United States, the vast majority of whom were Negroes.

POPULATION TRENDS. The basic population trend in the United States is one of numerical growth, at a higher rate than was the case earlier in the century. Vital statistics bear out this conclusion. The birth rate has stabilized at something over 24 per thousand per year; the death rate has steadily declined to its present rate of slightly over 9.6 per thousand. As long as these trends continue, the American population will grow steadily at a slowly increasing rate. One result of the decline in the death rate has been the slow rise in the median age, now stabilized around 30 years.

DEMOGRAPHIC CONCLUSIONS. From the point of view of sheer statistics, the American manpower situation is absolutely favorable except in comparison with China, India, and the Soviet Union. Americans constitute a numerous people whose steady increase to 200 millions is—barring unexpected catastrophe—probable.[4] There is no reason for us to assume that any likely American policy would fail because of a shortage of raw manpower.

---

[4]Some demographers of repute, however, are not convinced that the birth-death rate patterns of the last fifteen or twenty years are anything more than a statistical aberration. They do not share the opinion expressed in this paragraph, and we should note that such a dissent exists. For a strong statement in support of the stated position, however, see Harrison Brown, "The Prospective Environment for Policymaking and Administration," in *The Formulation and Administration of United States Foreign Policy*, pp. 140–143.

In addition, the United States has certain intangible manpower advantages that do not show up in a mere population tally. We shall consider them at greater length in a later section of this chapter, but we may say at this point that they rise generally from the demographic "quality" of the American people. The high levels of literacy, tool skill, technological orientation, formal education, and cultural homogeneity require that the verdict of size be revised upward. Except for certain situations involving sheer weight of numbers (such as a large-scale ground war), the manpower of the United States is thought to be adequate for any probable purpose.

NATURAL RESOURCES

THE AMERICAN RESOURCE ENDOWMENT.   The United States is among the more fortunate states of the world in its natural resource endowment. Many of the materials most critical to the capacity to execute foreign policy are present within the United States or immediately available outside its borders. Crucial shortages exist and are increasing in number; other reserves are nearing depletion. The general picture is not so serious, however, as to warrant deep anxiety. Most of the resource problems that exist promise to be soluble by the normal devices of foreign policy and do not present major dilemmas.[5]

The most basic category of materials includes coal and iron—the foundation of modern industry. American known coal reserves are conservatively estimated to be adequate—at present rates of consumption—for a thousand years. Domestic iron ore reserves of high quality are dropping rapidly—production from Minnesota's Mesabi Range fell 65 per cent between 1953 and 1954—but recent discoveries of rich deposits in Labrador and Venezuela open the prospect of ample supplies for certainly the next forty or fifty years, and perhaps for a century.

Energy sources—in addition to coal—are also substantial. The United States leads the world in the production of hydroelectric power and has vast untapped resources for further exploitation. Exact American petroleum reserves cannot be formulated because the rate at which new reserves are "proved" exceeds that of actual production by approximately one billion barrels a year. Other rich petroleum pools exist in Venezuela and Canada, and American industry has made extensive investments in the incredibly rich oil fields of the Middle East.

---

[5]Extensive data on resources may be found in the Report of the President's Materials Policy Commission, *Resources for Freedom* (Washington, D.C.: Government Printing Office, 1952). See also Percy W. Bidwell, *Raw Materials: A Study of American Policy* (New York: Harper & Row, Publishers, 1958), and Hans H. Landsberg *et al.*, *Resources in America's Future: Patterns of Requirements and Availabilities* (Baltimore: Johns Hopkins University Press, 1963).

The United States is in a less favorable position with regard to other industrial raw materials. The common ferroalloy metals—manganese, chromium, nickel, vanadium, cobalt, and so on—must be largely imported and stockpiled. So must large percentages of the critical nonferrous metals, including tungsten, copper, tin, and lead. Food, fiber, and timber resources, on the other hand, are generally adequate, although certain commodities within this class —such as coffee, hemp, and wool—must be procured abroad.

THE DEPENDENCE ON FOREIGN SUPPLIES. Thus we can see that the United States, for all its enviable position with reference to the basic raw materials, is nevertheless dependent on foreign sources for what are yet small—though critical—amounts of those resources vital to the maximum realization of its potential. What does this mean for American policy?

Nature distributed the important resources very unequally throughout the world. Whereas the early industrial centers grew up where coal and iron appeared in reasonably close proximity, today the major deposits of the newly important minerals are frequently in Africa, Central and South America, and Asia. American policy has concerned itself with the problem of guaranteeing adequate supplies of these items.

The protection of sources of supply is a fixed dimension of American action, and it is fortunate that at the present time enough of each material needed can be found within the portions of the world outside the communist sphere to which the United States can gain access. Any increase in the territory controlled by Moscow or Peking might have serious repercussions for America's resource position.

INDUSTRIAL AND AGRICULTURAL PRODUCTION

Of the tangible elements of capability, the one most directly pertinent to the contemporary role of the United States is that of industrial and agricultural production. The three we have so far discussed are relatively fixed; there is little a state can do about its geography, its population, or its resource endowment—at least in the short run. But what a people does on its own land to transform raw materials (which are, after all, only a potential source of power) depends to a great extent upon human will. Industrial and agricultural production is an index of the results derived from purposive activity by individuals and by government.

THE MEASURE OF AMERICAN INDUSTRIAL STRENGTH. Industrial production is at the same time the predominant economic activity in the United States and the major contributor to American power in international affairs.[6]

---

[6]For analyses centered around this point, see John K. Galbraith, *The Affluent Society* (Boston: Houghton Mifflin Company, 1958), and Massimo Salvadori, *The Economics of Freedom* (Garden City, N. Y.: Doubleday & Company, Inc., 1959).

Americans are generally sensitive to the major role played in their own lives by industry, and many have some appreciation of its place in foreign policy, but the exact configuration of American industrial strength is difficult to visualize.

The United States includes less than 6 per cent of the land area of the world and slightly more than 8 per cent of its people, yet since 1945 the United States has consistently outproduced all the other states of the world combined, at least as far as strategic commodities are concerned. The American industrial machine has a nice balance between capital and consumer production; war and postwar experience have indicated that it is technically a relatively simple matter to shift emphasis from one to the other. The flexibility and versatility of American industry is an important element in national strength.[7]

Few economists today would venture to predict a production ceiling for American industry. During World War II industrial production expanded to two and one-half times its 1935–39 level in the face of the loss of a substantial portion of the labor force to the armed forces.[8] Since 1950 industry has proved capable of handling up to $50 billion annually of government orders for military goods while at the same time increasing its output of consumer items.

WEAKNESSES AND VULNERABILITIES. The overall picture of American industry is one that makes it a central element in American strength. This optimistic generalization must be tempered by the recognition of certain shortcomings that may be classified as inherent weaknesses or as vulnerabilities to external pressures.

By "weaknesses" we mean only those built-in difficulties that bear on industry's contribution to American capability; no judgment is intended here on the social, economic, political, or psychic values that may attach to any of the conditions we shall mention.

In these terms we may briefly stipulate five such weaknesses in the American industrial machine. (1) Being a private enterprise system posited on competition, maximum efficiency through unified and coordinated effort is often difficult to achieve. (2) The industrial plant is so closely knit that maladjustment in one small segment may be rapidly transmitted to all parts of the economy. (3) There is a growing shortage of certain categories of key personnel, particularly middle- and high-level executives. (4) Long-range prospects are clouded by a relative overemphasis on applied research at the expense of more fundamental (although less obviously profitable) basic research. Dramatic demonstration of the inadequacy of American basic research was afforded by the entire nation's embarrassment at Moscow's technological

[7]Klaus Knorr, in *The War Potential of Nations* (Princeton, N.J.: Princeton University Press, 1956), qualifies this judgment sharply but concludes that it retains a good deal of its validity, even under conditions of nuclear weapons.

[8]See Geoffrey H. Moore, *Production of Industrial Materials in World Wars I and II* (New York: National Bureau of Economic Research, 1944).

leap forward after the launching of "Sputnik" in the autumn of 1957. (5) Certain key sectors of the economy, such as the machine-tool industry, are inadequately developed; strains and delays follow any unusual demand on these sensitive areas.

The vulnerabilities of the American industrial plant are somewhat better known; we shall list what are perhaps the three most significant. (1) The heavy concentration in the northeastern quarter of the nation and along the New York-Chicago axis; this has been only partly alleviated by planned and unplanned dispersal.[9] (2) The critical role played by labor relations; the growing sense of responsibility of organized labor has not yet obviated the danger inherent in work stoppages of various sorts. (3) The dependence of so much of American industry on stockpiles of key raw materials that must be imported. Any interruption in the flow of ferroalloys, other critical metals, or certain chemicals would disrupt great areas of American industrial production.[10]

THE AGRICULTURAL BALANCE. Agricultural production in the United States is remarkable for the enormous output derived from the efforts of only a small portion of the national labor force. In 1962 there were less than 7 million persons employed on the nation's 3.7 million farms; of the nation's 1.1 billion acres in farms, only some 287 million acres were planted to crops. The remainder was largely pasture or grazing land, with a smaller portion in timber. Farm income in 1962 was almost $36 million. The total number of American farms has been slowly decreasing ever since 1920, whereas the mean acreage has shown a corresponding steady increase. Farm tenancy is also on a slight rise.

From American farms pours a steadily increasing flow of agricultural products that far surpasses American capacity to consume, making possible both the export of farm goods and the accumulation of embarrassingly large surpluses. The United States leads the world, usually by a large margin, in the production of corn, raw cotton, wheat, and oats. The beef cattle, dairy cattle, and hog population of the United States is the largest in the world; America leads in the production of meat, milk, and dairy products.[11] The

---

[9]"Planned dispersal" is a problem complicated by the reluctance of interests adversely affected to cooperate. An apt example is provided by real estate and labor groups in such areas as New England.

[10]For the interrelationship between American defense policy and industrial production, see Henry Rowan, *National Security and the American Economy in the 1960's* (*U. S. Congress, Joint Economic Committee Study Paper No. 18*) (Washington, D.C.: Government Printing Office, 1960); Max E. Fieser, *Economic Policy and War Potential* (Washington, D.C.: Public Affairs Press, 1964); and Charles J. Hitch and Roland McKean, *The Economics of Defense in the Nuclear Age* (Cambridge, Mass.: Harvard University Press, 1960).

[11]In this connection, it is noteworthy that the Soviet Union has for more than a decade been attempting—with indifferent success—to "catch up" with the United States in the production of meat and milk. Successive Soviet attempts to reorganize its agricultural program in order to make this goal attainable have thus far had little result. It is obvious that Soviet leadership envies American agricultural preeminence.

only agricultural products that Americans cannot grow themselves are those requiring tropical or other special weather conditions.

The only food products imported into the United States in significant quantities are coffee, sugar, and cocoa; imported fibers include sisal and wool. Although there is considerable importation of other goods, such supplies are either unessential luxuries or are in direct competition with domestic sources. The enviable agricultural situation of the United States not only gives it the capacity to resist pressure on its food supplies to which other states might be vulnerable, but also—in an era of widespread food shortage—gives it a weapon of great versatility and sometimes controlling effect. The availability of food has several times been of real value to American policymakers.

MILITARY POWER

Military power is at the same time the most obvious element in a state's capability and the most difficult to assess accurately except in the most short-run of situations. Power-in-being is never more than a (possibly large) fraction of a state's potential; the men and materials available to a state in any context are susceptible of being employed according to different strategic and tactical theories. The mission to which armed force is put influences the techniques of its employment; the new technology of warfare has increased the relative importance of power-in-being. The most that we can do is to sketch the outlines of the problem.

AMERICAN MILITARY POWER. Unless the United States should be put to the ultimate test of survival, it is impossible to set a maximum figure for American military power. In mid-1945, during the mobilization peak of World War II, there were 12,300,000 Americans in the armed forces; during 1945 the armed forces spent $78.7 billion. At the same time, there yet remained a surplus—both of manpower and of resources—that had been untapped during the war.

The military establishment maintained by the United States in a combat-ready condition during the postwar era represented the best guess of what was necessary and varied with the rise and fall of the level of international tension. There was always some time lag, however (usually about two years), between the appropriation of funds and the mustering of forces-in-being. In 1963, for example, military manpower totalled some 2,700,000: The Army had almost exactly one million, the Air Force approximately 900,000, the Navy some 660,000, and the Marine Corps just under 200,000. While manpower totals had been remaining fairly static, budgets were edging upward from one plateau to another; between 1958 and 1960 they hovered at about $40 billion, whereas after 1962 they seemed to stabilize near the $50 billion mark. American participation in the war in Vietnam promised still another "quantum jump."

The radical advances in missiles and rockets that accompanied the space race after 1957, plus the Soviet policy of cutting its military manpower and emphasizing weapons of strategic deterrence, brought on a continuing debate in the United States about both force levels and budgets. In an era when evaluating the real contribution of men and weapons to national security was the most difficult in history, the dispute (which we shall examine in Chapter 11) was inevitably inconclusive (or perhaps we should say interminable). Neither the "budgeteers" nor the "security" group had enough concrete data to give their arguments the strength needed to win a consensus.

THE IMPORTANCE OF STRATEGIC AND TACTICAL THEORY. In the 1960's, the basic strategic posture of the United States has been most commonly known as the principle of "flexible response." The notion involves the maintenance in readiness in the United States of a broad range of military capability so as to be able to meet a wide variety of provocations. This represents a sharp departure from the so-called "massive retaliation" doctrine of the Eisenhower years in which primary reliance had been placed on strategic nuclear power as the primary deterrent and the ultimate decision-forcing weapon. According to current thinking, the United States will "escalate" any conflict only one step at a time, leaving the enemy the responsibility of initiating the final level. It is to be noted, however, that the abandonment of automatic and massive response does not deprive the United States of the capability (or the right) to employ its nuclear arsenal in retaliation for a subnuclear assault.[12]

Although the tactical doctrine of the armed services has been worked out in great detail in terms peculiar to each branch, we may nevertheless suggest some principles common to all three. Stripped to their essentials, they can be stated as follows. (1) American armed forces stress mobility, speed, and flexibility in performing their missions. (2) Aggressiveness is emphasized as being most parsimonious of both manpower and material. (3) Machine power—in the broadest sense—is both more efficient and more expendable than manpower; in tactical situations emphasis is placed on weapons and machines rather than on the commitment of large bodies of men. (4) The tactical goal of all branches, is firepower, whether from the ground, from the sea, or from the air; the object of maneuver is to subject the enemy to overwhelming fire.

HOW MUCH MOBILIZATION? One of the ubiquitous problems facing any responsible statesman, and one that endlessly complicates judgments on absolute or relative state capability, is the sliding relationship between actual

---

[12]For a representative sampling of recent works on this subject of continuing debate, see Morton Berkowitz, ed., *American National Security: A Reader in Theory and Policy* (New York: Free Press of Glencoe, Inc., 1965), and William W. Kaufmann, *The McNamara Strategy* (New York: Harper & Row, Publishers, 1964).

military power-in-being and theoretical potential. For the United States it has proved difficult in the postwar era to decide on a mobilization level that satisfies all the categories of requirements.

American military theory, relying on citizen-armies and heavy industrial production as the preferred ways of winning wars, has always insisted that the peacetime military establishment has only one real mission: to buy time against the enemy until war-level mobilization is attained. This system served well throughout the nineteenth century and brought victory in World Wars I and II. The technology of modern war, however, has reduced the value of mobilization and production planned to occur after the outbreak of hostilities. The advantages of surprise are so great that a three-week war (or, for that matter, a three-hour war) is a real possibility. The United States might well have to fight and win a total war with only the personnel and equipment available at the moment the first bomb fell.[13]

But to remain constantly prepared to retaliate overwhelmingly to any possible attack is beyond the capacity of any people. Americans, for reasons at the same time economic, political, ideological, and psychic, refuse to live forever on a total-war footing. Some bearable compromise between all-out readiness and underpreparedness has had to be devised. Any solution must take account of the changing nature of the threat confronting the United States, of its relative imminence, of the tolerance of Americans toward taxation and conscription, and of the general climate of world politics.[14] The result has been that since 1945 a persistent struggle, no less fierce because it was confined within a reasonably narrow range of alternatives, has raged over the amount and the kinds of the American mobilization potential that should be kept in readiness.[15]

Intangible Elements of Capability

We now turn to the intangible factors that affect the way in which the tangibles are employed and that often set outer limits to their usefulness.

---

[13]On this point see Bernard Brodie, *Strategy in the Missile Age* (Princeton, N.J.: Princeton University Press, 1959).

[14]See Arthur Herzog, *The War-Peace Establishment* (New York: Harper & Row, Publishers, 1965).

[15]The debate between limited and total war strategists is well covered in Seymour J. Deitchman, *Limited War and American Defense Policy* (Cambridge, Mass.: Massachusetts Institute of Technology Press, 1964); Robert A. Goldwin, ed., *America Armed: Essays on United States Military Policy* (Skokie, Ill.: Rand McNally & Co., 1963); and Paul Peeters, *Massive Retaliation: The Policy and Its Critics* (Chicago: Henry Regnery Co., 1959). For a contrary point of view, see James R. Newman, *The Rule of Folly* (New York: Simon and Schuster, Inc., 1962).

We must first, however, make one final remark about the catalogue in the preceding section: Even the most concrete element of capability has intangible implications that modify its significance in practice. Geography, population, and resources seem to be fixed entities that can be manipulated objectively, yet each of them gains its final relevance and value only in terms of human assumptions about them. Production and military power are even more obviously functions of human perception and will, and no automatic answers about state capability can be derived from any generalizations about these two. Even the tangible elements of capability, therefore, have indefinite dimensions of choice; at the level of all-out effort, this is often thought of as the "will to fight."[16]

This is even more the case, of course, when we take up the group of considerations that we are calling the intangibles. Here there are by definition very few concrete data on which to found generalizations; here each element is measured on a sliding scale, and any conclusion we reach is subject to immediate revision.

POLITICAL, ECONOMIC, AND SOCIAL STRUCTURE

This broad heading refers to the way in which the American people are organized for the accomplishment of political, economic, and social purposes. Each area deserves extended treatment, but our consideration of the American social order will be confined only to the most direct implications of the political, economic, and social system of the United States for the accomplishment of American foreign policy.

THE NATURE OF AMERICAN SOCIETY. The American political, economic, and social system remains, despite the massive strains to which it has been subjected during the past half-century, one of the most impressive monuments to human freedom the world has ever known. Founded and operated on the principle of encouraging the maximum of meaningful individual choice commensurate with the accomplishment of common goals, the United States has preserved its essential doctrine in the face of pressures both internal and external.[17]

Politically, the United States is organized into a federal democracy that institutionalizes private rights, limits government, and determines policy by the mass will. Economically, the partially-free enterprise system retains its

---

[16]See Knorr, *War Potential of Nations*, Part II: "The Will to Fight."

[17]For investigations of contemporary American society, see Denis W. Brogan, *American Aspects* (New York: Harper & Row, Publishers, 1964); Oscar Handlin, ed., *American Principles and Issues* (New York: Holt, Rinehart & Winston, Inc., 1961); and Daniel J. Boorstin, *The Image: Or, What Happened to the American Dream* (New York: Atheneum Publishers, 1961).

vigor although subject to extensive and increasing public control. The American social system is one of the least stratified in the world, permitting broad mobility both upward and downward as well as laterally.

The energizing principle of freedom in the major areas of life, however, has become subject to broad limitations largely stemming from the rising concept of bigness. Big government menaces much of the democratic myth as people stand outside the political process rather than participate in it; the major function of the mass is often conceived as that of serving as audience for the deliberations of the ruling elite. Big business and big labor together control much of economic life, and their struggles work great inconvenience and frequent hardship on the unorganized public.[18] Socially, the cult of conformity and the rise of "middle-class America" have given much of American life undertones of drabness, uniformity, and rigidity that do violence to the dream of a free society.[19] These trends, rather than proving the total collapse of the American system, are instead a measure of the extent to which American professions fall short of actuality. Their influence on the vigor of the foreign-policy effort of the United States is not yet great, although some observers are confident that it will increase.

STRAINS IN THE BODY POLITIC. In addition to the generalized threat of bigness in American life, there are specific maladjustments within the political, the economic, and the social spheres that create internal stresses. Each of them has direct influence on the broad questions of foreign policy and on the way in which it is executed.

In government, two issues defy final solution today and each is engaging the attention both of scholars and of practitioners. The first is the problem of discovering a working basis for federalism in the twentieth century. There are extremists on both sides: the states rights advocates who insist on the denigration of national authority and the transfer of broad grants of power to state and local governments and the supernationalists who argue for increased federal power and the abasement of the states to the status of administrative districts. Somewhere between these two positions a more satisfactory balance must ultimately be found.[20] The second problem concerns the accurate determination of the majority will. When apathy limits voting in presidential

---

[18]This theme is elaborately developed in John K. Galbraith, *American Capitalism: The Concept of Countervailing Power* (Boston: Houghton Mifflin Company, 1952).

[19]David Riesman, Nathan Glazer, and Reuel Denney, *The Lonely Crowd* (New Haven: Yale University Press, 1950); William A. Whyte, *The Organization Man* (New York: Simon and Schuster, Inc., 1956); and Thomas Griffith, *The Waist-High Culture* (New York: Harper & Row, Publishers, 1959). See also August Heckscher, *The Public Happiness* (New York: Atheneum Publishers, 1962).

[20]See, for example, Max Beloff, *The American National Government* (New York: Oxford University Press, Inc., 1959); James MacGregor Burns and Jack W. Peltason, *Government by the People*, 6th ed. (Englewood Cliffs, N.J.: Prentice-Hall, Inc., 1966); and William B. Graves, *American Intergovernmental Relations* (New York: Charles Scribner's Sons, 1964).

elections to 60 per cent of the eligibles, and if "engineers of consent" can mobilize public opinion on call by the use of techniques of advertising and mass communication, there is obviously something out of tune in American democratic processes.

In economic life, problems abound. Perhaps two assume primary importance. The first is the trend toward larger and larger units of production, symbolized by the rash of corporate mergers that broke out during the 1950's. How to continue to enjoy the advantages of large-scale production while avoiding monopolistic trends is a many-sided problem. The second issue, as much social as economic, has to do with the future of agriculture. The family farm, as a way of life as well as an economic unit, seems to be heading toward extinction. The consequences of any such outcome would be of deeper significance than to the limited number of persons directly involved.

In social relations, the two leading issues (or at any rate, two leading issues from among several) are the troublesome questions of interracial adjustment and the changing nature of the family in American society. Both racial conflict and family disorganization have results that extend into many other areas of social life, and both have a stubbornness that defies simple solutions. Some observers fear that either or both of them threaten to work basic changes in America that would radically alter the fundamentals of the entire American system. Whether or not their eventual importance will be this great, there is no doubt of their constantly eroding effect and the need for their resolution.[21]

EDUCATIONAL AND TECHNICAL LEVEL

Modern political power is inseparably wedded to modern technology, and the capacity of a state to exert pressure to accomplish its objectives depends in large measure on the extent to which its people have mastered contemporary techniques. An examination of the educational level and technical competence of Americans throws some light on American capability in this respect.

AMERICAN EDUCATION AND "KNOW-HOW." The American people are the beneficiaries of the most elaborate program of mass education in the world. Free public education is available to everyone through high school, and low-cost higher education at public expense is almost universal. Just what results has the United States had from its extensive educational effort?

---

[21]Racial relations in the United States are treated analytically in Gunnar Myrdal, *An American Dilemma: The Negro Problem and Modern Democracy* (New York: Harper & Row, Publishers, 1962), and Oscar Handlin, *Fire-Bell in the Night: The Crisis in Civil Rights* (Boston: Little, Brown and Company, 1964). A Negro point of view is expressed in Whitney M. Young, Jr., *To Be Equal* (New York: McGraw-Hill Book Company, 1964).

By 1965 more than 98 per cent of the population over 14 years of age was at least minimally literate. The school population, fed by the increased birthrate since 1945, passed 43 million in 1961 and showed no signs of ceasing its growth. In 1950 the median level of educational accomplishment was 9.3 years of schooling; by 1960 it had risen to 10.8 years, and projections called for stabilization at around 12 years by 1970. In 1962, over 420,000 bachelor's degrees were granted by American institutions of higher learning, 85,000 received some form of master's degree, and 11,622 doctorates were awarded. Americans seem to be making extensive use of the formal educational opportunities afforded them.

We should also recognize a factor more difficult to measure. Americans live in a technological culture, and they have shown remarkable aptitudes for coping with it. The facility with which Americans use the tools and techniques of technology—what is often called "know-how"— has become a byword in much of the world. Americans think of themselves as well-educated, and to a considerable extent the assumption is justified—at least by their scores on literacy and tool skill tests.

POTENTIAL SHORTAGES: ENGINEERS AND SCIENTISTS. The American educational and scientific picture is not so attractive, however, when certain categories of highly trained specialists are examined. In 1962, 34,735 engineers were graduated from American colleges, and 8,909 master's degrees and 1,207 doctorates were awarded in engineering. These totals fell far short of actual and anticipated needs for these specialists; the estimates of what could profitably be absorbed per year ranged from 40 to 60 thousand engineers, 15 to 20 thousand scientists, and three times as many Ph.D.'s and Sc.D.'s as are now being produced.

A whole new argument over education in the United States was touched off in the wake of the nation's embarrassment at the lead in the space race that the Soviet Union seized in 1957 and never relinquished through all the forms assumed by the contest for a decade. The world saw—and Americans realized—that the vaunted American educational system was not producing the scientists, the technicians, and the "know-how" specialists the United States was counting on to claim the first rank that Americans had confidently assumed was all but automatically theirs. A serious reexamination of educational philosophy was undertaken throughout the nation, with several immediate results.

The greatest stress in this rethinking of mass education was laid upon the deliberate reinculcation of the concept of "excellence" as the goal of intellectual achievement, a notion that had been seriously compromised through several generations of "life-adjustment" education. This new outlook had rapid results at all levels of education, spurred on by federal programs of many sorts aimed at upgrading educational efforts. One climax in this process was reached in 1965 when Congress not only passed the largest aid-to-education measure in history but also enacted separately an aid-to-higher-education bill that opened new horizons to almost all colleges and universities in the nation.

POTENTIAL SHORTAGES: EDUCATED PERSONS IN GENERAL. There is a more general and pervasive problem in American education. In 1954 the National Manpower Council's report revealed a chronic shortage of trained "brain-power."[22] Although the elementary schools are crowded and college enrollments are booming, there is an inadequate supply of thoroughly trained personnel in almost every area of scholarship, pure and applied.

As American foreign policy involves more and more areas of American life, the need for genuine experts becomes more pressing. Economic pressures, declining standards in public secondary education, the urge to conform and to avoid distinction (what David Riesman calls "other-directedness"), and a hyperconcentration on economic security have been suggested as explanations for the lack of interest among Americans in thorough intellectual training. Whatever the explanation, it is obvious that any inadequacy in the supply of educated men and women represents a substantial limitation on the capacity of the United States to accomplish the goals of its foreign policy.

NATIONAL MORALE

Morale is defined by Webster as "condition as affected by, or dependent on, such moral or mental factors as zeal, spirit, hope, confidence, etc." From the point of view of the operating statesman, morale is a measure of the extent to which his people are united behind their government and its mission and of the extent to which they will actively cooperate in accomplishing the ends of national policy.

AMERICAN MORALE: CHARACTERISTICS AND PROBLEMS. There is a constant "morale problem" in the United States, and policy-makers must always be alert to its requirements.

The state of American morale at any given time is materially affected by three factors. (1) There is a tendency for wide, relatively sudden, and frequently rapid shifts in the prevailing mood of the public. (2) American morale is notoriously sensitive to short-run or temporary influences, such as a sudden

---

[22]National Manpower Council, *A Policy for Skilled Manpower* (New York: Columbia University Press, 1954). It is noteworthy that the number of doctorates earned during the latter part of the 1950's did not increase in the same ratio as did the other degree totals. In 1954, 8896 doctorates were awarded; in 1955, 8840. In 1958, there were 8942—only a tiny increase. In the physical sciences, the number of doctorates actually decreased from 1661 in 1955 to 1589 in 1958. These trends, however, were reversed during the 1960's.

crisis or unexpected good news. (3) It is easier to maintain high morale on negative issues than on positive ones; that is, Americans traditionally are more at home when they are opposing some state than when they are pursuing an objective of their own.

Government morale policy, dealing with a public opinion and mass attitudes that are subject to extensive and frequent modifications, cannot be rigid. The continuing concern of American statesmen is to keep morale relatively constant in its acceptance of the objectives and procedures of the government. This requires effort to anticipate the swings of popular sentiment and to meet them with appeals designed to restrain both excessive optimism and extreme depression.

Not only is there a question about how much information to make public, but related issues of how to treat the information that is released are also pertinent. If relations with the public are wrapped in crisis, sudden and extensive popular reaction is to be expected; a more relaxed or unconcerned presentation will calm down some of whatever popular tensions exist. Both dictatorial and popular governments must be aware of the state of national morale, but a democracy like the United States must develop more elaborate strategies for dealing with it.

MORALE AND DISCIPLINE.   From the point of capability analysis, of course, national morale is an index of the degree to which a people will follow its leaders through the vicissitudes of foreign policy and, while doing so, exert maximum effort in the accomplishment of public tasks. We might say that by "morale" we really mean "endurability": the capacity to perform efficiently under prolonged stress. If this is what we mean by morale, then obviously another factor enters into its makeup besides "zeal, spirit, and hope"; this is the matter of mass discipline. It seems probable that some societies (Germany and Japan during World War II, for example) have been able to maintain a satisfactory level of performance by the sheer force of discipline even after hope and spirit had fled. There is a good deal of doubt, however, whether such would be the case in the United States; American behavior does not place as high a premium on discipline as does that of some other national groups.

MORALE: THE CENTRAL ISSUE?   A very good case can be made that the morale of the American people—their "zeal, spirit, hope, confidence, etc."—is the central problem of American capability. Whether the American effort in world affairs is well planned and energetically executed, whether American policy will "succeed" or "fail," will in the last analysis depend on whether or not the mass of Americans play their various parts effectively. Statesmen may plan and negotiate forever, but their efforts will be sheer futility without the active cooperation and allegiance of the people. It is not overoptimistic to conclude that the broad-gauge pattern of American policy is one that does not overtax the maximum capability of the United States; the major unanswered question is whether or not the American people will become sufficiently convinced of the worth and the desirability of their policy to make the necessary effort. On these grounds national morale becomes a matter of highest importance for American foreign policy.[23]

INTERNATIONAL STRATEGIC POSITION

Perhaps the most relative of the elements of state capability is the factor of strength or weakness that arises from the general strategic position of the state in the world. The situation of a state with regard to strategic advantage or disadvantage depends on the mission that the state sets for itself. If its goals are limited to what it can gain by its own resources, it is in a better position than if it needs help from other states to accomplish its objectives. If it must devote a large portion of its resources to the defense of its homeland against powerful and aggressive neighbors, it is deprived of part of its ability to prosecute its own purposes at greater distances. Here is the case of a state's ability to achieve its objectives being at least partially determined by the very objectives it selects.

AMERICA'S NEED FOR ALLIES. It is beyond doubt that the United States for the indefinite future is going to be required to work in close harmony and cooperation with other states. The objectives of American policy—summed up in an earlier chapter as the achievement of a world of peace, order, and stability—by their very nature require that the United States forge a series of close and long-lasting agreements with all like-minded states. The prosecution of the cold war also has necessitated that Americans ally themselves with over forty states and fit their policy into a common framework.[24]

To the considerable extent to which the United States is closely tied to its many allies, American freedom of action (and, consequently, American capabilities) is reduced. The kind of alliance the United States prefers to enter into (because of its greater usefulness and flexibility) is one that is genuinely voluntary and that springs from a sensed identity of interest. In dealing with its allies, Washington must therefore preserve the free and voluntary character of the alliance by minimizing the force component of capability and by

---

[23]It was obvious at the time, for example, that President Lyndon B. Johnson was as much concerned with the morale of the American people during the difficult days of 1965 when American entry into the Vietnam war was being undertaken as he was with the enemy. The solicitude with which poll data were analyzed and disseminated, by quick and strong rejoinders to all forms of dissent, and the reiteration of such powerful symbols as "national honor," "national will," and "keeping faith" all testified to a major involvement with the necessity of keeping popular support and commitment at a satisfactorily high pitch.

[24]For a succinct official statement of the United States' need for allies, see President Truman's *First Report to Congress on the Mutual Security Program* (Washington, D.C.: Government Printing Office, 1952), pp. 2–7.

seeking the maximum return from the exploitation of consent. Intra-alliance relationships are therefore sharply conditioned by America's need for allies.

An apt illustration of the inhibiting effect of alliances upon American freedom of action was provided by the Suez crisis of 1956 that grew out of Egypt's seizure and nationalization of the Suez Canal Company. Throughout the entire complex negotiations, including special international conferences, direct diplomatic negotiations, discussion before the Security Council of the United Nations, and extensive propaganda campaigns, American policy was at least partially governed by the necessity of maintaining a common front with France and Britain.[25] In the process, the United States was obliged to take a much less forthright stand than might have been the case had it been free to act completely according to its own desires. It was no longer under such compulsion after Britain and France had taken military action on their own initiative, and American policy then developed with unwonted speed.

ALLIES: STRENGTH OR WEAKNESS?   The vexations inherent in intimate and long-lasting cooperation among sovereign states have caused periodic resentments among segments of the American people. The whole idea of alliances is recurrently called into question; each crisis in the free world produces renewed pleas for the United States to "go it alone."

This position, however rationally it may occasionally be argued, is ineluctably based on a frankly emotional premise. It seems to grow out of two disparate sources: an evocation of a happier past and an urge to vent the inevitable frustrations attendant upon a multidimensional foreign policy. For the United States seriously to seek to dismantle the alliances it has so painfully put together would involve far more than merely abandoning one foreign-policy technique and substituting another in its place.

To take on a purely lone hand would require—if collapse were not to be swift and ignominious—a drastic truncation of the objectives of American policy and the abandonment of most of the world to its own fate (or to the clutches of communism). It would further the transformation of American society into the true "garrison state," heavily mobilized, constantly on the alert, and erosive of all remaining private rights in the name of national security. Put in terms of practical alternatives, the opponents of alliance find themselves defending a position whose costs would far outweigh the advantages alleged to accrue from a more extensive area of American "freedom."

A less extreme view of the pros and cons of the alliance structure of the United States would argue, even after admitting the embarrassments that have appeared and will continue to appear, that the United States cannot afford to do without them. So long as the current concept of national interest

---

[25]On several occasions, when Secretary of State Dulles intimated that the United States was following an "independent" course on some issues, strong British and French protests were immediately voiced. See *The New York Times* (October 3 and October 10, 1956).

retains its applicability, the American government must fit its policy within the framework of an alliance system. That valuable freedom of maneuver is sometimes sacrificed thereby no one will deny; that frequently the United States is forced to do things it really does not want to do seems obvious; that many of the alliances seem to be more advantageous to the other parties than to the United States is a suspicion that will not down.

Even after admitting all these—and many other—unpleasant side effects of the free-world pattern, it seems demonstrable that, save for two or three possible exceptions, the United States gains more than it loses from its arrangements with other states. For each diminution in capability vis-à-vis an ally, a greater gain is won in some other policy area. Under the policy pattern America is now following, some such calculation must lie behind each commitment undertaken.

Some Tentative Conclusions

Finally we now come to answer the question implicit in this entire chapter: Do American capabilities square with American objectives? Is the United States going to be able to meet the requirements of its own policy, at least under such conditions as we can foresee? At the end of our discussion, we may no more advance a categorical answer than we could at its beginning. The best we can do is to divide it into two parts, about one of which we have some certainty, but about the other of which we can do no more than conjecture.

First, there is little ground to quarrel with the general proposition that the pattern of American objectives is within the theoretical capacity of the United States, at least within any probable set of circumstances. Were Americans to mobilize all their potential and commit it to the accomplishment of their present foreign-policy goals, there would be adequate means at hand to achieve their ends. To put it briefly, we may say that the United States *can* eventually reach its objectives, at least as they are phrased today.

The other, equally blunt, question comes at the matter from another direction: *Will* the United States have available, at the appropriate place and at the right time, enough of its capability to surmount each of the obstacles it will be called upon to meet? The potential is there, at least as far as rational calculation can suggest, but whether the skill of American policy-makers and the understanding of the American people will prove equal to the operational mission of mobilizing, committing, and employing it is a question to which no one yet knows the answer.

THE ADEQUACY IN TANGIBLES. Taking into account the mission, the situation, the nature of the visible threat, and the operating principles of the

United States, the tangible raw materials of capability would seem to be adequate for the purpose as presently formulated. The American geographic situation is advantageous; the manpower balance—when modified by qualitative considerations—is satisfactory and promises to improve relatively and absolutely; the resource endowment is sufficient if prudently managed. Industrial and agricultural production have no inherent imbalances sufficient to threaten the continuation of their present and possible high levels; American military capacity, backed by technology and an elastic industrial plant, can be raised to almost any point that seems today to be possibly necessary. In each of the five tangible classifications are certain shortcomings; we have attempted to indicate at least some of the more important of them. None, however, seems beyond control or of such importance as to inhibit seriously future American efforts. On the score of the visible and tangible factors of capability the United States receives a satisfactory rating.

THE AREA OF UNCERTAINTY. It is, of course, the intangibles that provide the grounds for such doubts as may exist about the future. Questions bristle at every point. Will the American social order survive the strains of the coming decades, or is a quasi-totalitarian garrison state the only way to organize Americans for long-term coordinated effort? Will Americans match the Russian educational effort in training enough scientists, engineers, and technicians to meet national needs; alternatively, if American education should become science-oriented, will it mean the end of the humanistic, liberal education that has contributed so largely to the American version of the "open society"? Will American morale be equal to the task it faces; can rational calculation replace emotional fervor as the guide to mass attitudes toward foreign policy? Can the United States live indefinitely in close relationship with over 115 other nations, each of them bent on its own purposes and most of them aggravatingly different in culture, tradition, and social structure?

These questions, and the hundred more like them that could be raised, constitute the area of uncertainty about American capabilities. No one has any capsule solution to the problem they raise, but their relevance to our concern seems unquestionable. It is not the part of a textbook to exhort its readers, but it does not seem inappropriate at this juncture to suggest that in the ability of the American people to cope with the intangible factors determining the success or failure of the United States in its international mission will be found one of the most important tests of the applicability of the democratic idea to the conditions of the twentieth century.

CHAPTER **8**

The
Struggle with
the Soviet Union

For more than two decades, the struggle between the United States and the Soviet Union that Americans have long known as the "cold war" has been the supreme orienting factor in the foreign policy of the United States. Now that major rethinking about this massive enterprise has introduced some degree of coolness and detachment into a subject long marked by passion and emotion, we can attempt here what was hitherto almost impossible in a context such as this: a more or less systematic overview of two decades of conflict. In the discussion that follows, a conscious effort is made to avoid either heated polemics or the luxury of the superior wisdom granted by hindsight. Our point of view will instead be as analytical and as judicious as events—so many of which are still quite close in time—themselves permit.[1]

---

[1]The analysis and the argument in this chapter are generally based upon—but freely adapted from—the present author's volume, *The Cold War . . . and After*. A number of matters are treated briefly here that are covered in greater detail in the earlier study. From time to time, explicit citations of relevant material in *The Cold War . . . and After* will be found.

Origins of the Struggle

The Soviet-American conflict did not spring into existence overnight, nor was it the result of a single policy decision made in the Kremlin. Like most major developments in international politics, the cold war grew in the first instance from a complex of origins in a particular historical context. Because the era in which the struggle first appeared is so conceptually remote (although not nearly so far removed in time) from the present, it is a necessary as well as desirable exercise to recreate the original set of causes that launched the United States and the Soviet Union upon their conflict.

THE ENVIRONMENT

The cold war was in the first place the major outcome of World War II. Such a struggle would not have been possible, at least on the scale it assumed, at any earlier period in history. Its subsequent course as well has been shaped by the nature of the new environment we examined in Chapter 6. In every important way the Soviet-American struggle was the product of its age.

THE POSTWAR CLIMATE.   Earlier we analyzed in some detail the characteristics of the world arena in the aftermath of World War II. Here we need only identify a few of the major consequences of the war that contributed directly to the birth of the conflict. (1) The first was the drastic redistribution of power in the world that found the United States and the Soviet Union the only states with the capacity to conduct really independent foreign policies; under such circumstances it was only natural that both should think increasingly in terms of global strategies. (2) The second was the disappearance of the worldwide structure of empire that had been so familiar and so significant a feature of world affairs for at least two centuries. (3) The third was the new technology, symbolized most clearly by the birth of nuclear weapons, that seemed to presage an altogether new era calling for new policies by all concerned.

THE DECLINE OF TRADITIONAL INTERNATIONAL RELATIONS.   A second major component of the operational environment after the war was the obvious decline (almost to the point of disappearance) of the traditional concepts and doctrines of international political relations. A system three centuries in the making, built on informal but powerful consensus regarding the rules of the game, had been swept away in a holocaust. War was no longer the balancer of politics but rather its antithesis; the traditional system emphasized discrimination in objectives and techniques, whereas the new warfare elevated the means of destruction far above its historic end.[2]

Without its historic *ultima ratio*, the international political system was left almost directionless. Gone was the elaborately structured edifice of status and role that had for three hundred years made it possible to conduct relatively orderly relations in a context which was fundamentally disorderly because it was logically anarchic. Such a conceptual vacuum left the door open to the peculiar orientation of Soviet purposes and the equally unprecedented responses of the United States.[3]

REVOLUTIONARY CONCEPTS OF WORLD POLITICS. What we are saying here is that both the United States and the Soviet Union brought revolutionary doctrines of world politics into active application in the early cold war. American and Soviet approaches were both revolutionary because both emphasized the attainability of Utopia (although it goes without saying that the respective formulations were different). No greater break with tradition could be imagined than the (implicit or explicit) belief by the cold-war opponents that perfection was realizable by deliberate national action. When, after 1950, the two contesting Utopian visions were joined by a third, that of the emerging and "anticolonial" world, the stage was clearly set for struggles of massive proportions. It was not until well into the 1960's that traditional images began to reassert themselves and the fervor of revolution began to wear somewhat thin.

THE IDEOLOGIES

The one dimension of the Soviet-American struggle of which all Americans are aware is that of ideology. While we cannot investigate this question in any detail (it will be met frequently in the pages that follow), one or two points should be made here.

IDEOLOGY AS A GUIDE. Both the United States and the Soviet Union, we should remember, entered the postwar era with relatively little concrete experience in world affairs and few explicit formulations of interest to guide them. Both were therefore forced to rely heavily upon ideological imperatives to guide their decisions in the many unprecedented situations confronting them.[4]

---

[2]For an excellent analysis, see Raymond Aron, *The Century of Total War* (Garden City, N.Y.: Doubleday & Company, Inc., 1954).

[3]See John W. Spanier, *American Foreign Policy Since World War II* (New York: Frederick A. Praeger, Inc., 1965); John Herz, *International Politics in the Atomic Age* (New York: Columbia University Press, 1959); and George F. Kennan, *Russia, the Atom and the West* (New York: Harper & Row, Publishers, 1958).

[4]For a basic comparative study of twentieth-century ideologies, see William Ebenstein, *Today's Isms*, 3d ed. (Englewood Cliff, N.J.: Prentice-Hall, Inc., 1961).

Ideological decision is always marked by absolute terms of reference, inflexible commitments, one-dimensional actions, and a plenitude of moral judgments cloaked in historical inevitability. Certainly the Soviet attack on the postwar world demonstrated these characteristics in full luxuriance; candor forces the admission, however, that the early American responses to the postwar environment were not entirely free from the stigmata of ideological conformation.

IDEOLOGICAL CONFRONTATION. Soviet ideologists, facing a world in semichaos and enjoying an enlarged action capability, saw themselves as launching the final attack that would bring their new world into being;[5] American counterideologists characterized the mission of the United States as that of defending civilization, religion, and truth against forces demonic in their malevolence and awful in their strength.[6] Thus, both sides accepted as self-evident the proposition that their struggle was almost literally cosmic in significance and destined to decide ultimate questions of truth and reality.

From this overlofty formulation of mission neither side has ever officially departed, although the diminished militancy of their ideological confrontation today is a far cry from what it was in 1947 or 1950. That ideological issues remain important is not in dispute, but that they are the only important ones between the two states is today maintained only by dwindling bands of zealots on both sides.

THE STRATEGIC ORIENTATION

The third great root of the cold war is found in the disparity of strategic vision between the two states. They cast their policy problems in dramatically different terms; so great was the disjunction that this disharmony alone might well have led to the cold war.[7]

SOVIET STRATEGIC NORMS. Soviet strategists conceived of their national mission as one of incessant conflict against an inherently hostile environment. Struggle was thus neither good nor bad, only inevitable. There was no intrinsic value to agreement; what was important was the strategic goal, normally conceived of as monolithic, immutable, and absolute. Soviet thought, however, coupled inflexibility of purpose with the maximum

---

[5]For detailed expositions of Soviet ideological goals, see Elliot Goodman, *The Soviet Design for a World State* (New York: Columbia University Press, 1960), and Samuel Hendel, *The Soviet Crucible*, 2d ed. (Princeton, N.J.: D. Van Nostrand Co., Inc., 1963).

[6]For a representative exposition of this basic idea, see Robert Strausz-Hupé et al., *Protracted Conflict* (New York: Harper & Row, Publishers, 1959).

[7]The interrelationship of Soviet ideology and Soviet strategy in world affairs is examined in great detail in the present author's articles, "What's Behind the Russian Mask?" *United States Naval Institute Proceedings*, September, 1963, and "Contrasting Strategies in the Cold War," *United States Naval Institute Proceedings*, May, 1962.

tactical versatility and long accepted as a valid premise Lenin's dictum of "two steps forward, one step back."

AMERICAN STRATEGIC CONCEPTS. The United States, on the other hand, had a completely different and opposing norm. Conflict was abnormal, avoidable, and inherently undesirable; agreement founded upon mutual goodwill was the aim of strategic action. Agreement, furthermore, in American strategy was normally conceived of as growing from specific situations, and Americans were reluctant to think in terms of overall or absolute purpose. As we saw in earlier chapters, this orientation had authentic roots in American national tradition.

THE STRATEGIC CONFRONTATION. When the Soviet Union and the United States began to clash in the early postwar period, the disparity in strategy immediately had its effects. Moscow saw the reluctance of the United States to discuss questions of "principle" as a deliberate avoidance of real issues and as the unfolding of an anti-Soviet plot; Washington saw in the Soviet determination to proceed to ultimate purposes by flexible means a "blueprint for world conquest." Soviet lack of interest in abating particular disagreements was interpreted as proof of evil intent, whereas American demands for early agreements were viewed with profound suspicion. Although it is too much to say that both parties were acting in good faith and that conceptual and communications difficulties were responsible for their rapid descent to complete opposition, it is probable that strategic preoccupations were at least partially responsible for the peculiar form that the cold war developed almost as soon as it began.

THE THEORY OF CONTAINMENT

When two years of effort finally convinced the United States in 1947 that the Soviet Union could not be brought to accept a satisfactory arrangement by the prevailing doctrine of "patience and firmness," some more fundamental basis for policy was necessary. This was found in the concept of "containment," a theory and a policy that in its essentials has survived virtually unchanged to the present day.[8]

---

[8]Any discussion of "containment" must rely heavily on the writings of George F. Kennan who, as chief of the Policy Planning Staff of the State Department in 1947, made a major contribution to its conception and also helped make it public property by means of a justly famous magazine article ("X," "The Sources of Soviet Conduct," *Foreign Affairs* [July 1947]; reprinted in H. F. Armstrong, ed., *The Foreign Affairs Reader* [New York: Harper & Row, Publishers, 1948] and in George F. Kennan, *American Diplomacy 1900–1950* [Chicago: University of Chicago Press, 1951]). Although what we shall be discussing here is more the actual practice of American policy rather than its theoretical formulation by Mr. Kennan, any systematic analysis of recent American policy must be greatly in his debt. The catalogue of Soviet motivations included here is drawn largely from his writings.

SOVIET MOTIVATIONS

The fundamental assumption upon which the American government has proceeded is easily stated: Soviet policy is inherently expansionist. Left alone, the Kremlin would continue indefinitely to bring more and more of the world under its domination. Why did Americans conclude that Russia would always expand? What, in George F. Kennan's words, did the government believe were "the sources of Soviet conduct"?

THE ROOTS OF SOVIET ACTION. Soviet leadership, in making policy decisions, seems to be subject to three different pressures. The first arises from communist ideology, the second from Russian history and tradition, and the third from the peculiar dynamics of dictatorship in a police state.[9]

Thus Marxism-Leninism—and its later variants—impels them toward conflict with the capitalist world, assures them of inevitable victory, and teaches them that time is forever on their side. Russian historical tradition gives them a grip on their people and sets them in pursuit of objectives sanctified by time; the Kremlin has driven toward the Straits, has demanded Balkan hegemony, and has established spheres of influence in central Asia and the Far East.

The compulsions of dictatorship create certain imperatives for the ruling clique in Russia. The continued survival of the regime requires—as was the case in Imperial Rome—"bread or circuses." The expectations of a higher standard of living for the masses have not materialized in any significant way. The apparatus of the police state therefore becomes essential as the only way to guarantee the security of the regime as long as the better life for all remains out of reach. If no bread be forthcoming, circuses become vital; if the circuses fail, then the bread must be made available.

THE NEED FOR A CHOICE. In order to fashion a policy, however, the United States had to determine for itself the most deeply rooted of the three influences. What it felt to be basic to Soviet behavior made a great deal of difference to America's future policy. If ideology were fundamental, the United States would have to prepare to deal with fanatics who were immune to reason and who might well stop at nothing to achieve their goal of world communism. If "Russianism" were the inspiration for Moscow's policy, there were ample historical guides provided for the United States by the two centuries of British struggle with Czarist imperialism. If the Soviet

---

[9]For a good collection of basic analytical articles, see Alvin Rubinstein, ed., *The Foreign Policy of the Soviet Union* (New York: Random House, Inc., 1960).

leaders were first of all political adventurers who were most concerned with retaining their power, American statesmen again would be able to draw upon the rich store of experience that Western man had accumulated in coping with this type of political force. The direction of American policy depended on this initial decision.

THE REJECTION OF IDEOLOGY. It was apparent that Marxist-Leninist ideology was important to the Soviet as a tool of policy, as a guide in new and unfamiliar situations, and as an orienting and idea-shaping influence. The framers of American policy could not, however, bring themselves to believe that it was the ultimate answer to Moscow's behavior. The doctrine itself was simply too flexible.[10]

THE LIMITS OF HISTORICISM. In the same way, the influence of Russian history and tradition, although great, was finally not thought to be basic. Much of Moscow's policy was in the historic Russian pattern, but more of it was not. Lithuania, for example, was traditionally a Russian sphere but East Prussia never was. Tradition might serve a purpose in winning mass support for the regime and undoubtedly played its part in suggesting possible channels for expansion.[11] It failed, however, to explain enough of Soviet policy for the United States safely to accept it as controlling.

THE COMPULSIONS OF DICTATORSHIP. The conclusion was reached that the Soviet leadership, when finally judged, was composed of men who were first of all dictators with all the strengths and weaknesses of the breed. They were dictators under peculiar Russian and Marxist influences. But beneath the veneer of ideology and patriotism, the men in the Kremlin were driven by the same compulsions that have obsessed political adventurers in many other places: a lust for power and an urge to preserve and expand it.[12]

THE SIGNIFICANCE OF THE CHOICE. This judgment, if accurate, would have profound importance for the United States. It meant that, if driven into a tight corner, the leaders of Russia would probably react primarily from a desire to save their own power and to preserve their regime. It meant that the Soviet system was subject to the stresses and strains of any dictatorship, most conspicuously a conspiratorial psychology permeating the bureaucratic structure and an incessant competition for power. It meant that Soviet policy was, rather than a carefully worked-out timetable and

---

[10]On this point, see John A. Armstrong, *Ideology, Politics and Government in the Soviet Union* (New York: Frederick A. Praeger, Inc., 1962).

[11]A good collection of articles contrasting the differences among analytical approaches to Soviet foreign policy is Norman Graebner, ed., *The Cold War: Ideological Conflict or Power Struggle?* (Boston: D.C. Heath & Company, 1963).

[12]See Merle Fainsod, *How Russia Is Ruled* (Cambridge, Mass.: Harvard University Press, 1963), and Zbigniew Brzezinski and Samuel P. Huntington, *Political Power: USA/-USSR* (New York: Frederick A. Praeger, Inc., 1962).

battle plan, a highly experimental and pragmatic program subject to frequent revision in the light of changing circumstances. It meant that the dictators would be likely to stake their survival on a policy only after carefully calculating its probable effect on their own security. It meant, finally, that the leaders, although vicious and unprincipled men, were basically rational and could be dealt with by a rationally conceived policy.[13]

CONTAINMENT AS CONCEPT

The policy that developed from this analysis of Soviet motivations depended frankly for its validity upon the correctness of its initial premises. It called for a two-phase effort to blunt, to arrest, and eventually to modify Soviet expansionism on a worldwide front. Both its grandeur and its realism marked major new departures in American foreign-policy thinking.

THE PHASE OF HOSTILITY. The first phase, initiated in 1947 with the Greek-Turkish aid program (the "Truman Doctrine"),[14] called for the United States to take a stand all along the perimeter of the Soviet world and to resist any further advance by Moscow. America committed itself to meet each threat as it arose by such action as might be appropriate to the particular time, place, and conditions. No single pattern or technique of resistance was prescribed; the particular form of American response depended in essence upon the nature of the Soviet thrust.[15]

This decision pledged the United States to hold an enormous arc extending from the North Cape in Norway down through central Europe, the Middle East, and South Asia, and then turning northeastward and running up through Southeast Asia, China, Korea, and Japan. This was the geopolitical "shatter zone" abutting on the Soviet heartland. If Moscow were to be stopped short of total domination of Eurasia, America must draw a line and hold it before Russian power broke out to the open sea. Despite the loss of China, Cuba, and half of Indochina to communist control since 1947, however, the United States has held the line tolerably well.

---

[13]Thus Kennan says: ". . . it will be clearly seen that the Soviet pressure against the free institutions of the western world is something that can be contained by the adroit and vigilant application of counter-force at a series of constantly shifting geographical and political points, corresponding to the shifts and manœuvres [sic] of Soviet policy, but which cannot be charmed or talked out of existence." "X," "The Sources of Soviet Conduct," *Foreign Affairs* (July, 1947). Copyright by Council on Foreign Relations, Inc. Reprinted by permission.

[14]President Truman's message calling on America ". . . to support free peoples who are resisting attempted subjugation by armed minorities or by outside pressure . . ." is found in the *Department of State Bulletin* (March 23, 1947), p. 536.

[15]The necessity of a flexible and variable response is made very clear in the original Kennan article in *Foreign Affairs* in which he stresses the need for American capabilities in meeting Soviet threats of any nature in any area of the world.

This, however, was not all there was to it. As developed in practice, containment demonstrated an active dimension: the fostering of "situations of strength" in which local free-world superiority could force limited Soviet rollbacks. The theory was that a pragmatic, realistic Soviet regime, faced with stalemate in most of its efforts and deterioriation in some key areas, would eventually accept the bankruptcy of its aggressive designs and cast about for some new lines of action. It was clear, however, that the local victories the "situations of strength" might bring to the United States needed to be carefully (and tactfully) handled; too much zeal might have exactly the opposite effect on the Soviet leadership.[16]

THE ACCOMMODATION PHASE. Imbedded in the concept of containment——indeed, essential to its theory—was the idea of a second phase. This was not to become operative until Soviet expansive policies had been brought to a halt by American opposition and was to consist primarily of United States initiatives designed to offer the Soviet Union legitimate (if limited) satisfaction in return for peaceful and orderly behavior by the Kremlin. But such a turn in American policy could only be postulated on a "signal" from Moscow, probably in the form of a major Soviet concession on an important issue.

It would be frivolous for us to suggest any detailed terms on which Soviet-American accommodation could be based; they would have to depend on the particular conditions prevailing at the moment any such agreement was reached. We can, however, lay down the guiding principle of any American negotiator: The United States is willing to make any grants to Soviet interest that would ensure Russian cooperation in a peaceful world but that would not compromise the fundamental American position.

The United States cannot ever "trust" the USSR the way individuals trust each other (nations cannot ever safely "trust" each other in that way). Although this generalization does not invalidate the prospect for lasting accommodation, trust and good faith simply have never proved to be a solid base for viable international agreement.

The real stuff of lasting accommodation between states is a harmony of interest. We may assume that the Soviet leadership—never abandoning for a moment their conspiratorial outlook—will keep only those agreements that individual and mutual interest demands be kept. It is immaterial to the United States whether the Kremlin abides by its promises because of the

---

[16]Kennan says: ". . . it is a *sine qua non* of successful dealing with the Soviet that the foreign government in question should remain at all times cool and collected and that its demands on Russian policy should be put forward in such a manner as to leave the way open for a compliance not too detrimental to Russian prestige." "The Sources of Soviet Conduct." Reprinted by permission.

positive advantage accruing therefrom or because of its fear of the consequences of breaking faith.[17]

THE COMPONENTS OF RESPONSE

Thus, the theory of containment—or at least of its first phase—demanded that the United States develop a strategy of response to an assumed threat. Although the early days of the cold war saw Washington and the American people contenting themselves with an undifferentiated urge to "get tough with the Russians," by the time of the Berlin blockade (1948) "responses" had developed several distinct components. Each of these has turned out to have a long and active life.

MILITARY DETERRENCE. Since the American view of the Soviet threat assumed that Moscow was committed to military conquest of the world at the first favorable opportunity, the initial and basic element of containment has been military deterrence of the Kremlin.[18] The initial containment hypothesis was designed to deny the Soviet Union the possibility of exploiting any "soft spots" on its periphery by guaranteeing that American power would always confront Soviet initiatives. From this primary concern the United States has never departed. The aim of containment is to ensure that countervailing American power be available wherever the Soviets might be tempted to move.

With the weaponry revolution progressing so very rapidly, military deterrence has become less a matter of providing forces-in-being at the point of contact than one of shaping an overall deterrent doctrine and posture in strategic retaliatory capability—that is, in strategic nuclear weapons. American policy in the arms race (as well as in its antithesis, the struggle for arms control) is to maintain adequate military power to persuade Moscow that any military adventure would be disastrous.

---

[17]In this connection, Walter Lippmann, in criticizing the Kennan hypothesis in *The Cold War* (New York: Harper & Row, Publishers, 1947), p. 60, made this point about accommodation: "At the root of Mr. X's philosophy about Russian-American relations and underlying all the ideas of the Truman Doctrine there is a disbelief in the possibility of a settlement of the issues raised by this war. Having observed, I believe quite correctly, that we cannot expect 'to enjoy political intimacy with the Soviet regime,' and that we must 'regard the Soviet Union as a rival, not a partner in the political arena,' and that 'there can be no appeal to common purposes,' Mr. X has reached the conclusion that all we can do is to contain Russia until Russia changes, ceases to be our rival, and becomes our partner.

"The conclusion is, it seems to me, quite unwarranted. The history of diplomacy is the history of relations among rival powers, which did not enjoy political intimacy, and did not respond to appeals to common purposes. Nevertheless, there have been settlements. Some of them did not last very long. Some of them did. For a diplomat to think that rival and unfriendly powers cannot be brought to a settlement is to forget what diplomacy is all about." Reprinted by permission.

[18]See Peeters, *Massive Retaliation: The Policy and Its Critics*, and George E. Lowe, *The Age of Deterrence* (Boston: Little, Brown and Company, 1964).

THE ALLIANCE SYSTEM.   A second key element of containment was an elaborate system of alliances[19] to shore up the ring of containment. Alliances were thought essential for two reasons: First, they provided a rationale for the introduction of American power in potentially vulnerable areas close to the Soviet heartland; second, at least some allies (if efficiently and vigorously led by Washington) might contribute significantly to the common effort against Soviet aggression.

In accordance with this thesis, the United States moved quickly during the early cold-war years to the construction of an extensive alliance system. The western hemisphere, Western Europe, Southeast Asia, the southwest Pacific, and the "northern tier" of the Middle East were covered by means of regional multilateral pacts; in addition, certain key states (such as Japan and Taiwan) were tied bilaterally to the United States.

Each of these agreements was used as the springboard for more or less detailed arrangements for joint military planning, political consultation, and common policy on key questions. The "care and feeding" of the alliance system has been a major concern of American policy ever since 1949.

TECHNICAL AND DEVELOPMENT ASSISTANCE.   A third element of response has been the extensive supply of economic, technical, and development aid to underdeveloped and needy states throughout the (primarily non-Western) world. Although a very solid argument can be and is often made that this effort has no necessary relation to cold-war response, it is undeniable that its rationale has consistently been grounded upon its utility as a "weapon against communism." We shall be analyzing this question in some detail in a later chapter.

THE MOBILIZATION OF WORLD OPINION.   A fourth operational element of American response has been the constant—if unevenly successful—attempt to mobilize world opinion against Soviet aggression.[20] Before such world forums as the United Nations, in many international conferences, in unilateral propaganda programs, and in hosts of other ways, the United States has consistently attempted to show "a decent respect for the opinions of mankind" in its contest with Moscow. No more fundamental characteristic of the American approach to world affairs could be suggested.

THE WAITING GAME.   Implicit in this multilayered idea of response was, as we shall see in the next section, the idea of a "waiting game." All these disparate lines of effort were in the strategic sense preparatory and contingent; the real test of the policy would come only after a Soviet initiative had been attempted. This has been a frustrating and exasperating posture for the United States; complaints about the shortcomings of a merely "reactive" policy have long been widespread. Yet any other formula would

---

[19]On this point, see Arnold Wolfers, ed., *Alliance Policy in the Cold War* (Baltimore: Johns Hopkins University Press, 1959).

[20]On this point, see Norman J. Padelford and Leland M. Goodrich, eds., *The United Nations in the Balance* (New York: Frederick A. Praeger, Inc., 1965), Sections II and III.

have demanded a completely different concept of national mission and purpose, one fundamentally at odds with the very self-image of the American people. The definition of response that was adopted, therefore, was the only one that suited both America's posture and the operational needs of the postwar situation.

The Strategic Confrontation

We have briefly analyzed the theoretical components of the American attack on the problem of the Soviet threat. In the attempt to recreate some of the thinking of the early years of the cold war our point of view has necessarily been somewhat retrospective. It is now appropriate for us to change our analytical stance to some extent and to inquire how the original American hypothesis has stood the test of application. What have been the operational characteristics of the great strategic confrontation of the cold war?

THE DOCTRINE OF BIPOLARITY

One intellectual prerequisite to American strategy requires our attention briefly: the idea of "bipolarity." Originally largely a rhetorical device, it developed a structuring and directive effect on American thinking the consequences of which are readily identifiable today. To comprehend many of the concrete manifestations of American policy, we must first examine the bipolar view of the world.

THE CONCEPT OF BIPOLARITY.   In its early stages, the concept of bipolarity was no more than a simple and quick means of referring to an obvious fact of the postwar world: The only two states with the capability to conduct extensive and self-determining national policies were the opposing giants, the United States and the Soviet Union. From this descriptive use, however, there developed a prescriptive formula of portentous effect.

Using the easy if deceptive method of analogy, it was widely accepted in the United States during the late 1940's and early 1950's that Moscow and Washington were truly "polar": that is, they were centers of power that repelled each other absolutely on the one hand and exerted a powerful attraction on all other states on the other. Around each there was imagined a "field of force," a zone of influence that pulled third parties back and forth until all fell under the influence of one or the other. The control of each bipolar center, furthermore, over its minor associates was deemed to be inevitably absolute.

Thus, if it was natural and therefore inevitable that the world was destined to be divided into two mutually hostile camps each grouped around its power leader, there was no room for nonalignment or noncommitment. Early American cold-war rhetoric was quite explicit that "power vacuums"— that is, states who did not choose sides—were literally unthinkable in such an all-embracing conflict.

The operational focus of bipolarity was the reduction of the complex of American national policy to a single issue, that of the Soviet threat. If all issues of American interest were reducible to the great concern of containing the Soviet Union, the intellectual task of the policy-maker was greatly simplified. A built-in yardstick for evaluation of all alternatives was conveniently available, and criteria of success or failure were also easily deducible from the bipolar hypothesis.

THE EFFECTS OF BIPOLARITY ON AMERICAN POLICY. The consequences of the bipolar construct on American policy are readily seen today. First, bipolarity led immediately to single-minded concentration by American policy-makers on the problem of the Soviet Union, with a resulting minimization and even actual neglect of positive American purposes. Second, the bipolar assumption led the United States to believe that the Soviet camp was truly monolithic and that the "free-world" alliance was in fact far more united than it actually was. Third, the identification of all major problems as little more than "spin-offs" of the original cold-war confrontation has resulted in a consistent American underevaluation and misinterpretation of many issues that are outside the immediate Soviet-American context. Finally, bipolarity has made it extremely difficult for the United States to analyze evolution and change in direct Soviet-American relations themselves.

On the positive side, we must admit that the bipolar concept has aided American policy-makers in imposing a conceptual and operational unity on policy and in suggesting concrete lines of action to them. So long as whatever offended Moscow could be automatically assumed to be desirable to the United States, policy decision was much simplified. A nonbipolar universe is a much more complex environment in which to make national policy for the United States.

STRATEGIC STYLES IN CONTRAST[21]

Earlier in the chapter, we pointed to a disparity in strategic vision as a root of the cold war. Moscow and Washington saw their respective national purposes in different lights and as a result developed very divergent doctrines

---

[21]For an expanded discussion of the following section, see the present author's *The Cold War . . . and After*, esp. Chaps. 3, 4, 7, 8.

about how to proceed in achieving their ends. These strategic concepts, applied in the real world, have given rise to a distinct contrast in "strategic styles" that has given the cold war much of its operational coloration.

SOVIET STRATEGIC STYLE. The Soviet Union sees itself as pursuing a strategy of *finality*. This is to say that Soviet policy-makers consider the intellectual problem of making and executing strategy as a unitary task, with each mental or physical move gaining its force or its logic only from its relationship to the central and architectonic strategic concept. Its focus is upon the victory to be achieved at the end of the struggle; intermediate maneuver, tactical victory or defeat, or extensive delay and digression are all tolerable if their cumulative effect is to advance the ultimate strategic purpose.

Here, we are tempted to speculate, can be identified the true Marxist-Leninist inheritance of contemporary Soviet leadership. Communist goals in their pure Utopian form have been drastically modified by contact with a stubborn environment. But ideological habits of problem-solving remain, even if put to nondoctrinaire purposes; the Soviet preference for a strategy of finality comports as well with the mentality of addicts to the dialectic as with that characteristic of historic Russian experience.

AMERICAN STRATEGIC STYLE. The United States, in contrast to the Soviet, employs a strategy of *opportunity*. The American strategic style conceptualizes foreign policy as consisting of a series of discrete problems, each to be attacked in chronological order and on its own merits. Each confrontation is a miniature strategic exercise in itself, to be analyzed, estimated, and dealt with in a way calculated to produce victory in the immediate conflict. Strategic fulfillment is thus to be achieved not in terms of one final triumph that realizes an ultimate goal but rather by the accumulation of the fruits of a relatively large number of small victories.

Thus the United States accepts a strategy that emphasizes relatively rigid conceptual frameworks coupled with great facility in extemporizing tactics to meet a broad variety of operational situations. Flexibility in devising techniques for dissimilar problems, however, has seldom been matched by an equal skill in meeting unexpected circumstances arising within a single crisis. The very stylistic traits that enable the United States to assume that each problem is a fresh strategic exercise seem also to require that a crisis strategy, once adopted, must be pursued to the end of the problem.

THE MEANING OF THE CONTRAST. The strategic style of the Soviet Union is reminiscent of that used in its national game—chess—whereas the American way of problem identification and solution is strongly redolent of a favorite American pastime, poker. This analogy suggests that Soviet strategists are better equipped than their American counterparts to apply criteria of feasibility and appropriateness to particular moves in a context broader than that of an on-going crisis. Washington's preference for treating each involvement as a unique problem robs the United States of much of its ability to impose priorities, granting as it does primary importance and transcendent relevance to whatever issue may be under consideration at the moment. By the same token, however, the unitary strategic concept of the Soviet Union leads to repetitiveness and a general lack of inventiveness. One should not overlook the forest for the trees, but neither should one ignore individual trees in the concern for the forest.

THE CONFLICT CONSTANT

Ever since 1945, Soviet-American relations have been assumed to be more than anything else an exercise in the prosecution of conflict. "Conflict" in this sense refers not so much to a condition in which relations are conducted as to an inherent characteristic of the relations themselves. Moscow and Washington, the history of the cold war suggests, must inevitably clash, and the major operational problem is how to conduct the struggle and not how to end it.

THE ASSUMPTION OF DISAGREEMENT.   Once the cold war had been joined, strategists on both sides built their analyses on the assumption of total and permanent disagreement. Certainly in the United States, it was axiomatic and beyond discussion that the United States and the Soviet Union would line up on different sides of any issue that arose. Ideology, history, and the logic of the cold war were all advanced as confirmation of the thesis that conflict was inevitable. This was an apt example of the self-fulfilling prophecy, as both sides first predicted the inevitability of conflict between them and then acted in a manner which made such an outcome impossible to avoid.

The constant of cold-war conflict, furthermore, has often made both sides act as if the maintenance of the highest bearable level of tension in their relations had become the new norm of international relations. Conflict, in this sense, is not only inevitable but necessary. Certainly, policy-makers could be identified on both sides of the Iron Curtain for whom prosecuting the struggle has become an end in itself, all but divorced from either the origins of the conflict or the ends to which the respective national efforts are ostensibly being put. Opportunities to make real progress or to attain specific objectives often tend to be overlooked among Americans in favor of the prevailing fixation upon "fighting the cold war."

TACIT AGREEMENT IN THE COLD WAR.   We must not ignore, however, the fact that both parties have been able to indulge in the rhetoric of total disagreement only because of a largely tacit substratum of agreement upon how to conduct the struggle. There are ground rules for the prosecution of conflict that both the United States and the Soviet Union recognize and respect.

This agreement may be put in terms of two major propositions: First, neither side will launch total war upon the other (a controlling principle since the mid-1950's); second, neither will seek to impose an unbearable provocation or an unacceptable humiliation on the other (dramatically confirmed during the Cuban missile crisis in 1962). Both propositions are procedural and do not affect the issues of the conflict; both, however, make it much more likely that the parties will not destroy each other by accident or miscalculation.

CONFLICT MANAGEMENT. Out of the necessity long felt by both governments to keep the cold war active but contained has grown a new skill, known in the United States as "conflict management." Cold-war conflict is conceived of as a permanent feature of international politics. The relationship cannot be permitted to escalate above a permitted "ceiling" of tension for fear of explosion; neither, however, should it be permitted by inadvertence or misjudgment to slide through a corresponding "floor." The working variable in conflict management is tension: As crisis comes closer and the tension level rises dangerously close to the ceiling, countervailing forces are set to work to restore relations to a less perilous level. In like fashion, if much less overtly, any prospect of a breakthrough to relaxation is actively resisted by elements in both governments. The overall effect is the confinement of Soviet-American relations within a relatively narrow range of high but controlled tension.

THE OBSOLESCENCE OF STRATEGY

In analyzing the conflict constant in the cold war we have come a long way indeed from the dramatic evocation of national purpose and mission with which we began our analysis of the struggle. So far indeed is the conceptual distance from the early days of the cold war to the contemporary era that we can speak of the "obsolescence of strategy."

THE INSTITUTIONALIZATION OF THE COLD WAR. In both states a generous and controlling investment of political, economic, psychological, and military resources has been made in the permanence of the struggle. For both sides, a sudden victory would be scarcely less embarrassing than a strategic defeat; either outcome would necessitate a painful rearrangement of complex and costly institutional patterns. The institutionalization of the cold-war relations has become a foundation for both the internal policies and the world positions of the antagonists.

Each government, of course, blames the other for prolonging the struggle and proclaims its own willingness to negotiate all problems out of existence if only the other would bargain in good faith. Yet it is not excessively cynical to point out that each side nearly always states its demands in terms that

often sound reasonable but which are carefully calculated t~~o~~
other's minima of tolerability. When agreement is reached o~~n~~
substance, both sides emphasize its limited scope, its lack ~~o~~
major issues, its allegedly hidden importance as a victory over the ~~other~~,
its lack of precedent-setting effect. This was the case, for example, when the
limited nuclear test-ban treaty was consummated in 1963.

THE UBIQUITY OF STALEMATE. Strategy has become obsolescent in another
sense as well. Neither side dares admit the truth that its struggle has become
stalemated in the literal chess sense that both occupy positions of tolerable
safety but neither can make any major positive move against the other without risking total defeat. Indeed, the less freedom of action either may enjoy
at any moment, the more far-reaching become its verbalized protestations
of victory. Yet this very preoccupation with administering the conflict at
the expense of serious planning for bringing it to a close speaks more loudly
of its contemporary nature than does any absolute or euphoric public
statement. It is an ironic footnote to history that the frankest Soviet formulations of the true dynamics of the cold war have not been addressed to the
United States but to Red China in an atmosphere of bitter controversy;
and the brutal realities of the Western alliances have likewise been exposed
by an angry Charles de Gaulle in speaking to the United States.

THE RISING TIDE OF COST AND RISK. The obsolescence of strategy is
most graphically portrayed in terms of two of its necessary variables, cost
and risk. Strategic decision in favor of a particular course of action has
always been based on the conviction that the objective sought was worth
the probable cost and that the risks of failure were sufficiently small to be
bearable. Under contemporary technological conditions, however, the
grim cost-risk calculation has begun to breach the bounds of prudent statecraft.[22]

With cost factors analyzed in terms of nuclear war, it has become painfully
evident that finding an objective that is worth such astronomical costs is
extremely difficult. With the risk factor of failure including the possibility
of national obliteration, finding favorable odds to justify initiatives has also
gone beyond achievement. Thus, both sides, painfully aware of the logic
of the positions in which they find themselves, are to a major extent trapped
between their far-reaching pretentions and their sharply limited parameters
of action. To talk of "strategy" in such a context is either to deceive oneself
or to face an unacceptable dilemma. It is therefore no wonder that conflict
management and the administration of endless struggle seem the best available bargain.

---

[22]For a contrasting analysis, see the two volumes by Herman Kahn, *On Thermonuclear
War* (Princeton, N.J.: Princeton University Press, 1960), and *On Escalation: Metaphors
and Scenarios* (New York: Frederick A. Praeger, Inc., 1965).

The Phases of the Soviet-American Struggle

The Soviet-American confrontation, like most great international political configurations, has throughout its history reflected the dominant characteristics of the operational environment. Thus the cold war divides itself into a number of phases, during each of which the struggle went on in a different way than in those that preceded and/or followed it. A comparison of these differentiated patterns will not only throw additional light on the history of the struggle itself but will also provide some base for conjecture about the future of the relationship.

We are not, of course, attempting to tell the full story of the cold war. We have neither the space nor any necessity for such detail, particularly since so many books already cover the period. What we undertake here is rather a schematic study of the ebb and flow of Soviet-American relations, told primarily in terms of the evolution of the practice of bipolarity. This more modest enterprise will serve our analytical purposes better than would a complete history.

We will recall that bipolarity as a concept implied that world politics after 1945 contained only one real issue, the cold war. In operational terms, bipolarity therefore meant that Moscow and Washington, in prosecuting their own controversy, would also control the totality of world politics. Issues would gain relevance and priority by their articulation with Soviet or American concerns; resolution of all problems would be found in cold-war terms; the entire world was little more than an arena for the greatest and most portentous political drama of history.

The question in which we are interested, then, is just how accurately reality has been congruent with the bipolar hypothesis during the two decades of the cold war. How bipolar was the cold war at any period, and how valuable is the concept today to American students and policy-makers?

THE FOUR PHASES.   In general, we may say that in these terms the cold-war era can be divided into four major phases. The first extended from the end of World War II to the onset of the Korean war, during which time both great powers enjoyed some success in applying the bipolar idea to the operation of the world political system. This was the period of maximum great-power domination of events. The second period was that of the wars in Korea and Indochina, from 1950 through 1954. This era saw the major states, while unable to shape major decisions themselves, at least able to freeze world affairs in a military stalemate. The third period, that of the liquidation of the bipolar idea (in the face of great-power resistance), extended from the end of the 1954 Geneva Conference through the failure of the 1960 Paris summit conference. Finally, the fourth period that began in 1960 and continues to the present is characterized by the growing acceptance by both great powers of the fact that their scope of dominion has been sharply decreased and by a consequent willingness to deal bilaterally with one another.

THE LANDMARK CRISES. Within each phase, furthermore, we may isolate a single crisis, or at most two, that epitomizes the period and in a microcosmic way portrays the nature of the struggle. The Berlin blockade of 1948 sums up the first phase. The Korean war itself represents the second. The twin 1956 crises of Hungary and the Suez Canal Zone symbolize the third. The Berlin wall of 1961 and the Cuban missile crisis of 1962 are fairly representative of the contemporary phase. We shall pay particular attention to these events.

BIPOLARITY EVOLVING, 1947–1950

The first period of the cold war was marked by the systematic application of the bipolar concept by both major powers. Operating on the premise that their controversy was the single important issue of world politics, they sought to universalize their dispute and divide the entire world into two well-organized and hostile camps.

CHARACTERISTICS OF THE PERIOD. From the point of view of the United States, the earliest years of the cold war were also the most creative. Beginning in late 1946 and 1947 with the acceptance of the responsibility for world leadership and continuing through the beginning of open war in Korea, one original and unprecedented move followed another. At no time since has the United States matched its performance during this era on the count of creative innovation.

The major step taken by the United States was the decision to meet the Soviet threat in the terms in which it presented itself in 1946 and 1947: a combined military-political menace to a Europe that was unstable and vulnerable. Thus the first phase of the cold war may also be identified as one of "Europe first"—in distinct contrast to later periods.

Focusing on European questions, therefore, the United States developed and implemented in rapid fashion four great enterprises that have formed key elements in American policy ever since. These were: the Greek-Turkish aid program of 1947, in which the principle of American assistance to nations menaced by communist subversion was laid down; the Marshall Plan, given official form by the Foreign Assistance Act of 1948, in which the policy of economic aid to build bulwarks against communism was first established; the North Atlantic Treaty of 1949, in which American military guarantees of areas threatened by Soviet power were first given; and the

Mutual Defense Assistance Program (1949), in which American military aid for the armed forces of friendly states was first put in the pipeline.

Also during this early period, a major beginning was made at the creation of the alliance system that was to grow so large in the next decade. The Inter-American Treaty of Reciprocal Assistance (the Rio Pact) was negotiated in 1947. The North Atlantic Pact of 1949 incorporated ten European states into alliance with the United States and Canada.

Also noteworthy—primarily for their future significance—were three issues that arose outside the bipolar context: the partition of Palestine and the creation of Israel; the partition and independence of India and Pakistan; and the independence of Indonesia, an early harbinger of the flight from empire that was later to become such a major feature of world affairs. In each of these cases the United States was forced to move cautiously, since the bipolar cold-war construct offered no guidance and little else was available as a principle in these unfamiliar areas.

THE BERLIN CRISIS. The most open confrontation between East and West before 1950 was the Berlin crisis of 1948 and 1949.[23] Its details are complex, but certain of its aspects are relevant to the broader trends of the cold war.

Berlin was the first open test the Soviet made of American determination and American strength. It was important for Moscow to know that the United States was both willing and able to meet coercion with counterpressure. Berlin also stiffened the United States' position; the Soviet's stubborn and uncompromising attitude hardened American determination to carry containment through to completion.

Throughout the entire crisis, the tone and the context of the dispute were set by the two major powers. Moscow and Washington were quarreling over a prostrate Germany. The Soviet initiated the crisis to suit its own strategic and tactical purposes, but the United States chose the speed, the extent, the intensity, and the character of the Western response. The crisis endured only as long as both wished to keep it going. In many ways Berlin illustrated the rising tide of bipolarity in its starkest terms; during the crisis the United States enacted the Marshall Plan into law and negotiated the North Atlantic Pact, and the Soviet Union consolidated its hold on the rebellious satellites of Poland, Czechoslovakia, and Hungary while reconciling itself to the loss of Yugoslavia.

Most significant of the implications of Berlin was the fact that the issue was finally brought to the point of a time-buying compromise. Moscow, faced with a stabilized power situation, was willing to call a halt to its dynamism.

---

[23]One of the best accounts of the Berlin blockade is still Lucius Clay, *Decision in Germany* (Garden City, N.Y.: Doubleday & Company, Inc., 1950). For the relation of the Berlin crisis to the early stages of the cold war, see *The Cold War . . . and After*, p. 96.

The Soviet, confronted with equal pressure, had shown it would stop; it seemed reasonably safe to conclude that the Kremlin would recoil if faced by superior power. American assumptions had been vindicated.

BIPOLARITY DOMINANT, 1950–1954

We cannot specify the precise date at which the United States and the USSR lost their freedom of maneuver and became caught by the inexorabilities of the logic of the two-power system. We can come closest by placing it somewhere in the period beginning with the final victory of the communists in China and ending with the outbreak of the Korean war, although the atomic explosion in the USSR in September, 1949, was undoubtedly the major single event signalling the culmination of bipolarity. By the beginning of 1954 other forces had asserted themselves to the point that the maintenance of bipolarity became impossible.

CHARACTERISTICS OF THE PERIOD. The 1950–54 era of the cold war was marked, as suggested above, by a diminishing zone of free maneuver on the part of both bipolar states. During most of the period, the bipolar hypothesis of a one-issue, two-camp world remained at near-realization. The consequence was a generous measure of frustration that was to reach expression at the Geneva Conference of 1954.

Probably the most important new element of the cold war to appear during this period was the shift of its major battleground to Asia.[24] The fall of China to communism, subversion and revolt in the Philippines, a worsening situation in Indochina, and, of course, the Korean war itself combined to force a major shift in American thinking from Europe to the Far East.

The appearance of open war in Korea had another effect on American policy. The context of foreign-aid programs was declared to be one of "mutual security": that is, the United States saw itself as extending assistance to other states only as part of an overall defense of the free world against communist pressure. Military considerations regarding foreign aid became primary as early as 1951 and were not to lose their centrality until well into the 1960's. Several allies of the United States, notably in Europe, protested at this time against what they felt was a cavalier American attitude toward their needs and interests in aid, but their arguments received no hearing for a decade.

Europe, meanwhile, was initiating its renaissance. In 1951 the "Schuman Plan" for integrating the coal and steel industries of six western European

---

[24]See A. Doak Barnett, ed., *Communist Strategies in Asia* (New York: Frederick A. Praeger, Inc., 1963), David Rees, *Korea: The Limited War* (New York: St. Martin's Press, Inc., 1964), and *The Cold War . . . and After*, pp. 86ff.

nations was put into effect, and Europe's great adventure was under way. America's initial response to integration was favorable, even going so far as to extend grant aid of dollars to any supranational bodies formed in Europe.

West Germany's own miracle was also in full swing in this period. Economic recovery, aided by the Marshall Plan, was spectacular; politically, the rising emphasis on bipolarity meant that the United States moved quickly to tie the Federal Republic of Germany irrevocably to the West by a peace treaty (1952), by a decision to permit German rearmament, and by the final inclusion of Germany in the defense system of the West. The latter move, however, was not made until 1955 when West Germany—under certain safeguards—was admitted into NATO.

The climax of the period was reached at the Geneva Conference of 1954, called to bring the Indochina war between France and the local communist forces to a halt. The Geneva agreements (which the United States did not sign) institutionalized stalemate: Each side could hold back the other, but neither could push to a clean victory under the conditions of bipolarity. The next phase was to suggest a way of escape from this problem.

THE KOREAN WAR. American leadership thought of the Korean war as a part of a larger policy whole.[25] Korea was an example of a different technique—military force—put to serve the standard communist goal of expansion. The United States reasoned that its real enemy in Korea was neither Korea nor China, but the Soviet itself. American policy was therefore derived from an application of the basic principle of containment to the peculiar conditions prevailing in Korea. General MacArthur's more extreme views confused the issue but did not alter the outcome.[26]

One consequence of Korea was the identification of Red China with the Soviet. The active entry of Chinese troops in the Korean fighting and the participation of China in the truce negotiations removed whatever doubt remained about the direction the new regime would take. Henceforth Peking was assumed to be Moscow's most faithful ally.

Although military action in Korea was carried on in the name of the United Nations, we must admit that the United States did not fight there in support of any abstraction called "collective security." National interest governed American action as it did that of the fifteen other participating states. The only other United Nations members who entered the fighting were those whose concern about Soviet expansionism approximated that of the United States or whose interest demanded the closest possible relations with Washington.

---

[25]For a thorough study of American policy during the Korean episode, see Leland M. Goodrich, *Korea: A Study of United States Policy in the United Nations* (New York: Council on Foreign Relations, 1956).

[26]See *The New York Times* (April 20, 1951).

On the other hand, the polarizing effect of the cold war created stresses within the ranks of the noncommunist world. Americans had fallen into the habit of using the term "the free world" to refer to all states outside the Soviet orbit and of assuming that all of them were in general agreement with United States policy. This generalization, always an oversimplification, broke down as a result of the Korean struggle. Serious rifts were caused in what had seemed in 1950 to be an unbroken front against the Soviet Union.

The end of the war, furthermore, brought no settlement. The major point had been made that communist expansion by force would be resisted. This was really all that could be proved by containment. In these terms the Korean effort of the United States was a success.

But in a larger sense the issue of Korea epitomized the dilemma of the cold war. The Soviet was seeking to expand the frontier of the communist world; the United States was dedicated to frustrating this policy. Once both sides had committed their power, an inconclusive quarrel ended by mutual consent was inevitable, at least if neither side was interested in total war. Neither dared go further without risking too much; by the same token, neither could conveniently retreat. Diplomacy could discover a point of rough equilibrium at which to stop, but it could not dispose of the issues.

BIPOLARITY IN DECLINE, 1954–1960

The six years that followed the Geneva Conference of 1954 saw bipolarity lose most of its value as a guide to foreign-policy decision by the cold-war antagonists and as a base for the analysis of international politics. The political world escaped from its two-power vise during the latter years of the 1950's, even though the full significance of this development was not grasped until the next decade.

CHARACTERISTICS OF THE PERIOD. The most important and portentous characteristic of the period was the rapid rebirth of flexibility in world politics. Not only did the approaches of the United States and the Soviet Union to each other undergo major decreases in militancy, but the entire context of world politics changed as well.

Two parallel developments underscored this trend. First, it was not until after 1955 that any appreciable number of new states was born out of the decaying colonial empires and appeared on the world scene as active and assertive participants; some twenty-five new states made their appearance between 1954 and 1960. Second, and related to the first, during the 1954–1960 period "neutralism," or "nonalignment," in the cold war became an intrinsically respectable position in world affairs and the accepted posture of almost all the new states. By 1960 the original bipolar concept dividing the world into two camps had become no more than an historic anachronism.

Connected also to the fact of new participants in world politics was the rise of new issues that could no longer be fitted into a bipolar context. Anti-colonialism, technical and development assistance, radical change in the United Nations, and a number of other problems which we shall discuss in the next chapter simply defied formulation in simplistic cold-war terms. Both the antagonists were hard put to develop the new approaches these issues demanded.

The splits in the alliance structures, already foreshadowed in earlier periods, began to make themselves openly felt in this phase. It was the United States that felt the pressure most directly at first; Soviet mono-lithism made it possible for the Kremlin to conceal somewhat longer the rifts that were developing in its own camp. But with the stalemate of the cold war so obvious to all concerned, it was simply too much to expect that the minor allies would indefinitely put off their own concerns in favor of the protracted maintenance of an undesirable status quo.

As a result of these factors, both the United States and the Soviet Union found it necessary to make major modifications in their policies—all the while insisting that no such changes had been made. The United States was forced to deal with tensions within its own camp, to develop responsive and realistic approaches to the growing group of neutrals, and to undertake tentative feelers toward Moscow. On its part, the Soviet Union espoused a "soft" approach, seeking to win support and friends within the uncommitted world, to split the Western alliance by honeyed words, and to market "competitive coexistence" as the formula for stabilized relations with the United States.[27] Although no concrete results were obtained, the peaks of this effort to restructure great-power relations were the Geneva summit of 1955 and Premier Khrushchev's visit to the United States in 1959.

The fact that the period ended in a bitter fiasco, the collapse of the 1960 summit conference in the wake of the U-2 crisis, did not obscure the conclusion that the bipolar cold war was finally abandoned during this period. After 1960, it was a matter of great importance to both sides to find some new basis for their relations.

HUNGARY AND SUEZ. Summing up the dilemma of the bipolar enemies were the twin crises of 1956, the Hungarian rebellion and the Anglo-French-Israeli invasion of the Suez Canal Zone. Beyond the fact of their simultaneity, the two affairs were tied together by a single conceptual thread: Both were attempts by minor allies to pursue their own interests in defiance of their leaders' wishes, and both required the use of coercion to hold the alliance in minimally tolerable unity.

---

[27]See Crankshaw, *Khrushchev's Russia,* and the present author's *The Cold War . . . and After,* p. 51.

Again, it is not our purpose to analyze either issue in detail.[28] Suffice it to say that each leader was able in the immediate event to put down the rebellion against its leadership. The Soviet used naked force to destroy the Hungarian rebels, whereas the United States called into being a non-Western majority of the United Nations effectively to put down the Suez invasion. Yet, in the aftermath, both lost more than they won.

Each has suffered a continuing loss in its capacity to lead its own group; since 1956 each has found itself obliged to court, to woo, and to cajole the very allies it once could control. The major casualty of the crises, however, was the concept of bipolarity itself. Once it had been admitted that minor allies had interests of their own to which major states must defer, the illusion of a single-issue world conflict was dispelled for all time. Although Hungary and Suez took place relatively early in the period, in all important ways the crises symbolized the entire era. After 1956 bipolarity dissolved at an even more rapid rate than previously.

BIPOLARITY ABANDONED, 1960-

The contemporary phase of the cold war, which we date from the failure of the Paris summit in 1960 but which really opened with the inauguration of John F. Kennedy as President in 1961, has been marked by the abandonment of the bipolar construct in Soviet-American relations. Moscow and Washington, through crisis and relaxation alike, are seeking somehow to develop a meaningful and useful direct relationship to each other in a context which is less cosmic than that of bipolarity and more hopeful because it is more realistic. No one knows today where this effort will lead. All can be certain, however, of its importance and its relevance.

CHARACTERISTICS OF THE PERIOD. From the point of view of the United States and the Soviet Union, international politics in the 1960's has seen the continuation, the intensification, and in some ways the fruition of the major trends of the later years of the 1950's.

Each state has seen, for example, the continued erosion of its own alliance structure.[29] The United States has been forced to witness the weakening of its mutual-defense systems in Asia, the Middle East, Latin America, and even

---

[28]For a discussion of the 1956 Hungarian revolt, see Paul E. Zinner, *Revolution in Hungary* (New York: Columbia University Press, 1962), and Ferenc A. Vali, *Rift and Revolt in Hungary* (New York: Harper & Row, Publishers, 1961). On the Suez crisis, see A. J. Barker, *Suez: The Seven-Day War* (London: Faber & Faber, Ltd., 1964), and Herman Finer, *Dulles Over Suez* (Chicago: Quadrangle Books, Inc., 1964).

[29]On polycentrism East and West, see Steel, *The End of Alliance* and Laqueur and Labedz, eds., *Polycentrism*.

in Europe. The Soviet Union has not only drifted into an all-but-open break with its erstwhile key ally, China, but has suffered ignominious defiance from several of its eastern European satellites. Neither can any longer assume that it leads a unified and homogeneous bloc in world affairs; instead each spends more and more of its time in coping with increasingly recalcitrant junior associates.

The 1960's have also seen an acceleration in the rate at which new states—most of them located in the non-Western world—have insisted on playing major parts on the world scene. Most conspicuous, of course, have been several of the young states of sub-Sahara Africa who have moved from colonial status to freewheeling participation in important questions in a matter of only a few months. Neither Moscow nor Washington has yet developed a satisfactory attack upon the problem of the new states.[30]

Even more ominously, both giants are now menaced by rival candidates for leadership within their own camps. The Soviet Union has had no success at all in reconciling its tangled relations with Communist China; the latter is today an open competitor and a frequent adversary of the Soviet. The United States has had corresponding difficulties with the Fifth Republic of France, led by President Charles de Gaulle. France now is attempting to reclaim its ancient heritage of leadership, at least in Europe, and is also seeking a world role at least comparable with that of the United States, the Soviet Union, and China.

Another rival to great-power hegemony in the contemporary era is the United Nations. Largely at the instigation of the new states of the non-West, the General Assembly of the United Nations has taken advantage of great-power stalemate to play a major role in a number of important issues. "Peacekeeping" by the United Nations, a technique invented during the Suez crisis in 1956 and featuring small-state military forces that act under United Nations auspices, represents a far cry from the global role once envisaged for the major states. The United Nations must be accepted as a force minimizing the effective span of control of the former bipolar leaders.

Further complicating the Soviet-American controversy has been the lack of decisive advantage of one over the other. The arms race, the space race, the prestige race, the economic-growth race, and all the other dimensions of competition that have been advanced as surrogates for open political and military conflict have produced much activity but few results. Neither is able effectively to score victories over the other, and the permanence of stalemate seems self-evident.

---

[30]For the problems engendered by the emergence of the new states, see Thomas P. Thornton, ed., *The Third World in Soviet Perspective* (Princeton, N.J.: Princeton University Press, 1964), and C. L. Sulzberger, *Unfinished Revolution: America and the Third World* (New York: Atheneum Publishers, 1965).

THE BERLIN WALL AND THE MISSILE CRISIS. It is in such a context that the two great Soviet-American crises of the 1960's—the Berlin wall in 1961 and the Cuban missile crisis in 1962—must be placed. Although at one level it may be argued that Moscow and Washington drifted closer to Armageddon during these two affairs than ever before, it is also obvious that both sides maintained the strictest possible control over their commitments and that both accepted something less than full satisfaction from each crisis as an adequate reward.

In the Berlin case,[31] Moscow forced the United States to acquiesce in the erection of the wall but failed to bring about any change in the status of West Berlin; the United States established the principle that it would not be forced out of Berlin but did not push its putative "rights" in the eastern part of the city. The grim spectacle of Soviet and American tanks facing each other across the wall frightened people throughout the world, but it was also an eloquent symbol of how far each side dared to go in bringing pressure on the other.

The Cuban missile crisis, so vivid to Americans because of the physical proximity of the crucial area, was cut from the same conceptual and operational cloth. Even though the rhetoric of total war flew freely during the critical two weeks of October, 1962,[32] in retrospect we can see again that both Moscow and Washington were anxious to avoid a final "showdown" and were eager to discover a mutually acceptable formula for backing away from each other. The United States claimed a victory in Cuba, since Khrushchev "backed down"; the Soviet Union could claim both that its actions preserved world peace (which, in a highly technical sense, they did) and that the upshot of the affair left Soviet influence in Cuba unimpaired.

So the two crises established the point that the major powers had really very little freedom of action in pursuing their quarrel. Another aspect of these questions, however, merits a brief comment: Through both Berlin and Cuba, the two great powers dealt directly with each other.[33] Although the facade of intraalliance consultation was maintained, in essence these two crises were bilateral Soviet-American matters. Thus we can contend that the major impact of Berlin and Cuba was to reinforce the tendency (already present in both governments) to explore their future relations privately and directly, free of many of the appurtenances of bipolarity that had by now grown so burdensome.

---

[31]For a chronology of events leading to the construction of the wall, see *The New York Times* (July-August, 1961).

[32]For the major statements and President Kennedy's address to the nation on the crisis, see *The New York Times* (October 1–18, 1962).

[33]This tendency has since been made strikingly apparent through the installation of the Moscow-Washington "hot line."

A NEW CONTEXT FOR SOVIET-AMERICAN RELATIONS

Since the Cuban missile crisis, indeed, we can discover an evolving context of Soviet-American relations that is dramatically different from that of the fifteen years preceding 1962. Neither side has yet come to the point of openly admitting that it has in any real sense abandoned the formulas upon which it has long based its approach to the other, but the actions of the two states belie their continuously militant words. After two decades of struggle—two decades that we have seen to be marked by continual evolution—Soviet-American relations are slowly moving toward a new basis.

NEW PERCEPTIONS OF THE SOVIET. The first great step of the United States in this direction came only some seven months after the Cuban missile crisis. In June, 1963, President John F. Kennedy's speech at American University called upon the American people to take a "fresh look" at the Soviet-American conflict. He argued that if such a fresh look were in fact taken, Americans would realize that the conditions of the great confrontation had changed so drastically as to require major reassessment of American policy.

In the few months that remained to him, the President did what he could to move the United States along such a new tack. In this effort he was tacitly joined by the Soviet leadership. The change of administrations that occurred in the United States in November—and the change in Soviet leadership that took place a year later with Khrushchev's ouster—slowed down but did not arrest the process of rethinking that was obviously going on in both capitals.

THE RISE OF COMMON INTERESTS. The "fresh look" at Soviet-American relations of which President Kennedy spoke produced one immediate and moderately startling result: It was discovered among Americans that they shared a number of important interests with the Soviet Union. Only upon such a basis could a new relationship be built.

The leading common interest uniting the two states was, of course, the desire to avoid nuclear war. As the two most powerful states in the world, they had the most to lose by holocaust. An immediate consequence of the new approach, for example, was the negotiation in the summer of 1963 of the limited nuclear test-ban treaty[34]—a document that was unprecedently thrown open to signature by all states in the world.

But other interests tied Moscow to Washington and vice versa. It was apparent by the 1960's, for example, that the degree of control each individually—or both together—exercised over world affairs was slipping badly as long as their relationship was one of complete opposition. What could

---

[34]For the text of the treaty, see *The New York Times* (July 26, 1963).

not be brought about by conflict, however, might at least partially be recouped by joint action. In the non-Western world, in the United Nations, in such questions as arms control and development assistance, the possibility of a common Soviet-American policy opened horizons of a possible restoration of something like the situation of the early 1950's when all important decisions were made either in Moscow or Washington.

Both, also, had an inherent interest in turning back the challenges of their new rivals, China and France. Great-power status, to be valuable, cannot be shared widely; neither the United States nor the Soviet Union saw any attraction in the devolution of a two-power world into one of three, four, or even more major states. Again, it seemed probable that only joint action might suffice to hold back these threats.

THE BEGINNINGS OF DETENTE. And so since 1962 the Soviet Union and the United States have been grappling, hesitantly and up to the present moment ineffectually, with the problem of dismantling their struggle without causing major upheavals throughout the political world. We must admit that no major breakthroughs in the form of solutions to long-standing problems have been achieved to date; but since intent is always the precursor of action, it is of major significance that both sides are grimly determined not to permit the progress they have made—little though it may be—to be lost and also to keep open the doors to further advance.

It is remarkable, for example, that even during the most critical early days of American entry into the war in Vietnam, the Soviet Union went to great lengths not to overstate its objections to American policy and constantly to evoke the images of "good and friendly relations" as a spur to its efforts to bring about a change in the American posture. Nor, as a matter of fact, did the United States fall into the trap of any indiscriminate condemnation of "communism" as the enemy in Southeast Asia; Washington was explicit that it was "Chinese imperialism" against which it was fighting and expressed hope that the Soviet Union would join it in its programs for rehabilitation and development in Vietnam after the fighting ended. Of such gossamer threads was the early Soviet-American détente made; but no serious student should overlook their importance, especially when he realizes how far such restraint is removed from the early rhetoric of a total, bipolar cold war.

PART IV

CONTINUING ISSUES
IN AMERICAN POLICY

CHAPTER **9**

Continuing
Political Issues in
American Policy

Within American foreign policy today there are a number of "continuing issues." These are problems stemming from the general policy line the United States has been pursuing that are peculiar in that they do not seem to permit of any final resolution. Each has been met often within the context of a given set of circumstances, but each change in the situational milieu has required that new answers be given to the old questions. Because they promise to be of long duration, we would profit by discussing at least the most important of these continuing issues.

As we take them up in this section of our study, we will break them down into four functional areas, corresponding roughly to the four channels by way of which states usually execute their policies: the political (or diplomatic) area, the military area, the economic area, and the psychological area. This chapter deals exclusively with issues of a political import; there follows one devoted to each of the other three. These classifications are valid primarily as convenient foci of discussion. In practice the political, military, economic, and psychological dimensions of foreign policy blend into one another and form component parts of a single operational entity.

In this chapter we shall examine four diplomatic-political areas of continuing and fundamental concern to the overall structure of American policy. Each represents a significant complex of issues;

each has great relevance to American action in other areas, both geographic and functional; each has had a variety of answers recommended and, in some cases, attempted. The four we have selected are the issues (1) of American relations with the great powers, (2) of American relations with the free-world alliance, (3) of American relations with international organization, and (4) of American policy toward the smaller states generally and toward the issue of anticolonialism specifically.

The United States and the Great Powers

By the "great powers" in the world of the 1960's we mean (in addition to the United States) the Soviet Union, China, France, and Great Britain. This is a much longer list than we would have drawn up during the latter years of the 1940's, when only the United States and the Soviet would have qualified. We would also have constructed a somewhat different list during the middle 1950's; at that time France was not included, but India would have been. The rise of de Gaulle's France and the relative diminution of India's world role both illustrate the dynamic ups and downs of contemporary world politics.

These few states constitute the contemporary elite of the world political system, and American relations with the group as a whole and with each of its fellows individually are obviously critical. The political issues raised in this area are the key to many other problems.

THE FUTURE OF AMERICAN-SOVIET RELATIONS

No one can envisage any possible situation—barring the total eclipse of civilization in the wake of a general war—in which the United States and the Soviet Union would not remain the two most powerful states in the world. If this be so, it follows that Soviet-American relations will continue to be the bedrock of American policy, as they have been since 1945. There has been surprisingly little inclination in the United States to consider the long-term future of Soviet-American relations; as American experience accumulates, however, a greater sensitivity toward the necessity of such speculation seems to be dawning.

THE "FRESH LOOK."   In the closing pages of the preceding chapter, we noted that the United States, following the lead of President Kennedy, has begun to take a "fresh look" at the Soviet Union and that this reevaluation at least held out the promise of some new policies. Although it is very risky to predict the final outcome of an ongoing trend, we may nonetheless suggest a few of the directions in which American thinking has been tending.

As we pointed out earlier, the United States has already rejected (in fact, if not yet in word) both ideological and operational bipolarity as conceptual bases for its policy approach to the Soviet Union. A total noncommunity and hostility of interest have not only proved to be extremely difficult to implement in practice but such a dichotomy has also served too long to obscure the requirements of effective action in many areas.

Instead, the United States has begun to appreciate the force of the logic of great-power status in an unstable world. World leadership demands that common interests with the Soviet be postulated as possible (not to say desirable), that they be explored in a nonideological context, and that parallel—if not common or joint—policies be undertaken by the two great states on as many important matters as possible. Thus Soviet-American relations may well be on the brink of a new and very different phase. Whether or not such a development materializes depends primarily on the Soviet Union and its leadership.

"COMPETITIVE COEXISTENCE." The Soviet Union has for more than a decade contended that the only possible formula for the permanent resolution of the cold war is "competitive coexistence." This is a phrase of notoriously elastic meaning, but in all its several manifestations it incorporates two related points: (1) The Soviet-American struggle will continue indefinitely, but (2) it should never be permitted to escalate out of control.[1]

Thus "competitive coexistence" leaves the Soviet-American conflict untouched in concept but drastically modified in content and implementation. There is indeed little left of the original militancy of Soviet ideology—whatever its semantics—if its advocates admit that they intend to pursue their Marxist Utopia only within narrowly circumscribed limits of safety—limits, furthermore, that grow steadily narrower. Revolution, we are tempted to observe, is not accomplished by men whose dominant characteristic is prudence.

Many Americans, however, have found and still find today that "competitive coexistence" is an unpalatable and unacceptable formula. Instead they demand from the Soviet rulers nothing less than a formal repudiation of their cherished dogma and the abandonment of the major lines of Soviet policy since 1945.[2] Such a position may be ideologically symmetrical and emotionally satisfying, but it makes any realistic improvement in Soviet-American relations impossible. Moscow, whatever its ideological mutations, is less disposed today than in 1945 to surrender its hard-won world position and to submit to an American blueprint for peace. Any further accommodation of Soviet and American politics must take place in an extraideological context.

---

[1] See former Premier Khrushchev's attempt to define the concept in his article, "On Peaceful Coexistence," *Foreign Affairs* (October, 1959).

[2] See, for example, Strausz-Hupé, *et al.*, *Protracted Conflict*.

In spite of the questionable origin of the phrase, there are no rational grounds for an American rejection of "competitive coexistence" as either an unattainable ideal or as a concealed Soviet plot to "lull" the United States into false confidence. It is, after all, no more than a truism that underscores the stark dilemma of the bipolar powers: Real peace between the two states is unattainable in the foreseeable future, but real war is politically idiotic. What practical course lies open to either except to continue their dispute while at the same time seeking in every way possible to strengthen and fortify the parameters of safety? This line of attack has seemed inescapable to both governments.

THE DANGER OF EXPLOSION.   Yet the great change in the climate of Soviet-American relations that has already taken place and the regularization of relations that we are forecasting here should not blind us to the ever-present danger of explosion and catastrophe. The bipolar cold war offered a number of operational advantages to both sides, not the least of which was its relatively high level of stability. Each side knew quite well where the other stood and where it was likely to go. Once the well-established framework of cold-war semantics, policies, programs, and institutions begins to be dismantled to any significant extent, major instabilities in world affairs will become endemic.

Rapid transitions are always potentially dangerous, as unfamiliar situations force difficult and unprecedented decisions on statesmen. Here the risks of miscalculation are multiplied; here excesses of either optimism or pessimism, confidence or fear, may well tempt one state or the other to attempt too much or to hold back from a step which is vital. The resulting holocaust would be no less awful because it had been accidental.

So the changes in Soviet-American relations that we project here will probably come slowly, will begin (or, rather, have already begun) on the periphery of the struggle rather than with important issues, and will have a clearly ambivalent effect. They will frustrate those who want more rapid change as much as they will frighten those who oppose any relaxation at all. Bringing about major modification in Soviet-American relations is not a simple task, but it is a necessary one. Both states are well launched on the effort.[3]

BRITAIN AND THE UNITED STATES

Anglo-American relations have been the core of affirmative American policy since the end of World War II. Despite some inescapable controversy and considerable misunderstanding, the problems of American policy toward

---

[3]See Amitai Etzioni, *Winning Without War* (Garden City, N.Y.: Doubleday & Company, Inc., 1964).

Britain have been matters more of detail than of fundamental orientation. Agreement on basic premises is as great as can ever be the case between two major states, and prospects for any different basis of relationships are remote.[4]

BRITAIN: THE KEY ALLY. From the moment that the United States began to implement its postwar policy decisions, Britain has been its key ally. A high degree of coincidence of interest, both in general terms and on a remarkably large number of specifics, has resulted in a long series of joint policy moves and a group of more elaborate collaborative enterprises. In the network of American alliances, Britain has bulked large. The United States has resisted all Soviet invitations to negotiate directly with Moscow on most questions of interest to Britain. In the United Nations close Anglo-American cooperation has been the normal practice, whether in the Security Council, the General Assembly, or any other organs. In the fields of technical assistance, of military and economic aid, and of propaganda, British cooperation has given American policy an extra impact. Recent diplomatic history provides few such impressive examples of close and mutually satisfactory relations between allies in time of peace, considering that both states play the role of "great power" to the hilt.

ANGLO-AMERICAN DISPUTES. The closeness of Anglo-American relations has been affected to some significant—although minor—extent by a series of annoying disagreements. These have been most apparent when open breaks between the allies have taken place (the most serious was American opposition to Britain's invasion of the Suez Canal Zone in 1956), but there has been a constant undercurrent of tension that has colored relations when it has not directly controlled them.

These conflicts between Britain and the United States grow out of causes both general and specific. Perhaps most fundamental is the inevitable stress caused by the great disparity in power between the two states. For Britons, long accustomed to considering themselves as citizens of the world's leading power, to take second place to a young and inexperienced America has been difficult.[5] Anti-Americanism has complicated the partnership from its very outset. We must also admit that American attitudes have often not been calculated to soothe outraged British sensibilities, and frequently Anglo-American controversy has been a matter of embattled nationalisms nagging at each other.

---

[4]From among the many studies of Anglo-American relations, we may suggest Henry L. Roberts and Paul Wilson, *Britain and the United States* (New York: Harper & Row, Publishers, 1953) and Leon Epstein, *Britain: Uneasy Ally* (Chicago: University of Chicago Press, 1954).

[5]Britain's dependence upon the United States was embarrassingly highlighted when, late in 1962, the "Nassau accords" forced Britain to abandon its hoped-for independent nuclear deterrent in favor of arrangements that made London a "nuclear satellite" of Washington. See, for example, Kissinger, *The Troubled Partnership*, esp. Chap. 3; see also Joint Communiqué on Nuclear Defense Systems, *Department of State Bulletin* (January 14, 1963), pp. 44–45.

On a number of issues of considerable importance to the United States, furthermore, significant differences exist with Great Britain. London recognized Communist China many years ago and has consistently supported Peking's annual attempts to gain admission to the United Nations. Britain shows much more reserve toward the aspirations of West Germany than American policy thinks appropriate. Britain's Middle East role is frequently condemned as opportunistic. More generally, the United States consistently disparages any British attempts to play a lone hand in world affairs—that is, to act on a major question without consultation and coordination with the United States.

MAINTAINING THE TIE. Anglo-American controversy is always fuel for headlines on both sides of the Atlantic; the question is deeply involved in domestic politics in both nations, and each frequently finds in the other a convenient scapegoat for its own frustrations. Yet there is little possibility that the working agreement or the harmony of interest between the two states might dissolve. Both are status-quo powers; both recognize the need for substantive change in many world relationships if stability is ever to be attained; both insist that the necessary change be peaceful. Real disagreement arises only from the differing specifications each has for what would be an optimum solution to its own problems. The identity of purpose, however, is sufficiently great that each has ample room in which to adjust its differences in behalf of maintaining the tie that is so profitable and so necessary for both. Anglo-American relations will never be idyllic, but they will probably continue to be largely harmonious and cooperative. "Anti-Americanism" and anglophobia alike cannot affect a real coincidence of interest.

FRANCO-AMERICAN RELATIONS

Of all the perplexities of the 1960's, the one that has come to the American people with the greatest sense of shock has been the rapid deterioration in relations with France. Once identified as the "keystone of Western defense,"[6] in the few short years following the return to power of Charles de Gaulle in 1958 France has become an open rival of the United States in many parts of the world and a direct opponent on some critical issues. American policy, while admitting the urgency of the situation, has been at a loss to cope with it.

THE FRANCO-AMERICAN ALLIANCE. The United States came to France's rescue in both world wars. France and America, therefore, have a long history and great experience in cooperation. It was thus both expedient and simple for them to associate closely in the postwar world. France became one of the

---

[6]Edgar S. Furniss, Jr., *France: Keystone of Western Defense* (Garden City, N.Y.: Doubleday & Company, Inc., 1954).

inner circle of the free world as soon as the United States began to organize its sphere.

Almost from the beginning, however, France sought to make clear that it found unacceptable the major portions of the American theory of the alliance. American claims to political and military "leadership" were questioned; we shall examine this issue in the next section of this chapter. France, furthermore, felt throughout the 1950's that its own interests were not receiving adequate attention from the United States and that the American image of a free world unified in task and structure was simply unrealistic.

From the American point of view, France's importance as an ally was not matched by its cooperativeness. Paris refused to meet its military commitments, did not maintain an adequately solid front vis-à-vis the Soviet Union, and showed a disconcerting tendency to prefer its own parochial, imperial, and regional concerns to the global struggle against communism.

THE PROBLEM OF STATUS. At bottom, Franco-American relations have been plagued by an issue of status. To the United States, the natural relationship between Washington and Paris is one of leader and follower; to France it is one between equals dealing with each other in a climate of mutual respect. To the United States, the postwar power disparity between the two states is to be permanent and normal, whereas to France it has always been no more than a temporary embarrassment, to be eliminated as early as possible. As long as the bipolar cold war forced an approximation of unanimity on the free world, France's claims could be safely ignored. The renaissance of flexibility, however—symbolized, as we recall, by the Suez Canal crisis in 1956—gave Paris its opportunity. Two years after Suez, de Gaulle had come to power and France was off on its renewed pursuit of greatness.

DE GAULLE AND THE UNITED STATES. President de Gaulle sees France as a world power, with its own interests and its own policies. As a result he rejects American leadership as well as the bulk of the substance of American policy. He seeks the elimination of direct American influence in Europe and prefers his own formula for further integration of the continent to that supported by Washington. He demands the major overhaul of the Atlantic alliance away from the concept of integration and threatens to withdraw if he does not have his way. He has repeatedly defied the United States on United Nations matters, on Communist China, on the war in Vietnam, on colonial issues, and—most exasperating for the United States—on nuclear weapons. He has even had the temerity to challenge American hegemony in Latin America.

What de Gaulle's France is seeking from the United States may be stated simply: It is that most difficult of all concessions, complete equality of status and deference. Paris insists today that France will deal with the United States only as a full sovereign, including total freedom in military and political affairs. All of this, of course, the United States finds unacceptable, since the adoption of de Gaulle's formula would not only destroy much that the United States has painfully built in Europe and elsewhere but would also encourage other allies to attempt the same thing.

A POSSIBLE COMPROMISE. France and America, it goes without saying, need each other. The relations between them cannot and will not be permitted to deteriorate to the breaking point. Their present positions, however, are irreconcilable, and any salvaging must involve some modification on both sides. The United States cannot keep France forever subordinate, nor can France ever make good its claim to complete equality. Both parties, therefore, must relax their protestations and actively seek the common interests upon which to build a new relationship.[7]

THE PROBLEM OF COMMUNIST CHINA

Chinese affairs, long a concern of the United States, acquired a new dimension after 1949. The problem of China has had three novel features since that date. First, China is now free from (at least Western) tutelage and is aggressively prosecuting its own foreign policy. Second, China is a communist state and constitutes the most populous unit in the camp hostile to the United States. Third, China is openly revisionist, seeking in a variety of ways to improve its international position. American policy has been slow to devise a strategy adequate to cope with this new Chinese political dynamism.[8]

THE FIRST DECADE. The base of American policy toward China after 1949 was a determination not to accept the fact of communist domination of the mainland. The United States withheld recognition of the Peking regime, blocked communist representation of China in the United Nations, and openly supported Chiang Kai-shek's regime on Taiwan. In general American action toward the Peking government seemed built on the premise that Mao's victory was only a temporary interruption in the rightful occupation of power by the Kuomintang. Open American combat against Chinese "volunteers" in Korea and Peking's provocative and belligerent behavior subsequently hardened American determination not to yield an inch to the communists either in principle or in practice.

Throughout the latter half of the 1950's, the United States remained stalled on dead center in its relations with China. Despite a widespread American realization that some regularization of relationships would be

---

[7]See, for example, the rather back-door approach taken in Kissinger, *The Troubled Partnership*, esp. Chap. 2.

[8]See, for example, Robert A. Scalapino, *The Communist Revolution in Asia* (Englewood Cliffs, N.J.: Prentice-Hall, Inc., 1965); Russel H. Fifield, *Southeast Asia in United States Policy* (New York: Frederick A. Praeger, Inc., 1963); and Willard L. Thorp, ed., *The United States and the Far East* (Englewood Cliffs, N.J.: Prentice-Hall, Inc., 1962).

desirable, no satisfactory terms could be arrived at and no favorable opportunities for action appeared. Negotiations with Peking, carried on intermittently throughout the period, were fruitless; Mao Tse-tung and his associates appeared determined to maintain relations at the maximum bearable tension. Aggravating the situation was the recurrent danger of open war with China if Peking set out to seize the American-protected island territories of the Kuomintang regime.

THE SINO-SOVIET SPLIT. Throughout the 1950's the United States accepted the thesis of the monolithic character of communism and viewed China as little more than the largest satellite of the Soviet Union. In fact, Washington once went so far as to hold Moscow "responsible" for Chinese actions.[9] The growing rift between the two communist giants after 1960, however, destroyed this simplifying postulate and brought new complications to American policymakers.

From a strategic point of view, two aspects of the split were especially important to the United States. First, China rejected "competitive coexistence" and insisted instead on a fundamentalist doctrine of activism, revolution, and war as the only route to Leninist perfection. Second, China developed an active world policy of its own in clear defiance of Soviet wishes, not only becoming dangerously aggressive along its southern and southwestern frontiers but also setting itself up as a rival to Moscow and Washington in many parts of the world.

The cleavage in the communist world—quickly dubbed "polycentrism" by the experts—forced difficult and unpleasant judgments on the United States. Is the split on balance advantageous, perilous, or irrelevant to Washington? Dare the United States hope for Soviet support against China, or even vice versa? Should the United States relax or intensify its pressure on Moscow, particularly since China has begun to accuse the Soviet of being secretly in collusion with America? Is it in the interest of the United States to have Soviet influence weakened within the world communist movement? To none of these questions has the United States yet discovered a persuasive answer, nor have any major modifications in policy been attempted as a result.[10]

---

[9]See the statement of John Foster Dulles which implies some sort of overall control linking all members of the Sino-Soviet bloc: "I doubt that Communist China is a satellite country in the same sense, or the same degree, that the East European satellites are. I would say that there is perhaps this difference: I think that both the Soviet Union and Communist China are under the domination of what might be called international communism. I believe that the countries of Eastern Europe that we call the satellites are, you might say, in addition under the domination of the Soviet Union as a state, and in that respect there is perhaps a difference." News Conference of April 23, 1957, *Department of State Bulletin*, XXXVI, No. 933 (May 13, 1957), 768.

[10]See, for example, Dean Rusk, "Unfinished Business," *Department of State Bulletin*, XLIX, No. 1266 (September 30, 1963), 493, in which the Secretary states: "I have repeatedly emphasized that we should not take comfort from that . . . break. It eliminates none of the dangers that hang over us and makes none of our immediate tasks appreciably easier."

AMERICAN-CHINESE HOSTILITY.   The entry of the United States into the war in Vietnam has made official what has long been an implicit assumption of American policy. The United States is now openly committed to "stop China." Americans generally agreed at the time that the nation's real enemy in Vietnam was China and that the frustration of Peking's aggressive designs was their primary purpose. It has become a commonplace in America, furthermore, that China is in fact a greater danger to world peace than the Soviet Union and that the cold war is now primarily an Asian matter.

EROSION OF A POLICY.   It was, therefore, all the more disheartening to Americans to realize during the 1960's that their increased determination to oppose China's policy was not being matched by their allies. On the contrary: The more the United States stiffened its position, the fewer of its allies agreed. In Vietnam, for example, the United States not only had no European allies but faced a chorus of condemnation from most of its NATO partners.

Even on an issue of great symbolic importance to all Americans, the nonadmission of Communist China to the United Nations, the United States position was slipping steadily. After a number of years of dwindling majorities in favor of rejecting Peking, in 1965 the American margin disappeared completely in a tie vote that maintained China's exclusion for another year but was a shattering prestige defeat for the United States.[11] Included among those voting against the United States were both Britain and France.

By the mid-1960's it was obvious that the long-established American policy toward China had run dry of result. Any new direction, however, was difficult to justify. The advocates of relaxation were bemused by the fact of Chinese aggression and a pronounced stiffening of Peking's attitude toward the United States; those who argued for a harder line, on the other hand, could point to no logical outcome of their policy except a major war with a China newly arrived at nuclear status. The problem of Communist China was no nearer solution in 1966 than it had been a decade and a half earlier.

American-Allied Relations

Having to maintain relationships with more than forty allies in time of peace is a completely novel experience for the United States. "Allies" traditionally are a by-product of war; when the United States has been at peace American tradition has insisted on the working minimum of fixed commitments. The cold war, however, forced the United States to accept the leadership of a massive coalition for the prosecution of free-world policy. This new

---

[11]On November 17, 1965, the General Assembly vote on the question of Communist Chinese admission was 47 to 47, with twenty nations abstaining and three nations not voting. See *The New York Times* (November 18, 1965).

posture has required that Americans accustom themselves to the peculiar requirements of policies framed and executed within a multistate context. Problems both of theory and of practice have grown out of this situation, and the subject of American-allied relations is one which the United States has yet to resolve satisfactorily and one which is growing more acute.

AMERICAN THEORIES OF ALLIANCE

THE MYTH OF THE "FREE WORLD." The basic bipolar assumption of American policy after 1947 contributed to the development of what we might call the "myth of the free world." Americans tended to assume that the world consisted of two groups of states, the communist and the noncommunist blocs, the one led by Moscow and the other by Washington. If every state in the world were on one side or the other, and if the dividing line between them was the choice between freedom and communism, it was then only a short step to reason that all anticommunist states shared the same value system and the same general foreign-policy pattern.

This is the notion of the "free world." Americans seem to feel that the alliance of which their government is the leader is (or ought to be) a monolithic entity that opposes communist pretensions with a single purpose and a single effort. United States policy often purports to speak for all its allies on a great variety of questions, and the revelation of intraalliance disagreement often throws much of American public opinion and leadership into a strange catalepsy. Americans are fond of the shibboleth of "the unity of the free world," a notion often more pervasive than relevant. The "free world" is a concept of great importance, but in practice it has demonstrated significant limitations as an analytical focus for policy.

Students of international affairs know that the Western alliance, like all alliances, is founded on coincidence of interest among its members and that it cannot be interpreted as covering any substantive or procedural points by sheer implication. Cooperation among the allies is ensured only in those areas of action for which ironclad agreements, embodying predetermined degrees of harmony, have been worked out. To assume that agreement on any single point implies agreement on any other point is not only to prepare the way for later disillusionment and disappointment but frequently also to weaken the working effectiveness of such alliances as exist.[12]

THE UNITED STATES: LEADER OR PARTNER? Equally important to the issue of American-allied relationships is the question of the role of the United States within the alliance pattern it has worked out. There is considerable

---

[12]This point is elaborately developed by George F. Kennan in *Realities of American Foreign Policy*, Chap. 2: "The Non-Soviet World."

disagreement among Americans and foreigners alike about the nature of American responsibility to its associates and the degree of authority the United States is to be permitted in committing other members to courses of action they may not wish to follow.

During the first two phases of the cold war, the United States followed the self-imposed path of leadership.[13] Both in the development of intraalliance relationships and in the common front presented to the Soviet world, American wishes were paramount. The weakened condition of many noncommunist states made it difficult and often impossible for them to resist American pressure, and a number of European, Asian, and Latin American countries were (as they saw it) coerced into accepting purely American formulas for the solution of joint problems. This tendency reached its height during the Korean war, when American militancy caused serious rifts in the Western alliance and forced India and its associates to break with the free world and to adopt a self-styled neutrality.

What caused considerable disquiet, even among the states most in agreement with the United States, was what American "leadership" of the alliance often meant in practice. Western Europe, particularly, harbored serious doubts about the wisdom and the skill of American policy-makers, and its leaders questioned the implicit (and sometimes explicit) claim that only the United States knew the right answers to the questions facing the free world.[14] The inclination among many Americans to regard any deviation from the American line as evidence either of a lack of moral fiber or of a half-concealed admiration for communism often irritated Europeans who considered themselves guilty of a no more reprehensible offense than that of differing with Washington over how to accomplish a particular objective. American leadership also showed a disconcerting tendency to interpret "Western" objectives in purely American terms and to assume (in a paraphrase of a statement attributed to then Secretary of Defense Charles E. Wilson) that "what is good for the United States is good for the free world." Some plaintive voices were even heard to inquire what in practice was the difference between Soviet satellitism and American leadership of its allies.

After about 1955, the United States changed to a "partnership" concept of alliance and placed greater emphasis on persuasion and adjustment as a means of securing allied unity. This "softer" approach, however, rapidly developed its own pattern of difficulties. Its implementation required the United States to accept rather extensive modifications of its own demands on the alliance as well as open disagreement and occasional defiance from its

---

[13]Reitzel, Kaplan, and Coblentz, *United States Foreign Policy, 1945–1955*, p. 492.

[14]Raymond Aron, *The Century of Total War* (Boston: Beacon Press, 1954), pp. 322–324. Mr. Aron, a distinguished French publicist, argued here that the real cause of Europe's resentment of American leadership was Europe's realization of its own weakness. See also Steel, *The End of Alliance*.

associates. Both of these results had unfortunate repercussions among the American people. Partnership to a critical observer often looked perilously like a lack of decision, a failure of will, or an unworthy search for popularity abroad. The American government, once it relaxed its efforts to enforce conformity from the other states of the free-world complex, was attacked by its own constituents for being too weak and by its allies for being yet too dominating.

The growth of neutralism, a predictable outcome of the partnership concept, brought down new torrents of criticism among Americans. As long as the United States was committed to avoiding coercion in its relations with the noncommunist states, it was obliged to accept the possibility that some of them would use their newly guaranteed freedom of action to develop independent courses. When this actually happened, objections were heard both from those who condemned the government for weakness in permitting the neutrals to stray and from those who argued that a more sympathetic American policy would have prevented any such deviation.

In the period since 1955, America's approach to the free world has swung between the poles of leadership and partnership without finding a satisfactory resting place. The result is that the United States is attacked alternately (and sometimes simultaneously) for being too strong or too weak in dealing with its allies. In the 1956 Suez crisis, for example, the United States was accused of attempted dictatorship over its associates; during the post-1957 space race, on the other hand, it was criticized for not offering the leadership the free world demanded. Whenever the United States conspicuously accedes to its allies' wishes, it is attacked at home and frequently abroad as well for lack of will and purpose; when it pushes its side of an intra-allied conflict with vigor, the same critics accuse it of insensitivity and bungling. No simple formula for happy interallied relationships exists. All the long quarrel really proves is that the major power's lot in a large coalition is seldom a satisfying one.[15]

TRANSITION AND CRISIS IN AMERICAN ALLIANCES

At its peak, the American alliance system numbered forty-four states tied in one way or another to the destiny of the United States. Throughout the 1950's these arrangements, especially the "regional security systems" of NATO, the OAS, SEATO, and CENTO, were viewed generally as the core of America's world policy and as monuments to the intelligence, determination, and perspicacity of the policy-makers who had created them. The concepts of

---

[15]For one set of interpretations of American-allied relationships, stressing military implications and the primacy of Europe among the various groups of allies, see Wolfers, ed., *Alliance Policy in the Cold War*.

free-world unity and American leadership were self-evident foundations of all joint action against communism.

Today, however, the system of alliances of which the nation was once so proud is in serious trouble. None of the relationships, whether bilateral or multilateral, is free from tension. Political disagreements impair military and psychological efficiency, and popular ill-feeling both within the United States and within the allied countries threatens to become worse instead of better.

Some of the causes for this unwelcome development are intrinsic in the nature of alliances themselves, whereas others can be traced more directly to the policies pursued by the members—especially to the policies of the United States. In any case, because the weakening of the alliance spheres of both the United States and the Soviet Union is obviously a part of the operational climate of the 1960's, some analysis of the state of American alliances today is appropriate at this point.

THE RELAXATION OF THE THREAT.   Alliances do not simply spring into being spontaneously; they are carefully constructed arrangements for joint action to meet a stipulated contingency. The free-world alliance was created to turn back the menace of Soviet aggression. The vitality of any such arrangement obviously depends upon the willingness of the members to cooperate voluntarily, which in turn is a function of a shared appreciation of the threat. Any alliance, in other words, is no more effective than the consensus among the members about the problem faced by all.

Rightly or wrongly, many—perhaps most—of the allies of the United States feel that the threat from the Soviet Union has significantly relaxed. Feeling less menaced than previously, they now find the tight bonds of alliance favored by the United States to be oppressive limitations instead of sources of protection. Throughout the several alliances, there is encountered today a recurrent protest against what is frequently called an American tendency to overexaggerate the danger.

THE PURSUIT OF NATIONAL INTEREST.   What the relaxation of the threat means to most of the allies is a greater opportunity to pursue their own interests instead of constantly having to subordinate themselves to the cold-war policies of the United States. This tendency was present as long ago as the mid-1950's, as was seen in the case of the Suez crisis. Since 1960 it has become widespread.

Leading examples of allies that seek their own satisfaction at the possible expense of the unity of the free world are France in NATO and SEATO, Pakistan in SEATO and CENTO, and Mexico in the OAS. But their examples are only moderately more pronounced than those of the bulk of their fellows. Everywhere, arguing that the inhibitions imposed by emergency conditions have been lifted, associates of the United States have begun to seek their own fortunes at the risk of displeasing Washington.

Their logic is simple: What really counts to them, in the final analysis, is the guarantee of their protection by American nuclear power. This assurance, furthermore, is realistically independent of any reciprocal pledges but remains effective regardless of whatever its beneficiaries might do, short of actually surrendering to communism. This, for example, is the position taken by France. As annoying as it may be to Americans, it must be admitted that the argument is extremely difficult to refute.

THE REVOLT AGAINST AMERICAN LEADERSHIP. The allies, in a word, are rebelling against the leadership of the United States in any area except the specialized (although important) one of military defense. The alliances themselves have become all but useless as instruments for the formulation of common stands in support of American arguments. They serve still, although to a decreasing extent, as vehicles of consultation and discussion among the members, but these negotiations are frequently marred by political tension and acrimonious debate.

In several alliances, there are powerful movements afoot today in favor of major reorganization. The general thrust of these efforts is toward the elimination of the privileged American position of "leadership" in favor of some less restrictive concept of "partnership," in which the United States would be only one (although perhaps first) among equals. Up to now, Washington has been able to fend off these attempts at the repudiation of its key role, but each year its task grows more difficult.

THE FUTURE OF THE ALLIANCE SYSTEM. Which way the alliance system of the United States evolves depends to a great extent upon the overall course of world politics and the nature of the American response. If flexibility becomes the dominant characteristic of the next era of political history, it seems inevitable that some major modification in the alliances will be necessary. The only real question will then be whether the United States will play a leading role in shaping the changes or whether it will only reluctantly accept those that are forced upon it. If, however, a recurrence of high tension and the possibility of nuclear war reintroduce a renewal of the bipolar era, the alliances will quickly revert to their original structure and dynamic.

The United States and International Organization

American attitudes and behavior toward international organization provide one of the most impressive and instructive contrasts with the period of the 1920's and 1930's. The rebirth of isolationism that followed World War I took its characteristic form from the spontaneous and consistent effort to avoid "entanglement" in the League of Nations system; for millions of Americans the League epitomized the devious world of diplomacy that they were seeking to shut out. Throughout the entire period since 1945, on the other hand, American commitment to the principle of international organization, though not total, remained consistently high, and the maintenance, strengthening, and employment of the United Nations endures as a cardinal procedural principle of American policy.

THE UNITED STATES AND THE UNITED NATIONS

THE UNITED NATIONS IDEA IN AMERICAN POLICY. The framers of the Charter knew better than anyone else that they were not drafting a constitution for a world government and that the United Nations could never be any more than a mechanism for the more efficient implementation of such will to cooperate as existed among the membership. The "United Nations idea" that made the organization such a hopeful portent was the hope that states generally would accept the principle that United Nations procedure was the type of action most conducive to permanent improvement of world relations; the goal was to funnel the great majority of all national policy moves through United Nations channels. The organs of the Charter were thought of as instruments for the harmonization of national interests rather than for the creation of entirely new policies.[16]

How has the United States reacted to the challenge of the "United Nations idea"? On balance, we may say that America has established a reasonably good record in acting through United Nations channels, but it is by no means an exceptional one. The major elements of postwar American policy have been executed both within the United Nations and outside it; the most important cold-war moves, such as the alliance system and economic assistance, have generally been independently executed. Washington has taken great care, however, to make all its actions square more or less directly with its obligations and privileges under the Charter.[17]

Th most spectacular single example of American reliance on United Nations procedures was, of course, the series of General Assembly resolutions in 1956 condemning Soviet behavior in Hungary and the Anglo-French-Israeli invasion of Egypt. Here, at a crucial moment in American policy, President Eisenhower placed American trust almost entirely in the mechanisms of international organization and—to the surprise of considerable

---

[16]See Daniel S. Cheever and H. Field Haviland, *Organizing for Peace* (Boston: Houghton Mifflin Company, 1954), Chap. 28: "The New Diplomacy and World Order."

[17]The mutual-security pacts of the United States, for example, make specific reference to the obligations of the parties under the Charter. See *Disarmament and Security: A Collection of Documents, 1919–1955* (Washington, D.C.: Government Printing Office, 1956), pp. 531, NATO; 599, Philippines treaty; 600–601, ANZUS; 607, Japanese treaty; 608–609, Formosa treaty; 612–613, SEATO; 650, Rio Pact. See also Bloomfield, *The United Nations and U.S. Foreign Policy.*

segments of American public opinion—discovered that at least in this case the essentials of American policy were adequately achieved. American popular reaction to this move reflected a major upsurge in public support of the United Nations.

Other leading examples of American reliance on the world organization have been furnished by Washington's support of a number of United Nations "peacekeeping" enterprises, most notably in the Congo after 1960. On the other hand, the United States (and the Soviet Union as well) has been very reluctant to permit United Nations participation in purely great-power issues, of which a prominent example is arms control.

THE UNITED NATIONS AS A TOOL. In general the attitude of the United States toward the United Nations has been the same as that shared by the other great powers. To a major state with global interests, extensive commitments, and a sensitive nationalism, the notion that all policy is to be executed in the chambers of the United Nations cannot help being considered somewhat naive. The characteristics of United Nations action—publicity, majority vote, the preponderance of small-state opinion, leisureliness, and the disavowal of other than collective force—often are felt to be overly constraining to great powers.

The normal view among the permanent members of the Security Council (who, with India, constitute the group of "major powers" in the organization) is that of considering the United Nations as a tool of national policy. Like any policy technique, on appropriate occasions its use is mandatory, at other times either expedient, immaterial, undesirable, or inimical. The decision by such a government whether or not to "go to the United Nations" is not based on any preference for such action in the abstract but upon the circumstances of the case and the nature of the objective sought.

These generalizations roughly characterize the American approach to the United Nations. It has been appropriate for the United States, as a status-quo state interested in stabilizing world relationships, to find working through the United Nations expedient a larger share of the time than would such revisionist states as the Soviet Union or Yugoslavia. But despite the relatively favorable record America has made compared with the USSR, many of the smaller states complain that American policy has often bypassed international action in behalf of unilateral procedures, in spite of such conspicuous instances as Suez, the Congo, and Cyprus.

In defense of American policy, it might be pointed out that the first twenty years of the world's experience with the United Nations have demonstrated that the organization has definite limits beyond which it has no usefulness. Constructed on the principle of great-power cooperation for peace, it has proved itself powerless to cope with the cold war in any but the most indirect ways. The United States was obliged to take direct action in prosecuting the anticommunist struggle simply because no effective means existed to act through the United Nations.

A good case could be made to the effect that significant portions of longer-range American planning (looking beyond the cold war) did take the United Nations into account and that the "tool" view of the organization in no way embodied a negative judgment about its usefulness in appropriate situations. According to this argument, direct American cold-war policy was in preparation for the day that the United Nations would be able to function effectively in affirmative action for a more stable world.

THE UNITED STATES, THE UNITED NATIONS, AND "WORLD OPINION." One dimension of the United Nations policy of the United States is difficult to specify but is obviously very important. The stalemate in the Security Council caused by the cold war has focused great attention on a General Assembly swollen to over 115 members. Lacking any of the enforcement "teeth" conferred by the Charter on the Security Council, the larger body has sought instead (especially since the first great increase in membership in 1955) to crystallize and apply "world opinion" to political trouble spots.

During the 1950's, the United States was quite sensitive to world (that is, non-Western) opinion as expressed in the General Assembly. This tendency reached a crest in 1956, when the vast majority of the membership overwhelmingly supported American policy in the Middle East and in Hungary. On colonial issues as well, Washington tended for some years to defer to anticolonialist sentiments in the General Assembly.[18]

During the first years of the 1960's, however, as the communist challenge grew simultaneously more ambiguous and more complex, the United States began to launch more and more unilateral and direct policies that frequently flew in the face of mass opinion at the United Nations. In Laos after 1961, during the Cuban missile crisis of 1962, and especially during the twin American interventions in force in the Vietnam war and in the Dominican Republic in 1965, the United States clearly defied large segments of world opinion and opened itself to the charge of demeaning the United Nations.[19]

THE UNITED STATES AND SUPRANATIONAL ORGANIZATION

The drastic redistribution of power brought about by World War II caused a renewed interest in the question of supranational political organization. The concentration of strength in the two new giants made most of the states of the world acutely aware of their own insecurity and set them thinking about ways to escape this unhappy situation. One of the frequently discussed techniques of doing so—particularly in the early postwar period—was the creation of political entities on some basis greater than the national state.

---

[18]See, for example, the first chapter of Gardner, *In Pursuit of World Order*, and Secs. II and III of Padelford and Goodrich, eds., *The United Nations in the Balance*.

[19]For United Nations reaction to American intervention in the Dominican Republic, see *The New York Times* (April 28–May 25, 1965).

The extensive discussion and the tentative beginnings at the implementation of the idea raised an issue of some pertinence to the United States. It did not become a central question during the first decade and a half after the war, but no one dares say unequivocally that the problem will never become critical to Americans. In its details it is relevant at two levels, those of regional federation and of world government.

THE UNITED STATES AND REGIONALISM. As far as the noncommunist world was concerned, American policy toward regionalism was and is favorable.[20] The more tightly organized the free world became, the better for the United States. We must point out, however, that this sympathy with regional supranational groupings did not go so far as to suggest that the United States itself might join seriously in such an undertaking. The creation of new vehicles of government was up to smaller and weaker states; the United States was determined to preserve its own freedom of action.

Thus Washington spurred the creation of the European Coal and Steel Community, the European Defense Community, the European Economic Community, and the Europe-wide atomic pool known as "Euratom," but until 1962 turned a deaf ear to the proposals from private sources on both sides of the Atlantic suggesting the creation of some federal superstructure incorporating an "Atlantic Community." Even such a natural grouping as the states of the North Atlantic region was kept at the intergovernmental level of NATO rather than carried forward in any more elaborate framework.

As Europe began to split into rival trading blocs, as American business began to suffer from European competition, and as France's de Gaulle began to show signs of political megalomania, the United States began to rethink its position. On July 4, 1962, President John F. Kennedy spoke of a new "declaration of interdependence" between the United States and Europe.[21] For some months thereafter there was extensive public discussion of the President's "grand design," which incorporated an economic (but not, be it noted, either a political or a military) Atlantic community under American leadership. It was in consummation of this project that the Trade Expansion Act of 1962 was passed by Congress, opening the way to wholesale tariff reductions vis-à-vis Europe.

These hopes were dashed early in 1963, however, as President de Gaulle vetoed British entry into the Common Market and made explicit his distaste for any larger American role in the new Europe. Since that time American opinion has been articulate in condemning France for its opposition to a truly integrated Europe, but little further has been heard about any possible American entry into any such arrangement.

---

[20] An interesting analysis of the problem in a context of "sociological jurisprudence" was made by Northrop in *European Union and United States Foreign Policy*.

[21] For the text of President Kennedy's speech, see *The New York Times* (July 5, 1962).

THE UNITED STATES AND WORLD GOVERNMENT. The same general theme ran through the less-than-cursory attention paid to the question of world government after 1945. Official policy, backed by the bulk of public opinion, usually dismissed the entire idea as the crackpot scheme of a group of visionary idealists; some patriotic organizations hinted darkly that the movement was at least quasi-communist.[22] It is true that under the cold-war conditions between 1947 and 1966 there was little immediate relevance to a discussion of whether or not the United States should forthwith merge its sovereignty with that of the Soviet, its Western allies, and all the neutrals in a single mechanism of world government. The problem of the United States was phrased more in terms of a formula for survival rather than for the transformation of all political relationships.

And yet the ultimate implications of American national interest in the postwar era could not be dismissed indefinitely. If peace, order, and stability on a worldwide basis were actually the interests that the United States was pursuing and was determined to pursue in the future, at some point the question of supranational organization would have to be faced. The history of societies everywhere demonstrates that social stability is feasible only within an elaborate pattern of institutions; the more complex the working institutional structure, the greater is the stability and predictability of human behavior. If peace, order, and stability were to mean anything in terms of final purposes, the issue of whether or not the United States would be willing to carry its interests to the point of promoting world government would have to be resolved eventually.

Small States and Anticolonialism

An issue that was relatively late in making its appearance in American policy and that could only with difficulty be fitted into an exclusively cold-war mold is the bifurcated question of American policy toward the small states of the world generally and toward the related burning problem of anticolonialism. After 1954 some analysts insisted that this question, rather than the more widely discussed one of direct Soviet-American relations, would hold the key to the success or failure of American policy over the long term.[23]

---

[22]For an examination of the position of the John Birch Society and other extremist groups in the United States, see Harry and Bonaro Overstreet, *The Strange Tactics of Extremism* (New York: W.W. Norton & Company, Inc., 1964).

[23]See, for example, Chester Bowles, *Africa's Challenge to Americans* (Berkeley, Calif.: University of California Press, 1956).

The two issues are distinct but so closely connected that they can conveniently be discussed together. Not all small states are anticolonial, nor are all ex-colonial states small. Enough states fit both categories, however, and the questions grow from such similar roots that their combined impact on American policy is exerted in the same general direction.

THE SMALL STATES AND THE COLD WAR

The "small states" of the world include the fifty or so smallest members of the international society, although drawing a definite line between small, medium, and medium-large states is difficult.[24] Their general approach to the cold war has been governed essentially by the fact of their absolute and relative weakness and their groping attempts to find some common cause in restraining the super-powers.

SMALL-STATE GROUPINGS. As of early 1966, there were seven more or less distinct small-state groups active in world politics. These were: (1) the Latin American bloc; (2) the Commonwealth nations except for Britain; (3) the small states of western Europe led by Scandinavia and the Benelux countries; (4) the Soviet satellites; (5) the minor Asian powers, usually led by India; (6) the Arab states; and (7) the evolving bloc centered in Africa south of the Sahara. The latter three had made up the former "Afro-Asian" bloc; increase in membership and growing divergencies of interest led to fission into the three distinct groups. The effect of these clusters was most obvious in the United Nations, where the requirements of public voting and overt alignments made them apparent; in the patterns of diplomatic maneuvering, significant intra-group solidarity was shown by all of them after 1954.

SMALL STATES AND NEUTRALISM. We have already noted the tendency of smaller states toward neutralism and abstention from the cold war. Increasingly interpreting it as a great-power struggle in the direct issues of which most of them had only peripheral interest, the small states found that the cold war offered them both responsibilities and opportunities. They assumed the duty of keeping the cold war within the limits of safety and urged its eventual accommodation, but as long as it continued they were perfectly willing to fish in troubled waters and to gain what profit they could from the great-power dispute.

The increasing initiative of the small states foreshadowed a possible revolutionary reorientation of world relationships. The cold-war era of the 1950's saw three more or less formalized vertical groupings in the world: the United

---

[24]One interesting attempt to establish criteria of size (both in area and in population) is made in Samuel Van Valkenburg and Carl L. Stotz, *Elements of Political Geography*, 2d ed. (Englewood Cliffs, N.J.: Prentice-Hall, Inc., 1954), pp. 54–55.

States and its coalition, the communist bloc, and the neutrals. Each of these included major powers, middle powers, and small states. As long as the military danger was acute, smaller states were forced to cling to the coattails of a massive leader. But with nuclear stalemate reducing the imminence of the threat, small states of all blocs are showing a stiffer resistance to any and all great powers. If this development continues through the 1960's, the world may be moving in an era of horizontal rather than vertical cleavages: The small states will form the most numerous group in opposition to the group of giants, with the middle powers holding the balance. Any such outcome would pose major problems of policy reorganization not only for the United States but also for the Soviet Union, China, Britain, France, and the other members of the nuclear club.

AMERICAN POLICY. American attitudes and policy toward the small states between 1947 and 1966 passed through four perceptible stages, corresponding roughly to the phases into which we divided the cold war in Chapter 8.

Up to about 1950, the bipolar assumptions of the United States considered all small states as actual or potential allies of one of the two great leaders, and a neutral small state was unthinkable. American policy was therefore aimed at winning as many as possible of these states to the camp of the United States.

Between 1950 and 1954, the United States became officially aware of the distinct groups into which the small states were dividing themselves, with the first obvious ones being Latin America, the Commonwealth, and the Afro-Asians. The strength of the new group orientation of these states was first shown in the General Assembly and later in various regional conferences (such as Commonwealth Conferences, the Bandung Afro-Asian Conference in April, 1955, and various inter-American meetings).

The third stage of American comprehension of the small-state problem came with the recognition of the basic identity of interest of all minor powers when they have a free opportunity to express it, demonstrated most dramatically in the United Nations votes on the Middle-East crisis of 1956. In the most important vote, every member of the small-state group except Australia and New Zealand agreed in demanding a cease-fire and the withdrawal of the forces invading Egypt.[25]

The contemporary phase of American policy toward the small states began with the realization by the Kennedy administration (certainly by the time of the Cuban missile crisis but perhaps even earlier) that in many ways the United States had at least as much in common with the Soviet Union as it

---

[25]See Laurence W. Martin, ed., *Neutralism and Nonalignment* (New York: Frederick A. Praeger, Inc., 1962); Crabb, *The Elephants and the Grass;* and Eugene Staley, *The Future of Underdeveloped Countries*, rev. ed. (New York: Harper & Row, Publishers, 1961).

did with the small-power world. At the very least, Moscow shared with Washington the desire to protect the concept of great-power status and its incident freedom of choice and action against the onslaught of the lesser powers who were interested in limiting it. Since about 1961, therefore, the United States has sought to escape the effect of the small states while simultaneously (especially under President Johnson) attempting to control their actions.

How successful this approach will be is an open question. If great-power status retains anything like its historic meaning, and if the great powers should succeed in closing their ranks against lesser interlopers, then the impact of the small states might well be minimized for many years. But with more than one hundred members—almost all of them highly vocal—and a United Nations in which all can be heard, the small states may well prove very difficult either to silence or to render impotent.

THE UNITED STATES AND ANTICOLONIALISM

"Anticolonialism," a word symbolizing a potent force in world affairs today, is a product of the contemporary era. Since 1945 the great colonial empires of the nineteenth century have all but melted away; coincidently with this development (and to some extent its cause) there has appeared a vast current of opinion that condemns as immoral and illegal the very principle of imperial rule. The source of this attitude is found in the nationalist aftermath of the successful colonial revolutions in Asia and Africa after 1945, but it is by no means confined to ex-colonial peoples. There has always been something of a guilty conscience in the Western world about the subjugation of alien peoples, and this has come to the surface since the end of the war. The ex-colonial states and the mass support they command in the West (to say nothing of the encouragement they receive from the USSR) have combined to make the word a rallying point for some of the most potentially explosive forces in the modern world.[26]

THE MEANING OF ANTICOLONIALISM. Anticolonialism has meaning in a variety of contexts. At its simplest, it stands for the rapid and total dismantling of all forms of imperialism. To borrow the language of the Charter (Article 73), anticolonialism insists that the category of "non-self–governing peoples" be eliminated from the world's political vocabulary. It is the right of one people to rule over another—regardless of any extenuating circumstances—that the missionaries of anticolonialism are busy denying.

---

[26]See, for example, David E. Apter, ed., *Ideology and Discontent* (New York: Free Press of Glencoe, Inc., 1964), and Louis L. Snyder, ed., *The Dynamics of Nationalism* (Princeton N.J.: D. Van Nostrand & Co., Inc. 1964).

But anticolonialism in practice goes much further. It does not stop with attacking the legal relationships of ruler-colony but challenges what some of its practitioners call the "colonial mentality." This means that the task of anticolonialism is not ended by a declaration of independence but that it goes further to a variety of social, economic, and (especially) psychic goals. Anticolonialism will not be content until ex-colonial states are accepted as full and equal partners in the world political process, until equality of deference is accorded them, and until their purposes and objectives are judged to be as important and as inherently worthy as those of older nations. This has meant inevitably that anticolonialism has come to carry unmistakable overtones of racial equality, of the relative merits of different civilizations and cultures, and of a demand for industrial and technological parity.

THE IMPACT ON THE UNITED STATES. The United States was totally unprepared for the violent effect of anticolonialism on the pattern of international politics. At a time when Washington was laboring to construct a framework of unity for the free world, and when some of its major partners were the world's leading colonial powers, it seemed a regrettable and almost irrelevant digression when the new states of Asia began to raise the issue of anticolonialism.

The slowness of American response to the new forces led many Asian and African leaders to conclude that the United States had proved false to its own revolutionary and antiimperialist tradition. They feared that Americans had been seduced by Britain and France into becoming apologists for an "outworn" imperialist outlook and that American policy had acquired a racist character that classified the new states as "lesser breeds without the law." With some reluctance and regret, many anticolonialists turned to the Soviet as being more sympathetic toward the aspirations of freedom and equality that they harbored.

This development again caught the United States off guard. The new turn in the anticolonial attitude caused sharply divided opinions among Americans. Some argued that this proved the essentially communist nature of the revolt against imperialist authority and urged that the United States join vigorously in suppressing independence movements aimed at destroying the bonds of empire. Others contended that the liquidation of empire and the appearance of new states was inevitable and that several hundred millions of newly independent people were soon to be added to the world political community. These new states and peoples would constitute a powerful factor, one that the United States would ignore only at its own peril.

AMERICAN POLICY. The early 1950's found the United States caught with a consistently unclear policy. The Suez crisis of 1956, however, provided a turning point. At this juncture, the United States came down squarely on the side of the anticolonialists against its imperialist allies. From 1956 onward, the United States has not departed from its basic commitment to the justice and validity of the anticolonialist hypothesis. On many occasions, however, specific American actions have brought down anticolonialist wrath.

Perhaps the most serious blows suffered during the entire postwar period by the United States came in 1965 with the twin American interventions in the Dominican Republic and Vietnam. With American military force being used openly against weak and unstable non-Western states, the accusation was widely heard from noncommunist sources that the United States, fatigued with merely supporting imperialists, had become an imperialist nation itself.

The United States position, on the other hand, was quite clear—at least to Americans. Although subscribing to the tenets of self-determination and freedom of choice for all peoples, and especially for ex-colonial states, the United States was determined not to permit any new or emerging state to be taken over by communist subversion. At whatever cost to its image in the eyes of professed anticolonialists, Washington was to defend its interests (and, as Americans saw it, the interests of all free peoples) by stopping communist aggression in the ex-colonial world. This, after all, was the greatest service the United States could render, and Americans felt that history would prove the justice of their course.

CHAPTER **10**

Continuing
Military Issues in
American Policy

At various points in the preceding chapters we noted that one of the characteristics of the post-1945 era is the closer interrelation of military, political, and economic factors in the foreign relations of the United States. Americans, to whom military affairs were a matter to be traditionally dealt with in a crisis atmosphere of war or near-war, have been obliged to devise a consistent military policy for times that, if not truly peaceful, were at least not marked by all-out warfare. With little of consistent tradition to guide the United States, and with the stakes in national and international power and prestige so high, it is no wonder that the postwar era has produced no entirely satisfactory resolution of the military issues in American policy.

In this chapter we shall examine three of the broader and more persistent questions that have arisen since 1945. We shall first deal with American military policy in general, considering the military mission of the United States and examining the controversy between the advocates of a theory of "flexible response" and those of some doctrine of "massive retaliation." Next we shall take up American overseas defense obligations, both in extent and in nature. Finally we shall summarize the problem of arms limitation, reduction, and control, often stereotyped in the popular term "disarmament."

United States Military Policy

THE AMERICAN MILITARY MISSION

The military establishment of any state is an instrument of the state, to be used for the implementation of appropriate policies. As such, it is a part of the arsenal of techniques any government has at its disposal. The military mission of the United States, therefore, is inseparable from the totality of American policy objectives and is comprehensible finally in terms of the contribution it makes to their accomplishment.[1]

Granted the nature of American foreign policy and the concept of national interest which it serves, we may say generally that the American military mission is to put the armed might of the United States at the service of international peace, order, and stability. In this way, American armed forces exist for the purpose of deterring a potential revisionist state (an "aggressor") from seeking to advance its policy by armed attack on the United States security sphere and of warding off such an attack by active combat if one should occur.[2]

THE DETERRENT MISSION. The story is told that General Curtis LeMay, former Commander of the Stategic Air Command of the United States Air Force, once said: "If war comes, SAC will have failed in its primary mission." Whether or not this is an accurate quotation, the idea it expresses is central to much of American military thinking. American military power has the primary mission of preventing wars from happening, for to a status-quo nation such as the United States, the most successful wars are the ones that never have to be fought.

Under conditions of modern technology, deterring a potential aggressor is only partially a matter of defensive ability. Although the race to develop effective neutralizing techniques against nuclear bombs, supersonic aircraft, guided missiles, rockets, and so on is never ending, the offense in warfare still enjoys the advantage over the defense that it gained at the beginning of World War II. Today, the most elaborate and expensive defenses can afford only partial protection against modern weapons. Military security, therefore, tends to be largely a function of a nation's ability to retaliate to attack.

---

[1]See W. D. Puleston, *The Influence of Force in Foreign Relations* (Princeton, N.J.: D. Van Nostrand, Co., Inc., 1955), esp. Chaps. 2: "Land, Sea, and Air Forces as Factors of Peace" and 7: "Averting War by Means of Force"; see also Council on Foreign Relations, *Basic Aims of United States Foreign Policy*, pp. 14–16.

[2]See Edgar W. Furniss, Jr., *American Military Policy* (New York: Holt, Rinehart & Winston, Inc., 1957).

No sane leader will attack another state if he is certain he will be over-whelmed in return; only a foolhardy one will launch a modern total war if he is convinced that his enemy can and will reply with an equal amount of force. Modern warfare, to be a good bargain, requires an enormous margin of superiority. Deterrence, therefore, in theory does not require absolute superiority over any possible enemy or even equality with him; adequate reprisal power to discourage attack is sufficient to accomplish the mission, even if the total available is less than that of the enemy.

THE COMBAT MISSION. But the American military machine must be pre-pared to deal with the situation arising from an overt resort to arms by an enemy; it must be prepared to fight and win any probable war. This is a more familiar problem to Americans; it has seemed to many as if this is the true and natural mission of the United States Army, Navy, and Air Force.

But here again the impact of modern weapons has complicated what was once a reasonably clear and simple problem. Modern war, in practice, can assume either of two forms: total war for total objectives or limited war for limited goals (what is sometimes called today the "brush-fire" war). Each presents its own technical problems, and each—and this has been the source of much difficulty—requires its own strategy and its own level of "preparedness."

Total war will probably be won by the side that achieves absolute surprise and buries its enemy in a rain of nuclear bombs. It is conceived of as a quick and sudden assault on a scale sufficient to destroy or to impair fatally the enemy's capacity to strike back. Limited war, however, refers to a struggle prosecuted without recourse to total weapons and for objectives that are by that fact themselves limited.

The major question surrounding limited war since 1945 has been one of utility. It is possible, even under modern conditions, to prevent a limited war from growing into an all-out struggle; Korea, Indochina, and Palestine all proved this point. But since the era of total weapons was born, no limited war directly involving major states has been able to bring about a final solution to the political problems that were responsible for the conflict in the first place. This is an inhibition that affects the United States perhaps less than it does the revisionist states, because a stalemated war for America can never be anything less than a qualified victory; for all states, however, it throws much doubt on the efficacy of any form of war other than total war.[3]

American military missions, therefore, must take two forms. The United States must be prepared to accept the challenge of total war if any aggressor presents it. Americans must also face the necessity of coping with limited

---

[3]On the problem of limited war, see Halperin, *Limited War in the Nuclear Age*, Heilbrunn, *Conventional War in the Nuclear Age*, and Klaus Knorr, *Limited Strategic War* (New York: Frederick A. Praeger, Inc., 1965).

wars of all types; "brush fires" may break out at any moment, and the United States must have the ability to extinguish them if it be thought desirable. America should recognize, however, that the probability of winning any meaningful affirmative victory by limited war is at best a very low one and that stalemate will often be the most that can be achieved by any such effort. Short of winning a war of survival, it can be argued that the most important American military mission is preventing big wars rather than winning small ones. This is true not because the small conflicts are unimportant in themselves but because of the difficulty of "winning" them while keeping them small.

"MASSIVE RETALIATION"

This formulation of the American military mission has been controlling within American government circles since the onset of the cold war, but it is by no means the only one that has been advanced. We alluded earlier to the controversy over the optimum form of the American military establishment. Although fought out before the public largely in terms of the conflicting responsibilities of the three armed services, it actually was (and is) an outgrowth of a fundamental disagreement over the nature of the military problem facing the United States and the theory to be adopted in solving it.

LITTLE WARS OR BIG WARS? We will recall that the original containment hypothesis of American foreign policy called for the United States to resist further communist expansion at whatever time and in whatever form it appeared. In military terms, this meant that American armed forces would repel any Soviet-inspired attempt to break through the ring by war and that adequate American military power would be committed to holding the line. The Korean war provided the first clear test of this principle.

Korea proved to be an extremely frustrating experience for Americans; no enterprise could be imagined more calculated to fray American nerves and to destroy American perspectives than a war fought under such conditions. There were technical military reasons for questioning American policy in Korea. The indefinite fighting of a holding action and the refusal to force a battlefield decision defied the historic American theory of war.[4] There was also some doubt about the worth of a policy that left it up to the enemy to decide when, where, with what weapons, and for what objectives to fight. It became popular to warn of the "bleeding" effect of such a policy: Moscow, according to this argument, could use its initiative to force a series

---

[4]This was the major point in General MacArthur's attack on administration and United Nations policy in Korea. See Charles A. Willoughby and John Chamberlain, *MacArthur, 1941–1951* (New York: McGraw-Hill Book Company, 1954), pp. 421–422.

of profitless little wars on the United States and thus to bleed America to death.

As an alternative to Korea-type wars, there was developed a new military policy, one that came to be known popularly as "massive retaliation." According to this doctrine, the United States—although not totally abandoning the "little war" field to the communists—came to concentrate instead on the big-war problem. Instead of meeting each "brush fire" directly, the United States emphasized the true source of the difficulty, the Soviet itself. The United States reserved the right to meet any new war not by equivalent resistance at the point of outbreak but by "massive retaliation" at "places and times" of America's own choosing. Thus deterrence became the preferred method of dealing with the danger of limited war as well as with that of total war.

THE NEW LOOK IN DEFENSE.   Beginning in 1953, the Eisenhower administration began reshaping the structure of the American military establishment in conformity with the new doctrine. The "new look"[5] had two major components: (1) a reduction both in expenditure and in manpower—headlined on occasion as "more bang for a buck"; and (2) a new strategic theory based frankly on American industrial and technological superiority.

Defense budgets were scaled down to approximately $33 billion in fiscal 1955. After that year the total moved slowly upward again as the cost of new weapons programs continued to mount, reaching over $40 billion in fiscal 1961 and leaping again to over $50 billion in fiscal 1966. Manpower was likewise reduced, dropping from three and a half million in 1953 to less than two and a half million in 1959.

These new directions were possible, acccording to official doctrine, because of the new strategic theory. Essentially this new dogma involved a concentration upon air power as the central vehicle of applying force and upon nuclear weapons as being most appropriate to the mission the United States was adopting. Underlying both of these foci of concentration was the basic assumption that the American military problem was one "no longer calling for rearmament by a specific date of peak danger but one requiring a gradual build up and steady maintenance over an indeterminate period."[6] For the long pull America was to put its trust in science and technology as a means of offsetting Soviet preponderance in manpower and in conventional weapons. Despite the strenuous objections of some military personnel

---

[5]The term apparently was first used by Defense Secretary Charles E. Wilson in June, 1953, while testifying before the Senate Committee on Appropriations on the 1954 defense budget. Wilson promised "a new look at the entire defense picture." *Hearings on the Department of Defense Appropriations for 1954*, Senate Committee on Appropriations, 83rd Congress, 1st Session (Washington, D.C.: Government Printing Office, 1953), p. 6.

[6]Reitzel, Kaplan, and Coblentz, *United States Foreign Policy, 1945–1955*, p. 347. Reprinted by permission.

who felt themselves slighted in the redefinition of missions and of other observers who found partisan politics at least partially at the root of the new principles, the United States government moved steadily to make the "new look" a reality.

THE ASSUMPTIONS OF "MASSIVE RETALIATION." The doctrine of "massive retaliation," if it were to be taken seriously as the operating principle of American defense policy, rested on a number of assumptions that were independent of the technical issues of budgets and the conduct of warfare. Five of them were of primary importance. (1) All three services would agree on the principle of the "new look." (2) American superiority (qualitative and quantitative) in nuclear weapons would be maintained. (3) The only threats to United States military security would come from the communist world. (4) The decision to employ the weapons of totality would be a unilateral one by the United States. (5) Public opinion, inside the United States and the free world and among the uncommitted nations, could be safely ignored.

One need not be a partisan in the triangular Army-Navy-Air Force dispute to be convinced that these assumptions have never been simultaneously realized in practice. None of them has been constantly operative, and it has been rare since 1953 to find as many as three of them applying at one time. Each is open to serious question.

The argument against the first simply denies that interservice agreement and consensus, let alone unanimity, has ever existed. The second is challenged on the ground of the history of the development of Soviet nuclear weapons; in the spring of 1956 General LeMay could assert the possibility of early Russian leadership both in aircraft and weapons.[7] The General's point was dramatically confirmed in 1957, when in rapid succession the Soviet fired a hydrogen bomb, announced a successful intercontinental missile, and launched several space satellites. During the next four years, as the USSR maintained its lead in both long-range rocketry and the penetration of space, Americans were warned of a "missile gap" opening against them, at least in ICBM's. Despite the overall success that the United States continued to enjoy in preventing the appearance of a corresponding "deterrent gap" in broader capabilities, serious problems resulted from the invalidation of the easy assumption of American strategic dominance.[8]

The third assumption is the least open to question, although many security threats to the United States can be suggested that might arise from

---

[7]See General LeMay's testimony before the Symington subcommittee of the Senate on April 27 and 30, 1956. *The New York Times* (April 28 and May 1, 1956.)

[8]Most of the concern about the "missile gap" was generated during the presidential campaign of 1960, as Senator John F. Kennedy threw the Eisenhower administration on the defensive with his claims of the inferior position of the United States with respect to ICBM's. Shortly after taking power, however, the New Frontier announced that there had been no missile gap after all but that steps were being vigorously taken to ensure that none developed.

other than Soviet sources. The fourth runs counter to the entire alliance system of the United States and was invalidated by the success of Great Britain and France in independently acquiring a nuclear capability. The fifth was never more than conjectural and, by as early as 1960, had obviously become totally invalid; public opinion, far from remaining quiescent, was instead forcing all the nuclear powers to discuss both test cessation and control of nuclear weapons.

The "new look" was not inseparable from the doctrine of "massive retaliation." It was possible to justify a smaller and more efficient armed force geared into a retaliatory strategy on some basis other than that of meeting every danger with the threat of nuclear assault. The increasing inexpediency of the doctrine stimulated a series of bitter arguments among service personnel, the public, and policy-making officials, and within the free-world alliance. By 1956 there were indications that the rigor of the massive retaliation thesis had been somewhat relaxed;[9] by the beginning of the Kennedy administration, even its one-time violent partisans were reluctant to use the term itself or to defend its concepts.

INTERSERVICE DISPUTES. Complicating the objective evaluation of the "new look" in defense and of "massive retaliation" as the theory for its implementation was the continuing squabble among the three uniformed services. Basic strategic development was obscured by well-publicized barrages of claims and counterclaims by the Army, Navy, and Air Force for privileged positions in the new military machine. In the course of the running battle by the three, however, the various alternatives were thoroughly aired.

Underlying the controversy and dating back to its initial flareup at the time the armed services were "unified" by the National Security Act in 1947, was the widespread notion among professional military men of all branches that the future belonged to air power. The older services hoped to redefine their own missions so as to give them authority over such air weapons as were appropriate to themselves; the Air Force, itself newly independent of Army control, sought to acquire and to perpetuate a monopoly.

A large, if undiscoverable, share of the devoted care with which each service prosecuted its own case was due to the sincere conviction each held that its own strategic principles, tactical doctrine, and dedicated personnel were best fitted to provide for the security of the United States. We must also recognize, however, that all three services were not unaware of the career implications of the new nature of defense. The service that was granted central responsibility would receive the lion's share of prestige, high

---

[9]Reitzel, Kaplan, and Coblentz, *United States Foreign Policy*, pp. 444–445.

rank, and appropriations. Each service felt impelled, therefore, not only to press its own claims but also to deprecate and often to deride the assertions of the other two.

"FLEXIBLE RESPONSE"

"Massive retaliation" as a doctrine and as a policy is identified with the Eisenhower administration and is considered today an historical anachronism, long since abandoned in favor of a better theory. The new and presently controlling doctrine of defense is that of "flexible response," as clearly linked with the Kennedy-Johnson era as its predecessor was with the Republicans. Although the general idea has a long history stemming from the Army position in the interservice disputes of the 1950's, in the public mind today the idea of "flexible response" is considered to be the creature of one of the most remarkable men ever to hold public office in the United States: Robert McNamara, Secretary of Defense under Presidents Kennedy and Johnson.

THE SEARCH FOR OPTIONS. The attack on "massive retaliation" came eventually to center, at least in operational terms, upon its denial of options to the United States. In its effort to accomplish a complete deterrence of Soviet aggression, it emphasized American ability and willingness to launch nuclear war in response to the merest pinprick; in order to make this extreme threat credible, the United States under the Eisenhower administration deliberately reduced its capability to act in any way other than automatically and totally. Critics claimed that this was neither a strategy nor a doctrine, only a prescription for suicide. Its deterrent worth, furthermore, was drastically reduced by its very lack of credibility, as no government at all acquainted with the United States could take seriously an American threat to incinerate the world for a trivial cause.[10]

After 1961, the Kennedy administration set about creating a pattern of options for use in situations of threat that would provide a more rational—and therefore more credible and persuasive—spectrum of response. This initially called for building a "pause" into American action (in contrast to what critics called the "knee-jerk" response intrinsic to "massive retaliation") to provide time, first, for a complete evaluation of a tense situation and, second, for a very broad range of action alternatives—involving all three armed services in a variety of combinations—that vastly augmented the choices open to the American government. Thus "options" became the essence of "flexible response."[11]

---

[10]See, for example, Lowe, *The Age of Deterrence.*
[11]See Kaufmann, *The McNamara Strategy.*

THE THRESHOLD OF PROVOCATION. Implicit in "flexible response" was the basic commitment by the United States to react in some less-than-total fashion to minor provocations and to force on the aggressor the onus of a decision to escalate the conflict to a nuclear level. This dogma, however, had one serious weakness as we have stated it here: In a way reminiscent of the Korean war, it presented to an enemy the power to determine the level at which any conflict would be fought. But the theorists of "flexible response" were unwilling to make such a concession and specifically reserved to the United States the right to respond to a subnuclear provocation with nuclear weapons.[12] Thus the essential deterrent effect of massive retaliation was preserved at the same time that the doctrine itself was being abandoned.

COST EFFECTIVENESS. Secretary of Defense McNamara was faced in 1961 with the necessity of rebuilding the American military machine into an instrument capable of giving reality to "flexible response." A major corporation executive prior to his entry into government service, he brought to his position all the tools of modern management. Within four years he had revolutionized the Pentagon, molding a cumbersome military establishment into an effective arm of the national will.[13]

He approached the "Pentagon jungle" by means of certain tried-and-true executive techniques, of which the most famous is "cost effectiveness." This catchphrase means simply that weapons systems are to be evaluated in terms of the missions they are to perform; those judged to be inefficient will be summarily phased out, and only those will be selected for production that can accomplish the preselected mission most economically. It is perhaps only a coincidence that "cost effectiveness" is reminiscent of former Secretary Wilson's "more bang for a buck" and interesting that Wilson, like McNamara, was an automobile executive before coming to the Pentagon. In any case, it is undeniable that management methods realized great savings in procurement and deployment of advanced weapons, in spite of the fact that the total dollar cost of defense increased steadily throughout McNamara's tenure.

"PROGRAMMED DEFENSE." It must not be assumed from the foregoing, however, that Secretary McNamara's years in the Pentagon have been either smooth or happy. The American military establishment is a caste- and tradition-ridden body, and McNamara's ruthless drive for management efficiency upset many cherished taboos. Resistance appeared from the outset.

---

[12]On this point, see Stewart Alsop, "Kennedy's Grand Strategy," *Saturday Evening Post* (March 31, 1962).

[13]Secretary McNamara's abilities as a manager of the Defense establishment have been widely touted since 1961. Among the articles on his approaches and methods, see C. J. V. Murphy, "Education of a Defense Secretary," *Fortune* (May, 1962); Joseph Kraft, "McNamara and His Enemies," *Harper's* (August, 1961); and Theodore H. White, "Revolution in the Pentagon," *Look* (April 23, 1963).

The major charge against McNamara was (and is) his depersonalization of the problem of defense. His conception of his own mission as above all one of management, his addiction to concepts like "systems analysis" and "computer gaming," and his selection of advisers from among a group of youngish academic civilians (pejoratively identified as the "whiz kids"), all led the uniformed military to feel that their own expertise and dedication were being deliberately minimized. "Cost effectiveness," for example, was subtly challenged by the subjective concept of "combat effectiveness," and computer programming was held not to be an adequate substitute for battlefield experience.[14]

Secretary McNamara, however, showed little inclination to yield to pressure, although the realities of life in Washington forced him after 1964 to be somewhat more sensitive to congressional feelings than he had been during his earlier years. The Pentagon appeared to be irrevocably committed to his principles of a unified and flexible military capability kept at top fighting pitch and backstopped by all the modern management techniques available.

THE TEST: VIETNAM.   The first major test of "flexible response" and of the military machine created to realize it was the war in Vietnam. Ever since the Kennedy administration had decided in mid-1961 to give all-out support and advice to the beleaguered government of South Vietnam, the situation had steadily deteriorated; by early 1965 the United States faced the prospect of a communist victory and a consequent major material and prestige defeat for itself. Under the standard principles of response, therefore, rather than accept such a setback the United States resolved instead to escalate the level of the struggle by air bombardment of North Vietnam and by ever-increasing commitment of American ground and tactical air forces to the jungle war in the South.

How far the American involvement would eventually go, and how high a price would be finally exacted for success, no one in Washington or in Saigon knew when the early decisions were being made. What is important for our purposes, however, is the extent to which the military task in Vietnam was cast within a doctrinal frame. "Victory" in the familiar sense was not established as an objective of American action. The conceptual base of the entire effort was the theme of "counterinsurgency," the tactical purpose of which was to communicate a "message" to the communists: The United States was prepared to do whatever was necessary to deny victory to the communist forces. Thus each level of American response was calculated as

---

[14]By no means has Secretary McNamara been exempt from criticism of his handling of Defense Department matters and defense policy. Among the critiques are Hanson W. Baldwin, "McNamara's Monarchy," *Saturday Evening Post* (March 9, 1963); Cato, "From Washington Straight," *The National Review* (March 12, 1963); and W. J. Coughlin, "Fallible Man," *Missiles and Rockets* (April 29, 1963).

precisely as possible to convince the enemy of the futility of his effort rather than to inflict a defeat on him.

Thus Vietnam was the field exercise designed to test "flexible response" in action. The United States found itself in the unfamiliar role of fighting a war within the requirements of a theory instead of merely crushing identi- fied enemy opposition. It proved not to be an altogether pleasant experience but one obviously fraught with potential significance for the future.

American Overseas Defense Commitments

A major feature of American policy during the cold war has been the development and elaboration of a series of overseas defense commitments. For the first time in its history, the United States had found it necessary both to enter into firm alliances with foreign states and to deploy its military forces on the territory of its allies. A logical consequence of this develop- ment has been the adoption of the policy of supplying the associates of the United States with materiel for their own defense and for the security of the alliance.[15]

As of 1966 the United States was formally allied with forty-three different states. These ties included four multilateral treaties and a number of bilateral arrangements. The obligations covered the major areas of the world. Western Europe was protected by NATO. Southeast Asia was covered by SEATO, the southwest Pacific by ANZUS, the western hemisphere by OAS, and the Middle East by the series of bilateral pacts that linked the United States to CENTO. The Far East was tied together by a network of bilateral agree- ments with the Philippines, Nationalist China, the Republic of Korea, and Japan. These pacts together created the greatest peacetime "Grand Alliance" in history.

THE PATTERNS OF ALLIANCE

Although all the forty-three states with which the United States had military agreements were, in one sense or another, "allies," the nature of the obligation incurred by the American government differed from one pact to another. Each merits mention in order to clarify just what Americans have obligated themselves to do.

---

[15]Two books which make the general case for the American need of close allies and structured defense alliances within the specific context of NATO are Klaus Knorr, ed., *NATO and American Security* (Princeton, N.J.: Princeton University Press, 1959), and Alastair Buchan, *NATO in the 1960's* (New York: Frederick A. Praeger, Inc., 1963).

THE NATO COMMITMENT. Both the most binding commitment accepted by the United States and the most elaborate institutional implementation are found in American action under the terms of the North Atlantic Treaty of 1949. NATO is, as American leadership delights in pointing out, the keystone of all contemporary American policy, and our consideration of American alliances should begin with it.

The principal obligation under the Treaty is contained in Article 5. Its language is important enough to merit quotation:

> The parties agree that an armed attack against one or more of them in Europe or North America shall be considered an attack against them all; and consequently they agree that, if such an armed attack occurs, each of them, in exercise of the right of individual or collective self-defense recognized by Article 51 of the Charter of the United Nations, will assist the Party or Parties so attacked by taking forthwith, individually, and in concert with the other Parties, such action as it deems necessary, including the use of armed force, to restore and maintain the security of the North Atlantic Area.[16]

Later provisions define the geographic area included by the pact and the relationships of the treaty to the Charter of the United Nations and provide for the creation of a North Atlantic Council for implementing the execution of the treaty. It was thrown open to adherence by any other European state "in a position to further the principles of this Treaty" upon unanimous invitation of the members. Under these terms, the original twelve signatories have accepted the later membership of Greece, Turkey, and West Germany.

THE SEATO OBLIGATION. The Southeast Asia Collective Defense Treaty of 1954 is not as precise as the North Atlantic Treaty in specifying either the action to be taken by the parties or the danger which the treaty is designed to meet. Article 4 contains the general pledge of collective defense, resistance to aggression, and joint action:

> 1. Each Party recognizes that aggression by means of armed attack in the treaty area against any of the Parties or against any State or territory which the Parties by unanimous agreement may hereafter designate, would endanger its own peace and safety, and agrees that it will in that event act to meet the common danger in accordance with its constitutional processes.[17]

Section 2 of the same Article deals with a slightly different contingency. If the "inviolability or the integrity" of any party or of any protected territory

---

[16]*Disarmament and Security: A Collection of Documents, 1919–1955*, Committee Print, Subcommittee on Disarmament, Committee on Foreign Relations, United States Senate, 84th Congress, 2d Session (Washington, D.C.: Government Printing Office, 1956), pp. 530–531.

[17]*Disarmament and Security*, p. 612. The "State or territory which the Parties may hereafter designate" referred to the Associated States of Indochina (Laos, Cambodia, and Vietnam), barred from entry into any such pact.

"is threatened in any way other than by armed attack or is affected or threatened by any fact or situation which might endanger the peace of the area," the parties will consult together immediately to agree on measures to be taken for the common defense. We will note that Section 1 does not provide for consultation in the case of armed attack but that Section 2, covering other dangers, requires consultation and the formulation of common measures.[18] Later provisions of the treaty, in much the same way as had the North Atlantic Treaty, define the area covered, establish a Council, and relate the treaty to the Charter.

THE ANZUS OBLIGATION. The Australia-New Zealand-United States security treaty, negotiated in 1951 and put into effect in 1952, involves a commitment less comprehensive than the North Atlantic Treaty and more akin to the SEATO obligations. Articles III and IV are the pertinent provisions concerning consultation and common defense:

ARTICLE III. The Parties will consult together whenever in the opinion of any of them the territorial integrity, political independence or security of any of the Parties is threatened in the Pacific.

ARTICLE IV. Each Party recognizes that an armed attack in the Pacific Area on any of the Parties would be dangerous to its own peace and safety and declares that it would act to meet the common danger in accordance with its constitutional processes.[19]

It is noteworthy that nowhere in the treaty is the term "Pacific Area" defined, although what would constitute an armed attack on a Party is declared to include "an armed attack on the metropolitan territory, . . . on the island territories under its jurisdiction in the Pacific, or on its armed forces, public vessels, or aircraft in the Pacific."[20] Other provisions are not exceptional, except that Article VIII authorizes the ANZUS Council to maintain a consultative relationship with "States, Regional Organizations, Associations of States, or other authorities" in the Pacific area in a position to contribute to the security of the region.

THE OAS OBLIGATION. The Inter-American Treaty of Reciprocal Assistance of 1947, the first of the mutual-security pacts brought about by the United States and to some extent the model for all subsequent ones, is both more detailed in its provisions and more complex in its structure than are the others we have considered.

---

[18]This distinction is generally thought to be a gesture in the direction of the Asian neutrals, who—led by Nehru—distrusted the narrowly anticommunist orientation of NATO and were interested in provisions offering protection against any renewed Asian colonialism.

[19]*Disarmament and Security*, p. 600.

[20]*Ibid.*, p. 601.

Article 3 contains the general guarantee and authorizes individual action on behalf of the group:

ARTICLE 3. 1. The High Contracting Parties agree that an armed attack by any State against an American State shall be considered as an attack against all the American States and, consequently, each one of the said Contracting Parties undertakes to assist in meeting the attack in the exercise of the inherent right of individual and collective self-defense . . . .

2. On the request of the State or States directly attacked and until the decision of the Organ of Consultation of the Inter-American System has been reached, each one of the Contracting Parties may determine the immediate measures which it may individually take in fulfillment of the obligation contained in the preceding paragraph and in accordance with the principle of continental solidarity.[21]

Article 6 defined the kinds of situations that would make the treaty applicable:

ARTICLE 6. If the inviolability or the integrity of the territory or the sovereign or political independence of any American State should be affected by an aggression which is not an armed attack or by an extra-continental or intra-continental conflict, or by any other fact or situation that might endanger the peace of America, the Organ of Consultation shall meet immediately in order to agree on the measures which must be taken in case of aggression to assist the victim of the aggression or, in any case, the measures which should be taken for the common defense and for the maintenance of the peace and security of the Continent.[22]

Article 7 authorized the parties to terminate a conflict between two or more American states on the basis of the "*status quo ante bellum*," and to take action to maintain inter-American peace. Article 9, without attempting a definition of "aggression," listed as examples "unprovoked armed attack by a State against . . . another State" and "invasion, by the armed forces of a State, of the territory of another State" by trespassing "boundaries demarcated in accordance with a treaty, judicial decision, or arbitral award" or "territory under the effective jurisdiction of another State." Article 17 provided that the Organ of Consultation should make its decisions by a two-thirds vote of the signatories. Thus the treaty made a major attempt to minimize inter-American conflict.

THE UNITED STATES AND CENTO. American security relations in the Middle East are somewhat less explicit. The principal vehicle is the Central Treaty Organization (CENTO), an association of Great Britain, Iran, Pakistan, and Turkey, of which the United States is not a member. Having lost its name of "Baghdad Pact" after Iraq's withdrawal in 1958, CENTO

---

[21]*Ibid.*, p. 650.
[22]*Ibid.*, p. 651.

itself is a very generalized cooperative agreement among the signatories. In 1956, the United States established permanent liaison with the pact; in 1957 it joined its economic and military committees. In 1958 the United States associated itself with a declaration by the members that emphasized the pact's defensive nature. On March 5, 1959, the United States virtually closed the circle by concluding bilateral defense agreements with Iran, Pakistan, and Turkey, whereby in case of aggression the United States "in accordance with the Constitution, will take such appropriate action, including the use of armed forces, as may be mutually agreed upon and is envisaged in the Joint Resolution to Promote Peace and Stability in the Middle East [the 'Eisenhower Doctrine' of 1957]."[23] With these agreements, the question of whether or not the United States should become a "member" of CENTO became purely academic.

BILATERAL OBLIGATIONS. The United States has entered into bilateral security arrangements with five states: the Philippines, Japan, Korea, and Nationalist China in the Far East, and Spain in Europe. Each of these has its own pecularities.

The earliest was with the Philippines, negotiated virtually simultaneously with the ANZUS agreement in 1951. Its language is in some parts exactly the same. Article IV, for example, makes the identical pledge as Article IV of the ANZUS treaty, and Article III, providing for consultation, differs from the ANZUS provision only in specifying that the vehicle of consultation shall be the Foreign Ministers (or their deputies) of the two states.[24]

The treaty with Japan was first negotiated in 1951 and was completely one-sided because of the limitations on Japanese military strength imposed by the 1946 constitution. Under the pressures of the evolving Asian cold war and the revival of Japanese nationalism, a new pact was negotiated in 1959. Its ratification touched off a major crisis in Japan and caused the cancellation of a projected goodwill visit by President Eisenhower in June, 1960. The treaty itself pledges both parties to "maintain and develop their capacities to resist armed attack," to consult regularly on carrying out the treaty, and to recognize that an attack on either "on the territory of Japan" is a threat to itself. Japan further renewed the authorization given the United States in the 1951 treaty to maintain land, sea, and air bases on the territory of Japan.[25]

---

[23]The complete texts of these three agreements are to be found in *United States Treaties and Other International Agreements*, Vol. 10, Part I, 1959 (Washington, D. C.: Government Printing Office, 1960), pp. 314–322.

[24]*Disarmament and Security*, pp. 598–599.

[25]Text of 1951 treaty, *United States Treaties*, p. 606. An analysis of the crisis surrounding the negotiation and ratification of the 1960 treaty can be found in Richard P. Stebbins, *The United States in World Affairs, 1960* (New York: Harper & Row, Publishers, 1961), Chap. 6, Sec. 41: "Japan: A Narrow Escape."

The pact with the Republic of Korea, negotiated after the truce in the Korean war in 1953, included most of the concepts that this brief catalogue has made familiar. Article II provides for consultation if either party is "threatened by external armed attack." Article III states that an armed attack on the territory of either party would be dangerous to the peace and safety of the other. Article IV confers the right to "dispose United States land, air, and sea forces in and about the territory of the Republic of Korea."[26]

The 1954 treaty with Nationalist China followed what was by this time the standard pattern for Far Eastern pacts: It provided for consultation, action according to "constitutional processes" to meet the danger of armed attack, and the disposition of American forces on Taiwan and the Pescadores. Because of the somewhat anomalous status of the Chinese government, the territorial limits of the treaty were restricted for China to "Taiwan and the Pescadores" and for the United States to "the island territories in the West Pacific under its jurisdiction."[27] This provision was widely interpreted as constituting official American recognition of the Taipei regime's claim to *de jure* sovereignty over Taiwan.

The agreement with Spain, entered into late in 1953, was much less specific and much more restricted in scope than any of the other bilateral pacts. The United States agreed to extend military aid to Spain "during a period of several years to contribute to the effective air defense of Spain and to improve the equipment of its military and naval forces. . . ." Spain, on its part, agreed to permit the United States to construct bases in Spain and engaged itself to acquire the land necessary for that purpose; such areas, however, were to remain "under Spanish flag and command," and Spain was to "retain the ownership of the ground and of the permanent structures which may be constructed thereon." Despite the limited nature of the obligation assumed by both sides, the agreement was generally regarded as bringing Spain within the alliance framework of the United States.[28]

MILITARY-AID PROGRAMS

Beginning with the first Mutual Defense Assistance Act in 1949, the United States has consistently supported its political and military commitments to its allies with programs of military aid. The various major

---

[26] *Disarmament and Security*, pp. 607–608.

[27] *Ibid.*, pp. 608–610. It is interesting that the treaty is silent on the question—so fruitful of later controversy in the United States—of whether the American guarantee also extended to the "offshore islands": Quemoy and Matsu.

[28] *Ibid.*, pp. 537–539.

phases of the effort to equip the military establishments of friendly nations have been considered in earlier chapters. At this point only the policy in its present more or less stabilized form need be considered.

WHAT IS "MILITARY AID"? "Military aid" has for many years been classified by Americans as a part of the larger concept of "foreign aid," the other components of which are "economic" and "development" assistance. Over the years, furthermore, military aid has proved to be the form of aid most politically acceptable to the American Congress and the American voter. Military assistance to allies of the United States has often seemed a more useful way to use American funds than visionary schemes of development in politically unreliable and unstable non-Western countries.

This consideration led the United States during the 1950's (following the passage of the Mutual Security Act of 1951) to attempt to lump all foreign aid, except development assistance, under the rubric of "mutual-security" aid. As the President put it in 1956:

> Direct military assistance under the mutual security program is extended by providing weapons and other military supply items, by carrying out training programs, and by sharing in the financing of joint military facilities.
> Nonmilitary assistance is extended in one of three ways, depending on how the needs and circumstances of the participating country relate to the policy objectives of the United States: (1) defense support and technical cooperation; (2) development assistance and technical cooperation; or (3) technical cooperation alone.[29]

"Defense support" is defined in the same document as being

> designed to help certain countries which are receiving military assistance to support appropriate levels of military strength while also maintaining and promoting political and economic stability. Such support involves furnishing economic resources to enable the recipient country to undertake defense activities that otherwise would not be possible or to increase the recipient's capacity to do so in the future.[30]

This device, however, was abandoned by the Kennedy administration. Following the recommendations of a special committee appointed by President Eisenhower to study the aid program (the "Draper Committee"[31]), the administration proposed and Congress passed the Foreign Assistance

---

[29] *Report to Congress on the Mutual Security Program*, September 20, 1956 (Washington, D.C.: Government Printing Office, 1956), p. 14.

[30] *Ibid.*, p. 14.

[31] House Committee on Foreign Affairs, *Conclusions Concerning the Mutual Security Program*, Document No. 215, Report of the Draper Committee, 86th Cong., 1st sess., House 1959 (Washington, D.C.: Government Printing Office, 1959).

Act of 1961. This law put military aid on a more forthright and realistic basis and, as annually renewed, controls the military-aid program today.

The Act does not define military aid in any restrictive way but authorizes the President to do any or all the following things for friendly nations or organizations:

1. Provide by loan, lease, sale, exchange, grant, or by other means any defense article or service.
2. Make financial contributions for joint overseas bases.
3. Provide financial assistance for regional or collective defense organizations.
4. Assign United States military personnel to perform noncombat actions of training or advice.[32]

The act also establishes a number of criteria to guide the President—criteria that have been attacked as undesirable limitations on the freedom of the executive branch but that have not thus far served as real inhibitions to presidential decision. Among the more important are the requirements that no recipient country can be "part of the international communist conspiracy" (although programs are possible with communist states that are not so designated), or trade with Cuba, or have seized United States property without compensation, or have "aggressive plans" against the United States or against another country receiving United States military aid.[33] Further limitations apply to all grant (as opposed to loan or sale) programs as well as to all kinds of aid to Latin America.[34]

THE MILITARY-AID PROGRAM. The dollar cost of the military-aid program—even allowing for the vagaries of government accounting—has declined more or less steadily from its high of $4.0 billion in fiscal 1953 to its fiscal 1965 figure of $1.05 billion. Through fiscal 1965, the overall total of expenditures for the twenty years since World War II was in the neighborhood of $33 billion—an amount roughly equivalent to the cost of the Lend-Lease Program with Britain alone during World War II. Military aid, by most standards, has been one of the greatest bargains purchased by the United States since 1945.

The exact breakdown of aid among its recipients has never been fully revealed, but the major beneficiaries of the program during the 1960's have been a relatively small number of states in Asia who are conceived to stand in the most imminent peril from communist aggression and who also give

---

[32]Foreign Assistance Act of 1961, Sec. 502.

[33]*Ibid.*, Sec. 620.

[34]*Ibid.*, Sec. 511. No assistance to Latin America, for example, may be used for internal security purposes, although other recipients may do so.

the most serious promise of using the aid effectively. South Vietnam, Taiwan, South Korea, Pakistan, Turkey, and Iran are among the leading recipients of military aid today, at least on a regular basis.

Arms Control in United States Policy

Our final military issue—which is only partly military in nature, since it carries heavy overtones of political, economic, and psychological relevance— is the troublesome question of the international regulation and control of armaments. In some respects, the history of the attempt to devise a workable system of arms control since 1945 is a continuation of the story of the interwar period. Certain factors peculiar to the contemporary era, however, have made the issue both more frustrating and more important than ever before.

At the beginning of this brief examination of the issues and problems of arms control, we should point out that we are not discussing here the emotion-packed concept of "disarmament." Although planning for "general and complete disarmament" (known as "GCD" in government circles in the United States) is a part of the overall American effort, it ranks relatively low on the scales of priority and probability. The less explicit but paradoxically more accurate phrase "arms control" covers what we are considering here: a system permitting a multilateral reduction in the level of national armaments and guaranteeing that interstate relations will remain confined within the limits demanded by these more modest military establishments.

THE ARMS RACE WITH THE SOVIET UNION

What has changed the issue of arms limitation from a nonspecific concern for a better world to a matter of practical urgency for the United States is the ominous dimensions assumed by the massive arms race with the Soviet Union. In international affairs (as in other areas of social life) there operates a concept known as the "expectation of violence." When social conditions habituate individuals to the probability of a recourse to violence, the prospect of its employment in settling disputes increases. In the relations of rival states, there seems to be positive correlation between the respective levels of armament and the expectation of war. This suggests, but by no means proves, that an arms race between the USSR and the United States tends to make war between them more likely.

In any case, since 1956 the intensity of the arms competition between the two giants has become a cause of much concern, both within the United

States and among America's allies. Public pressure has multiplied on both governments to make some new efforts to break through the obstacles and to release the world both from the economic burden of armaments and from the menace of nuclear holocaust.

THE ARMS RACE AND THE COLD WAR. How the arms race began was well known. As soon as the cold war began in earnest, the United States started to rearm. Never planning to match Soviet preponderance in manpower generally and in ground armies in particular, America's effort centered on the development of mobile and highly effective air and naval defense units; the principal weapons in which the United States placed its trust were atomic. Moscow's reaction to the failure of atomic-control discussions was to intensify its own "crash" program for the development of nuclear weapons; its success in 1949 prompted the United States in turn to strengthen its own ground defenses and to construct the extensive alliance system to contain Soviet expansionism. Since 1950 the cold war has had a clear arms-competition dimension.

CATEGORIES OF COMPETITION. Any discussion of armaments since 1945 must take account of the fact that the military equipment of both major states falls today into two categories: "conventional" and nuclear. One of the most vital—but yet unsettled—questions is the relationship of these two to each other. In totalling up a nation's armed power, how many infantry divisions equal one hydrogen bomb? No easy formula has yet been devised to answer this obviously pertinent question, and without one it is extremely difficult to make intelligent estimates of military parity.[35]

The United States has recognized that it would be politically inexpedient for the free world to attempt to match Soviet ground power. The United States has sought instead to keep its own and its allied armies superior to the Soviet on a man-for-man basis and to maintain a sufficiently large ground force to serve as a deterrent in time of peace and as a delaying factor in the event of combat. The major American effort has been in maintaining a controlling lead over Russia in strategic air power, in nuclear bombs, and in missiles of all types. As this lead first began to narrow after 1957 and then all but disappeared after 1959, the United States found itself trying to catch up (at least in ICBM's) rather than exploiting a safe advantage. It was generally agreed that any missile gap would not lead to a "deterrent gap" in the future if the United States followed a rational arms policy,[36] but the arms race was a much more complex thing for Americans after 1959 than it had been previously.

---

[35]This problem is discussed in Knorr, *The War Potential of Nations*, Chap. 14: "The Present State of War Potential."

[36]See *Developments in Military Technology* . . . by the Washington Center of Foreign Policy Research, The Johns Hopkins University, Part C, Chap. 5: "Stability and Instability in the Equation of Strategic Power."

The Kremlin, however, has followed a peculiarly ambivalent line. It would seem obvious that if Moscow could develop its nuclear capacity to the point where it effectively neutralized American strategic power, its advantage in conventional forces would confer a great military preponderance upon the Soviet. The actual course of recent Russian policy, however, has been to match each nuclear-missile breakthrough with a corresponding reduction in Soviet conventional forces. If this policy is carried through, Moscow's arms pattern will correspond to Washington's, with both committed to strategic deterrence and a defensive posture.

In the tense climate of East-West relations, however, clear policies were difficult to discover. The unprejudiced observer might feel justified in feeling that the arms race was nearing totality as each side made every effort to gain some sort of leverage over the other.

THE PROBLEM OF PROLIFERATION. Complicating the arms race in the 1960's was the fact that it had become much more than a two-power affair. The "nuclear club" had expanded to five members (the United States, the Soviet Union, Britain, France, and Communist China) by 1964, and other powers were both in a position to develop nuclear capability of their own and apparently preparing themselves politically to do so. Proliferation posed a very serious problem for the two giants, since they shared an interest in preventing it but could not do so effectively without placing major limitations on their own competition. Certainly the realization that theirs was no longer a private discussion sharpened the urgency with which both Moscow and Washington approached the problem after 1964.

THE UNITED NATIONS AND DISARMAMENT

The United Nations has been the focus of all postwar attempts to limit and control armaments. The history of the negotiations in that body over this question is a complex, confusing, and only intermittently interesting one. From it, however, certain important lessons have been learned about the future possibilities of armaments control.

THE CHARTER AND ARMS LIMITATION. It is worth noting at the outset that the Charter does not call either for "disarmament" or the "reduction of armaments"; it speaks instead of the "regulation of armaments."[37] It was expected at San Francisco that armed force would exist in a United Nations-dominated world but that it would be put only to the purpose of guaranteeing international peace and security. Charter provisions calling for the creation of a United Nations armed force and for the temporary earmarking of certain national contingents for United Nations use further underscored the

---

[37]Article 26.

point. Military power and armaments were to have a place—limited, controlled, and subordinate, but a place nonetheless—in the world of the United Nations.

"THE DIPLOMACY OF EMBARRASSMENT." The long and tortuous course of negotiations in the various organs of the United Nations looking toward the creation of a system of regulated armaments is of little interest to us here. As soon as the issue got caught up in the cold war, any real prospect of arms control was dissipated. The inability of the United Nations mechanisms to check the course of the great-power conflict was nowhere more dramatically demonstrated than in the failure of disarmament.[38]

What was remarkable about these unproductive discussions, however, was the tack taken by both the USSR and the United States. Each was interested in and advocated an arms-control formula that would give it a policy advantage; Washington advanced proposals that would have forever denied Moscow nuclear parity while the Soviet plainly wished to pull America's atomic teeth while maintaining its own primacy in conventional weapons. Each saw the impossibility of achieving its major goal and settled down instead to what we might call the "diplomacy of embarrassment." Each was hoping to extract the maximum policy and public-relations value from an obviously foredoomed negotiation. By early 1948 disarmament discussions were hopelessly deadlocked; no more serious attempts were made until 1955.[39]

SECOND WIND. President Eisenhower's famous "open sky" proposal at the 1955 Geneva summit conference (asking for a system of aerial inspection designed to guard against surprise attack) reopened the question and gave the search for arms control its "second wind." From 1955 to 1961, activity both within and outside the United Nations was constant. Although progress was miniscule, both sides obviously felt a greatly increased urgency.

The United Nations Disarmament Commission, however—especially after its membership was enlarged in 1957 and 1958—proved incapable of shaking off its cold-war impotence. Late in 1959, the United States, Britain, France, and the Soviet Union announced the creation of a special ten-member group (five from each bloc) to negotiate independently of the United Nations but to report to the Disarmament Commission.[40] This body

---

[38]This point is made clear in Leland M. Goodrich and Anne P. Simons, *The United Nations and the Maintenance of International Peace and Security* (Washington, D.C.: Brookings Institution, 1955), Chaps. 21, 22.

[39]See John W. Spanier and Joseph L. Nogee, *The Politics of Disarmament* (New York: Frederick A. Praeger, Inc., 1962).

[40]Secretary-General Dag Hammarskjöld, while welcoming the new body, made it clear that the United Nations "retains the ultimate responsibility" for disarmament negotiations and insisted that the ten-nation group could only "prepare the ground" for later United Nations decisions. *The New York Times* (August 14, 1959).

set to work early in 1960, awaited instructions from the 1960 summit conference, and collapsed when that meeting produced nothing but a burst of bad temper from Premier Khrushchev. In June, 1960, the Soviet Union walked out of the body completely, and the point was again made that even a special negotiating body was helpless in the absence of great-power political understandings.

The negotiations on nuclear test cessation that had begun in 1958, a separate and distinct problem, were likewise carried on by special emissaries: initially a commission of scientists from the nuclear powers and subsequently official political spokesmen. Since nuclear-test cessation was generally regarded as the most hopeful area of negotiation with the fewest obstacles to agreement, both the scientists and the political figures were able to make considerable progress in their discussions. In this case, the special-body technique proved workable, because enough of the prerequisites to success were available.

EAST-WEST POSITIONS. During the era of intensive negotiations, the positions of the two camps have come much closer together, but major differences still keep them apart. At the risk of drastic oversimplification, we may say that the Soviet has been most interested in substantive reduction of arms levels on the basis of a declaration of principle and intent by both sides and that the United States has focused primarily upon the control system that would police any agreement. It is hard to escape the conclusion that each side chose its emphasis because of its known unacceptability to the other. The USSR is pathologically frightened by the espionage possibilities of any inspection system on Soviet soil; the United States is equally obsessed by the danger of Soviet cheating on any unpoliced (or imperfectly policed) agreement. Both sides, but especially the Soviet, have also tended to inject political issues into disarmament talks as a means of warding off an agreement. Perhaps the most effective has been Moscow's idea of "geographic disarmament": some tactic of disengagement in central Europe that would effectively wreck the American alliance and defense system based on NATO.

ARMS CONTROL SINCE 1961

The Kennedy administration, as was the case in so many other areas of American foreign policy, moved with unprecedented vigor and imagination into the thorny thickets of arms control. New approaches—not all of them successful—have been attempted by the United States on many occasions since 1961. Partially due to increased commitment at home and partially to major changes in the world environment, the United States is more serious about arms control today than it ever has been during the postwar era.

NUCLEAR TESTING. In March, 1958, the Soviet Union scored a propaganda coup by announcing a unilateral suspension of nuclear tests. The

United States (after having completed a test series of its own) followed suit on a one-year basis in October, 1958. Negotations were initiated looking toward making the test ban permanent and progressed more or less smoothly until 1961.

In both the Soviet Union and the United States, however, major pressures in favor of resuming tests were building up within the governments. Technical developments were being made in weapons systems that could not be realized without further testing, and President Kennedy was strongly urged during his first few months in office to find some pretext for ending the moratorium. The President stood fast, however, in his determination to pursue to the end the possibility of a firm test-ban agreement.

The Soviet Union, however, had other ideas. In late August, 1961, Moscow announced its intention to resume testing and did so forthwith. The United States almost immediately followed suit, although its explosions were smaller (and therefore less "dirty" with fallout than those of the Soviet). What exasperated American policy-makers, however, was the tenor of world opinion: Although the case seemed clear that it was the Soviet that had broken the moratorium and that should therefore be subject to international condemnation, the nonaligned states seemed to parcel out the blame for the renewal of testing rather impartially between Moscow and Washington.[41]

A NEW FORUM AND NEW PROPOSALS. In December, 1961, a General Assembly resolution recommended that the ten-nation special body be expanded into an Eighteen Nation Disarmament Committee (ENDC), to meet in Geneva and to work steadily for some agreement. To this proposition both the United States and the Soviet Union agreed, and the ENDC began its work in March. Interestingly enough, the general proposal that tended to receive the most serious and searching analysis—perhaps reflecting the expanded influence of the nonaligned nations—was that for "general and complete disarmament (GCD)"—a proposition that was taken in complete earnest by most of the members in spite of the general lack of enthusiasm for it by the great powers. Each major power submitted a broad blueprint for GCD and the Conference began to grapple with the old dilemma: Technically GCD was possible, politically it was—as had been the case ever since 1945—out of the question.

NEW ORGANIZATIONAL ARRANGEMENTS. The Kennedy administration also moved to strengthen its organization for arms control. In September, 1961, Congress passed a law creating an Arms Control and Disarmament Agency[42] that, under the general direction of the Department of State, was to conduct the long-range disarmament studies necessary for preparation for a final agreement. This action was in conformity with the President's

---

[41]Richard C. Stebbins, *The United States in World Affairs 1961* (New York: Vintage Books, 1962), p. 92.

[42]Public Law 87–297, September 26, 1961.

pledge to "make arms control a central goal of our national policy."[43] A "Directorate for Disarmament" was also established in the Pentagon, located within the purview of the Assistant Secretary of Defense for International Security Affairs.

THE TEST-BAN TREATY. During the first two years of the Kennedy administration there was little progress made in arms control, as major crises in Berlin and Cuba and the resumption of nuclear tests seemed to becloud the atmosphere rather than to lighten it. But in the wake of the Cuban missile crisis, a narrow but portentous breakthrough came with surprising speed. This was the limited test-ban treaty of August 5, 1963.

In one sense this treaty—thrown open to adherence by all nations and eventually ratified by over one hundred—was no more than the culmination of the five years of effort that had gone into negotiations about the problem. In another sense it was not very important: It did not cover all tests, only those in the atmosphere; it made no provision for the tight inspection, control, and verification procedures for which the United States had long contended; it did not touch any of the other areas of arms competition or deal seriously with the question of proliferation (since neither France nor Communist China had signed it). Yet, when all was said and done, the test-ban treaty was the first concrete step "back from the abyss" that the cold-war antagonists had been able to take in nearly two decades of struggle. As such it had an importance far beyond its explicit provisions.

ANTIPROLIFERATION. There was little immediate follow-up to the test-ban treaty. The major reason was, of course, the change in administrations in the United States and the rising tide of crisis in non-Western areas of the world. Yet as the Johnson administration began to face the grim realities of the arms race, certain propositions became obvious.

The most important point was that the danger of proliferation was becoming acute. The two newest nuclear powers, France and Communist China, were refusing to cooperate in any projects looking toward further controls; at the same time, at least half a dozen states—several of questionable responsibility—were threatening to develop their own nuclear weapons. If the nuclear-arms race was to be halted before it ran away with the human species, early action to arrest proliferation was vital.

At this point the American argument began to run into difficulty. To cooperate with the Soviet Union in antiproliferation measures was one thing, difficult and complex but not impossible. To do so in any real way, however, required major modification in two areas of policy very important to America in the mid-1960's: the effort to give a "sense of participation" in nuclear weaponry to West Germany, primarily as an offset to France; and the long-standing refusal to deal publicly with Communist China.

---

[43]In his State of the Union Message, January 30, 1961. *The New York Times* (January 31, 1961).

The European difficulty centered around an American impulse to head off a German thrust for nationally-owned nuclear weapons by dissolving this urge in some multilateral or interallied nuclear force. Several projects—all abortive—were attempted after 1964; each ran afoul of objections from other European allies and the stern warning that any form of nuclear capability in German hands would be interpreted by Moscow as the *coup de grace* to any effort at an antiproliferation agreement.

China was a different problem. China could be brought into the scope of any such agreement only by its own consent, given in free and open negotiation. As long as the United States refused to participate in any such conference with China, there was no hope of any treaty that would bind Peking.

At the beginning of 1966, it finally seemed as if the United States was beginning the painful process of reevaluating these cherished positions in behalf of making some progress toward an understanding with the Soviet Union. Strong opposition to such modification was to be found in many places in the American government, and the war in Vietnam served to cast something of a pall over the whole matter. Yet the brutal logic of modern weapons was having its effect, and there was considerable reason to believe that the United States was bracing itself eventually to pay the price for a realistic and workable system of arms control.

THE PROSPECTS FOR ARMS CONTROL

Where did the arms-limitation issue stand after more than twenty years of more or less serious attempts to solve it? What can we say about the prospects for regulation and control of national armaments? Is there any realistic ground for hope?

DISARMAMENT AND SECURITY. The postwar arms-reduction issue teaches much the same lesson as that taught by the experience of the interwar years. Disarmament, by itself, is not a cause of peace, rather a reflection of it. Since 1945 it has proved impossible, just as it was between 1922 and 1932, to separate the issues of disarmament and security. As long as armed force remains the only ultimately efficacious method of guaranteeing national security, states are going to retain their military machines. They will agree to a reduction in arms levels only to the extent that they become convinced that their security problems will be solved by other methods.

Within the area of academic speculation there is a real cleavage on the point of the relative importance of disarmament and security. There is a sizeable body of opinion that finds certain "positive" values in disarmament. This argument contends that even—or especially—at a moment of crisis, measures to reduce arms levels and to call off an arms race result in affirmative gains in security for everyone involved. On this basis, the time to disarm is just at the moment when affairs seem at their most tense; the beneficent effects of a reduction in armaments will extend to other policy areas, and the creation of an atmosphere of mutual confidence will be expedited.

On the other hand, an equally strong argument is frequently made that disarmament cannot ever precede the establishment of binding security agreements. This was the theory behind Premier Bulganin's suggestion in the summer of 1956 that the first step in arms reduction be the negotiation of a nonaggression pact between the United States and the Soviet Union. It has also been the apparent basis of American action; implicit in United States policy has been the assumption that disarmament could be implemented only if and when Moscow fundamentally changed its foreign policy and minimized its threats to the peace and security of the world.[44]

It seems unnecessary for us to attempt a solution to this "chicken-or-egg" dilemma as to which condition leads to the other. We can be just as informative and on much safer ground if we merely stipulate that disarmament and security are inextricably intertwined and that no formula for one can permanently exclude the consideration of the other. As long as a reduction in arms cannot be imposed by fiat on a major state, if it is to come at all it must come voluntarily. No state will consent to a reduction in its military capacity unless it is convinced that the arms it is giving up are genuinely surplus and not needed. The problem of arms control must be attacked within a total context if it is to yield a solution.

ARMS REDUCTION AND ACCOMMODATION. What is this total context? Of what larger whole is the issue of arms limitation a part? In attempting to answer this question we come back very nearly to our original starting place.

The arms race is not the cause of the cold war, but is rather one of its symptoms. The original root of the disarmament issue lies in the fundamental divergence in national interest between the United States and the Soviet. So long as this conflict continues, and so long as there remains the remotest possibility that the disagreements might be prosecuted to the point of open warfare, each side will insist on retaining the practical maximum of armed strength. The arms race is thus one facet of the total policy controversy between the two contemporary giants and can be dealt with only in connection with the other points at issue.

The road to large-scale arms limitation and reduction will really open only at some time in the future of Soviet-American relations when the trend toward mutual accommodation has accumulated sufficient momentum. Only when the resolution of outstanding issues on a basis of substantial

---

[44]For a summary of the issues and some suggestions, see J. David Singer, "Threat-Perception and the Armament-Tension Dilemma," *Journal of Conflict Resolution* (March, 1958).

compromise is a dominant concern, and when "coexistence" is not a propaganda phrase but rather a formula for problem-solving, can large-scale plans for arms control be discussed realistically.

This might be thought a pessimistic view. Yet, if our analysis in the earlier part of this book has any validity, it would seem to be the most probable one. Weapons are tools of policy; when new policies no longer call for execution by military means, the weapons can be discarded. Any proposal for disarmament advanced before substantial political agreement has been reached (or at least before some sort of "agreement to agree" has been ratified by both parties) is at best irrelevant and at worst dangerous. It may be that the first fruit of any such joint decision to reduce the level of conflict might be an understanding on arms control. There is, however, no way for this to happen before an appropriate broader decision is made at the highest policy level.

CHAPTER **11**

Continuing
Economic Issues in
American Policy

"Economic issues in American policy" is a phrase with two possible meanings; which of them we select will affect the nature of our discussion in this chapter. On the one hand, it may refer to the general range of concerns that are included in the notions of "economic foreign policy" or "international economic relations," primarily involving the pattern formed by the economic objectives and interests of the American people and the techniques used to serve them. The phrase may equally accurately connote, however, the purely economic dimension of total American policy, including both the economic components of American national interest and the economic techniques the United States Government employs to advance it.

What makes this dual meaning important to us is that there is a considerable degree of contradiction in the implications of the two meanings. An "economic foreign policy," with objectives drawn from the free-enterprise doctrine accepted at least in principle by most Americans, cannot be thoroughly reconciled with the course of American foreign policy since 1945. The larger questions of national security and foreign policy have imposed a number of policies on the United States that cannot be squared with any traditional or rational image of "economic foreign policy" that would call for the maximization of private profit and the free flow of goods, services, credit, and persons.[1]

Our discussion will, as it must, select one of the two meanings upon which to concentrate and will consider the other only to the extent that it is relevant to the first. We shall deal in this analysis, as we have attempted to do throughout this book, with the broader aspects of American foreign policy: The "economic issues" we shall consider are those that bear upon the overall mission that the United States has set itself and problems that it encounters. We shall discuss initially the basic issue of the impact of American foreign policy upon the national economy. We shall then take up two of the more significant problems of American policy with a uniquely economic pertinence: American economic assistance to foreign states and American trade policy. These subjects fall under the second meaning of the term.

Foreign Policy and the American Economy

It is obvious that the major weapon upon which the United States has relied in its struggle against the Soviet camp has been its economic power. Unable to match the communist world in manpower, military mobilization, "political warfare," or subversion, America has counted on balancing the scales by its unique ability to produce and distribute goods and its possession of a highly organized and effective economic machine.[2] The key role of economic capability has given rise to certain fundamental questions about the relationship of foreign policy to the American economy.

THE COSTS OF FOREIGN POLICY

Foreign policy, involving as it does such a large share of the expenditures of the government, is admitted to cost a great deal of money. So much, indeed, that sectors of the general public, egged on by ideological, political, or opportunistic opponents of the trend of American policy, have come to entertain a genuine fear that the expenditure forced by international affairs

---

[1]"In short, although economic and military developments tend to be shaped by the same forces, a considerable gap separates our strategic and economic interests. How to bridge this strategic gap—rather than any dollar gap—is the central problem our foreign economic policy must overcome." Samuel Lubell, *The Revolution in World Trade and American Economic Policy* (New York: Harper & Row, Publishers, 1955), p. 40. Reprinted by permission.

[2]James P. Warburg, in *The United States in a Changing World* (New York: G.P. Putnam's Sons, 1954), pp. 425–431, gives a dramatic account of how this decision was originally reached in 1947–48.

will "bankrupt" the United States. Generally speaking, this attitude tends to go hand in hand with a relative unawareness of the exact costs of foreign policy and their relation to the national wealth or the gross national product. It would be salutary, therefore, to begin our discussion with some consideration of just how much foreign policy does cost.

THE DOLLAR COST OF FOREIGN POLICY: 1965. Expenditures for foreign policy fall into two major categories: national security and international affairs and finance. The dollar cost for a single year is instructive: We have selected fiscal 1965 and used the budget estimates as a basis. Expenditures in this year were typical of recent trends.

Estimated Foreign-Policy Expenditures, Fiscal 1965 (In Millions)*

National Security:	
Department of Defense (military)	51,200
Atomic energy	2,735
Stockpiling, defense-related programs	82
Military assistance	1,225
Total national security	55,242
International Affairs and Finance:	
Economic and financial programs	2,150
Relief, Peace Corps, P.L. 480	422
Foreign information, exchange activities	228
Conduct of foreign affairs	314
Total international affairs and finance	3,114
Total expenditures	58,356
Less receipts	30
Net Cost of Foreign Policy	58,326

*Data from *The Budget of the United States for 1965*, pp. 72, 82.

Thus, out of a total estimated government expenditure for fiscal 1965 of $97.9 billion, over $58 billion was earmarked for purposes directly connected with foreign affairs. Within the remaining $39 billion, another large amount—perhaps as much as $9 billion—financed programs with almost as direct an impact on foreign policy. The costs of foreign policy are not only large in themselves but constitute the most important single charge on the government's budget.

FOREIGN POLICY AND THE GROSS NATIONAL PRODUCT. But billions of dollars printed in a table are difficult to visualize; the sheer volume of amounts involved serves to obscure both the meaning and the relationships of the totals. More relevant for our purposes is the portion of the gross national product (GNP) that is devoted to foreign-policy purposes. The following table shows this relationship during recent years.

Gross National Product and Its Distribution Between Foreign Policy and Other Uses, in 1954 Dollars, 1950–1964*

Year	GNP (Billions)	Foreign Policy (Billions)	Other Uses (Billions)
1950	318.1	16.7	301.4
1955	392.7	44.9	347.8
1958	401.3	48.2	353.1
1959	428.6	50.5	378.1
1960	439.9	49.3	390.6
1961	447.7	50.9	396.8
1962	474.8	55.1	429.7
1963	492.9 (est.)	56.9	446.0
1964	516.6 (est.)	53.7	462.3

*Data from *Statistical Abstract of the United States: 1965* (Washington, D.C.: Government Printing Office, 1965), p. 234.

From these figures a few conclusions can be quickly drawn. In the first place, the increase in the total production of goods and services has been much more rapid than that in foreign-policy expenditures, thus making more available for general consumption each year. Other figures indicate that the steady increase in the "other uses" category has been more rapid even than population growth, thus increasing per capita personal income by over 59 per cent. In 1965, America's GNP surpassed $600 billion in current dollars, while foreign-policy expenditures were slightly over $53 billion. That year, the per capita share of goods and services was the highest in history.

The data contained in this table would suggest that the costs of foreign policy have not represented any great strain on the American economy. Americans have been able to bear the burden of maintaining a sizeable military establishment and of conducting a foreign policy heavily loaded with economic programs without impoverishing themselves. On the contrary, with the share of the GNP available for maintenance of the standard of living increasing both relatively and absolutely, large foreign-policy expenditures have had no measurable inhibiting effect on the much-lauded American standard of living.

Trends in Foreign-Policy Costs. The costs of foreign policy, viewed historically, follow certain clear trends, as shown in the following table.

Yearly Totals for Major Foreign-Policy Expenditures (In Billions)*

	1950	1955	1956	1957	1958	1959	1960	1961	1962	1963	1964	1965†
Economic, technical assistance	3.5	1.8	1.5	1.6	1.6	1.9	1.9	2.0	2.5	2.3	2.4	2.2
Foreign military aid	0.1	2.4	2.9	2.1	2.4	2.1	1.7	1.4	1.4	1.8	1.9	1.8
National security	13.0	40.7	40.7	43.4	44.2	46.5	45.7	47.5	51.1	52.8	55.3	54.0

*Data from *Statistical Abstract of the United States: 1965* and *The Budget of the United States for 1965*.

†Data for fiscal 1965 are estimated.

It appears from these figures that American spending on national security had reached something of a plateau in the neighborhood of $45 billion during the Eisenhower years but immediately rose to over $50 billion under the Kennedy and Johnson administrations; the major reasons for the higher costs (in addition to a steady upward movement of the price level) were the obligations entered into to make the doctrine of "flexible response" a reality. Throughout the period covered by the table, furthermore, it can be seen that economic and technical assistance has been until recently on a slow rise, while foreign military aid has held more or less steady between $1.5 billion and $2 billion. The grave new obligations the United States assumed in Southeast Asia during 1964 and 1965, however, promised major upward revision of cost estimates. Whatever the outcome of the war in Vietnam, it was quite probable that the dollar cost of foreign policy would remain indefinitely at a much higher level.

CAN THE UNITED STATES AFFORD ITS FOREIGN POLICY?

In one sense, the question at the head of this section is unnecessary; there is no doubt that the United States can afford the foreign policy it is presently carrying on. It has been doing so for a decade and a half and—despite some danger signals in the economy—there seems to be no real danger that the demands of foreign policy will place any insuperable burden on the economic capacity of the United States.

But there is another sense in which the question has great relevance. We may refer momentarily back to our discussion of American capabilities. We concluded that American capacities are in general adequate to the mission the United States has set for itself. The United States *can*, we suggested, meet all the foreseeable tests; what was much less certain, however, is whether the United States *will* do so. So long as there remains an area of relatively free choice, no one dare state unequivocally that Americans will decide that they can afford their foreign policy.

THE "LAYER OF FAT" IN THE ECONOMY. Economists point out that despite the great expenditures that the United States has been making in the foreign-policy field and the constantly rising GNP and standard of living, the national economy has not been operating at peak efficiency. There remain segments of plant, manpower, and finance capital that are not being used at full effectiveness; there is, in other words, a residue of productivity that has not yet been fully called on. Speaking theoretically, therefore, it seems reasonable to assume that the United States could if it wished increase its foreign-policy expenditure by an indefinite but certainly considerable amount without significantly affecting the standard of living. A simple expansion of productivity to take up the slack would make available great amounts of goods and services for public purposes without reducing the total available for other purposes.[3]

This "layer of fat" in the national economy—the unused (or inefficiently used) productive capacity—may well be the secret economic weapon of the United States. As long as it exists it provides something of an answer to the question we asked above: The United States can afford its foreign policy as long as it retains in uncommitted reserve considerable increments of economic power. Until international requirements force the United States to go beyond this point—that is, until the demands of foreign policy require that serious inroads be made in the goods and services available for civilians— the United States will live within its means.

THE IMPACT OF POPULAR PREFERENCES. Webster defines "afford" in the sense in which we are using it as "to incur, stand, or bear without serious detriment (as to financial condition . . . etc.)." Whether or not the United States can afford its foreign policy, therefore, depends in the final analysis on whether the American people, acting through their political channels, decide that the cost of international relations is causing "serious detriment" to their standard of living. A popular decision at any time that foreign affairs are costing too much would be immediately reflected in a cut in government outlays to a level felt to be tolerable.

There is no doubt that Americans are willing to support great deprivations in private economic life if they are convinced that the external peril is real enough to justify them. This fact is at least a partial explanation for the "crisis technique" that has surrounded so much of American programming between 1947 and 1953. The policy of the Eisenhower and Kennedy administrations, however, made much of eschewing this approach and of concentrating instead on commitments of a long-term nature and planning for coordinated policies extending over a period of several years. This method, although minimizing the risks of going "too far, too fast," involved dangers of its own.

In view of the mercurial swings of American public sentiment in response to stimuli frequently slight or even irrelevant, a long-range plateau-type

---

[3]In his provocative study, *The Revolution in World Trade*, Samuel Lubell has a typically suggestive statement on this point (p. 40):

"Currently the tendency is to think of our surpluses as costly liabilities. But two world wars and the whole course of the postwar period have shown that the free world's strongest *single* asset is the ability of the American economy to generate sizable surpluses of every kind, from food and machinery, to medicine and clothing . . . .

"Although the heads of many foreign governments do not seem to realize it, our productive reserves are the cushion which permits them to sleep in political stability and freedom. For some time ahead most of the world is likely to continue to be living on the thin edge strategically and, in many cases, economically as well. By far the greatest contribution the United States can make to the well-being and security of the rest of the world is to remain economically strong, a reservoir of productive resources capable of meeting any emergency." (Italics in original; reprinted by permission.)

policy may sometimes be thought too expensive and sometimes too niggardly. Particularly in moments of relative relaxation may the public pressure for a lower rate of expenditure become politically impossible to resist. At these times the danger of unwise retrenchment is the greatest.[4]

THE BALANCE-OF-PAYMENTS DEFICIT. In recent years a familiar economic problem has acquired ominous new dimensions and has become a matter of grave national concern. This is, of course, the chronic deficit in the American balance of payments. Put simply, the United States spends more abroad than it takes in at home in payment for exported goods and services. The payment deficit can be made up only by the export of gold drawn from American reserves.

We should first emphasize that the deficit is not a new problem; it has existed every year since 1945. In the first postwar decade, however, it was considered to be in the interest of the United States to transfer purchasing power abroad as rapidly as possible, both as an anticommunist maneuver and as a major contribution to rapid economic recovery. During those years, therefore, the deficit in the balance of payments was regarded as either a substantial irrelevancy or else as a positive indication that United States policy was on the right track. The economic recovery of Europe and Japan that featured newly competitive export industries, the increase in imports of merchandise by American consumers, the rapid increase in American tourism abroad, and a substantial rise in private investment abroad by American corporations all combined after 1961 to focus attention on the serious depletion in American gold reserves.

Looked at in detail, certain characteristics of the deficit are obvious. The "ordinary" transactions that enter into the balance of payments are all "favorable" to the United States. In 1963, for example, the nation exported $21.9 billion worth of goods and services, and imports amounted to only $16.9 billion. The deficit (that amounted to $2.6 billion in 1963 and approximately the same in subsequent years) arose almost entirely from two major sources: Private investment abroad was the second most important factor, and United States government expenditures outside the country (military forces and bases, foreign aid, and the like) contributed the largest share.[5] It could be said, in other words, that the balance-of-payments deficit represented in one important sense one of the major costs of conducting American foreign policy.

The Kennedy and Johnson administrations moved to deal with the problem but with no more than minimal success, at least during the early 1960's.

---

[4]See, for example, the table on pages 593–594 of *Hearings Before the Committee on Foreign Relations, United States Senate: Foreign Assistance 1964* (Washington, D.C.: Government Printing Office, 1964). Since 1963, there has been an average cut of $500 million from the President's requests for development and other forms of economic aid, whereas military assistance requests have nearly always been met or exceeded.

[5]*Statistical Abstract of the United States: 1965*, p. 856.

The government's policy was two-sided: On the one hand efforts were made to increase earnings from abroad by stimulating exports and encouraging foreign travel in the United States; on the other hand, tentative beginnings were made at reducing the net outflow of dollars. Tourism abroad by Americans was discouraged, pressures were felt to "buy American" rather than foreign goods, and—most importantly—"voluntary guidelines" were established to control private investment overseas. The one part of the deficit-producing complex that officials were unwilling to consider reducing was government expenditures abroad. These, it was felt, were so essential to national security that at all costs they should be kept at their existing levels or even increased. No concern about the balance of payments was voiced, for example, during the commitment stages of American entry into the war in Vietnam.

The future of the effort to control the balance-of-payments deficit was unclear in the mid-1960's. There was some evidence, for example, that major producing nations in Europe and Asia were becoming concerned lest the deficit either lead the United States onto a path of unhealthy economic restrictions or else actually undermine world confidence in the dollar (which was still, as it had long been, the major reserve currency of the world). Discussions looking to the discovery and exploitation of ways to assist the United States with its problem were initiated among international bankers after 1962. There was some irony in this development: After helping put the world on its economic feet during the early 1950's, it would be a strange reversal of roles for the United States to be helped out of its difficulty by the very economies it had once nurtured.[6]

CAN THE UNITED STATES AFFORD PEACE?

A question of only remote significance in contemporary affairs but of potentially major importance is whether or not the United States can afford peace. We have seen that the cold war, at least at its present level, is bearable; we know also that the United States has fought a major war and avoided a postwar depression. But what if the economic stimulus provided by foreign-policy spending of all sorts (consuming, as we have seen, roughly 12 per cent of the GNP), should suddenly come to an end? Would there be, as some political figures contend, an immediate depression? Does the United States need the cold war to maintain its prosperity?

---

[6]A general treatment of the problem can be found in a study done by the International Bank for Reconstruction and Development, Dragoslaw Avramovic *et al.*, *Economic Growth and External Debt* (Baltimore: Johns Hopkins University Press, 1964). The increasing concern of the Johnson administration over the balance-of-payments problem is illustrated by the repeated calls from the President and from Secretary of the Treasury Fowler for "voluntary" controls over overseas investment and by the President's "see America first" campaign to reduce the outflow of tourist dollars.

THE ECONOMIC EFFECT OF PEACE.   These are questions which no one can answer *in vacuo;* the proof of the American economic pudding must be in the eating. Certain points, however, permit some generalization.

We must initially distinguish between two different ways in which peace could "break out." If the whole pattern of American postwar policy were to be made suddenly obsolete by a dramatic collapse of communism, the economic questions that would then be posed would indeed be formidable and would call for rapid, perhaps emergency, action. On the other hand, if the cold war were to relax gradually, the American government would have time to shift its policy emphasis little by little from a quasi-war basis to some other areas of expenditure.

To be more specific, major saving in the cost of foreign policy—of an amount sufficient to present a problem to the adjustment capacity of the American economy—can be achieved in only one major category: armaments spending. Other areas of government outlay for foreign policy represent only relatively negligible totals. The economic problem of peace would most probably be presented in the form of a great reduction of government appropriations for military purposes, and it is in this area that the clearest difference between a rapid shutoff and a gradual slowdown is demonstrated.

Were there to take place wholesale demobilization, speedy contract cancellation, renegotiation of purchases, and the other apparatus of rapid transition with which Americans became familiar during 1945 and 1946, one-sixth of the GNP would suddenly become surplus. If no corrective action were taken, massive unemployment, price drops, and deflation would bring on an economic crisis potentially rivaling the depression of 1929. On the other hand, if the cutback in military expenditures were more gradual, its impact could be spread out over a longer period and—even in the absence of palliative government action—the pressure at any one time would not be so great.

GOVERNMENT POLICY.   In the event that the cold war relaxes gradually, the United States stands committed to maintain a high level of international spending for an indefinite time. As long ago as 1953, President Eisenhower pledged that the United States would devote substantial portions of any savings brought about by disarmament to a fund for "world development and reconstruction."[7] From the domestic point of view, maintaining prosperity while readjustment takes place is primary; it is a happy coincidence that one technique for accomplishing this purpose also directly advances the foreign policy of the United States. If world stability and order are to follow peace, American financial assistance will be needed. The fact that such a policy will also play a part in maintaining domestic economic health only makes more probable the fulfillment of the pledge.

---

[7]In his speech to the American Society of Newspaper Editors, April 16, 1953. See *The New York Times* (April 17, 1953).

In the event of a sudden shutoff in the cold war, however, the major problem would be that of emergency action. The American economy contains a number of built-in stabilizers and antidepression mechanisms that would cushion the shock,[8] including the Social Security System, the Full Employment Act, and the Federal Deposit Insurance Corporation. But emergency action to "prime the pump" (in the phrase of Depression days) would be needed to get the economic wheels turning again at full speed.

Foreign Economic Assistance

We have discussed in another chapter some of the aspects of military aid and defense support extended by the United States to friendly nations. In the present connection we are primarily interested in the overall economic implications of foreign aid, not only that portion oriented toward defense but also including development assistance, technical assistance, and private overseas investment.

FOREIGN AID: AMOUNT AND IMPACT

THE ECONOMIC DIMENSIONS OF FOREIGN AID.   How large have American aid programs been, and of what size are they today? The summary figures indicate both amounts and trends.

Foreign-Aid Expenditures, Fiscal 1950-Fiscal 1965 (In Billions)*

Year	Military Assistance	Economic and Technical Development	Total Foreign Aid	Total Expenditure, U.S.
1950	0.05	3.6	3.6	39.6
1951	1.0	2.6	3.6	44.1
1952	1.4	1.9	3.4	65.4
1953	4.1	1.9	6.1	74.2
1954	3.2	2.2	5.5	67.7
1955	2.3	1.8	4.2	64.5
1956	2.9	1.5	4.4	66.2
1957	2.1	1.6	3.7	69.0
1958	2.4	1.6	4.0	71.4
1959	2.1	1.9	4.0	80.3
1960	1.7	1.9	3.6	76.5
1961	1.4	2.0	3.4	81.5
1962	1.4	2.5	3.9	87.8
1963	1.8	2.3	4.1	92.6
1964 (est.)	1.9	2.4	4.3	98.4
1965 (est.)	1.9	2.2	4.1	97.9

*Data from *Statistical Abstract of the United States: 1965*, p. 863.

---

[8]For an interesting (if somewhat out of date) study of this point, see David Cushman Coyle, "Leaning on the Kremlin," *Virginia Quarterly Review* (Spring, 1954), p. 192ff.

The decreasing share of the GNP taken by foreign aid appears clearly from these figures, the cumulative effect of which is heightened by the well-known steady increase in the price index. Dollar costs of foreign aid of various categories are holding steady in contrast to increasing total expenditures by the government.

Our earlier discussions of the overall impact of foreign policy on the American economy made the point that to the extent that international obligations constitute a net drain on the available goods and services, the primary stress occurs at the point of military expenditures rather than in foreign-assistance programs. This generalization appears to be borne out by the statistics we have quoted. At particular pressure points in the economy, however, there could be some cause for complaint that foreign assistance might actually work a hardship on Americans. This contention is offset, however, by the considerable, if immeasurable, extent to which foreign-assistance programs have stimulated other, more normal trade activities and thus brought about a net economic gain to the United States.

THE GLOBAL SCOPE OF AMERICAN AID.   Despite its relatively small dollar volume as compared to the total expenditures of the American government, the aid program has brought the United States into direct contact with the economies of virtually all the countries of the free world. Whether American economic assistance is by means of direct supply of military end-items, defense support, development aid, or technical cooperation, the United States and its policy exert a significant effect on economic affairs in the entire noncommunist world.

During the period between July 1, 1964 and December 31, 1964, the total cost of foreign assistance was $96.0 billion. Of this total, $33.8 billion was the cost of military aid, while $62.1 billion represented "grants, credits, and other assistance." During the two decades, western Europe was the major overall recipient: A net total of $39.7 billion (reflecting repayments of some $2 billion) was transferred to the states of western Europe. The Near East (which included Greece and Turkey) had received $19.4 billion, Africa $2.0 billion, the western hemisphere $5.9 billion, and the Far East $24.7 billion. As indicated above, the bulk of western Europe's bill had been piled up during the 1950's, and in recent years there has been a greater flow-back of funds. In fiscal 1964, for example, the only states included in western Europe to receive continued nonmilitary aid were Iceland, Italy, Portugal, and Yugoslavia. In contrast, the figures for the Far East, the Near East, and Africa showed a fairly steady increase during the first half of the 1960's.

The bill for military aid—$33.8 billion—showed that western Europe (principally France, Italy, Belgium, and the Netherlands) had received the largest share: $15.8 billion. Following in order were the Far East ($10.9 billion), the Near East ($5.6 billion), the western hemisphere ($0.9 billion), and Africa ($0.2 billion). Nonmilitary aid showed the same general pattern of distribution: western Europe led with $23.9 billion, the Far East came next with $13.8 billion, the Near East was almost equal with $13.7 billion, the western hemisphere lagged behind with $5.0 billion, and Africa (which had received virtually no aid at all through the 1950's) had received $1.8 billion by the end of 1964.

The recipients of the major share of nonmilitary aid (exact figures on military aid are classified) were, in order: the United Kingdom ($6.4 billion), France ($4.4 billion), India ($4.2 billion), Korea ($3.7 billion), West Germany ($3.0 billion), Italy ($2.8 billion), and Japan ($2.5 billion). We should recall that the United Kingdom, France, and West Germany have all substantially reduced their totals in recent years by significant repayments.[9]

THE FUTURE OF AMERICAN AID. No issue has caused more bitter debate among Americans than the question of foreign aid and its future. To some it is simply a "giveaway," inspired by quasi-socialists who want to dissipate the American substance in a mad burst of vapid philanthropy; to others it is a foredoomed attempt to "buy friends" who cannot be bought; to still others it is stupid to arm, modernize, and develop potential rivals, adversaries, and competitors. On the other hand, its defenders claim it is—in one form or another—not only the most efficient weapon of American policy but indeed an absolutely essential method of holding back communism without war.[10] The ups and downs of the aid budgets over the years not only reflect the changes in the international scene but also roughly indicate the currents of public opinion and legislative interest in the question.

Considering the trends of contemporary world politics, there seems to be no prospect of an end to American foreign aid. Programs may change in response to new conditions and indeed should so do. Administration and planning undoubtedly can be improved. But to some form of aid the United States is indefinitely committed; there is too much in the American interest that can be accomplished only by such measures for anyone seriously to indulge himself in the illusory hope of their early termination. The appropriate argument with existing philosophy and implementation is in favor of a greater emphasis upon tailoring programs to meet actual needs rather than allowing them to develop out of American domestic politics or to take form via an unimaginative perpetuation of time-sanctioned practices. Foreign aid has a future; Americans should be bending every effort to make sure that this future is a good one.

---

[9]Data from *Statistical Abstract of the United States: 1965*, pp. 863–865.

[10]Of the enormous volume of literature available on American foreign-aid programs, a balanced appraisal is found in Liska, *The New Statecraft: Foreign Aid in American Foreign Policy*. Also useful are Feis, *Foreign Aid and Foreign Policy*, and James Wiggins and Helmut Schoeck, eds., *Foreign Aid Reexamined* (Washington, D.C.: Public Affairs Press, 1958).

DEVELOPMENT ASSISTANCE

A special form of foreign aid with its own set of problems has been assistance to underdeveloped countries. First broached in 1949 in President Truman's inaugural address, the "bold new program" grew in complexity throughout the 1950's and 1960's. It still remains a constant concern to policy-makers and a perplexity to Americans, with both its goals and its techniques in constant dispute.

TECHNICAL ASSISTANCE. The original conception underlying the effort to aid underdeveloped (today more commonly called "developing" or "emerging") states was that of technical assistance and cooperation: the export of American "know-how." Beginning with the creation of the Technical Cooperation Administration in the Department of State in 1950 as an immediate reply to President Truman's original proposal, the United States has been continuously in the business of providing technical personnel and information to over eighty countries. The major areas in which American experts are made available to states that request them are education, health (private and public), agriculture, industry, and community development.[11]

Technical assistance and cooperation by the United States has been a clear success, but its record has been much less impressive than at least some of its early advocates had hoped. Providing teachers or agricultural agents for a developing country may indeed be the most valuable service the United States can perform for the recipient nation, but it must be admitted that this kind of policy cannot win any quick or immediately satisfying victories over communism.

It is also true that technical assistance has been forced to subsist on a budgetary diet that can only be called niggardly. Congress, sensitive to the immediate crises arising from the danger of communism, has never perceived any clear relationship between the major problems of United States foreign policy and, for example, community development in a valley of the Andes. As a result, technical cooperation has never bulked really large in the total American policy picture, although it has long served as a valuable outlet for the innate philanthropic inclinations of the American people. The Peace Corps, for example, is an apt example of an enterprise that both performs a real—if limited—service in the field and also contributes to better morale at home.

FINANCING DEVELOPMENT. The problem of the economic and social development of the non-Western world, the United States realized very

---

[11]Jonathan B. Bingham, *Shirt-Sleeve Diplomacy, Point 4 in Action* (New York: The John Day Company, Inc., 1953), is a very enthusiastic analysis of the early stages of Point 4. Mr. Bingham was Acting Director of the Technical Cooperation Administration.

early in the 1950's, involves far more than merely supplying technical personnel. It also demands capital in large amounts, and—except for those few states with extensive petroleum deposits—this capital must come from outside the developing state itself. As a result, the United States has long been involved in a variety of programs designed to make development capital available to friendly countries. Three distinct approaches have been developed.

The first has been the encouragement of private investment in the developing countries. Although recently contradicted to some extent by other policies aimed at restricting further drains on the balance of payments, the principle remains valid today. AID sells investment insurance to private investors for certain types of operations, partially subsidizes studies of possible investment opportunities, and performs other services for private capital. By and large, however, American corporations and lending institutions have been relatively reluctant to make high-risk and low-return commitments in emerging countries, preferring instead to invest in the more profitable markets of stable economies, such as those in western Europe.[12]

It was this realization that led the United States to undertake the second line of attack on the problem of financing development, the use of direct government financing.

An old (1934) instrument for this purpose that has gained new relevance in the postwar era is the Export-Import Bank of Washington. EIB has concentrated since 1945 on making commercial-type loans abroad for low-risk development enterprises, almost all for industrial expansion or the creation of new facilities. In the two decades from 1945 to the end of 1964, EIB had made $9.3 billion in loans and had collected $5.7 billion in repayments. The percentage of loss has been very small.[13]

EIB, however, suffers from one handicap from the point of view of overall American policy: Its loans are commercial and thus are confined to enterprises that are almost certain to succeed. This leaves a large area of need uncovered for somewhat more speculative and low-return—but politically and socially necessary—investments. Such arrangements call for longer terms, more favorable interest rates, and even repayment in local currencies rather than in dollars.

This problem was attacked in 1957, when Congress created the Development Loan Fund. The DLF was supposed to make "soft" loans both to

---

[12]For a discussion of this problem with particular reference to Latin America, see Edward S. Mason, *Foreign Aid and Foreign Policy* (New York: Harper & Row, Publishers, for the Council on Foreign Relations, 1964), pp. 87–97.

[13]An overall summary of the activities of the EIB is available in U.S. Congress, House of Representatives, *Hearings Before a Subcommittee of the Committee on Appropriations: Foreign Operations Appropriations for 1965; Part 1* (Washington, D.C.: Government Printing Office, 1964), pp. 1–47.

private enterprise and to governments to finance development projects. It never grew to major stature, and in 1961 it was integrated into the newly formed Agency for International Development. Since AID has taken over development lending, the pace has quickened moderately, surpassing $1 billion in fiscal 1963, 1964, and 1965.[14]

The third avenue of attack has been through United States membership in international organizations. These are of two types: those that plan and coordinate development enterprises and those that actually finance them.

The most significant of the first type are the Development Assistance Committee (DAC) of the Organization for Economic Cooperation and Development (the successor body to the OEEC of Marshall Plan days) and the Alliance for Progress (1961). Other examples are the regional Economic Commissions of the United Nations for Asia and the Far East, Africa, and Latin America and the Consultative Committee of the Colombo Plan for development in South and Southeast Asia.

Four major international financial institutions play leading roles; the United States is a member of each and makes a major financial contribution to all of them. They may be characterized serially:

1. *The International Bank for Reconstruction and Development* (World Bank). The IBRD has 101 members, none from the communist world. Its total subscribed capital in 1965 was $21.6 billion. The Bank is, like the Export-Import Bank, a conservative lending agency which makes only "hard" loans and which has proved to be a very successful business enterprise. Its total loan disbursements are in the neighborhood of $10 billion during its history. While its overall contribution is relatively small in comparison to American unilateral commitments, its impact on the practice of financing development has been very great due to its high prestige and the all-but-universal character of its membership.[15]

2. *The International Finance Corporation* (IFC). The IFC was created in 1956 as an affiliate of IBRD for the purpose of encouraging the growth of productive private enterprise in the less-developed countries. Its purpose is to invest in promising private projects in association with private capital when adequate private funds are not available. IFC in 1965 had seventy-eight members, with a total subscription that year of $98 million. Most of

---

[14]On the general topic of development loans, see Antonin Basch, *Financing Development* (New York: The Macmillan Company, 1964) and Robert L. Heilbroner, *The Great Ascent* (New York: Harper & Row, Publishers, 1963). See also the annual reports of AID and the International Development Association.

[15]For a summary of the operations of the World Bank see Alexander K. Cairncross, *The International Bank for Reconstruction and Development* (Princeton, N.J.: Princeton University Press, 1959). For yearly accounts of activities see the *Annual Report of the International Bank for Reconstruction and Development and the International Development Association*, published in September each year by the Bank.

its some $80 million of commitments have been in Latin America for industrial purposes.[16]

3. *The International Development Association* (IDA). IDA, also an affiliate of IBRD, was created in 1960 to provide even more flexible terms for international development assistance. All its credits are extended for a term of fifty years and without interest. In 1965 IDA had ninety-four members and a total subscription of almost exactly $1 billion. Its credits, amounting in all to some $500 million, were extended primarily to Asia, Africa, and the Middle East and went primarily for assistance in the building of highways and port facilities.[17]

4. *The Inter-American Development Bank*. The Inter-American Development Bank and its companion agency, the Special Operations Fund, were created in 1959. These bodies include all Latin American states, except Cuba, as well as the United States. The Bank has a subscription of $1.7 billion, the Special Operations Fund $219 million. The Bank makes most of its loans on a commercial basis in dollars for wealth-producing projects; the Fund makes loans that would normally be regarded as unacceptable bank risks, have easier terms, and are repayable in local currencies. The Bank also administers the Social Progress Trust Fund of the Alliance for Progress. As of the end of 1965, the Bank had approved loans amounting to $545 million, the Special Operations Fund $171 million, and the Social Progress Trust Fund $450 million.[18]

United States Trade Policy

An economic issue of immediate pertinence to the total of American foreign policy is the question of the status of international trade. Perhaps in no area has it proved more difficult to bring together the competing requirements of a cold-war orientation to immediate issues and a long-term interest in the economic implications of peace, order, and stability.

America's strategic economic position has made it possible for the United States to use international trade as a weapon against the Soviet. Denying exports to hostile nations or extending trade and exchange concessions to friendly ones and the employment of promises or threats to do either while bargaining have proved generally useful to American negotiators. The use of trade control as a tool of policy has meant, however, a systematic denial

---

[16]For the latest data on the IFC, see the *Annual Report of the International Finance Corporation: 1964–65*.

[17]For yearly surveys of IDA activities, see the annual reports cited above.

[18]The activities of the Inter-American Development Bank are extensively reported in U.S. House of Representatives, *Foreign Operations Appropriations for 1965*, pp. 97–161.

of the pledges of "normal" trade relations made by the United States on other occasions. Freely operating "multilateralism" in international economic relations has been a casualty of the cold war. The United States has been unable thoroughly to rationalize this confusion of purpose.

Domestic developments have also complicated the problem. The free-enterprise economy of the United States has resisted both forms of government pressure, either toward greater control of trade in the national interest or toward a genuine attempt at the liberalization of international trade. Instead the American economy has been greatly affected by the worldwide urge toward economic nationalism, and considerable pressure-group agitation toward protectionism, boycotts, government-subsidized trading, and other manifestations of "unilateralism" have been constant factors in government decisions. All of these matters enter into United States trade policy and affect the broader pattern of American policy.[19]

THE PROBLEMS OF TRADE

International trade, for the United States, has presented a series of problems since 1945 that have made the development of a coherent trade policy very difficult. As we shall discuss them here, they break down into three broad categories: the announced pledge of multilateralism and what has happened to it, the "dollar gap" and its eventual conversion into a balance-of-payments deficit, and the political significance of trade, both with the communist bloc and the noncommunist states.

THE PLEDGE OF MULTILATERALISM. The United States entered the postwar era committed in principle to multilateralism in international economic relations, the increase of international trade, and the maximum possible freedom for all forms of interstate economic contacts.[20] The American position in 1945 was flatfootedly in favor of immediate and extensive action to reduce the barriers to trade and to stimulate the flow of goods and services in all directions across national frontiers. The concrete measures the United States (in association with Britain) proposed included tariff reduction and cooperative action by all trading states to create a climate

---

[19]Samuel Lubell, in *The Revolution in World Trade*, says (p. 26): "To attempt to reassert the doctrine of free trade or free competition in its old laissez-faire sense is unworkable in view of the prevailing pressures for government intervention, from both domestic and foreign sources. Yet expanded government intervention, in itself, offers no solution either, if only because the pressures for government action that arise from domestic sources, are so often in such violent conflict with the needs of international stability." Reprinted by permission.

[20]See, as the most forthright statement of this position, *Proposals for Expansion of World Trade and Employment*, Department of State publication 2411 (Washington, D.C.: Government Printing Office, 1945).

more favorable to trade; particularly important in American (and British) thinking was the early negotiation of the General Agreements on Tariffs and Trade (GATT) and the creation of the International Trade Organization (ITO).

Unfortunately, neither economics nor politics permitted the pledge of multilateralism to be effectively translated from the realm of principle to the area of practice. The first postwar decade saw the United States Government clinging to its pledge of ultimately freer trade but unable to make any major progress toward that goal in the face of constant political crisis provoked by the Soviet and recurrent economic trouble at various points in the free world.

THE DOLLAR GAP. From the point of view of pure economics (assuming for the moment that in this context "economics" can be separated from "politics"), official American policy asserted that the reopening of trade channels after 1945 was obstructed by four factors: (1) restrictions imposed by governments; (2) restrictions imposed by private combines and cartels; (3) fear of disorder in the markets for certain primary commodities; (4) irregularity and the fear of irregularity in production and employment.[21] In practice, however, all of these proved less important than one that American economists and policy-makers foresaw only dimly in 1945: the dollar gap.[22]

In essence the dollar gap after 1945 meant that the free-world nations wanted and needed American goods but lacked the means to pay for them. In international trade, payment for American goods in the first instance may be made in dollar credits, but ultimately the payments must balance; if Europe (for example) were to continue purchasing American commodities over any protracted period, it would be obliged to sell an equivalent amount of goods in dollar markets. In 1945 the free world could neither produce salable goods nor gain access to dollar markets. This was the dollar gap: the margin between a nation's import requirements from the dollar area and its available dollars or dollar-earning capacity.

So great was the dollar gap for all except a very few states that to talk about "normal trade" was preposterous. The United States was forced (both for economic and for political reasons) to undertake large-scale programs of aid to the free world ("unilateral transfers," to use the delicate phrase) in order to keep some trade flowing and to accomplish the minimum objectives of foreign policy. This program was concentrated in Europe, where (in an industrialized society) the problem was more acute; the elimination of the dollar gap in unindustrialized nations (primarily raw-material

---

[21] *Proposals for Expansion of World Trade and Employment*, pp. 12–18.
[22] See, for a theoretical discussion, J. E. Meade, *The Balance of Payments* (London: Oxford University Press, 1951).

producers) was to be accomplished by longer-range programs, primarily development assistance. We have seen some figures earlier indicating the magnitude of the American effort in this regard.

So effectively did American action reduce the dollar gap that a real (although invisible) balance-of-payments deficit quickly opened up for the United States—exactly the purpose of the program, especially as regards Europe. It was not until the recession of 1958, however, that Americans generally awoke to the existence of the deficit, and then only after it had impinged directly on the import-export rates with Europe. Despite the fact that the bulk of the deficit arose as the result of military and other overseas expenditures of a noneconomic sort, protectionists began their attack on the American trade position. Americans by 1960 no longer were worried about a dollar shortage in Europe; instead, there was talk of a "dollar glut." The deficit primarily affected American economic relations with Europe. It was of much less relevance to the underdeveloped nations unless it brought on a totally unexpected loss of confidence in the dollar.

We have already mentioned the variety of measures the United States Government is taking to cope with the balance-of-payments deficit. What concerns us here, however, is how Washington can effectively reduce the deficit—granting that military and foreign-aid expenditures remain at their present level—without doing serious damage to the normal flow of trade. One small—really symbolic—gesture, for example, has already caused considerable backlash of ill feeling abroad and even some threats of reprisal: the reduction of the duty-free allowance granted American tourists returning to the United States from a high of $500 to its present low level of $100 retail-price value. Simple logic dictates that if the United States wishes to sell abroad, it must buy abroad also. Except in the very shortest of runs, attempts to bypass this principle can lead only to unfortunate retaliation and the worsening of an already unsatisfactory situation.

THE POLITICAL IMPLICATIONS OF TRADE. But there were additional reasons why multilateralism was ignored. When the nature of the Soviet threat was made clear and the outlines of an American policy were inked in, America's strategic economic position dictated the use of trade as a political weapon. Since 1945, the use of trade as a tool of foreign policy has taken two forms: (1) The Soviet bloc has been generally excluded from the American trading area; (2) trade concessions have been used to weld the free world into a more cohesive entity. Bipolarity as a policy demanded that the Soviet sphere be boycotted by the entire free world, and American policy has worked to this end. The Battle Act, passed by Congress in 1951, was designed to deny American economic aid to any nation that traded with communists, and much effort was expended by American negotiators to persuade allies and neutrals alike that they should have no dealings with Moscow.

The policy, however bravely it might be stated, was never fully implemented. Too many noncommunist states were faced with economic problems that the United States could not (or would not) solve, and the communist bloc offered too many tempting bargains. From the point of view of allied nations, American tariff policy left a great deal to be desired. There was always a certain amount of trading across the Iron Curtain, even at the height of bipolarity; the rise of neutralism after 1954 and the coincident decline of the two-power concept made it out of the question to restrict free-world trade with the communist empire. After 1957, although the United States was careful not to undertake any full-fledged reconsideration of its policy, the volume of East-West trade was at a postwar high and promised to increase steadily.[23]

Just as the effectiveness of bipolar control of East-West trade diminished, so did the utility of using intra-free-world trade as a means of unifying the American bloc. This is not to say that the economic interdependence of the Western world diminished; what declined was the ability of the United States to hold its allies in line by economic means. In the first place, the economic revival of western Europe and its consolidation by means of the European Economic Community gave those states great economic leverage against the United States. Smaller states as well exploited their freedom of economic maneuver. The 1958 recession taught Americans the hard lesson that economic power was no longer their monopoly, to be put to political purposes at will. Instead the United States was forced to think once more in terms of competition, a concept once generic to the American genius but almost forgotten in the highly political atmosphere of the post-1945 world.

ITO AND GATT

In the postwar world multilateral international trade has been subordinated to the twin pressures of domestic planning and economic nationalism on the one hand and of the demands of foreign policy on the other. A clear demonstration of this generalization is the history of the attempts to formalize multilateralism into international institutions. The International Trade Organization, the Charter of which was hailed as a great forward step, has never come into existence; the General Agreement on Tariffs and Trade,

---

[23]After 1956, each time the subject of "improvement in East-West relations" came up in Soviet-American exchanges, Soviet spokesmen were quick to raise the prospect of an increase in trade as an augury of better times. See, for example, the proposal voiced by then Deputy Premier Kosygin asking for a "normalization" of East-West trade and an extension of long-term credits to the Soviet Union as reported in *The New York Times* (March 7, 1964).

although provocative of much negotiation and some reduction in tariffs, has had only a negligible effect on trade patterns.

THE FAILURE OF ITO. The ITO Charter was drawn up at the United Nations Conference on Trade and Employment, held at Havana in 1947–48.[24] It was the culmination of the 1945 American *Proposals* and, in general, provided for an organization charged with the duty of bringing about an increase in the flow of international trade. Even though the Charter contained many exceptions to the general principles of free trade (made on behalf of nations that were in difficulties and that demanded the right to take unilateral remedial action), the theory of the document was clearly in the tradition of multilateralism.

The ITO was stillborn; the Charter remains as a monument to the hopes of the early postwar era, but the organization never came into existence. Failure of the United States to ratify the instrument doomed the entire undertaking, and after 1950 the executive branch ceased even to attempt to win congressional approval. In 1955 President Eisenhower attempted to gain consent for American entry into the Organization of Trade Cooperation, a less elaborate offshoot of ITO. This also proved too much for newly protectionist Senators to accept, and there was little hope after that date that the United States would—at least in the contemporary climate of domestic and foreign policies—take this step in implementation of its promise of freer trade.

NEGOTIATIONS UNDER GATT. The General Agreement on Tariffs and Trade was entered into in 1947.[25] It is actually an understanding providing for multilateral tariff bargaining among the signatories. Under its terms periodic meetings of the contracting parties are held. Discussions go on, either for reciprocal tariff reductions or for ironing out particular trade difficulties.

The GATT negotiations, in addition to bilateral and multilateral tariff discussions, have concentrated upon certain semipermanent problems obstructing free trade. Among these have been the issue of import quotas[26]

---

[24]United Nations, *Charter for an International Trade Organization*, United Nations Conference on Trade and Employment, Havana, Cuba, 1947–48 (New York: United Nations, 1948).

[25]U.S. Department of State, *The General Agreement on Tariffs and Trade and Texts of Related Documents* (Washington, D.C.: Government Printing Office, 1950).

[26]The State Department press release discussing the eleventh session of the contracting parties made the following comment about American action on import restrictions at this 1956 meeting: "... the U.S. delegation held bilateral consultations with the delegations of thirteen countries. . . . These discussions covered import restrictions maintained by these countries on specific commodities which created a hardship to U.S. producers or were unduly discriminatory toward U.S. goods. In each case the U.S. delegation suggested that the other country consider whether a relaxation of the restriction could be made without disrupting that country's balance-of-payments position. Industrial products were discussed with eight countries, agricultural products with five, and fisheries products with four." Quoted in *Department of State Bulletin* (December 3, 1956), p. 895.

(imposed usually by nations in serious balance-of-payments difficulties), currency convertibility, and price stabilization on primary commodities (usually agricultural). Despite the fairly general goodwill with which these problems were attacked, most of the participating states have sincerely felt that their own problems were important and unique enough that exceptions to general rules should be made in their case. Understandable as this was, and justifiable as many of the claims were, this emphasis on discovering loopholes in GATT rather than attempting to make forward progress could not but be a disappointment to those who hoped for an increase in trade as a contribution to stability in the world.

THE UNITED STATES AND THE EUROPEAN TRADING BLOCS. One of the most troublesome trading problems facing the United States in the 1960's was that of coming to terms with an increasingly united Europe. In 1957 six states of continental Europe—France, Italy, West Germany, and the three Benelux states—formed the European Economic Community. This body was for the purpose of creating a customs union among its members within a ten-year period,[27] and during 1958 and 1959 it began to make changes in the tariff schedules of its members, looking toward the day of internal free trade and a common external tariff. Great Britain, meanwhile, had not been idle. Opposed to the economic consolidation of the continent on political grounds and unwilling to join EEC because of a reluctance to compromise its position in the Commonwealth, London first suggested an eighteen-member free-trade area to comprise all the OEEC states. This failed to win any support from France, and Britain then succeeded in 1959 in negotiating a rival trading bloc, the European Free Trade Association. This seven-nation group included Britain, Portugal, Austria, Switzerland, and the Scandinavian states. EFTA was purely a free-trade area with no common external tariff contemplated.

With Europe threatening to split into rival blocs, the United States became involved. It intervened in the dispute and proposed early in 1960 the conversion of OEEC into the Organization for Economic Cooperation and Development, in which the United States would hold membership.[28] In this way the United States might act as a "bridge" between the groups and at the same time act to protect its own interests from being adversely affected. Although OECD did not move rapidly toward realization, later developments indicated that Britain was actively seeking closer relationships with EEC and perhaps eventual membership; if this were to come about, the other EFTA members would inevitably join the Community as well—

---

[27]Both a customs union and a free-trade area involve the elimination of tariff barriers among the countries composing the area. A customs union, however, establishes a common tariff applicable to all imports from outside the area, whereas in a free-trade area each nation retains its own tariff schedules except vis-à-vis each other.

[28]See remarks of Under Secretary of State C. Douglas Dillon, *The New York Times* (February 24, 1960).

where several of them belonged anyway because of their normal trade-flow patterns.

Although thoroughly sympathizing in principle with European integration, the United States saw several potential difficulties in the prospect of a unified trading Europe. One was the possibility that for certain countries and certain commodities, the new common tariff would be higher than the old single-nation one as it applied to American goods. A second was the worsened competitive position of United States goods in the European market once the equalizing factor of tariffs on intra-European trade was removed.[29] A third was the possibility that the European bloc (or blocs) would not move toward multilateralism but instead toward a larger-scale bilateralism.[30] A fourth centered on Britain. If London proved unable to reach satisfactory arrangements with EEC, there was a possibility that she might "turn to the East" and enter into much more extensive trading with the Soviet bloc.

THE TRADE EXPANSION ACT OF 1962

It was in the face of this serious situation in western Europe and the annoying deficit in the American balance of payments that the Kennedy administration decided late in 1961 to undertake some basic changes in the American policy on trade and tariffs. President Kennedy set the tone himself on May 4, 1962, when he said: "We must either trade or fade . . . . For the whole pattern of trade is changing, and we must change with it."[31] The result was the Trade Expansion Act of 1962, the first major modification of American trade and tariff policy since 1934. Although until now the results of the new measure have been disappointing, considerable optimism remains that the different approach will eventually bear fruit.

AMERICAN TARIFF POLICY. The basic American tariff law is still the Smoot-Hawley Tariff of 1930, the highest tariff in American history and a major contributing factor to the Depression of the early 1930's. The Roosevelt New Deal never repealed this law; such reduction in its prohibitive rates as was accomplished prior to 1941 was by means of the Reciprocal Trade Agreements program (1934). By this device the President negotiated

---

[29]One estimate was that 32 per cent of American exports to the EEC countries would be adversely affected and that another 27 per cent might be. Howard Piquet in *Commercial and Financial Chronicle* (January 15, 1959).

[30]It is for this reason that GATT specifies that any free-trade or customs union should not result in tariffs or other protections higher under the new arrangement than they were before, and that tariff preferences for particular outside countries should not be increased. GATT also requires that any trading-area agreement be submitted to the contracting parties for review.

[31]Speech at New Orleans, printed in *Department of State Bulletin* (May 21, 1962), p. 824.

executive agreements for tariff reduction with one nation at a time. He was authorized to lower existing rates by up to 50 per cent in exchange for corresponding concessions. Under the widely used most-favored-nation clause, such reductions in American duties were extended to most other countries as well.

The Trade Agreements program is often thought of as a landmark of New Deal foreign policy, and yet in retrospect we can see that it failed to bring about really important reductions in American tariffs. Congressional pressure has been constant ever since the enactment of the original law in 1934 against any thorough-going overhaul of American imposts, and each legislative renewal of the Act has brought more limitations on the freedom of executive action. Most revelatory was the so-called "peril point" legislation, originally added to the Act in 1947. Under its terms, the Federal Tariff Commission was required to fix the point at which foreign goods could compete with any American industry. If tariffs were below this point, Congress must be informed. This carried the implicit threat of legislative increase of rates if the President were to persist in cutting tariffs below what Congress felt to be tolerable.

THE PROPOSALS. In essence, what the President asked for when he submitted the bill to Congress in January, 1962, was a somewhat broadened power to do what he already could do under the expiring Trade Agreements Act (most recently renewed in 1958): negotiate trade agreements with foreign countries to reduce American tariffs by up to 50 per cent.[32] The novel features of the proposal, however, concerned the trade relations of the United States with the European Common Market.

The President proposed that the United States and the EEC could reach agreements under the terms of which United States tariffs might be further reduced—even to zero—on those items in which America and the EEC together dominated world supplies and in which their combined exports surpassed 80 per cent of the free world's total. These provisions were obviously based on Britain's early admission to the EEC and were hailed at the time as a great step toward the realization of the President's "Grand Design" of an "Atlantic Community" in at least an economic sense.

THE FIGHT FOR SUPPORT. The President felt that he dared not risk an all-out battle with American protectionists—no President has taken such a risk since the passage of the Smoot-Hawley Tariff in 1930. Accordingly, he adopted the standard technique used by his predecessors in all the postwar renewals of the Trade Agreements Act: disarming enough segments of protectionist opposition in advance by granting them concessions to ensure their support of the final measure. During the spring and early summer of

---

[32]President Kennedy presented the bill in a special message to Congress on January 26, 1962. See *The New York Times* (January 27, 1962).

1962, therefore, such industries as petroleum, textiles, lead and zinc, lumber, carpets, and sheet glass were appeased either by provisions built into the bill or executive actions designed to persuade them that their interests were, and would continue to be, adequately protected by the national government.

In the meantime, the Administration was mounting a powerful public-relations campaign to win a popular consensus in support of the general principles of the bill. So extensive was the effort and so euphoric was the picture painted of the consequences of the measure's passage that some fears arose that the public was in danger of being "oversold" and that any disappointment of unreasonable expectations might have unfortunate consequences on mass opinion. The Administration, however, appeared confident that its analysis of the situation was sound and that it was not arousing any unjustified hopes in the public. Even the concessions to protectionist sentiment were not looked upon as diluting the general scope of the act, and the New Frontier pressed for its passage with great determination.

VICTORY AND FRUSTRATION. The Trade Expansion Act passed the House of Representatives on June 28 and the Senate on September 19 with its important provisions substantially unchanged from the President's original request. The Administration looked forward to an early implementation of its new capability to deal with the EEC. It was high time; several of the protectionist moves of the United States had already aroused great indignation in Common Market circles and even a few gestures toward retaliation. The New Frontier, however, was certain of its ability to deal with all such difficulties once the EEC began to bargain seriously.

The hopes—and the basic concept of the "Atlantic Community" as well— were seriously jarred in January, 1963, when President de Gaulle of France vetoed Britain's application for membership in the EEC. In one blow most of the Administration's assumptions were all but invalidated. Instead of there being a long list of products whose exports were dominated by the United States-Europe combine and on which American tariffs could be reduced to zero, there were only a very few; common parlance limited them to jet aircraft and oleomargarine. Furthermore, the United States found itself facing a Common Market become assertive, suspicious, and incipiently protectionist.

THE "KENNEDY ROUND." It had been anticipated from the outset that serious tariff bargaining under the terms of the Trade Expansion Act would take place under the auspices of GATT (the press and the public in the United States took to calling these negotiations the "Kennedy Round"). During 1963, however, only preliminary and preparatory conversations at the ministerial level with the EEC were possible, since full-dress GATT negotiations were scheduled to open at Geneva early in 1964.[33]

---

[33] *Department of State Bulletin* (June 3, 1962), pp. 585–586.

The 1963 discussions to lay down the "ground rules" for the formal meeting of GATT were bitter, provocative of hard feelings, and narrowly failed to end in a serious breakdown.[34] The EEC did not wish to discuss tariffs on agricultural products; the United States, anxious to preserve the markets for its exports of agricultural commodities in Europe, insisted on the point. The EEC imposed what Americans thought were discriminatory regulations on the import of a number of food products, notably poultry, and the United States began to consider some retaliation. The ensuing dispute came almost immediately to be known as the "chicken war." A compromise was patched up by Chancellor Ludwig Erhard of West Germany that permitted the real "Kennedy Round" to begin, but only an incurable optimist could feel that the prospects for success were bright.

These low expectations were confirmed when the GATT negotiations finally opened, with the name "Kennedy Round" acquiring an added poignancy because of the President's recent and tragic death. During the first year and a half of desultory negotiations, very few real agreements were reached and little hope was expressed for the future. The rationale of the Trade Expansion Act had been thrown into question by a series of unforeseen events.

THE FUTURE OF AMERICAN TRADE POLICY.   Yet, as we have had occasion to observe already at a number of points in this book, history has its own logic and events continue to move. The imperatives that drove the United States to pass the Trade Expansion Act are still operative, and Europe cannot remain economically split indefinitely. The opportunity of 1962— never, perhaps, as glowing as it appeared to be at the time—has apparently been lost. This does not mean, however, that no similar opportunity to make progress will come again. It is, therefore, a net gain that the United States now has the capability to move somewhat more directly and forcefully in the direction of the liberalization and expansion of international trade. The true verdict on the Trade Expansion Act is not yet in.

---

[34]Richard C. Stebbins, *The United States in World Affairs, 1963* (New York: Harper & Row, Publishers, for the Council on Foreign Relations, 1964), p. 105.

CHAPTER **12**

Continuing
Psychological Issues in
American Policy

The only permanent victories that the United States can win in its search for a world of peace, order, and stability are to be found in the realm of human preferences and desires. This necessarily means that mass states of mind everywhere have a central relevance to the accomplishment of American objectives and the advancement of American interest. The "psychological" area of policy is as replete with continuing issues as are the others we have been discussing.

Of course, every move made by the United States has its psychic overtones, and Washington no longer uses the concept of "psychological warfare" to denote a distinct dimension of action. We shall not, therefore, discuss narrowly psychological concepts in this chapter. Instead, adopting the same general posture used in the two preceding chapters, we shall consider a number of issues of broader import, each involving a specific psychological implication.

We shall first comment on the question of whether or not the cold war is a "battle of ideas": that is, we shall attempt to discover the extent to which the Russian-American controversy has been an "ideological conflict" and what place ideological considerations have within it. We shall next attempt to analyze American propaganda as to content and purpose. A final section, on the maintenance of American morale, will include a discussion of American popular reaction to the propaganda of foreign states and the various "morale policies" used by the government to achieve and maintain the desired level of public morale.

The Cold War as a Battle of Ideas

Among the more hotly disputed points stemming from the general line of American policy since 1947 has been a basic disagreement among analysts and the general public about whether or not (and if so, the extent to which) the cold war is actually a struggle between ideologies. That there has been an ideological quarrel between East and West seems beyond question. The controversy, at least among Americans, grows out of the conclusions that can safely be drawn from this admitted divergence in ideological outlook.

Some of the most frequently argued points are the following: (1) Is America's real enemy communist ideology or communist expansionism? (2) Is ideological conflict inevitable between communism and democracy? (3) Must ideological disagreement result in overt policy clashes? (4) Is ideological war inevitable? (5) Can the cold war ever be adjusted amicably? (6) Must the cold war go to the point at which one ideology exterminates the other? (7) Can the behavior of the USSR (or, for that matter, the behavior of the United States) be predicted on the basis of ideological imperatives? We should note, however, that the discussion in this section will not attempt to answer these questions in detail; its purpose will be rather to suggest a few factors that might influence the responses that any citizen would make to them.

THE IDEOLOGICAL FRONT

What has been the ideological front of the cold war? In what forms have ideological differences been prosecuted?

IDEOLOGICAL DISAGREEMENTS. There is no need for us to examine the many detailed points of disagreement and differences between communist ideology and the American belief system. To do so would require an elaborate analysis of both societies and the roots of their beliefs.[1] We may perhaps make the central point, however, that both ideologies are "total" in the sense that from either may be derived an ideological position on almost any foreign-policy issue. Taking opposing positions on a number of basic philosophic dichotomies—such as free will (democracy)-determinism (communism), or individualism (democracy)-collectivism (communism)—the ideological confrontation of the two systems is as nearly absolute as we can imagine.

We should also note here that it is important to keep clear which level of ideological disagreement we are discussing. Although each belief system

---

[1]See, among studies on this point, Ebenstein, *Today's Isms*, and H. B. Mayo, *Democracy and Marxism* (New York: Oxford University Press, Inc., 1955).

exists in a "pure" form to which people and government alike render homage (Marxism for communists; the "natural-rights" dogma of the Declaration of Independence for Americans), the officially sanctioned credo of each government today represents a significant departure from such original formulation. The ideological controversy most pertinent to our analysis is that between the presently controlling belief systems within the respective societies and governments, not that between the relatively rigid philosophical formulations of Karl Marx and Thomas Jefferson.

IDEOLOGICAL CONFLICT. The ideological issues between American-style democracy and Russian-style communism are infinite, but we may conveniently group them under three main headings:[2] (1) the world role to be played by the two states and their relations vis-à-vis each other; (2) the preferred political system for all states—Western parliamentary democracy vs. communist "people's democracy"; and (3) the preferred economic system on which ultimately to organize the entire world—capitalism vs. socialism. In each of these three broad areas, absolute disagreements exist; in each, ideological controversy is prosecuted vigorously.

IDEOLOGY AS OBJECTIVE

Any ideology has as one of its essentials a vision of the world as it ought to be and as it will be when truth finally triumphs. This means that an ideology incorporates a set of ideological objectives: goals derived from the summary absolutes of the dogma. If the ideology is accepted by the bulk of the people of a state, the attainment of those objectives in the real world becomes the putative responsibility of that state's government.

It is clear that both the Soviet and the American ideologies as officially enunciated today lay down such policy objectives. Such ideological concerns can be classified as positive and negative: that is, some call for the destruction of conditions inimical to the doctrine, whereas others demand the affirmative accomplishment of states of affairs deemed desirable.

SOVIET IDEOLOGICAL OBJECTIVES. Soviet ideological objectives can be grouped in three categories, called for convenience economic, social, and political.

1. *Economic objectives.* Negatively, Soviet ideology calls for the destruction of private property as an institution and capitalism as a system of production. Positively, capitalism is to be followed by "socialism," which will provide a cure for each of the evils for which private property is responsible.

2. *Social objectives.* Negatively, the social classes whose existence depends on private property—the aristocracy, the capitalists, and the bourgeoisie— are to be liquidated, either by conversion and "reeducation" or by violence.

---

[2]See, on this point, the present author's *The Cold War . . . and After*, pp. 8–12, 78–79.

Positively, the class structure is to be replaced by a reconstituted classless community of "workers, peasants, and intellectuals."

3. *Political objectives.* Negatively, all regimes dominated by socioeconomic groups hostile to Soviet beliefs (the capitalists and the bourgeoisie) are to be either destroyed or transformed, and all foreign policies opposing Soviet aims are to be defeated. Positively, anticommunist democracies and autocracies alike are to be remade into "people's democracies" on the Soviet model, and an era of total ideological peace is to be ushered in.[3]

These objectives as we have stated them are drawn fairly directly from orthodox Marxist-Leninist-Stalinist sources. Since Stalin's death in 1953, however (and to some extent previously), successive official reinterpretations of communist doctrine have blurred the sharper edges of the ideological blueprint. It is no longer necessary, at least according to some formulations of the official line, for the Soviet to act incessantly to destroy the capitalist democracies; coexistence is ideologically respectable.[4] "Socialism" itself, as defined today, permits private property, savings banks, and some free-market economic activity. The newer exegeses of Soviet holy writ so inhibit the impact of the older ones that it is extremely difficult for us to be precise about just what contemporary Soviet ideology demands as objectives.[5]

AMERICAN IDEOLOGICAL OBJECTIVES. The United States—fortunately or unfortunately—has no such rigid belief system that purports to impose a set of controlling foreign-policy objectives. Americans, proud of being a pragmatic people—and so ill-equipped historically for foreign policy—have no detailed and consistent set of traditional ideological objectives.[6] We may, however, extrapolate certain foreign-policy concerns from the general pattern of American beliefs.

Generally speaking, America's ideological objectives in foreign policy tend to be more negative than positive, to concentrate more on enemies to be defeated and obstacles to be overcome than on concrete aspirations. Ideologically the United States opposes any form of authoritarian regime, although the extent to which this opposition becomes active depends largely on the

---

[3]Many detailed analyses of Soviet ideological goals have been made. We shall cite only two: R. N. Carew Hunt, *Theory and Practice of Bolshevism* (London: Bles, 1950); and Hans Kelsen, *The Political Theory of Bolshevism* (Berkeley and Los Angeles: University of California Press, 1948), esp. pp. 26–39.

[4]Less than a month after the ouster of Premier Nikita S. Khrushchev, the new Soviet rulers stressed the "correctness" of continuing a policy of peaceful coexistence. See *The New York Times* (November 14, 1964) for accounts of a major editorial in *Pravda* and Western commentary and reaction to it.

[5]For analyses of the evolving role of ideology in contemporary Soviet society, see Armstrong, *Ideology, Politics and Government in the Soviet Union* and Brzezinski and Huntington, *Political Power: USA/USSR.*

[6]In our earlier discussion of the "American tradition" in foreign policy, we pointed out that long-standing American *objectives* grew out of history and experience, whereas such ideological tradition as Americans had was concentrated on *methods* of foreign-policy implementation rather than on specific objectives.

extent to which the particular autocracy impinges directly and unpleasantly on the American consciousness. Violations of individual freedom contradict American predispositions, whether in the economic or political realm. Once involved, American ideological hostilities tend to become extreme and to harden in stereotyped—almost absolute—terms.

Positively, American mass beliefs hold that all people everywhere will eventually accept the essentials of the American system.[7] The victory of American ways over all competitors is foreordained; ultimately the world will consist entirely of democratic political systems, fluid societies, and capitalist economies. This ideological objective is deemed certain of eventual achievement; many people seem to think that ideological vindication will come to Americans as the result of no more taxing an effort than that of setting a good example and remaining faithful to their own beliefs.

With the destruction of ideological enemies bulking so much larger than the accomplishment of positive ideological ends, it is natural that official and semiofficial analyses of the American ideological position should stress the inherent conflict between the communist world and the United States. There is a minor tendency to emphasize the positive solidarity of the United States with the free world, but such efforts are usually aimed at the practical end of buttressing the working alliance against the USSR and Red China. So little ideological concern has been given to the shape of any world after the cold war that a cynical observer might be pardoned for wondering if American ideology today teaches that the destruction of the Soviet empire and the elimination of the threat of communism would usher in Utopia.

IDEOLOGICAL OBJECTIVES VS. OPERATING POLICY. How important have the rival ideologies proved to be as controlling elements in the foreign policies of the two adversaries? In hazarding an answer to this important question, we must again seek to generalize as the only way to avoid a long and detailed comparison of preachments with practices.

The history of the cold war reveals that both states have used ideology as the dominant guide to policy only when no more trustworthy criteria have been available. When either Moscow or Washington was faced with a decision for which history, experience, logic, or a clearly understood concept of interest failed to prepare it, ideological considerations were most likely to be called upon.[8] In other situations, in which the demands of time and place and the compulsions of history and interest were more clearly grasped, policy was at least to some extent liberated from ideology.

---

[7]For an expression of this, see Robert Strausz-Hupé, "The Balance of Tomorrow," *Orbis* (April, 1957).

[8]Early American policy toward the war in Indochina and early Soviet attempts to penetrate the Middle East (in both cases prior to 1954) are examples of policies grounded more on ideology than on more concrete bases.

Most of the policy decisions originally rooted in ideology have been eventually modified by both sides. Some, proving to be good and workable programs in their particular contexts, were retained; the Soviet approach to the Asian revolution, for example, was thoroughly feasible as a working policy (at least up to the Hungarian massacres of 1956), although it grew initially out of an ideological base.

We may conclude, however, that the actual conduct of both the United States and the Soviet Union—as apart from what both sets of leaders have said—indicates that ideological considerations are not primary in their respective foreign policies. Objectives, the motivations of which are purely belief-centered, have been accepted only in default of better ones. To the extent that any may be clearly identified in operative policy decision, we may safely conclude that they remain distinctly subordinate to other, more immediate concerns.[9]

IDEOLOGY AS TECHNIQUE

If we accept the generalization that ideological objectives are of relatively little importance to the participants in the cold war, how then can we explain the great extent to which ideological issues figure in its conduct? It seems probable that ideology, although of limited value as a goal-setting mechanism for either the Soviet or the United States, is of great service as an instrument for executing policy and for achieving ends determined by other criteria. Ideology's major pertinence to the cold-war would then seem to be its use as a technique of policy implementation.

"Psychological instruments of policy" or the "psychological channel of power" are concepts long familiar to students of international affairs.[10] The nature of the cold war and the perhaps controlling importance of winning the allegiance of uncommitted millions of men have raised this vehicle of policy to an unprecedented strategic significance. If the only permanent

---

[9]A number of well-qualified analysts, however, differ sharply with this conclusion. Some argue that the Soviet's orientation is totally ideological and that communist theory is the enemy the United States must defeat; others see the cold war simply as a titanic struggle between truth and falsehood and call for unremitting effort by the United States not only to vanquish communism but to make good the final victory of American beliefs. The best-known advocate of the latter position is James Burnham. See esp. Chap. 3: "The End of Traditional Diplomacy," in his *The Coming Defeat of Communism* (New York: The John Day Company, Inc., 1950). A somewhat different development of the same theme is found in Robert Strausz-Hupé, *Protracted Conflict* (New York: Frederick A. Praeger, Inc., 1959); see also Robert Strausz-Hupé, William R. Kintner, and Stefan T. Possony, *A Forward Strategy for America* (New York: Harper & Row, Publishers, 1961).

[10]See, as an early example, the sophisticated discussion in Frank L. Simonds and Brooks Emeny, *The Great Powers in World Politics*, new ed. (New York: American Book Company, 1939), pp. 149–152.

victories are those won in the minds of men, it would seem to make good sense to argue that the most significant weapons of foreign policy are those that have their effect on the human psyche.

SOVIET IDEOLOGICAL TECHNIQUES.   We have previously alluded to many specific examples of Soviet ideological technique. We may summarize it here as a continuing attempt to identify communism everywhere with the dissatisfactions, aspirations, animosities, and fears of whatever group in any state Moscow feels is most useful for its purposes.[11] In some states this may be the submerged mass just beginning to stir, as in much of Asia and Africa; on the other hand, the Kremlin has no aversion to sustaining or supporting an oligarchy of power even against the wishes of the bulk of the local population.

Moscow's negative ideological emphasis is on portraying the United States as the enemy of the downtrodden everywhere. America is identified with monopoly, capitalist exploitation, imperialism, and war.[12] By discrediting the United States in ideological terms, the Soviet hopes to accomplish two purposes: first, to weaken American influence and the effectiveness of American policy; second, to procure a more favorable hearing for its own claims. The Soviet's primary goal is to alienate people from the United States and then, on the old principle (made much of by Moscow's propaganda) that "the enemy of my enemy is my friend," to win them to the acceptance of its own position.

Moscow's major victory on the ideological front, of course, has been its success in establishing a communist party in virtually every noncommunist state. These parties, serving under the Kremlin's orders, provide a ready-made pipeline into the social structure of every host state, and the message is more effective when propagated by natives. Soviet emissaries maintain close contact with local communists and coordinate their activities. It has been for this reason that the split between the Soviet Union and China that came into the open after 1960 has caused such havoc in the ranks of the communist parties of the world. In many states, pro-Russian and pro-Chinese factions have appeared within the ranks of the party, and they have spent at least as much time struggling for control of the apparatus as they have prosecuting the party's cause. There is little doubt that the rift in the facade of communist unity has seriously weakened the utility of ideology as a technique for the Soviet Union.

AMERICAN IDEOLOGICAL TECHNIQUES.   American ideological techniques are generally the reciprocal of the Soviet's. Like the Russians, Americans

---

[11]A provocative analysis of Soviet ideological methods, interpreted in the light of the doctrines of modern psychology, is " 'Ferreus,' The Menace of Communist Psychological Warfare," *Orbis* (April, 1957).

[12]In this connection, it is undeniable that the American participation in the war in Vietnam after February, 1965, played directly into the hands of Soviet ideologists. They were enabled to argue that United States policy confirmed exactly that they had been saying about America for many years and thus to warn their "détente-minded" associates against the dangers of a too-close association with Washington.

insist that they are interested in the welfare of all men everywhere and that American beliefs promise the most for the future. American ideology stresses human freedom, national self-determination, and individual economic well-being.

This last point has been hotly debated. Some observers argue that emphasizing economic betterment under American-style capitalism is a total refutation of the materialistic philosophy of communism, whereas others insist that the incessant reiteration of the material comforts resulting from adherence to American ideas makes the United States an advocate of a "bathtub and television" culture that entirely neglects the spiritual side of man.[13] Whatever its impact on foreigners, however, there is no doubt that most Americans feel that their high standard of living is in some way an outgrowth of their system, and it is only natural for an export ideology to make much of what so many Americans feel is important.

The major use to which American ideological weapons have been put has been the forging of the free-world complex. In this endeavor the ideological concept of the "free world" has been put to extensive use in developing a common ground on which all noncommunist nations could stand. The operative ideology seems to presuppose a simple dichotomy between communism and freedom and to count as ideological brethren all nations on the non-Soviet side of the dividing line. Some difficulty has arisen, however, because of the natural but unfortunate popular tendency to make "freedom" (in the sense of opposition to communist expansionism) a working synonym for "democracy," peaceful intent, or a shared interest in the American version of the status quo.

The major complaint we can level against the use of ideological techniques by the United States has been the glaring disparity between American professions, and the actual policy of the United States. If self-determination, individual freedom, and economic well-being are the cornerstones of America's ideological position, the extent to which American action fails to exemplify these abstractions is one measure of the inadequacy of American policy. Either because ideology has been neglected in shaping decisions or because the American position has been inadequately presented to the world, a considerable gap exists between principles and practice, and this opening in American defenses has been exploited by the Soviet.

During the middle years of the 1960's, as the cement of the "free world" began to wear thin, as several allies of the United States undertook to defy American leadership, and as the rhetoric of democracy lost a good deal of its former persuasiveness, something like ideological weariness could be detected at times in the United States. Journalists began to call for more

---

[13]Barbara Ward addresses herself to this problem in *The Interplay of East and West* (New York: W. W. Norton & Company, Inc., 1957); she further treats the point in *The Rich Nations and the Poor Nations* (New York: W. W. Norton & Company, Inc., 1962). For a theoretical analysis of the issue in a cultural framework, see F. S. C. Northrop, *The Meeting of East and West* (New York: The Macmillan Company, 1947).

candor from the United States and to speak of a "credibility gap" between American ideological pronouncements and the understanding of large sectors of the body politic.[14] If this were the beginning of a real trend, major readjustments in America's ideological position could not be long delayed.

THE UNITED STATES AND "POLYCENTRISM"

The ideological issue in American foreign policy has been seriously clouded since 1960 by the Sino-Soviet split and the revelation that communists can differ violently with one another on matters of doctrine, strategy, or tactics. The simple dichotomy of "we or they" that had served so many Americans so faithfully as a guide to decision and judgment has been compromised by being stretched to accommodate an increasing number of separate but simultaneous communisms and communist regimes; discrimination of an increasingly complex sort has been forced upon a people and a government who had once been all but persuaded not only that ideological questions were really simple but that all the important ones had already been answered. The rise of "polycentrism" has not been an entirely happy experience for the United States. Many interpretations of the ideological significance of the split have been advanced; we here reduce them to three broad schools of thought.

THE "OLD BELIEVERS." The first position is that taken by the militant anticommunists to whom the cold war has always been an ideological struggle and who have advocated ideological vindication as the only fit purpose to which American power should be put. To these analysts, the Sino-Soviet split is either a mere ruse or else an irrelevancy. Either Moscow and Peking are only seeking to lull the United States into a false security—in which case the only thing for America to do is to double its vigilance—or else their quarrel is about power rather than truth. In either case, the conceptual unity of the enemy is retained, and therefore the essentials of the American task are likewise unchanged.[15]

---

[14]See, for example, James Reston, "The Quiet Disasters," *The New York Times* (December 1, 1965); see also Murray Marder, "Credibility Gap: Greater Skepticism Greets Administration Declarations," *The Washington Post* (December 5, 1965).

[15]Representative of this point of view is Professor Franz Michael of the Institute for Sino-Soviet Studies at George Washington University. On page 12 of the report of the Subcommittee on the Far East and the Pacific of the House Committee on Foreign Affairs, House Document 237: *Sino-Soviet Conflict* (Washington, D.C.: Government Printing Office, 1965), he states that the United States still faces "a double strategy from the two Communist headquarters. Even if the Communist movement is half divided the common purpose still remains. ... The division can weaken the Communist effort, but it can also broaden the Communist attack which we must counter in all its aspects." On page 356 of the same report, Secretary of State Rusk skirts this view by stating: "In other words, I think we have to proceed on the assumption that cooperation between the two is possible, or, indeed, probable, where our own interests are concerned. Otherwise we would get caught short and underestimate the formidable opposition we face in this great struggle between the free world and the Communist world."

THE "DISCRIMINATORS." A second position, most commonly seen in official United States Government statements, recognizes the ideological split between China and the Soviet Union as real and important but refuses to draw any operational conclusions from it. The argument seems to be that the ideological rift may have indeed fractured the unity of the communist world, but as far as the United States is concerned its major effect is to increase the number of major adversaries from one to two. America will discriminate between the Soviet Union and China and will not ascribe a synthetic monolithism to any communist posture, but the challenge remains unquenchably hostile and will be dealt with accordingly.[16]

THE "PRO-RUSSIANS." A third school of thought, identified as clearly with liberal groups in the United States as the "old believers" tend to be with the "new conservatism," finds in the split the basis for some basic policy orientation for the United States. They purport to see the Soviet ideological position today as somewhat more "advanced" than that of China: that is, Moscow is seriously interested in peaceful coexistence, arms-control agreements, political stability, and the like, whereas China remains militantly revisionist on all such points. This group concludes, therefore, that the span of common interests uniting the United States and the Soviet Union continues to grow— with a common hostility to Chinese ambitions an important component—and therefore tends to downgrade ideological dispute between Moscow and Washington as anachronistic though finding it a continuing reality in connection with China.[17]

CHINESE-AMERICAN IDEOLOGICAL DISPUTE. One thing, however, is certain in this confused picture: Most Americans feel that in the mid-1960's China is a more serious ideological enemy than is the Soviet Union. Possibly because of the general climate of relaxation that has characterized Soviet-American relations since the Cuban missile crisis of 1962, but primarily because of the frequency with which all but open confrontations with Peiping have arisen during the past few years, there seems to be general agreement that the "cold war" is a more apt title for Chinese-American relations than for the state of affairs with Moscow. Thus much of the ideological baggage of an earlier stage of Soviet-American dispute has been transferred almost bodily into the

---

[16]Secretary of State Dean Rusk, in a speech justifying discrimination among the various versions of "national communism," nevertheless strongly reiterated the basic American position: "We, in this administration, and in this country, are under no illusions as to the designs of the Communists against us and the entire free world. No one needs to tell us that the Communist menace is deadly serious, that Communists seek their goals through varied means, that deception is a standard element in their tactics, that they move easily from the direct attack to the indirect, or to combinations of the two." Yet the main body of the speech was a defense of administration differentiation between the various communist states. See "Why We Treat Different Communist Countries Differently," *Department of State Bulletin*, L, No. 1290 (March 16, 1964).

[17]Walter Lippmann is representative of this school of thought in the United States. See especially "Today and Tomorrow" in *The Washington Post and Times-Herald* (September 28, 1965) on Soviet-American "parallelism."

context of the conflict with China, and many of the same absolutist assumptions about motivation and behavior that once formed the stock-in-trade of hard-line Kremlinologists is now applied, *mutatis mutandis*, to Mao Tse-tung and his cohorts.

VERDICT ON TWENTY YEARS

To the extent that the Soviet-American struggle has actually been a battle of ideas, how has the tide run during the first two decades of the cold war? Can we reach any general conclusions about the relative success of the United States and the USSR in the struggle for the minds of men? Although recognizing that these are treacherous waters indeed, we may suggest some general conclusions.

RUSSIAN BALANCE SHEET.   Before venturing any estimate of Soviet success in winning converts, we should establish some rough criteria of measurement. The Kremlin has had several operational goals in mind and has made different degrees of progress toward each of them.

The Soviet's announced primary goal—its major "ideological objective"— has been to win converts to the total official ideology of the USSR, the entire communist apparatus of dialectical materialism, the dictatorship of the proletariat, the classless society, and so on. In this area its success has been minimal and, considering the entire period from 1945 to 1965, perhaps negative. Even before the dissension in the communist ranks became obvious after 1956, it was apparent that throughout the world communists were tending to organize into tiny, almost clandestine revolutionary groups instead of becoming major political forces in their own nations. In only a few states— France, Italy, and China, for example—did communism ever become anything like a mass movement organized under a rigid ideological roof. And here "polycentrism" has exercised its disruptive effect.

In their second ideological purpose—winning foreign support for the foreign-policy objectives of the USSR—the Soviet leadership had some greater success. Once the overtly "hard" line generally identified with Stalin had been suppressed in favor of an advocacy of peace, disarmament, and reconciliation, the Soviet discovered large segments of opinion, both in the neutral world and within the ranks of the West itself, that were becoming more disposed to listen to Moscow. Soviet espousal of the cause of under-developed and colonial peoples also gained considerable popular approval and some overt diplomatic cooperation from the Asian bloc. To these must also be added the augmentation in prestige that followed the Sputnik breakthrough, weapons development, the successful penetration of space after 1959, and other technological achievements.

Moscow's greatest ideological success, however, came in its effort to discredit the United States. Here both American failures and the inability of the United States to present its position convincingly made it possible for the Soviet to claim that events were corroborating its denunciation of everything American. Much of the noncommunist world, distressed by its own weakness, by the heavy-handed manner in which much of American policy was executed, and by its dependence on American largess found comfort in accepting Soviet attempts to explain United States action in the most sinister terms. This approach, although it led to only limited pro-Sovietism, nevertheless served Russian purposes by impeding American efforts and can be counted as a major ideological victory. No more impressive example of this can be advanced than Moscow's attack on American policy in Vietnam after 1964.

THE AMERICAN RECORD. The American record on the ideological front is (for Americans) one of the least encouraging aspects of the cold war. If we apply the same general criteria as we used for the Soviet record, we find little to justify American self-congratulation.

On the count of winning converts to the total American ideology, there is no indication of any but miniscule success. A lack of agreement at home about what the American ideology actually is and a general preference for emphasizing those aspects of American belief most likely to offend exotic cultures (material comfort, mechanization, and armed might) have resulted in only a relatively short list of converts. Americans today realize that they are much less "popular" throughout the world than they were two decades ago, and their perplexity at this development is matched by their resentment.[18]

The record of winning ideological support for American foreign policy is an uneven one; broad swings can be detected from acceptance to rejection of the American ideological defense of particular policy moves. The enactment of ECA was one high point at which American arguments were listened to sympathetically; United States opposition to Britain and France at the time of the Suez invasion of 1956 was another, although before a different audience. Other policies, such as America's insistence upon European rearmament after 1950 even though such a policy endangered economic stability, have caused widespread cynicism about American sincerity. Probably no single move did so much damage to the ideological commitment of the United

---

[18]Edward W. Barrett, in the concluding paragraph of his study of the American information program, *Truth Is Our Weapon* (New York: Funk & Wagnalls Co., Inc., 1953), makes this comment: "When we Americans consistently put our case before the people of the world in a way which shows we respect their intelligence, we will be well on our way. In the world of today there is an enormous stock of good will toward us. . . . America can mobilize this force of good will effectively when it determines to pursue vigorously and *consistently* the aim reflected in the Declaration of Independence—to behave and to speak out of a decent respect to the opinions of mankind." (p. 300; italics in original. Reprinted by permission.)

States to peace, self-determination, democracy, and freedom than the nation's entry into the Vietnam war. In spite of the very good arguments that could be advanced on the side of American policy, the fact of Americans killing Asians in the name of democracy and the more than modestly equivocal public presentations of America's objectives and intentions tended seriously to undermine whatever ideological support the United States retained in much of the non-Western world.

American ideological obstruction of communist designs was more successful. The constant exposure of the contradictions between Soviet beliefs and Soviet practice impeded Russian policy in many areas. American success was greatest in those regions, such as western Europe, where considerable ideological harmony already existed with the United States; in Asia, the American anticommunist message was so confused with other purposes that its edges were often blunted. Just as unfortunate American actions and statements helped the Soviet discredit the United States, occasional senseless Russian moves played into America's hand. The most impressive of these gaffes was of course Russia's unabashed brutality in dealing with the Hungarian rebellion in 1956. Khrushchev's grotesque distortion of the "U-2" incident of 1960 was so extreme as to retrieve much of the ground that inept American statements had lost; and his blatant obstructionism in the 1960 General Assembly alienated many of the very non-Western states he was obviously wooing.

THE STATE OF THE IDEOLOGICAL BATTLE. Ideological conflict within the cold-war context has been, on the basis of the record, inconclusive. Neither side has scored any great or convincing victory; the major effect of the ideological battle has been negative. Each side has had some profit from its attempt to demolish the other's position. One conclusion, however, emerged from the record of ideological disputation: The effectiveness of ideological argument as a technique of foreign policy seemed to depend, in the long run, upon the extent to which actual policy could be reconciled with purported beliefs. The mere advocacy of absolute principles of social, economic, or political organization had only a limited effectiveness by itself; when coupled with demonstrable implementing action, however, ideology not only heightened the effect of other tactics of policy implementation but acquired a significant impact in its own right.

United States Propaganda: Purpose and Content

The United States is deeply involved in a propaganda war, most obviously with the USSR and China but also to some extent with the great majority of the states with which it has relations. It is a relatively new, and for most Americans a somewhat distasteful, outgrowth of the new stature of their nation; Americans do not yet feel thoroughly at home in a systematic attempt to influence other peoples by overtly persuasive techniques. But to forego propaganda would be to concede the psychological battleground to the enemy, and the American situation is by no means so advantageous that the United States can allow other states to enjoy a field day in propaganda unimpeded by American countermeasures.

THE PURPOSES OF AMERICAN PROPAGANDA

What are the purposes of American propaganda? What does the United States hope to accomplish by its efforts? In judging the propaganda program of the American government we must keep in mind the objectives it is designed to attain.

WHAT CAN PROPAGANDA ACCOMPLISH? The many definitions of "propaganda" agree that it is generally a technique of persuasion and that its general objective is action taken by the recipient(s) of the sort desired by the propagandist. Appropriate action will not follow a propagandist's appeal unless the recipient's own attitudes are favorable to the receipt of the message. Attempting to persuade tribal groups of native Africans to purchase electric refrigerators would be pointless unless the Africans themselves were aware of what they were missing by not having these appliances. In the jargon of American advertising, this is known as "creating a demand." In the same way, urging a foreign population to rise against its oppressors is of no use unless the people themselves realize that they are oppressed, nor is there any value in begging such a people to support American policy unless they feel that the United States is actually trying to help them.[19]

We may thus subdivide the propagandist's purpose into two different tasks, one precedent to the other. Government propaganda may in the first place concentrate on the creation of a climate in which the propagandist's appeals are favorably received. Advertising men term this process "building good will" or "institutional advertising." After the image of the propagandizing nation as a friendly, likable, and well-wishing people has been constructed on a lasting basis, the second phase of propaganda can be undertaken. At this point open appeals for action may be made, drawing their effectiveness from the base of goodwill created by earlier programs.

This two-phase operation, as we describe it, is obviously schematic. In the case of the United States, there already exists a "reservoir of goodwill" in

---

[19]See D. Lincoln Harter and John Sullivan, *Propaganda Handbook* (Philadelphia: 20th Century Publishing Co., 1953), Chap. 7: "The Aims of the Propagandist", and Daniel Lerner, "Effective Propaganda: Conditions and Evaluation," in Daniel Lerner, ed., *Propaganda in War and Crisis* (New York: George W. Stewart, Publisher, Inc., 1951), pp. 344ff.

many parts of the world upon which Washington can draw to float its appeals for direct action. In such cases the United States need devote only a small amount of time and effort to the creation of a "set to action" and can move directly to its specific programmatic message. But in dealing with peoples whose attitude toward the United States is either indifferent or hostile, an indispensable first step is the discovery of some channel into the foreign society that will procure a favorable hearing for whatever America has to say. Only such a route, properly exploited, can serve to transmit propaganda with a political purpose.

THE TARGETS OF AMERICAN PROPAGANDA.   We must also distinguish the various groups that form the targets of American government propaganda. Each of them presents a separate problem; for each of them a separate program has been devised.

The first target of propaganda is, of course, the American people. Public support of the policies undertaken by the leadership is vital; full attention must be paid to the maintenance of public confidence. The second target group consists of America's allies; the object here is to maintain the solidarity of the alliance and to win continuing diplomatic agreement with American moves. The third consists of the states of the "neutral" world; the United States attempts to gain their friendship and support and, if that proves impossible, at least to strengthen their anticommunist orientation. Finally, and most obviously, the fourth propaganda target is the group of states in the communist orbit. In this area the United States seeks fundamentally to impair or destroy the loyalty patterns of the peoples of the communist world and to set them against their governments.[20]

THE VEHICLES OF AMERICAN PROPAGANDA

The direction of the American propaganda effort is under the administrative control of the United States Information Agency (USIA), operating from a headquarters in Washington through a network of posts abroad. Its functions are under the policy direction of the Department of State.

THE PROPAGANDA MEDIA.   USIA is organized into five "services" through which it serves its overseas posts. The first is the Press and Publications Service that not only publishes a great deal of printed material but also through its own wireless network services all posts (and countless local news media) with up-to-date news and information. The second is the Motion Picture Service that produces many films—some of them, like the story of John F. Kennedy, *Years of Lightning, Day of Drums*, of superb quality—for showing only outside the United States. The third is the Information Center Service, which maintains libraries and provides exhibits, classes in English, and so on,

---

[20]This listing is similar to the one suggested by Barrett, in *Truth Is Our Weapon*, p. 290n.

in the overseas installations. The fourth is the Broadcasting Service, the home of the famous Voice of America that in December 1964, was broadcasting over 800 hours weekly in 34 languages. The final service is the Television Service which is aimed at preparing television programs for use over the networks of the more than 50 free-world countries in which television has become an important medium.[21]

USIA at the end of 1964 had over 200 posts overseas, with a disproportionate number in the non-Western world. Under strong congressional pressure, the Agency's activities in Europe have been drastically reduced since the mid-1950's in favor of a constant upgrading of effort in Africa, Latin America, and South and Southeast Asia. In addition, there were in 1964 some 170 "binational centers," each supported in part by USIA but operated basically by the host country.

FIELD ORGANIZATION. USIA is organized for field operations into five regional groupings: Europe, Far East, Latin America, Near East and South Asia, and Africa. In each host country, the operation is known as the United States Information Service (USIS); the principal officer of each USIS is known as the Public Affairs Officer, who serves as a member of the American Ambassador's staff. Under him is a cultural affairs section headed by a Cultural Affairs Officer (sometimes known as a "cultural attaché"), and a press-public relations section. In many countries USIS maintains branch posts (usually information centers). There were, for example, 13 branches in West Germany in 1964, 12 in Japan, 10 in Brazil, and 8 in India.

THE MESSAGE OF THE UNITED STATES

What is the content of American propaganda? What message does the United States distribute abroad through the elaborate mechanisms that we have outlined? On what stimuli does the American government count to provide the action abroad that it hopes for?

"TRUTH IS OUR WEAPON." In his authoritative study of the early stages of the American propaganda effort, former Assistant Secretary of State Edward W. Barrett laid down what is still the controlling principle of American information policy:

In the contest for men's minds, truth can be peculiarly the American weapon. It cannot be an isolated weapon, because the propaganda of truth is powerful only when linked with concrete actions and policies. . . . Yet, because truth is generally on our side, it can be our decisive weapon if we will only profit from past lessons and employ it with wisdom, consistency, and responsibility.[22]

---

[21]United States Information Agency, *23rd Report to Congress, July 1–December 31, 1964* (Washington, D.C.: Government Printing Office, 1965), p. 43.

[22]Barrett, *Truth Is Our Weapon*, p. ix. Reprinted by permission.

Truth can indeed be the decisive American propaganda weapon only if it remains accurate to say that "truth is generally on our side." Less committed to the "big lie" as a policy technique than is the Soviet and free by its own decisions to implement its commitment to tell the truth, the United States enjoys a massive advantage in the battle of persuasion.

The development of modern methods of communication and the mass media by means of which simultaneous and instantaneous communication is possible with hundreds of thousands of people has placed a premium on the propaganda of truth. Maintaining the efficiency of lying propaganda is fantastically difficult when only a modicum of effort will enable almost any target people to check one nation's claims against another's. Any propagandist caught in a barefaced untruth thereby creates a barrier against all his subsequent efforts to penetrate; each exposed lie makes the lot of the persuader that much more difficult. Theodore C. Streibert, then Director of USIA, put the point this way in 1956:

If the "world's people" are to understand the issue in this contest, we must effectively counter the hostile propaganda of world communism and, at the same time, vigorously project abroad the truth of what we stand for.[23]

We must not suppose, however, that the "truth" that is the American weapon is (or even should be) always the whole truth. What goes into propaganda should be truthful—for reasons both of conviction and of expediency —but this does not imply that American messages must tell everything there is to be told. Propaganda, after all, is persuasive; it would call its very purpose into question to include—out of a single-minded devotion to the ideal of truth—information that might vitiate the persuasive message.[24]

UNDERSTANDING THE UNITED STATES. A most important aspect of the American message is that devoted to broadening foreign understanding of the United States and the American people. We must never forget that American ignorance of foreign cultures, particularly of the exotic ones of Asia and Africa, is matched by an almost equal lack of comprehension of the United States abroad. American policy is more likely to receive a favorable response abroad if sympathy for and sophistication about the United States are widespread.[25]

---

[23]USIA, *Sixth Review of Operations, January 1–June 30, 1956*, p. 1.

[24]No more dramatic demonstration of the danger of "telling the whole truth" could be suggested than the dilemma the United States created in 1960 by confessing to the espionage activities of the famous "U-2" airplane. Something less than full confession would have served the purposes just as well and yet not complicated the mission of American propagandists so extensively.

[25]"The job of USIA is to try, in every appropriate and overt manner, to inform the *people* of foreign countries about the United States." George V. Allen, Director of USIA, in USIA, *13th Review of Operations*, p. 1. Italics in original.

The heart of the continuing USIA mission, therefore, is the "cultural" program: a steady projection of the best in American life, presented in terms that even relatively untutored foreigners can grasp. During 1964, for example, the agency emphasized in its global programming the passage of the Civil Rights Act of 1964, the successful flight of Ranger 7 that photographed the moon, the presidential campaign (featuring elaborate election-night coverage all over the world), and the John F. Kennedy film, *Years of Lightning, Day of Drums.* In addition, the steady flow of books, exhibits, cultural exchanges, and the like continued.[26]

SPECIFIC PROPAGANDA LINES RELEVANT TO POLICY. American propaganda, however, does not confine itself to background conditioning. The USIA also stresses particular lines with immediate relevance to on-going policy, either by offsetting Soviet-Chinese propaganda or by advancing an effort of the other branches of the United States Government. During 1964 again, for example, USIA emphasized the American version of the first shooting incident in the Tonkin Gulf, the Sino-Soviet split, and a new "psychological offensive" in Vietnam.[27]

THE SHORTCOMINGS OF AMERICAN PROPAGANDA

We suggested earlier in this chapter that the cold war was marked either by a stalemate or by a relative Soviet victory in the ideological struggle. Unless we are willing to admit that there is an inherent superiority in communist dogma, it would seem that America's lack of success can be attributed to a failure in communicating American ideas to the world—in other words, in propaganda techniques. We cannot, however, explain away this difficulty on the ground of a lack of knowledge of the technical problems of persuasion since, after all, it is in America that advertising (the "engineering of consensus") has become both an art and a science. The shortcomings of the American propaganda effort must lie somewhere else than in the inadequacy of the message itself or in a lack of technical skill in its transmission.

The deepest-rooted cause of the ineffectiveness of American propaganda would seem to be found in the rather common lack of understanding, both in government and among the general public, of the nature, limitations, and effectiveness of the propaganda instrument. Far too often, the implications of propaganda have been either overestimated or underestimated, and the execution of the persuasive task has been either overenthusiastic or halfhearted. With such a record, the remarkable point is not that American

---

[26]See USIA, *22d Review of Operations, January 1–June 30, 1964* and USIA, *23d Report to Congress, July 1–December 31, 1964, passim.*
[27]*Ibid.*

propaganda has not been as effective as that of the Soviet but rather that the disparity between the two is not greater than it is.

We may list the major shortcomings of American propaganda under four heads, each varying in degree of importance but all of major pertinence to the future program of the United States.

THE EXPECTATIONS ABOUT PROPAGANDA. Americans have swung between extremes in their expectations of what could be accomplished by propaganda. One extreme may be represented by the abortive "political-warfare" movement in 1953, when official Washington seemed to think that a magic formula of persuasion could be discovered that would demolish the Soviet threat quickly and cheaply. At the other extreme we may put the niggardly attitude of Congress toward the entire propaganda effort in the backwash of Senator McCarthy's investigation of the Voice of America; during the early 1950's responsible lawmakers were arguing that the entire propaganda machine should be dismantled and the money put into bigger and better bombs and aircraft.[28]

Even as of the moment of this writing, we cannot say that the United States has a clear understanding of what its propaganda can do, what it is expected to do, and what will follow the achievement of any of its objectives.[29] There was something almost shocking, for example, in the insistence of the State Department that its "liberation" propaganda of 1952 and 1953 had had nothing to do with precipitating the Hungarian rebellion in 1956.

THE RELATIONSHIP BETWEEN PROPAGANDA AND POLICY. Edward L. Barrett's warning that "truth is powerful only when linked with concrete actions and policies" is particularly apposite. The American record of promises—both explicit and implicit—unfulfilled by action is too long for any partisan of the United States to feel comfortable. Americans are often perturbed when foreigners do not accept the unsupported word of the United States, either about its good intentions or about its willingness to act under certain circumstances. It goes against the American grain to admit it, but history (at least as viewed by foreigners) teaches that many American commitments have been repudiated, often in response to changing domestic political currents. To the extent to which American propaganda is not consonant with or implemented by policy, the propaganda itself becomes almost valueless and may on occasion actually prove harmful.[30]

---

[28]For an example of this argument, see Victor Lasky, "Can Propaganda Make Friends?" *Saturday Review* (September 17, 1955).

[29]Compare Barrett, *Truth Is Our Weapon*, Chap. 15: "Home-front Foes."

[30]It would appear, for example, that at least one of the reasons that the Johnson administration explained its role in Vietnam in 1965 as a single-minded determination to "fulfill" and "honor" its "commitments" was the fear that much of the world was coming to doubt the word of the United States. The very vagueness of the commitments in question made it all the more important in the minds of the leadership that they be fulfilled completely. See, for example, President Johnson's speech of December 9, 1965, *The New York Times* (December 10, 1965).

UNINTENTIONAL PROPAGANDA. Americans are also largely unaware of the broader dimensions of propaganda. Not all the persuasive messages from the United States are disseminated by USIA; Americans do not realize the extent to which every facet of their lives is under constant scrutiny throughout the world. The bitter language of politics; the isolated cases of racial violence and the much more common patterns of racial discrimination; the towering corporate structure of mergers, combines, and cartels; the vulgarity and ostentation of much of American life—these too are part of the American propaganda message. Often their effect is to vitiate much of the overt information activity of the government. How, USIA representatives abroad are often asked, can the United States be sincere about individual liberty, human dignity, and economic well-being when at home racial, religious, economic, and cultural discrimination is common, political rights are denied, monopoly capitalism is rampant, and cultural life is being reduced to a dead mediocrity? Such questions, of course, reveal inaccurate information and distorted inferences. The fact remains, however, that to the extent to which these propaganda devices (and others we might mention, such as the ubiquitous Hollywood film) are operative, the task of the official propagandist becomes more complicated and difficult of achievement.[31]

TRANSLATING ABSTRACTIONS INTO SPECIFICS. At the operating level, the major inadequacy in American propaganda shows up in translating the abstractions of American ideological predispositions into specific appeals. Making American propaganda intelligible to its targets has not been simple, nor has the record of performance notably improved during the latter period of the cold war.

What we are saying is that American propaganda, in making such concepts as individual liberty or economic well-being the bases of specific appeals, has failed to clothe these notions with referents intelligible to the actual wants or needs of the target people. The American criterion has instead tended often to be what the "average" American means by these terms, and the net impact of the American message has been to exhort the Greek, the Vietnamese, the Sudanese, or the Bolivian to become just like the middle-class citizen of Peoria, Illinois.[32]

Painting rosy pictures of life in America, complete with skyscrapers, television, and indoor plumbing, makes few converts among peasants whose

[31]See C. D. Jackson, "Private Media and Public Policy," in Lerner, *Propaganda in War and Crisis*, pp. 328ff. In this connection, in recent years a great concern for the effect of "the overseas American" has resulted in a widespread program of training Americans who live and work abroad to be better "ambassadors." Several universities (among them Syracuse University and the School of International Service of American University) have undertaken training programs for business executives on their way to overseas posts. See Harlan Cleveland *et al.*, *The Overseas Americans* (New York: McGraw-Hill Book Company, 1960).

[32]Barrett makes this point a number of times in *Truth Is Our Weapon;* see esp. Chap. 21: "The Quest for a Formula."

major concerns are with shaking free of the local moneylender and learning to read. Instead of inspiring a desire to emulate the United States, such appeals usually leave the observer unmoved; frequently, indeed, they stir up actual resentment and soften up resistance to Soviet persuasion. American self-praise, particularly when American policy can be interpreted as contradicting ideological professions, often helps no one except the Soviet.

To the extent to which American propaganda is pitched at a level to which its audience is responsive—whatever the audience and whatever that appropriate audience level might be—there is a greater likelihood that a sympathetic hearing can be obtained. As long as the specifics of propaganda fail to reach mass audiences because of their unintelligibility, mass responses are impossible. How to increase the audience for the American message is a problem of growing significance.

The Maintenance of American Morale

Perhaps the most crucial psychological issue of all has nothing whatever to do with United States propaganda abroad. It is, of course, the mental state of the American people; can it be maintained at a level adequate to provide the necessary support for American policy?

We discussed American morale as a capability factor in Chapter 7. At this point we shall discuss only one problem bearing on the state of national morale, that of American reaction to foreign propaganda; then we shall canvass briefly the various approaches to public opinion that we call the "morale policies" of the United States Government.

AMERICAN REACTION TO FOREIGN PROPAGANDA

"PROPAGANDA" AND THE AMERICAN PEOPLE.   Americans, we have pointed out, are a suspicious people in international relationships, and they also have a deeply rooted cultural antipathy to being taken in by any sort of oversmooth and glib sales talk. From these two sources has grown a prevailing popular attitude: "Propaganda" in international politics (and in many other areas as well) is a dirty word. In the mass mind, propaganda is put to an ulterior purpose, and that purpose is almost always against the better interests of whoever is being propagandized. Furthermore, propaganda carries distinct overtones of deceit: It is almost by definition thought to be compounded of untruths, half-truths, suppressed facts, and deliberate misinterpretations.

This attitude toward anything overtly labeled "propaganda" has made the lot of the foreign specialist in persuading Americans a particularly unhappy one. He must disguise his message so that it does not seem like propaganda at all; he must, in the jargon of the television commercials, do a "soft sell" rather than a "hard" one. Even so, the remarkable aspect of the total foreign propaganda effort in the United States is the relatively minor impact it has had—with certain important exceptions.

FOREIGN PROPAGANDISTS IN THE UNITED STATES. With perhaps one or two exceptions, each foreign diplomatic mission in the United States maintains some organization for the dissemination of propaganda and information. The name most commonly given them is that of "information service," and their clientele is divided between the American press (and other mass media) and the general public. Each foreign propaganda agency or individual is required to register with the United States Department of Justice, and its activities are subject to some government control. Perhaps most typically American is the requirement that each piece of literature must bear a notice that its source is a registered foreign propaganda agency and that "registration does not imply" that the information contained is vouched for by the United States Government. The Justice Department thus seems to be interested in giving the potential consumer fair warning of "foreign propaganda."[33]

Registration and labeling serve to inhibit the effectiveness of many "information services," although all of them have a large area of action—producing press releases, answering questions and requests for information, and in general attempting to gain as large an audience as possible for their material. Some of them, however, are further handicapped by small staffs and inadequate and inefficient facilities; in contrast we may point to the model propaganda service in the United States, the British Information Services. The BIS has a network of regional offices throughout the United States and offers an almost unending variety of materials.

Often much more valuable to a foreign state than its own information service, however, are the voluntary groups of Americans which, each for its own reasons, spring up to advance the "friendship" between the United States and the nation it is interested in supporting. Among the most important are the English-Speaking Union (Great Britain) and the Zionist Organization of America, which is affiliated with the World Zionist Organization and works in a variety of ways to advance the interests of Israel. These private organizations, led by prominent Americans and usually elaborately organized down to the local community level, can prosecute the cause of the foreign state in an effective way totally barred to official propagandists.

THE REJECTION OF SOVIET PROPAGANDA. The USSR has failed almost completely to gain any sympathetic audience among Americans. Its propaganda seems crude and banal, and its ability to affect American attitudes turns

---

[33]The statement used on British material reads: "This material is filed with the Department of Justice, where the required registration statement under 56 Stat. 248–258 as an agency of the British Government is available for inspection. Registration does not imply approval or disapproval of this material by the United States government."

out often to be the exact reverse of its intent. For this the Soviets can blame both their own ineptitude—their appeals aimed at Americans betray an appalling ignorance of what Americans are like and of what their mass wants, fears, and concerns actually are—and the large information establishments maintained by the American government. Washington attempts to bar Soviet propaganda from American distribution except on a strict *quid pro quo* basis and exerts considerable effort to warn the American people of the deceitfulness and evil intent of Soviet appeals.

Americans generally are aware that the Soviet is attempting to propagandize them—perhaps overly so. Although the militancy of American resistance has relaxed perceptibly since 1952 and 1953, there is no doubt that most people today are highly sensitized to the danger of being trapped by the wiles of communist arguments. Such a normal and ordinarily commendable concern was distorted out of all reason during the red scare of the early 1950's in which the late Senator Joseph McCarthy of Wisconsin figured so largely. During this period anyone who deviated from the Senator's version of orthodox Americanism ran the risk of being accused of "following the communist line"—an offense that, though never made specific, was made to seem treasonable. After the 1955 summit conference the controlling American attitude seemed to be one that no longer feared communist propaganda as a virus against which there was no defense but a closed mind, although it retained a near-total skepticism about the content of Russian arguments.

After 1957, as the Soviet-American struggle assumed its characteristic up-and-down pattern of tensions, the internal dispute over whether or not Americans were succumbing to Soviet propaganda rather faithfully followed the course of events. When relations were strained, patriotic Americans were quick to brand every Soviet initiative aimed at changing the climate as dishonest propaganda; as a matter of fact, it seemed almost an item of faith that to dismiss a Soviet proposal (regardless of its content) as "propaganda" sufficed as an American policy and that it was never necessary to make any more concrete response. When relations were more relaxed, as in the wake of the negotiation of the test-ban treaty in 1963, the popular threshold of acceptability of Soviet messages lowered perceptibly and there was greater willingness to listen cordially—if not sympathetically—to what Moscow had to say.[34] On the whole, however, Americans still find it difficult to take any Soviet material at face value, preferring still to find hidden motives and sinister purposes imbedded in the most innocuous-seeming communications.

---

[34]See, for example, Ambassador Harriman's speech, "Negotiating a Limited Treaty for Banning Nuclear Tests," *Department of State Bulletin*, XLIX, No. 1260 (August 17, 1963), 280.

SUCCESSFUL FOREIGN PROPAGANDA. A few states have been able to make their propaganda widely effective in the United States, both through direct contact with the public and via domestic informational media. Each of this small group of states has certain advantages—ethnic, cultural, or historic—that create affinities with a mass American audience and guarantee a sympathetic hearing. Each of them also (for perhaps the same reasons) has had the assistance of extensive private organizations in the United States that have worked in close cooperation with official representatives.

Certainly the most successful has been Great Britain. Based upon the superlatively efficient BIS and aided by virtually every Briton temporarily or permanently resident in the United States, the network of transmission centers established by Britain is extensive. Amicable relations with news media, friendships with national and local leadership elites, a delicate restraint in capitalizing on the fact of linguistic, cultural, and economic ties, and a uniformly helpful and courteous attitude have made British propagandists the envy of American informational personnel.

During the confused days of the Suez crisis of November, 1956, for example, the British position received extensive and friendly discussion in all media, to the point where serious doubts were raised among Americans about the wisdom and effectiveness of the policy their government had adopted. The crisis receded, however, before anyone could tell whether the British wedge had driven home to the point where American public opinion might force the United States Government to modify its policy. The success of the British campaign, however, eloquently testified to the efficiency of British propaganda, and the later evolution of American policy on the Middle East suggested that many of London's shafts had struck home.

Another state with a good record of influencing American attitudes is Israel. Here again something of a ready-made consensus has aided Israel's propagandists, and here also a voluntary apparatus has done yeoman service. But the Israeli government has also shown much imagination in its campaign (particularly in emphasizing the social-service aspect of Israeli domestic policy and in stressing the "Western"—pro-American—nature of its experiment in government), and the number and variety of pro-Israeli groups in American society are one indication of its success.

Vivid proof of the effectiveness of Israeli efforts to influence American attitudes was provided during February and early March of 1957. During the crisis caused by Israel's refusal to evacuate the Gaza Strip and the Gulf of Aqaba, the American government seemed inclined to accept the possibility of a General Assembly resolution to impose sanctions on Israel. Israeli propagandists, professional and volunteer, succeeded in creating a mass opposition to this move to the point that for Washington to have gone ahead with the project would have touched off a major internal dispute. Fortunately, the crisis was compromised and the full strength of the pro-Israel sentiment was never put to the test.

Nationalist China has also shown great ability to gain a hearing for its cause. Chiang Kai-shek's official governmental mechanism for propaganda in the United States is only a skeleton, but he has been aided by many volunteers. Whether or not there is a "China Lobby" of Nationalist officials and influential Americans—as has been charged[35]—it is a fact that Nationalist propaganda has won a large and highly sympathetic audience, both within government circles and in the public at large. Its major purpose has been to keep the United States committed to the defense of Taiwan and to oppose American recognition of Communist China; in both it has had a great degree of success.

THE LACK OF A MASS AUDIENCE. Except for the states mentioned and perhaps one or two others, however, the story of foreign propaganda in the United States is briefly told: It has had no great and continuing effect because of its failure to achieve a steady mass audience. The information services of such states as Spain, Laos, Paraguay, or Iceland—to cite a few more examples —reach large segments of the American public only under very special circumstances. If they penetrate news media, they have a somewhat greater impact, but in this effort there is such fierce competition that many states receive little more than routine coverage.

AMERICAN GOVERNMENT "MORALE POLICIES"

We know that government action in foreign policy must be backed by active mass support by the public. On any but the most minor, short-run matters mere passive acceptance of what is decreed in Washington is insufficient; what is needed over the long term is an informed, alert, and insightful public opinion that understands the reasons why the government acts the way it does, that has confidence in official leadership, and that cooperates with officialdom in executing the decisions out of which foreign policy is made.

One need not be a pessimist to point out that—if this be an accurate representation of what high "national morale" involves—American mass attitudes leave much to be desired. Mass apathy toward international issues is a problem of growing dimensions; mass emotional clichés all too often are substituted for rational attempts to perceive the national interest. Interest

---

[35]See the series of articles by Charles Wertenbaker and Philip Horton, "The China Lobby" in *The Reporter* (April 15 and 29, 1952); see also Robert Scheer and Warren Hincle, "The 'Vietnam Lobby' " in *Ramparts* (July, 1965).

groups and political parties are ever at work to impair public confidence in the leadership of opposition groups; and the level of public understanding and discussion of international questions is often discouragingly low.

The present state of national morale constitutes a continuing operating problem for the American government. Judicious care must be taken that the level of active committed support be retained sufficiently high to guarantee a workable consensus and that opposition forces be restrained at a safe pitch. A variety of different techniques have been developed for this purpose; which one is used in any particular circumstance depends upon the situational factors and the objective in view.

THE "CRISIS" APPROACH.   The "crisis" approach was most useful during the earlier stages of the cold war, when public comprehension of the nature and requirements of American policy was rudimentary. With its general outline all adult Americans are familiar; a particular policy move was identified with an international crisis calling for immediate American action, and speedy and unquestioning acceptance of the government's proposal was asserted to be the only way to stave off the danger. Disagreement, delay, or alternative proposals were dismissed as perilous; the official cry for "unity" attempted to drown out dissent.[36]

The methodology of crisis has had, and retains today, a real utility as long as the crisis is real and the government does not in fact have adequate time to use any longer-term method of developing adequate consensus. Certainly—particularly during the early days of the cold war—it made possible a number of American initiatives that otherwise might have been lost in a morass of highly emotional partisan debate. We may suggest, as leading examples, the passage of the ECA in 1948 and the decision to intervene in the Korean war in 1950.

As it matured during the 1950's, however, the crisis approach began to show several real shortcomings. It proved particularly vulnerable to two dangers: the risk intrinsic in crying "wolf" when the wolf never came and the risk of jading American sensibilities to the point where crisis became the only context in which Americans could be moved to act. This meant that as successive crises demanded quick action, the government found itself forced to escalate the level of tension higher each time in order to evoke the same level of response. This condition of diminishing returns raised a real difficulty: the prospect that some day mass attitudes might become oversold on the reality of a given crisis and would force undesired extremes of action upon the government itself.

---

[36] As an illustration, see the story of the unveiling of the Truman Doctrine and its public reception in J. C. Campbell, *The United States in World Affairs, 1947–48* (New York: Harper & Row, Publishers, 1948), pp. 34–38. The same technique, with only minor variations, was used during the Cuban missile crisis of 1962 and the Vietnam debate during 1965.

Although, as we shall see in a moment, ever since at least 1955 the executive branch of the government has been aware of the drawbacks of high-morale-through-unity-in-crisis, the United States Government has never felt itself able to dispense with it in situations in which it needed quick and extensive public support. In Lebanon in 1958, in Laos in 1960 and 1961, at the Berlin wall in 1961, in the Cuban missile crisis in 1962, and above all in Vietnam after 1964, the semantics and the stimuli of crisis have been the major instrument used by the government to achieve the desired level of consensus and morale.

THE "CALM AND FIRM" APPROACH. The administration of President Dwight D. Eisenhower, from 1953 to 1961, made a major effort to eschew crisis tactics and to develop the image of "calmness and firmness" in the face of adversity. The government sought to create an atmosphere of circumspection, of rationality, and of reflection as it faced its problems and to persuade the public to act in the same way.

This method was especially well suited to President Eisenhower, comporting neatly as it did with his own personality and with his theory of the Presidency. His popularity with the public and the widespread popular confidence in his judgment and his good intentions made his approach to morale-building a workable one.[37] Opinions of contemporary students differed as to whether the administration's commitment to the "calm and firm" technique tended toward popular apathy, but there was no doubt that the national temper was calmer after 1953 than it had been previously.

In spite of Mr. Eisenhower's best efforts, however, "calmness and firmness" never gained the total acceptance that he had hoped for. The public had apparently become too accustomed to crisis to react as quickly or as forcefully to any lesser stimuli. On a few occasions—notably the Suez crisis of 1956—a low-pressure appeal to reason in the general public produced an impressively mature popular response, but by and large rapid and strong consensus still depended upon a judicious massage of mass fears by a skillful bureaucracy.

KENNEDY AND THE "SENSE OF URGENCY." John F. Kennedy won the Presidency in 1960 by a campaign featuring a frontal attack on American "complacency" and a promise to "get America moving again." In his early months in office, there was much talk of a "sense of urgency" as a necessary prerequisite to American policy moves. It appeared as if "calmness and firmness" had been buried with the candidacy of former Vice-President Richard M. Nixon.

---

[37]An apt example of the Eisenhower technique was the President's radio-TV report to the nation on May 25, 1960, after the collapse of the summit. In this speech he refused to take the more extreme positions some of the Democratic leaders had urged and instead voiced his confidence that a more congenial climate of Soviet-American relations would again come about. His manner, as well as his words, emphasized calmness and restraint. Text of speech in *The New York Times* (May 26, 1960).

For all the flamboyancy of its rhetoric, however, the Kennedy administration was careful not to go all the way back to 1947. Crises there were in profusion during 1961 and 1962, yet the New Frontier showed a marked restraint in exploiting outraged public sensibilities in moments of tension. Partly because of its own interest in preserving maximum freedom of maneuver and partly because of its distaste for oversimplification or excess emotion, the Kennedy policy machine never gave as many hostages to public morale—even during its finest and most dangerous hour, the Cuban missile crisis of 1962—as had any of its predecessors.

THE "FRESH LOOK." Thus in 1963, when Mr. Kennedy turned to the improvement of relations with the Soviet Union, his approach was that of education. Inaugurating the new effort by what many consider his greatest speech, his commencement address at American University on June 10, 1963,[38] he called in sober and calm tones for a "fresh look" at foreign policy by all Americans. He seems to have seen himself and his advisers as the shapers of a new consensus, a high level of morale based less on extravagant emotional involvement than upon rational choice. Except for greater sophistication in thought and language, this was the Eisenhower "calm and firm" approach all over again.

In the few short months left to him, President Kennedy had an astonishing impact on public attitudes. The frenzied note all but disappeared from popular and official discussion of foreign-policy issues; there was an effort, unprecedented since 1945, to explore alternatives realistically and to search for new solutions for old problems. No great breakthroughs were achieved, of course; there was a general expectation, however, that major events lay not far in the future. All these hopes, unfortunately, were dashed by the tragic events in Dallas in November.

THE JOHNSON METHOD. Lyndon Johnson, after his succession to the Presidency, has followed an entirely different route. Especially after his smashing electoral victory of 1964, the care and nurture of his enormous consensus has been a major charge on his time. Not for him the perilous route of "public education," with its overtones of division and controversy, nor the extremes of crisis psychology that overexcite the people and put pressure on the government. He has preferred to stand on the middle ground, identifying his policies with "freedom," "honor," "justice," and all the other lofty abstractions so

---

[38]"Some say that it is useless to speak of world peace or world law or world disarmament —and that it will be useless until the leaders of the Soviet Union adopt a more enlightened attitude. I hope they do. I believe we can help them do it. But I also believe that we must re-examine our own attitude—as individuals and as a Nation—for our attitude is as essential as theirs. And every graduate of this school, every thoughtful citizen who despairs of war and wishes to bring peace, should begin by looking inward—by examining his own attitude toward the possibilities of peace, toward the Soviet Union, toward the course of the Cold War and toward peace and freedom here at home." For the full text of the speech, see *The New York Times* (June 11, 1963).

dear to the American self-image. At the same time, Mr. Johnson has been more successful than almost any other American President in surrounding his real policies with mystery and in cloaking the actions of his administration in the deepest secrecy. To focus public attention on attractive abstractions while operating virtually free of popular control in dealing with specifics seems almost a prescription for governmental Utopia.

But one real danger can be pointed out: The Johnson method generates adequate consensus in the short run, but by making meaningful public debate (debate, that is, about real issues) impossible it runs the risk of drying up spontaneous public morale at its source. There is more to high morale in a democracy than just "support" for or "approval" of the President's policy of the moment. The government must encourage serious public participation in the discussion of alternatives, something the Johnson approach avoids. Until such a condition prevails in the United States, even the most forceful and effective cultivation of an undifferentiated consensus cannot guarantee a satisfactorily high level of American morale.

PART **V**

WHAT LIES AHEAD?

CHAPTER 13

American Foreign Policy in a New Environment

Throughout this book, and especially in its later chapters, one theme has appeared and reappeared in a great variety of guises: The operational environment of American foreign policy has changed more rapidly and more extensively than has the capacity of the United States to cope with it. This has given rise to what we can call a "conceptual gap" in American thought and action on the major issues of foreign policy. This is to say that the picture Americans have of the political world no longer is adequately congruent with reality. Frustration, hurt feelings, and reckless action have been among the inevitable results of this discontinuity between idea and environment.

Here in our final chapter, it is appropriate for us to face this issue squarely. To what extent is American foreign policy as formulated and executed today no longer responsive to the real needs of the nation and to the opportunities and inhibitions intrinsic in a substantially changed milieu? Does American policy stand in need of a reappraisal and an overhaul? If so, in what directions should change be undertaken?

It would be both presumptuous and pretentious of us to attempt here to spell out all the details of a new foreign policy for the United States. No one not a major figure in the official hierarchy could make such an analysis with any claim to be heard. All we can do is to suggest a few basic guidelines and, in the closing pages of the chapter, to raise a few basic questions that would appear to strike at the heart of the entire matter. Our purpose is one of analysis and judgment rather than either captious criticism or lighthearted prediction. As such, it provides a justifiable climax to our effort in this book.

The End of an Era

By the mid-1960's, it had become obvious to all thinking Americans that their nation, and the world of which it was a part, had at some point a few years earlier come to the end of an era. The historical phase that had begun with the surrenders of Nazi Germany and Imperial Japan in 1945 and that had incorporated the entire period of bipolar cold war had been unceremoniously—almost cavalierly—brought to a close. Contemporary Americans are very much aware that the world in which they live is drastically different from the one in which they were functioning only a few years ago.

It is this fundamental—if still more or less obscure—change in the conditions of international political life that has given rise to the conceptual gap to which we referred above. The United States developed an image of power, responsibility, and action during the early postwar era that was perfectly adequate to the conditions of 1945 or even 1955, but almost shockingly irrelevant to the demands of the 1960's. Here is the basis for the reappraisal we shall attempt in this early discussion: What is the nature of the new era of international politics, and what has been the initial and early United States response to the change?

NEW OPERATIONAL CONDITIONS

The new era is marked by a number of peculiar operational conditions, each with roots running back decades or even centuries but each representing a sharp break with the recent bipolar past. These combine to impose a drastically changed set of requirements on a state like the United States that aspires to play a leading role in world affairs. We may list a few of these quickly.

THE FLUIDITY OF RELATIONSHIPS. The new era, in clear contrast with the cold-war decades, is marked by a great increase in flexibility of relations between states, a flexibility which is rapidly becoming comparable to that which followed the era of the French Revolution. In an operational sense, this means that international arrangements of all sorts are assumed to be inherently fluid and subject to rapid and all but constant change. The forces of revolution running free in many parts of the world and the general fraying of the bonds of alliance and alignment have combined to destroy much of the rigidity (or "stability") of the world on which the United States has long counted to hold intact the orientations of states, whether of friendship or of enmity.

THE COMPLICATION OF ISSUES. Another aspect of the new era that has left its mark on the American psyche has been the vast expansion in the agenda of international politics. At the height of the bipolar cold war, it could be—and was—argued that there was only one real issue in American foreign policy: how to frustrate the Soviet threat. It might be claimed that this simplification was invalid, even during the early 1950's, but it approximated reality closely enough to be workable. By the 1960's, however, no comfort can any longer be extracted from it. The old issues clustering around the traditional political values of sovereignty, security, and national well-being now must share a place with a host of new ones, many of very recent political vintage: population control, space exploration, water desalinization, and the like.

THE PROLIFERATION OF FORMS OF ACTION. Neatly paralleling the complication of issues has been the proliferation that has taken place in the forms of action available to states with major roles to play. Traditional diplomacy, propaganda, and military power remain as standard forms of policy implementation, but the new problems of world politics call for new methods—many of them without precedent. One of the perplexities of the expansion in the forms of action has been the lack of criteria to determine whether the outcome of any venture has or has not been "good" from the point of view of the initiating state.

THE CHANGING FORMS OF POWER. Equally upsetting to traditional lines of calculation has been the change in the politically relevant forms of "power." In the contemporary era, many of the old status-conferring aspects of capability—most explicitly military force—have lost much of their capacity to produce political victories; at the same time, many states considered impotent in terms of the familiar methods of power evaluation, have demonstrated a surprising ability to achieve their own purposes—which, after all, is the true mark of power. So far has this trend gone, at least in some contexts, that many observers have begun to speak acidly of the "tyranny of the weak" in international affairs. But this pejorative conclusion misses the point. It is not weakness which is in truth having its way but the possessors of the new forms of power appropriate to the requirements of the milieu who are enjoying freedom of action.

THE NEW ACTORS. A final aspect of the new era flows from the great increase in the number of substantially independent and self-determining actors in world politics. Two decades ago there were no more than some sixty participating states, and of these only a very small number (in the strict bipolar construct, only two) were relevant. Today, the number of participating states has more than doubled, at least thirty are permanently relevant, and none can be safely dismissed as totally irrelevant. No situation can be imagined more inappropriate to the American judgments of the early 1950's.

AMERICAN RESPONSES

The principal response of American mass opinion to the dramatic change in operational conditions has been one of perplexity and frustration. Convinced during the bipolar cold war that they had a firm grasp of the essentials of policy and that all that was needed to bring eventual victory was courage, persistence, and zeal, Americans have found the invalidation of many of their cherished hypotheses to be a traumatic experience. The growing disparity between effort and result in national policy, the ingratitude of allies, the unflagging implacability of enemies, the growing complexity of problems, the unrelieved ambiguity of choices, and the indefinite postponement of vindication have produced great and powerful public tensions. Evidence of the effect of these frustrations is easy to find in recent American policy.

At least four trends can be identified, some of them mutually contradictory. All, however, betray a common characteristic: an attempt to deny the reality of the new era or at least to escape its operational consequences.

"BUSINESS AS USUAL."   One very popular and pervasive approach to the new era is to assert—in the words of the cliché so beloved by the Department of State—that "nothing fundamental has changed." For all the surface indications of evolution, revolution, and metamorphosis, the argument runs, the basic situation in its essentials remains what it was in 1945. Thus no fundamental reorientation in American policy is necessary, and it would be dangerous to attempt one. If a particular enterprise is not going well, the fault is judged to be quantitative rather than conceptual: All that is necessary, in other words, is for the United States to increase its commitment and its participation without modifying its rationale in any important way. The classic example of this way of thinking in American policy is NATO. Each revelation of the serious difficulties into which the organization has drifted has been greeted by new American plans and projects to "strengthen" the alliance in a military sense—a line of action long sanctified by practice and one in which Americans feel very much at home.

THE SEARCH FOR SCAPEGOATS.   Another avenue of self-exculpation very popular today is the search for scapegoats, foreign or domestic, upon whom to blame the troubles of the United States. According to this thesis, the United States would not be suffering from its contemporary distempers were it not for the obstructive actions—sometimes malevolent, sometimes merely stupid—of particular men at home and abroad. The favorite scapegoats of all are the communist leaders of the Soviet Union and China; it has long been a basic premise of the world view of the United States that the frustration of every good and decent impulse in human affairs (epitomized, it goes without saying, in the foreign policy being pursued at the moment by the United States) is the top priority purpose of all communists. Thus it is very convenient to load all responsibility for American failures and disappointments on communist shoulders. But other foreign statesmen have played an important role here as well: Charles de Gaulle, Gamal Abdel Nasser, the late Jawaharlal Nehru, Achmed Sukarno, and Moise Tshombe have all served their turn. Among domestic scapegoats, none can rival the late John Foster Dulles in bearing the blame for contemporary American frustrations, although Harry Truman, Dwight Eisenhower, and Dean Acheson also rank high.

UNILATERALISM. A third line of response leans heavily upon Hamlet's alternative: "to take arms against a sea of troubles and, by opposing, end them." In recent years the United States, grappling with situations of ambiguity and complexity, has on occasion sought to cut the Gordian knot by unilateral action of a simple and forceful nature. In the military-political realm, the interventions in the Dominican Republic and the Vietnam war are prime examples, while in economic affairs the attempt to cope with the deficit in the balance of payments by restricting the flow of investment abroad is cut from the same cloth. Although such initiatives have provided some temporary relief from frustration by the sense of real participation, none has produced the clean-cut solution so urgently hoped for. Each attempt to escape complications by direct and unilateral action has served to reveal new layers of complexities and has compounded the real problem.

THE SEARCH FOR A SHOWDOWN. So powerful have the pressures of the new era become that a note has begun to be struck in recent years that had been muted since very early in the cold war: the argument, usually cast in a vein of melancholy but acquiescent fatalism, that the United States is irrevocably set on a collision course with its adversaries and that the whole drama is destined to find its denouement in some final "showdown." Most of those who seek the catharsis of an ultimate crisis do not in fact expect it to take the form of a nuclear war of obliteration; in essence they urge the United States to force each issue to the point where the (communist) enemy faces the choice of surrender or extermination. Brought thus to the final decision, few Americans of this persuasion doubt that the enemy would "get the message" and terminate his obstruction of American designs. Up to this writing, however, the search for a "crunch" to serve as the final escape from stasis has not emerged from the clouds of rhetoric in which it has normally been wrapped.

THE NEED FOR REAPPRAISAL

None of the American responses to the new era of international affairs has been successful in the operational sense, and none has offered any but the most transitory psychic satisfaction to the sensitized group ego of the American people. The world of 1949 has disappeared, probably forever; so also should the ways of thinking and the policies of that era be discarded in favor of new ones more efficacious in meeting the needs of the age. This is a simple and virtually self-evident proposition when put in abstract terms, but to carry it out in the concrete political world of the United States will require great and conscious effort and the courage to face and accept unpleasant and possibly embarrassing outcomes.

THE DANGER OF IRRELEVANCY.   Probably the gravest prospect facing the nation is the danger of becoming substantially irrelevant to real issues of contemporary world politics. This is not to be taken literally, of course; the United States can never become really irrelevant so long as it retains its military capacity to destroy and its economic capacity to build. But relevance is not merely a function of capability; it calls into direct question matters of intent as well.

So long as the United States is unable to develop problem formulations in operational terms and to apply its power to produce solutions acceptably close to its own wishes, the true relevance of American policy to world affairs will remain in serious question. What is more, many governments in even the noncommunist world appear to believe already that American purposes and American policy are becoming progressively less relevant to themselves and are increasingly ignoring American purposes as they seek their own destinies. To a nation at last convinced of the utility and desirability of a role of real leadership, such a development should be deeply disturbing.

THE DIFFICULTY OF DECISION.   Reappraisal is urgently demanded for another reason: Decisions—that is, choices among sets of alternatives—are becoming more and more difficult for the United States to make. The working criteria of choice are so eroded by time and change that American policy-makers often seek refuge in a synthetic but comforting illusion of inevitability: They are fond of projecting their policies as being the result of a situation in which "the United States had no choice."

For a great power, especially for the greatest power in the world, to argue that its policy moves are inevitable because no choices exist is to admit the hollowness of its claims to leadership of others. We must admit, however, that a refusal to decide and an acceptance of a postulated imperative at least makes some sort of action possible. To call this form of action a policy worthy of a great power, however, is to torture language and outrage logic. Choice is the essence of decision, and decision is the heart of policy. If the intellectual framework now relied upon does not make choices possible, then the only way to rediscover a new dimension of action is to recast the conceptual system on which national action must rest.

The New Requirements

It has been a fundamental premise of this book that foreign policy is more than anything else an expression of the prevailing value consensus among a people and that the foreign policy of the United States that is carried on by its government is in reality, as the title of this study stresses, the "foreign policy of the American people." If this is true, it follows that the reappraisal for which we are arguing here must first take place internally. Americans must, in other words, adapt themselves and their government to the conditions that prevail; what the United States has learned in the years of bitter head-to-head struggle with the Soviet Union must be expanded into a more sophisticated *Weltanschauung* that will adequately equip American policy-makers for the subtle and difficult tasks that lie ahead. Before examining the new directions in emphasis, content, and direction which should be imposed on American policy, therefore, we should first look into the new requirements to be imposed on the United States and its people.

CLARIFICATION OF PURPOSES

The first obvious need is for a clarification of purpose in American foreign policy. Before any improvement in American prestige or American power is possible in the new environment, the United States must come to much more specific terms with itself. Americans must be quite clear in their own minds about what they are seeking to accomplish and about the terms of settlement they will demand and accept.

"Purpose" in foreign policy was for many years not a popular subject of discussion in the United States. It was long obscured by the steady diet of crisis which Americans have fed upon and was rejected as irrelevant or diversionary by large sectors of "realistic" opinion. Such statements of long-range goals and interests as were formulated by official spokesmen tended to resemble little more than a string of windy clichés, chosen more for their oratorical effect than for their effectiveness in communication. Thanks to the explicit and (perhaps deceptively) simple way in which the challenges to the United States were formulated, the American people sensed no deficiency in policy; purpose was either assumed to be self-evident in "the American way of life" or ruthlessly imposed from without by the action of evil enemies. Public concern over what the United was seeking to do was slow in developing.

The ambiguities of the new era, however, have weighed heavily upon the United States, and since 1960 the tone of public discussion has reflected no little anxiety about the lack of direction in foreign policy. Perhaps the landmark episode of this whole discussion was President Kennedy's American University speech in 1963, although in retrospect it is clear that this large concern underlay much of his thought about international affairs. Out of the resulting clamor came little consensus except on the basic consideration that neither aimless drift nor violent response born of frustration will suffice in the future as a guide to successful American action. Unless Americans are reconciled to being buffeted helplessly by forces that they neither understand nor control, they must develop and articulate a clearer set of purposes than any they have yet generated.

THE END OF NEGATIVISM.   An early casualty of the search for a national purpose will be the easy negativism of much American policy. No longer will America content itself with opposing those men, those nations, and those forces with which it finds itself in disagreement; policies will be formulated increasingly in affirmative terms. Difficult problems will no longer be attacked by waiting for the communists to choose a side and then moving the United States to the opposing position. Importunate leaders and governments will no longer be measured on a single cold-war yardstick, and "No!" will no longer be considered a satisfactory answer to any proposals emanating from states and governments of which Americans may disapprove. The image of the United States as a state with a peculiar genius for rejecting, denying, and disapproving will be replaced by that of a government and a people who know their own minds, seek their own goals, and reach their own decisions.

THE DOWNGRADING OF ABSTRACTIONS.   Equally critical to the clarification of national purpose will be the substantial downgrading of the set of empty abstractions that have served as the substitute for real purpose for so long. "Security," "peace," "trust," "sincerity," and all their countless elaborations have—despite their intrinsic desirability—been used in fact as pretexts for refusing to come to grips with real problems in concrete contexts. For a long time, in view of the insolubility of the problems spawned by the cold war, the formulation of American objectives in abstract terms did little harm and occasionally considerable good. But issues no longer respond to either evasion or temporizing. If the United States is not to be left hopelessly behind events, it will be obliged to cast its objectives and its goals in concrete terms that are meaningful to other states, friendly, hostile, and nonaligned alike.

THE VINDICATION OF ENDS OVER MEANS. The translation of purpose into concrete terms will require a reversal of the American preference for the elaboration of means at the expense of a discussion of ends. The means of foreign policy—action capabilities and techniques of all sorts—will lose their status as fixed points in American policy and will instead be constantly evaluated in terms of their efficacy in attaining postulated specific purposes. Foreign policy, in other words, will again emphasize the "policy decision" and will minimize the inhibitions inherent in an institutionalized (and budgeted) "program." Nor will the United States any longer be able to afford infatuations with particular techniques automatically applied to widely varying situations; neither foreign aid, "controlled escalation," military assistance, nor General Assembly votes will have any particular preferability except as any of them advances an American purpose (cast, we remember, in concrete terms) in a particular context. Only by making the ends of policy paramount can rational choices be made among the several means that are available.

THE THRESHOLD OF ACCEPTABILITY. As the generalized concept of national purpose is translated into sets of concrete goals, something will be added to the discussion that has long been absent in American foreign policy: the formulation of a minimum level of acceptability, defined as the least the United States will accept as a satisfactory outcome of a problem. Nothing more helpful to an effective policy in a dynamic environment could be suggested.

Any state, in formulating its objectives, should appreciate that the infinite number of possibilities inherent in the situation virtually guarantees that any of several outcomes is possible in the train of the action to be taken. Although its policy-makers attempt to formulate these in terms of likelihood, any unforeseen contingency may intervene to produce an unexpected outcome. Wise statesmanship allows for this and develops (independently of any other considerations) a notion of which results would be minimally acceptable, which would be unacceptable, and which would represent positive gain beyond the stipulated minimum. Necessary to this exercise, however, is the predetermined threshold of acceptability.

Much of American policy toward the communist challenge has been marked by the lack of such a determination. The United States has behaved as if the only choices open to it were total victory or total frustration. Neither in the changed set of great-power relations of the future nor in the increasing number of new kinds of problems will the United States be able any longer to dispense with this guide to decision. With the pace of change rising so high, American insistence upon complete satisfaction or indefinite stalemate would be little short of suicidal. There are too many issues clamoring for resolution and too many forces at work for any such simple dichotomy to be valid. Only by exploiting the range of outcomes between the minimum and the maximum can America succeed in turning events meaningfully to its own advantage.

MATURITY OF ACTION

Underlying and giving increased emphasis to the specific requirements that the United States must fulfill if it is to operate effectively in the world of the future is a more generalized imperative. We may phrase it as the development of a heightened maturity of international action. Only by acting with the level of purpose and courage that is implicit in the notion of *maturity* and by abandoning patterns of behavior that in an individual we could call adolescent can Americans face the troubled future with any confidence in their eventual vindication.

Maturity as a desirable emotional condition to which individuals attain is a much-discussed concept in contemporary American life; each critic, however, tends to incorporate in it such behavior characteristics as he himself finds commendable. Nothing approaching consensus as to its exact meaning can be discovered. We must, therefore, specify what we mean by the term. In this discussion, maturity of international political action demands two traits that ordinarily distinguish adults from juveniles, at least in American life: first, the capacity to make difficult decisions even though the outcome is unpredictable and could be unpleasant; second, the willingness to accept the consequences of one's own action without seeking to shift the onus of responsibility. Both these characteristics obviously bear upon the way the mass of Americans have behaved and will behave as they confront foreign-policy problems. A democratic foreign policy, to be defensible, must have optimum public performance in both areas.

We shall list and comment briefly upon a number of the components of what in the aggregate constitute maturity in our sense of the term. On none of them is the record of the United States an especially impressive one during the period since 1945; on each, marked improvement will be necessary before real progress can be made toward the achievement of American purposes. Nor are we suggesting that this list, in spite of its (perhaps illusory) specificity, is either all-inclusive or precise. It does, however, point out some directions in which American mass responses to international issues should evolve.

SELF-CONFIDENCE. Although it would be impossible to assign any absolute priorities to the several points we shall make, we would not be far in error if we placed our major emphasis on the development (or rediscovery) of self-confidence among the American people. Volumes have been written about the crisis of confidence in contemporary American life and the blind search for some external source of security and reassurance to which it has given rise. This wave of anxiety and self-doubt has had immediate and palpable foreign-policy consequences.

Americans all too often doubt the validity and the worth of the purposes they purport to seek in foreign affairs. Taking refuge in the preference for techniques to which we have already referred, they either refuse to discuss purposes at all or else turn toward vague and quasi-Utopian formulations. Lacking confidence in their alleged goals, Americans seek to pursue a policy framed without reference to *a priori* postulations of ends.

This lack of confidence extends to the actual execution of foreign policy as well. Faced by evidence that they may have underestimated their difficulties, Americans tend to react by overestimating them. Unless the problem lends itself to easy solution, it frequently is classified as insoluble. Self-doubt permeates the American approach to the challenge of communism; only a people lacking self-confidence could fear the prospect of "competitive coexistence" as actually guaranteeing an inevitable Soviet victory.

On both counts Americans must muster the self-confidence worthy of the people of a great power before they can cut a truly impressive figure on the world stage. Goals must be chosen with confidence in their intrinsic worth as well as in their ultimate attainability; international encounters must be faced with trust in the capacity of the United States either to win through to victory or to endure a defeat.

The solution, as we all realize, is not to be found at all in world affairs or in the context of American foreign policy. The root of the difficulty is within American society. The failure of confidence in the American approach to the world only reflects a mass *malaise* that permeates American life. Excuses and explanations of this phenomenon are innumerable, but with issues of survival hanging in the balance, the finespun theories of psychiatrists, social psychologists, and anthropologists do not provide any answers. The stark fact is that a successful American foreign policy requires that Americans find again within themselves the confidence in their own capacity that was once the envy of the world.

PERSISTENCE. A second characteristic of mature behavior is what we might call persistence. Americans have shown a disconcerting tendency to react to problems in one almost convulsive effort. If it succeeds, the issue is forgotten; if it fails, the problem is written off as insoluble and little thought is invested in it thereafter except to justify inaction.

The United States could well learn a lesson here from the Soviet. The USSR, once it is firmly in command of its purposes, is unremitting in the effort it puts out in pursuit of an objective. Partial victories do not induce relaxation but instead serve as a base from which to launch the next move; defeats may cause a modification in tactics but do not dampen the ardor of the search. Communist pressure is constant, probing always for a favorable opportunity to advance; retreats are tactical and seldom represent abandonment of the original goal. In this regard, Soviet policy is a model for all states—not the least for the United States.

If a goal is worth striving for, it is worth long and persistent effort; if the goal, however, is considered to be of dubious worth, persistence is no great virtue. Here again we see the strategic part played by the formulation of goals in an effective foreign policy. Unless Americans can set their goals clearly and confidently, they will continue to lack the poise and determination to pursue them with tenacity.

The world of the future, however, will place a high premium on exactly this quality of persistence. Only by persistence can policies be constantly readjusted to meet rapidly changing conditions; only by persistence can satisfactory agreements be reached. Only by keeping purposes consistently in mind can the United States keep its balance among all the conflicting forces that buffet it.

PATIENCE. Closely related to persistence is patience. We have already considered the notorious impatience of the American people; results must follow swiftly upon the heels of any action taken by the United States if frustration and disillusionment are to be avoided. Such an attitude in foreign policy is always dangerous because of the unreasonable demands it makes upon policy-makers.

Under contemporary and future conditions, the time span between action and result will be much less predictable than previously. On occasion it will be very short; often, however, a very long interval will elapse before any result emerges from an American venture, and when it appears it may not be what was hoped for in the first place. Even more galling to Americans, as the cold war continues to lose its grip on world affairs, will be the instances when no action at all is possible for the United States. All Americans can do in such a case is to wait as patiently as possible, avoiding the hasty reactions induced by frustration, until circumstances again permit effective moves.

Foreign policy, as we have often suggested in this book, is not a series of unrelated crises, each a struggle to win a victory or avoid a defeat. Instead it is an unending process of adjustment to external situations, a set of responses to a constant flow of stimuli. Total success in foreign policy is so unlikely that there is little use in planning on it; the most any people can realistically hope for is perceptible (if frequently jerky) progress toward the goals they set. Granting these apparently inescapable limits on what any state can accomplish, it would appear that a generous supply of patience is no less an indispensable requirement for Americans than for any people.

SENSE OF PROPORTION. Of great assistance in the development of sufficient patience among Americans will be a sharpened sense of proportion: an increased sensitivity to the relative importance of the various goals they may be seeking. Under bipolar cold-war conditions, American policy largely lost this ordering quality, and each issue assumed the same transcendent relevance. Defeat on any problem was interpreted as utter ignominy; victory, even on small points, was heralded as a vindication of the whole of American policy and as an augury of total future success. Any concession to Soviet demands was branded as "appeasement" and rejected categorically without any serious analysis of what the United States might obtain in return or any determination of the relative worth of the two sets of considerations.

Such a fragmentation of policy means that real negotiation is impossible, since bargaining cannot be unilateral. If the United States remains unwilling to sacrifice lesser objectives to gain greater ones, all remain equally out of reach. But even if the United States were to resolve to bargain realistically with all comers (including the USSR), no beginning could be made until a reordering of priorities was undertaken and concepts of greater and lesser centrality were applied to the many objectives of American action.

Once equipped with a reasonably clear formulation of what is critical and what is peripheral to American interest, however, the task of the policy-maker and the negotiator will become immeasurably simpler. It will be possible to discover fairly quickly if accommodation of disagreements is possible and (if the finding is affirmative) to proceed to viable agreements by following the classic maxims of diplomacy. Unless such an ordering is made, however, true maneuver will remain unattainable. The United States, on the threshold of an age in which maneuvering will again be a key to success, cannot afford to be deprived of this capability.

THE ACCEPTANCE OF RISK. We have commented on the search for security in American life. In foreign affairs during the cold-war era, it has resulted in a profound mass reluctance to assume the burden of risk inherent in any political venture. The pursuit of risk-free policies has led to the avoidance of encounter, an unwillingness to venture, and a growing immobility in the American posture.

As we have pointed out, once the cold war had been stabilized it was possible for the United States at least to avoid increasing the load of risk it was carrying by maintaining the status quo vis-à-vis the Soviet Union. Today and in the future, however, the cold-war status quo has disappeared; the new world no longer permits the United States the luxury of framing policies upon the basis of minimum risk. Action is inescapable; more chances must be taken, for the stakes are higher. Political risk—the danger of miscalculation, of failure, of frustration—is the price that the United States and its fellow states must pay for the new opportunities that are opening. When nothing can be done, success or failure are equally unlikely; any increase in the possibility of success carries with it an equally augmented cargo of dangers.

Only with a generous supply of self-confidence, persistence, and patience, and with a highly developed sense of proportion, can these increased risks be borne by Americans. There is no automatic guarantee of success in the new world any more than there was in the old, no "security" in the sense of an infallible bulwark against the consequences of failure. But no people has the right to demand an unreasonably high level of performance from its government. The ubiquity of risk and the certainty of occasional defeat are characteristics of a flexible international order, and all states must accept them. To do so, and nonetheless to press forward on behalf of national purposes, is the mark of a mature people.

REASONABLE EXPECTATIONS. The paragraph above raises one or two points that demand some further attention.

In one sense, history has played an unfortunate trick on the contemporary generation of Americans. As they read the record of accomplishment of their ancestors, Americans discover a panorama of unbroken success in international affairs. The United States, its citizens believe, has never failed in foreign policy (at least in a major way) and success is its natural due. Thus Americans, alone among the people of great powers, do not admit ever having experienced a real defeat; they insist that a perpetual continuation of this string of victories is no more than a minimum demand that Americans have a right to make of the world. The United States expects, in other words, to win every time. Failure can always be traced to treason or inefficiency in office and is to be met by redoubled dedication and increased commitments until America's rightful possession of the laurel wreath of triumph is confirmed anew by all comers.

This is indeed a crushing burden to load upon a government. The unfortunate consequences of such extreme expectations are clearly visible today. Public officials oversimplify, suppress, distort, and on occasion admit to having falsified reality in order to maintain an effective consensus in their search for success. Success, furthermore, today seems less a matter of the internalized satisfaction of the American people than one of the admission (preferably grudging) by foreigners that the United States has indeed won the struggle.

It seems scarcely necessary to point out that no such concept of total success in a relativistic and rapidly moving world can for long be acceptable to a mature foreign policy. Whether one chooses to call it a "sense of tragedy" or not, the fact remains that just as no individual can anticipate total success in his own endeavors throughout life, neither can any nation. Only by accepting the possibility of defeat can the American people and their government prepare themselves adequately for the future. There is no celestial or constitutional guarantee that the United States must always win its encounters. Success or failure are, to Americans as to other people, functions of the skill that the nation shows in responding to environmental conditions in a purposive and intelligent manner.

Ingredients of an Effective Policy

We now come to the crux of our discussion. We have analyzed the trends and forces that will shape the world in which American policy must be made, and we have considered the new behavior patterns that Americans and their government must adopt if the United States is not to be merely an impotent spectator of world events. There remains for us now only the task of fusing these two sets of considerations and producing our estimate of the ingredients of an effective foreign policy for the United States.

We will divide our discussion of what American foreign policy should be and—hopefully—will be, into four parts. In the first we shall list the general characteristics of American policy. In the second we shall examine the nature of the relations between the United States and the other great powers. In the third we shall generalize about the American response to the challenge of the non-Western world. In the fourth we shall consider the changing role of international organization in American policy. Out of our discussion will perhaps develop something of a synthesis.

GENERAL CHARACTERISTICS

What kind of a foreign policy will be needed by the United States in the years ahead? Our first answer must be given in general terms. Above and beyond the discovery of solutions to specific problems, American foreign policy must consistently demonstrate a set of basic characteristics different from those marking the moves made by the United States during the 1950's. Here we shall attempt to list at least the most important features of such a different approach to international affairs.

Before examining our list in detail, however, we should anticipate at least two of the criticisms to which it might well be subject. In the first place, it is composed of abstractions and thus must always be susceptible to conflicting interpretations by friendly or hostile critics. Second, it is by no means peculiar to the situation of the United States, but instead represents the aspirations of every people as they frame and execute foreign policy. Neither of these points, however, need concern us unduly. Exactly what any of our preferred characteristics means in practice may be impossible to determine absolutely; what is more important, however, is that each is a legitimate goal at which to aim and a standard by which to evaluate performance. Nor is it particularly relevant that all states seek to demonstrate these same characteristics, except that it suggests the argument that the United States would indeed be well served to develop a policy that the other members of the international system would consider worthy of emulation.

IMAGINATION.   The first necessary characteristic of American policy is imagination. For a nation that has dreamed great dreams and worked near-miracles in realizing them, recent American foreign policy has been far out of character. Much of the response of the United States has been all too predictable; far too little has involved the exploration of new channels, the exploitation of new opportunities, or the advocacy of new ideas. Strategy may indeed be, as the mathematicians tell us, inherently conservative rather than innovative; this is not synonymous, however, with the abandonment of creativity and the acceptance of the uninspired and the routine.

American policy should consciously seek to broaden its intellectual horizons. New approaches should be actively sought, old limitations should be consciously overstepped. The increasing complexity and fluidity of the international order should not be blindly denied or fled from in fear but should instead be enthusiastically welcomed as offering a broader stage and freer play for the national imagination. Other states, and especially the communists, have already made their peace with the new world; the United States cannot dare to do less.

The United States, in other words, should consciously seek out new, untried, and unexpected responses and, when a choice is open between an imaginative approach and one that has been tested and found wanting, the decision should be in favor of novelty. Assumptions, objectives, and techniques alike should feel the impact of this heightened imaginativeness. At the very least, it will go far to restore movement to the United States; at best, it could contribute to the breakthrough in foreign policy that Americans have almost despaired of accomplishing under the conditions of the cold war.

SENSITIVITY.   Sensitivity, defined here as a deepened awareness of the points of view of other states, is also a critical aspect of an improved American policy. The United States has long been accused of an inability (or worse, a deliberate refusal) to appreciate any attitudes or points of view on world affairs other than its own. America, especially among the newer states of the non-Western world, is portrayed as arrogant, overbearing, and lacking in understanding; the wide acceptance of Soviet propaganda about American motives indicates the extent to which this impression has taken hold.

With the decline in the utility of the traditional techniques of coercion, the United States will be required increasingly to rely on the free consent of other states to support its policy. This will require a much greater willingness to accommodate American policies to the wishes of others. Such adaptability can be achieved only after the United States has learned better to sense the direction and the strength of the real motivations behind the policy moves of other peoples, and the empathy necessary to work such a modification in an exclusively nationalistic preoccupation is an inescapable requirement.

Even in situations of total opposition, a greater sensitivity will strengthen the American hand. Awareness of the real motives, concerns, fears, and preoccupations of an adversary would spare American policy-makers the temptation of ascribing any disagreement to stupidity, evil intent, pernicious ideology, or flawed national character. It would also clarify the dimensions of possible dispute-settling accommodation much more quickly and easily.

DARING. In like manner, the United States stands in dire need of greater daring in its policy. This is obviously related to our earlier discussion of the burden of risk; unless the American people are willing to bear greater risks, no policy-maker will venture far from the well-trodden and familiar path.

Why is daring so essential? Primarily because only by exploiting each situation to the full can maximum advantage be gained, and no less of a margin of success is adequate to the United States. No state can move forward in international affairs that confines itself to those courses of action the outcomes of which are fully predictable; no state can do any more than hold its own if it concentrates on neutralizing threats and ignores affirmative action. The United States must regularly launch policies with a sizeable element of unpredictability about them, and trust to its ability to capitalize on dynamic forces to maximize its success.

We are not recommending that American officials gamble recklessly with the nation's security or survival. Foolhardiness is not the appropriate antidote to an overcautious policy. But the dichotomy between a safe policy and a dangerous one is false; there is always risk in any action at all, and in inaction as well. What we are arguing for here is a clearheaded acceptance of the burden of risk and a willingness to increase it if the possible rewards justify such a course. Some such daring enterprises may, of course, fail, and defeat will be no easier than ever to bear; the most a venturesome policy can hope for is an increasing margin of positive success that will outweigh the failures. Yet the alternative of increased caution and minimal risk does not offer even as attractive a prospect. The United States cannot evade the necessity of daring more to win more.

RESTRAINT. What we have been saying about daring should be taken in context with a corresponding emphasis on restraint. Again, we must be scrupulous not to overinterpret our term; restraint here does not mean a narrow conservatism of thought and action, rather a wholesome understanding of the limitations on American freedom of action. The United States must develop a new version of "brinkmanship"; it must avoid contenting itself with less than the most the situation permits, but must also be alert not to attempt too much.

Verbalizations of policy would profit greatly by more restraint than has been common in recent history. The United States has often sought to compensate for inadequate action by excesses of words. Loose and reckless accusations, threats, justifications, or promises serve no policy purpose and only increase the load responsible officials must carry. The less Americans say about what they are going to do, the less remains to be explained if they later fall short of their goals.

Restraint is also a useful trait in thinking about policy and in implementing decisions. It will avoid self-deception in formulating objectives, it will help confine American efforts to the object at hand, and it will prevent the dangerous error of identifying every problem with the ultimate issues of survival, security, or prestige. In action, a greater restraint will minimize the innate American tendency toward overcommitment or overreaction and will make it more likely that the strength of an American response will be more appropriate to the intensity of the stimulus.

REALISM. Finally, we may mention realism as a desirable characteristic of American policy. Here too we run the risk of being misunderstood; Americans have been exhorted to be "realistic" about foreign policy ever since 1945. Why then do we list it among the marks of the new policy the United States must develop?

As it figured in political and academic debate during the cold war, realism tended to have either of two meanings. It was frequently used as a synonym for "cynicism" as opposed to "idealism" or "morality"; its advocates urged that Americans abandon their scruples and adopt a thoroughgoing *Machtpolitik* with a heavy emphasis on military power. In its other sense, realism was contrasted with "optimism"; a "realistic" position in world affairs was held to be a pessimistic or—more elegantly—a "tragic" one. In each case "realism" purported to be a value in itself, a preferred way of judging events, and a prescription for action.

Neither of these usages is appropriate to the international order of the future or to the concerns of the United States, nor are we recommending either of them here. The politics of old-fashioned power are hopelessly out of date, and pessimism is a certain guide to American failure and eventual defeat. What we are urging on the United States in the name of realism is nothing more than an open-eyed and clearheaded acceptance of the world as it actually is and a determination to meet events on their own terms.

A realistic approach to foreign policy, therefore, will involve an appreciation of the forces at work in the world, the real range of choice open to the United States, and the actions necessary to the fulfillment of American purposes. It will eschew both the dichotomous formulation of issues and the oversimplified explanation of events; it will forsake alike the unverifiable hypothesis and the ritualistic response. Instead it will seek to relate American policy to the real world, make its major purpose the arrangement of events to the maximum American advantage, and accept gratefully even a partial victory if that is the most that can be achieved. A realistic foreign policy, in sum, is a successful foreign policy.

GREAT-POWER RELATIONS

In spite of the shifting dynamics of the international order and the growing importance of smaller states to the course of world affairs, it is apparent that the relations of the United States with the "great powers" will remain critical for an extended period. By the "great powers" we mean that small number of states that have the interest and the capability to exploit a fairly large area of freedom of international action: the United States itself, the USSR, China, Great Britain, France, and the evolving entity of "Europe." Some thought on how the United States should approach each of these would be useful.

It would, of course, be presumptuous to go into any detail in prescribing American policy, since the essence of the problem is the extent to which each of these states has the capacity to control events. The most we can do safely is to suggest certain guidelines for the United States that might serve to channel events as they arise into patterns that will serve American interests.

THE SOVIET UNION. Soviet-American relations will continue to inspire a great part of American policy, in spite of the overall decline in the relevance of the bipolar cold war to international politics. Although there is little likelihood of any major change in the American view of the struggle, a finer tuning of United States action and reaction to the Soviet threat is obviously in order.

There seems, in other words, no reason to argue for an abandonment of the philosophy of containment (as we discussed it in Chapter 8) or of the general policy framework inspired by it. The United States must assume that the Soviet is as eager and likely to attempt expansionism under the new conditions as under the old and must be in a position always to oppose, neutralize, or repel such adventures. America must, however, recognize the changing terms of the cold-war process and concentrate upon meeting the dangers in the specific terms in which they are presented rather than in those of the 1949–1954 era.

Granting the probable continuation of Soviet-American hostility, however, does not imply any necessity of its perpetuation or intensification. The United States, beset at it will be with problems in many parts of the world, must do nothing on its part deliberately to exacerbate Soviet-initiated crises. Americans have nothing to gain by worsening the climate of Soviet-American relations. At worst, such an outcome could result in total war; at best, it would be little more than a digression from more important business.

If the general tenor of Soviet approaches to the United States after 1962 should turn out to be the controlling emphasis of Moscow's American policy, certain policy imperatives become fairly clear to the United States. The Soviet Union has been talking extensively in recent years (although, we must admit, not acting especially firmly) about the desirability of an "improvement" in Soviet-American relations. It would be clearly in the American interest—and probably a relatively high-priority interest—to seize whatever opportunities the Kremlin provides and to exploit them vigorously. Indeed, the United States should go further and should grasp the initiative in seeking settlements, subjecting the Soviet Union to a barrage of constructive proposals. These should not be thought of as propaganda embarrassments to Moscow, but should be aimed at the Soviet Union's minimum range of acceptability while also guaranteeing the interests the United States judges vital.

CHINA. There has been a widespread suspicion among Americans, especially in recent years, that the major problem facing the United States in the next decades will be China. The rift between Moscow and Peking and the open Sino-American confrontation in Asia have added aspects of criticality to what had been a constant but quiescent annoyance. The development of American policy toward China that incorporates the optimum mix of caution and daring will be one of the next critical tasks facing the United States.

A basic premise of any such effort will be that the possibility of direct American influence on Chinese behavior will remain slight and that the orienting principle of the United States must be reliance on a set of supple responses to the various moves China might make. In this regard, we may accept as axiomatic the necessity of keeping China on notice that the United States will oppose any expansionist move with at least as great a vigor in Asia as in Europe, the Middle East, or Africa. Containment is probably more vital in Asia than anywhere else, at least as long as Communist China remains militant.

Beyond this essential but negative preliminary resolve, the United States should support any trace of restraint and reasonableness in China's policy.

America should work to bring the Peking regime more fully into the international order, to involve China in multilateral discussions and negotiations, and in general to dissipate both China's revolutionary fervor and the cloud of emotion that surrounds the "China problem" in American minds. Obviously no such policy is compatible with the long-standing American commitment to nonrecognition and nonadmission of mainland China to the United Nations, and an early and thorough overhaul of this position is a matter of high priority for the United States.

Deliberately to bring China onto the world stage is admittedly a risky step; we should realize, however, that a China actively engaged in world affairs in company with the other states of the world would be susceptible to moderating pressures and influences, to which she is largely immune as a near-hermit. The increasing support among neutrals for Peking's admission to the United Nations also raises the danger of eventual defeat for the United States on this issue, a possibility to be avoided if at all possible. What the United States requires with regard to China is primarily room for maneuver instead of the straitjacket of the 1950's; a more flexible policy could hardly be less productive than the former one, and might indeed be much more effective.

GREAT BRITAIN.   The problems inherent in Anglo-American relations are of a different order than in the case of either the Soviet Union or China. The high degree of coincidence in British and American interests can be expected to continue; the partnership, and the "special relationship" on which it is based, will retain much of its vigor. The difficulties in Anglo-American relations stem not so much from policy differences as from the growing disparity in power and capability between the two allies. Britain's worsening world position, its military weakness, its recurrent economic crises, and its ambivalent attitude toward Europe all react unfavorably on the substance of Anglo-American policy. Today, although it is obviously an exaggeration to claim that London is in any way a "satellite" of Washington, it is unfortunately true that virtually nowhere in the world can Britain play an unequivocally independent role. Allies, neutrals, and adversaries alike tend to view London as no more than a puppet of the United States, and British policy is generally accepted as a surrogate for American policy. How long the United States can continue to maintain as effective a working relationship as it has in the past under these conditions is no better than an open question.

FRANCE.   As we suggested in an earlier chapter, Franco-American relations are a relatively new dimension of great-power confrontation. From its status as a key junior ally of the United States, France has quite quickly metamorphosed into a rival and even an adversary of American policy in many parts of the world. In some American circles, journalistic and official, there has been a tendency to think in terms of "coercing" France until Paris is brought to appreciate the folly of its independent course. Yet this counsel of irrationality and despair has not yet been accepted as a basis of action and very probably will never be. The United States faces a complex situation in its future relations with France, one that will not yield either to nostalgic evocation of the "good old days" of the early 1950's when France never obstructed American designs in Europe or to stern lectures on the necessity of a common front against the dangers of communism. France is now an independent variable in the international political equation and must be dealt with on those terms.

EUROPE.   What will be the American approach to the nascent political entity we have called "Europe"? Here we dare not be overly specific, since the final shape of integrated Europe has not yet been determined.

We may assume, however, that the new Europe will almost certainly be a powerful world force for stability. This almost dictates a close American relationship, perhaps even more intimate than that prevailing during the cold war. Detailed political and military arrangements will, of course, change; NATO as presently constituted will certainly be drastically modified. But new lines of association appropriate to the altered circumstances will appear. A self-energizing Europe with an adequate power base of its own will prove a far more effective partner of the United States than has the nationalistic mélange of the post-1945 period. The United States must not allow the inevitable outbursts of "anti-Americanism" among Europeans to divert it from the early establishment of the bases of this firm relationship.

THE NON-WESTERN WORLD

The non-Western world is of critical importance to contemporary and future international relations and to the foreign policy of the United States. We have already made many specific suggestions about the course American action should take. All that remains to be done here is to characterize broadly the policy emphases that must be built into American efforts to deal with the new forces loose in the non-Western world.

EMPATHY.   The United States, in the first place, must call upon all its capacity for empathy in dealing with the non-Western world. It must make a massive effort not only to understand the concerns of these peoples but to identify itself with them. These states simply do not accept all the values of international life that are almost self-evident to Americans. They are, on the other hand, quite explicit about what they want and not overly discriminating about who gives it to them. Unless the United States is prepared to forego any influence over two-thirds of the human race—as obviously it is not—it must somehow persuade itself that concerns of the non-Western world are legitimate, worthy, and deserving of support.

PEACEFUL ORIENTATION.   The non-Western states demand that the United States not only profess peaceful intentions but that it also move concretely toward the achievement of peace. Any increase in American cold-war militancy produces strongly hostile reactions in the non-West; the affirmative response to each peaceful gesture the United States makes is equally clear. At least three major issues of American policy are viewed in this context as tests of the peaceful intent of the United States: disarmament, accommodation with the USSR, and alliance policy. American judgments can no longer analyze these and other problems of like import solely in the familiar power-politics categories, but must allow for the impact of non-Western opinion.

ECONOMIC AID.   Economic and development assistance—with no political strings—is another of the minimum demands the non-Western states make of the United States. Considering the strength of the mass urge for development and the already demonstrated willingness of these states to ignore cold-war lines in seeking assistance, there seems no way for the United States to avoid reasonably large programs of economic aid for many years. Much of the strain on American emotions could be eliminated, however, if certain regions were ruled out of the cold war and all aid (from whatever national source) were funneled through the United Nations. There is some reason to believe that some such technique will eventually prove attractive to the USSR as well. We already know that the non-Western states themselves would prefer it.

STATUS.   In the last analysis, the non-Western world looks for a set of status symbols of equality as its credentials of full membership in the international system. No real international stability is possible until these states have reached satisfaction in deference values. Here the United States has a real opportunity open before it.

If American policy can escape the twin dangers of patronizing on the one hand or fawning upon the non-Western states on the other, a viable basis for lasting understanding can be built. The approach of the United States must display dignity, sensitivity, and firmness; neither an obvious sense of guilt toward them nor a proclivity to pass irritating verdicts of unsophistication or lack of understanding of communist wiles can do any more than further complicate relationships. Deference of the correct sort—if fitted into a carefully conceived and well-executed policy—is among the easiest forms of aid for the United States to give to the non-Western world, yet none would be more certain of producing rapid and beneficial political consequences.

INTERNATIONAL ORGANIZATION

Not the least important of the characteristics of the new international environment is its increasing organization. A larger part than ever of the total foreign-policy effort of the United States will be expended in evaluating these organizations as situational factors, in devising stratagems for use within the various bodies, and in participating in the several cooperative enterprises undertaken by international organizations.

Here we examine only three of the many facets of American policy toward (and within) international organization: first, the role of international organization as a conditioning factor in United States foreign policy; second, the place of the United Nations in the broad purview of American policy; third, the evolving issue of the United States vis-à-vis supranational organization.

INTERNATIONAL ORGANIZATION AS A CONDITIONING FACTOR. The great increase in the number and elaborateness of international organizations has created a markedly different environment for American policy-makers. In the first place, the Wilsonian dream of a world public opinion capable of being focused on specific international issues has already been realized. This will increasingly serve both as a limiting factor on American policy and as a powerful ally when it is enlisted on the American side. Second, international organizations of all types constitute in the aggregate an impressive array of alternative techniques of action, frequently more productive of results under contemporary conditions than the classic unilateral approach; the range of American choice is broadened accordingly. Third, international organization has made multilateral contacts the most useful and normal vehicle of negotiation. "Conference diplomacy," with its unique advantages and its inevitable complexities, will increasingly become a routine political technique. The new organizations can thus be seen to have played a major part in the creation of the different environment of world politics which we have projected.

THE UNITED NATIONS AND AMERICAN POLICY. We can be fairly precise in forecasting the elements of American approaches to the United Nations, since the controlling trends have already been operative for some years.

In the first place, more and more of United States policy will be funneled through United Nations channels. Not only obviously political-diplomatic matters but (and perhaps especially) the increasing family of so-called "non-political" issues as well will find their most propitious climate in the United Nations. Second, the increasing share of American attention demanded by United Nations matters will tend strongly toward the eventual minimization of the cold-war side of American policy; the inhospitability of the United Nations (particularly the General Assembly) to cold-war questions is already apparent. Third, operating in the United Nations and sharing in the construction of a very broad consensus will induce a more pronounced American preference for accommodation and honorable compromise as the preferred method of adjusting differences between states. Fourth, what remains of the influence of pure military power over world affairs will almost certainly come to rest in United Nations hands (as the only safe place for it to be). This will reinforce the first three factors mentioned and throw the United States even more directly into the United Nations arena as it searches for the most efficacious technique for the maximization of its interests.

We must not suppose that the new posture of the United States toward the United Nations will be greeted with total enthusiasm by all Americans. It is galling, so soon after the United States has attained full international status, to face a future marked by serious limitations on action and by the constant problem of adjusting to an unstable consensus. Yet, whether or not the United States is happy about the prospects, there seems little likelihood of any escape; the United Nations may well become the most important single factor influencing American foreign policy.

SUPRANATIONAL GOVERNMENT. We have said very little about the possibility of American entry into some supranational organization. It has never been a real issue before the United States. As international interdependence grows, however, and as the logic of some of the positions of the United States becomes more compelling, the question will be posed much more insistently.

It will probably present itself first in the context of the "Atlantic community": a merger (at least for certain economic, political, and possibly military purposes) of the states of western Europe with the United States and Canada. Brought to a new pitch after 1959 by the European moves toward a common market and the pressure on the United States to affiliate with it, the question can no longer be indefinitely evaded. Other possible federative enterprises, either regional or functional, that might involve the United States are of much less immediate impact.

What should the United States do? There is no virtue in supranational federation for its own sake; neither, however, is there any overriding significance (other than emotional) in the national state system. As Americans ponder the question in the future, their most reliable guide in particular choice situations can only be their basic national interest. In other words, if adherence to a supranational grouping is the most effective step open toward peace, order, and stability, then the step should be taken quickly and firmly. If, however, some other choice seems more promising, or even if the choice is not clear, membership should not be accepted. The irrevocable character of a transfer of sovereignty argues strongly in favor of making the move only in clear cases. Nevertheless, the trends in world affairs all run in the direction of increasing the attractiveness of supranational organizations; the United States must remain alert to discover and act upon opportunities as they arise.

The Foreign Policy of the American People

Now, at last, we come to our final discussion, and it is appropriate to end our study with what may be the central issue of American foreign policy: the ability of the democratic process to generate decisions and actions adequate to the expanded role of the United States. This is a basic and necessary inquiry. Twenty years of constant effort, great expense, and not a little bloodshed by Americans have not produced any clear or even persuasive affirmative answer. Indeed, the prevailing mood in the United States in the mid-1960's is, if anything, a conditionally negative one.

This brief analysis is not intended to provide a final answer. In it, however, we shall raise one or two questions in the hope that their discussion will throw some light on the larger concern. Definitive solutions, of course, must wait upon the verdict of history.

THE OBLIGATIONS OF DEMOCRACY

Democracy has long been known to be the form of government most difficult either to defend in theoretical terms or to operate efficiently in the real world, but it is also the system that has had the firmest grip on the imaginations of political men everywhere. In the last two decades in the United States it has often been argued that, however useful democratic processes might be in domestic affairs, they are pernicious and dangerous in foreign policy. Although usually cloaked in a pro-democratic guise, this is really a vicious antidemocratic argument, for if a system of government cannot meet its greatest challenges it is obviously doomed. This book has argued the opposite position throughout that democracy can produce satisfactory foreign-policy decisions. There is no need to go through the entire exegesis; one or two points can suffice to illustrate both the principle and its dangers.

THE RELATIONSHIP BETWEEN GOVERNMENT AND PEOPLE. As we discussed in an earlier chapter, the working relationship between a people and their government is the crucial variable in democracy. In foreign policy, it is essential that the general public understand its role in terms of both its imperatives and its inhibitions. A public that refuses to play its value-formulating, direction-setting, and parameter-establishing function is not only abdicating its democratic responsibilities but also making the task of its leaders all but impossible. Equally destructive is a mass opinion that steps out of its proper place and attempts to dominate official decision on matters of detail, either by insisting on a particular course of action or by absolutely forbidding it. The responsibilities of government in this context are equally clear: to treat the public as its master, to deal honestly, candidly, and maturely with private opinion, and to accept the additional roles of education and leadership with good grace and public spirit.

It is not captious to conclude that in many respects the relationship between government and people is not at its best in the United States today. Much of the public—especially the better-informed, serious segment—is substantially disenchanted with officials of the government and tends to assume that Washington is not dealing candidly with its own constituency. Many government officials profess disdain, suspicion, and contempt for private opinion on international questions. The general climate is one of hostile neutrality, and the overall effort of the United States in world affairs suffers markedly as a result.

THE TYRANNY OF CONSENSUS. One distortion of the relationship between government and the public merits particular attention. This is the official fixation, so obvious during the middle years of the 1960's, with "consensus" as the goal of government policy. Consensus, we must recall, means not agreement upon a particular line of foreign-policy effort but rather support of a single President and his administration; this is most commonly measured by a public-opinion pollster asking: "Do you approve of the way President So-and-so is doing his job?"

On this basis, any policy that keeps the consensus percentage sufficiently high is deemed a good one, whereas any policy that reduces the percentage of support (or even threatens to do so) is a bad one and is usually rejected out of hand. Since consensus also relies so heavily upon uninformed mass attitudes, policy tends to be cast in terms of simple, emotional, and action-oriented concepts comprehensible to the least common denominator of opinion. Thus, almost by definition, major issues of policy tend to be oversimplified, dichotomized, and reduced to an unsubtle choice between absolutes of moral good and evil.

This raises the possibility that a policy that is "popular" with mass consensus can be pursued past the point of no return to the moment of absolute danger with little serious consideration of possible alternatives. At this crucial instant, the government runs the risk of being literally trapped between the consensual juggernaut it has created (and benefitted from) and the inexorabilities of the operative environment. This unenviable position would, on its face, confirm all the pejorative judgments passed on the future of democracy.

THE CRISIS OF DEMOCRATIC LEADERSHIP. This sort of disaster, however, does not have to be. It is a truism of democracy that a people may on occasion act less maturely and responsibly than their government expects them to, but they can never surpass official expectations. This is to say that if Washington expects a level of public conduct marked by unsophistication, emotionalism, and slogan-mongering, that is exactly what the government will receive. If, however, the government's spokesmen show that they expect—even that they demand—serious, mature, and reflective behavior from the popular mass, at the very least the overall level of thought and action will rise perceptibly and on occasion will surprise (pleasantly) the responsible public officials. No more convincing proof of this thesis can be advanced than the public reaction to President Kennedy's "fresh look" approach during the summer of 1963, particularly with reference to the limited nuclear test-ban treaty that was the major issue of those months. On this occasion, the overall tenor of public response justified even the most optimistic evaluations of the vigor of democracy.

The lesson seems clear: In foreign policy especially, the level and the quality of public participation in the policy process lie in the keeping of officialdom. The President and his associates can determine whether public dialogue is puerile and cliché-ridden or broad-gauged and sophisticated. On this distinction much of the long-term prospect for the survival of democratic values may well depend.

THE INTERNALIZATION OF PURPOSE

A second problem particularly apposite to America of the 1960's is what we can call here the "internalization of purpose" in American foreign policy. This is to say that a large portion of the overall foreign-policy effort of the United States is aimed less at the creation (or preservation) of states-of-affairs in the real world judged to be in the national interest (the standard definition of an objective of policy) than at the satisfaction of certain powerful but ill-defined internal urges and drives in the American body politic. The United States, in other words, is less interested in achieving desirable outcomes of particular problems than it is in proving the truth of certain propositions— ideological and operational alike—about itself. Again, this development is a very disturbing one to those who hope for a foreign policy for America appropriate to its world position.

AMERICAN SELF-DOUBTS. The difficulty begins with the crisis of self-confidence in American life and policy of which we have already taken note. Gone is the nineteenth-century sublime faith in the ultimate destiny of the nation that for so long marked the American point of view; gone also, for that matter, is the smug apathy of the early twentieth century that enabled Americans to look on Europe's major wars as "none of our affair." In their places we find today instead a widespread anxiety, a lack of faith in either the capacity of the nation to devise workable policy or the national will to carry it through. Deprived of the internal evaluative machinery by which to measure its own behavior, the United States naturally enough has developed an almost obsessive concern with what other states—especially hostile ones— think of American policy and American conduct. To judge by public statements of much recent leadership, it is more important that communist dictators disapprove of American moves than it is that Americans—public and private —approve.

This is an overstatement, of course. The situation is not as serious as it is sketched out above. Yet it would be a brave man indeed who would deny the entire charge and claim that Americans and their government today are sure either of the principles on which they base their action or of the goals they are seeking to achieve. To the extent to which this indictment has validity, therefore, it is a serious one and also one which must sooner or later be faced.

THE SEARCH FOR REASSURANCE. To make the argument clearer, we may put it this way: The United States today seeks psychic reassurance as the major result of its foreign policy. Washington professes to fear that communists think the United States is a "paper tiger" and attempts to prove its virility in terms comprehensible not to the enemy but to the American public. The United States today is much concerned about its reputation for "keeping its commitments," although no one seriously accuses the United States of being a breaker of promises. "Victory," to an insecure people, demands that the enemy openly, overtly, and unmistakably be defeated—and admit it; there is no pleasure in winning unless the adversary acknowledges himself vanquished. Many other examples of this concern with winning reassurance from the outside world that America's tarnished self-image is as glorious as ever—in spite of national suspicions to the contrary—could be cited, but the point has already been adequately made.

Even a modest amount of psychological insight leads one to the conclusion that the world can never think better of a person (or a nation) than he thinks of himself; the search for psychic reassurance from outsiders to quiet internal doubts is intrinsically futile. As long as Americans insist that foreigners be kinder to them than they are to themselves, the frustration factor so obvious in contemporary American foreign policy will remain operative. All a successful foreign policy can do for a nation is to rearrange matters in the real world more to its satisfaction than would otherwise have been the case. Foreign policy cannot by itself generate a workable standard of satisfaction nor make up by external action for whatever internal traumas are distressing the society.

PRESTIGE AND "IMAGE." Two special applications of the search for reassurance and the internalization of purpose should be cited: the national concern with America's prestige and with its world "image."

Discussion of prestige in the context of American policy tends to be narrowly zero-sum: That is to say, American prestige can increase only to the extent that some other country's decreases—and vice versa. Thus any prestige "gains" for the United States must be at some other country's expense; in the space race, the opponent has been the Soviet Union, whereas in Europe it has recently been France. A "high" prestige factor is widely thought to be a major source of reassurance, and if Americans can win enough "victories" in prestige at the expense of enough opponents, the entire nation will feel gratified. Once again, it seems that the whole matter is complicated by the internalized orientation of prestige: Americans want to rank high in exactly those aspects of national life in which they feel they rank low and tend to ignore those points on which the world already rates the United States high as not being the major ones.

The issue of "image" is cut from the same cloth. What Americans mean when they speak of "projecting a favorable image" is that they hope that foreigners will see America as Americans would like it to be seen. But American propaganda—official and unofficial, deliberate and unintentional—can never be believed abroad unless the American people themselves accept it as a true reflection of their beliefs. As we observed above, the world will never think better of Americans than they do of themselves.

Before the United States can persuade others, it must first persuade itself. Before the audience for American propaganda can be made broader and more sympathetic, the United States must develop a purpose, a maturity, and a flexibility in keeping with its aspirations and its heritage. Let Americans, in a word, decide what they want and let them resolve to grapple with their problems with good sense, goodwill, and high devotion; the problem of projecting the appropriate image will then solve itself.

The world image of the United States is seriously blurred today. In the years to come the United States will need as sharp and well-focused an image as possible, both to guide itself and as a technique of communicating with other peoples. The discovery of its ingredients and the dedication to its principles is an imperative of American foreign policy; it will be the real measure of the success or failure of the United States. No greater or fairer test of the survival value of American democracy could be devised.

THE MEANING OF "WORLD LEADERSHIP"

One of the basic concepts that has seriously affected the workings of the policy process in the United States since 1945 has been the ideal of the "world leadership" role the American people have been called on to play. Because it is so inextricably bound up today with the problems of a democratic foreign policy and the internalization of American purpose, it furnishes an appropriate final point of departure for this discussion.

THE AMERICAN PEOPLE AND "WORLD LEADERSHIP." We already know that the broad range of responsibility implicit in the status of a "leader" was accepted only reluctantly by the American people after 1945. Indeed, after twenty years the semantics of self-evaluation popular in the United States are still based on such ideas as "history called," "the United States was forced," "the needs of mankind," and the like, all of which stress the involuntary nature of America's role of leadership. As Americans see themselves, in pursuing their vocation of world leadership they are the most reluctant of dragons.

Yet candor forces us to admit that the United States, for all its pose of unwillingness, has come to enjoy the status—if not the burdens—of the leader's role. If we may judge by the vigor with which Washington resists any attempt at a breakaway by any member of the free-world complex, Americans are convinced today that their responsibility for the security and the well-being of all men is not only inevitable but permanent. "Leadership" in this context is to be distinguished from "hegemony," of course; the United States, its citizens insist, is not a hegemonic or dominating power. America leads only for the good of all and devotes its resources unselfishly to the betterment of the lot of all peace-loving and law-abiding peoples.

THE FAILURE OF AMERICAN LEADERSHIP. In view of this lofty (and, we must admit, perfectly sincere) American image of the nature of leadership, it is a distressing fact that American leadership is failing—or at least is showing signs of incipient failure—in the contemporary era. American policy has not overawed the communist world, has not captured the imagination or the support of the nonaligned world, and is being resisted, repudiated, and defied in every organized alliance system of the free world. Repeated and sententious verbalizations by American officials of the central role of the United States in world affairs tend increasingly to be greeted by reactions ranging from indifference and tolerance to undisguised amusement, tempered only by a constant fear of the destructive capacity of American military might. Americans are fond of saying that they do not wish to be loved by foreigners, only respected. Today they are neither.

The crux of the matter is found in the concept of leadership that has grown up in the United States during the past two decades. As the free world grew in organization and rigidity during the 1950's, the United States came to look upon this enormous structure as an instrument of American policy, to be used by Washington for American purposes. No qualms were felt about this arrogation to themselves of the policy and power of all their allies, for Americans were certain that their policy was framed in the true interests of all and was therefore constructively synonymous with free-world policy—or at least with what free-world policy should be and would be if all the allies were as well-informed, well-intentioned, and capable as was the United States.

This identity of American interests with the interests of all was never as self-evident or as widely accepted by the allies as Americans expected it to be. From the very beginning, therefore, the associates of the United States exerted themselves to act independently, and in the mid-1960's the results are clear to see. The American leadership function in world affairs is today little more than a shadow of its former pretensions; in moments of crisis the United States is increasingly finding itself alone. The American public, furthermore, is at a loss to know what to do about it.

THE TRUE TASK OF LEADERSHIP. Leadership, we may remind ourselves, is not at all a lonely status. By its very nature it is a collective operation, because leaders must have followers. Furthermore, the leader-follower relationship (unlike the satellite-hegemonic power relationship) is voluntary. It is based upon a common perception of purpose and an explicit agreement upon objectives and procedures. The leader, in a word, is as much the creature of his followers as he is their master.

The crisis in American leadership today is the outcome of the fulfillment or the obsolescence of the original consensus that created the free world. The old structure and dynamics of American leadership have been rendered out of date by the new conditions of international affairs. At this point, we may oversimplify the issue by suggesting that the United States has only two viable choices open to it: either to attempt to impose its will upon its erstwhile associates—that is, to play the part of a hegemonic power—or else painfully to construct a new basis for true leadership. Put this way, it would seem that only one of the two courses is at all attractive to Americans.

American leadership can be reestablished in many parts of the world on a viable basis only by the discovery of a new consensus. When once again the United States meaningfully identifies itself with the operative purposes of free men and free governments and builds its policy upon common action aimed at shared goals, questions of the status and the role of the leader will substantially answer themselves. Nor does such a course run counter to any innate and basic American interests; it has been the essence of American policy that the United States is safe and prosperous only when the world is also safe and prosperous. The task facing the United States today is that of finding a way to give convincing expression to this preoccupation under the conditions that will prevail throughout the remainder of this century.

Recommended Readings

This reading list is highly selective. To include all the books of relevance and interest to a student of American foreign policy would require a list covering approximately as many pages as there are in this book. What follows here is a list whose selection of titles is based on at least one of the following criteria: unique relevance to the thesis of this study; major significance and lasting impact on the study and/or practice of American diplomacy; recent publication and promise of future importance.

Acheson, Dean, *Power and Diplomacy*. Cambridge, Mass.: Harvard University Press, 1958.

Almond, Gabriel, *The American People and Foreign Policy*. New York: Harcourt, Brace & World, Inc., 1950.

———, and James S. Coleman, eds., *The Politics of Developing Areas*. Princeton, N.J.: Princeton University Press, 1960.

Apter, David E., ed., *Ideology and Discontent*. New York: Free Press of Glencoe, Inc., 1964.

Aron, Raymond, *The Century of Total War*. Garden City, N.Y.: Doubleday & Company, Inc., 1954.

———, *The Great Debate*. Garden City, N.Y.: Doubleday & Company, Inc., 1965.

Beloff, Max, *Foreign Policy and the Democratic Process*. Baltimore: Johns Hopkins University Press, 1955.

Bemis, Samuel Flagg, *A Diplomatic History of the United States* (5th ed.). New York: Holt, Rinehart & Winston, Inc., 1965.

Black, Cyril E., and Thomas P. Thornton, eds., *Communism and Revolution*. Princeton, N.J.: Princeton University Press, 1964.

Black, Joseph E., and Kenneth W. Thompson, *Foreign Policies in a World of Change*. New York: Harper & Row, Publishers, 1963.

Bowles, Chester, *Ideas, People and Peace*. New York: Harper & Row, Publishers, 1958.

———, *The New Dimensions of Peace*. New York: Harper & Row, Publishers, 1955.

Brodie, Bernard, *Strategy in the Missile Age*. Princeton, N.J.: Princeton University Press, 1959.

Brzezinski, Zbigniew, and Samuel P. Huntington, *Political Power: USA/USSR*. New York: Frederick A. Praeger, Inc., 1962.

Buchan, Alastair, *NATO in the 1960's*. New York: Frederick A. Praeger, Inc., 1963.

Byrnes, James F., *Speaking Frankly*. New York: Harper & Row, Publishers, 1947.

Carleton, William G., *The Revolution in American Foreign Policy: Its Global Range*. New York: Random House, Inc., 1963.

Claude, Inis L., *Swords into Plowshares*. New York: Random House, Inc., 1959.

Crabb, Cecil V., Jr., *The Elephants and the Grass: A Study of Nonalignment*. New York: Frederick A. Praeger, Inc., 1965.

Crankshaw, Edward, *The New Cold War: Moscow vs. Peking*. Baltimore: Penguin Books, Inc., 1963.

Dahl, Robert, *Congress and Foreign Policy*. New York: Harcourt, Brace & World, Inc., 1950.

Dallin, Alexander, *The Soviet Union at the United Nations*. New York: Frederick A. Praeger, Inc., 1962.

De Conde, Alexander, *The American Secretary of State*. New York: Frederick A. Praeger, Inc., 1962.

De Visscher, Charles, *Theory and Reality in Public International Law*. Translated by P. E. Corbett. Princeton, N J.: Princeton University Press, 1957.

Dulles, John Foster, *War or Peace*. New York: The Macmillan Company, 1957.

Elliott, William Y., *et al.*, *The Political Economy of American Foreign Policy*. New York: Holt, Rinehart & Winston, Inc., 1955.

Etzioni, Amitai, *Winning Without War*. Garden City, N.Y.: Doubleday & Company, Inc., 1964.

Fainsod, Merle, *How Russia Is Ruled*. Cambridge, Mass.: Harvard University Press, 1963.

Feis, Herbert, *Foreign Aid and Foreign Policy*. New York: St. Martin's Press, Inc., 1964.

Finletter, Thomas K., *Foreign Policy: The Next Phase, the 1960's*. New York: Harper & Row, Publishers, 1960.

Fromm, Erich, *May Man Prevail?* Garden City, N.Y.: Doubleday & Company, Inc., 1961.

Fulbright, J. William, *Old Myths and New Realities*. New York: Random House, Inc., 1964.

Gardner, Richard N., *In Pursuit of World Order: United States Foreign Policy and International Organization*. New York: Frederick A. Praeger, Inc., 1964.

Griffith, Ernest S., *Congress: Its Contemporary Role* (3d ed.). New York: New York University Press, 1960.

Griffith, William E., *The Sino-Soviet Rift*. Cambridge, Mass.: Massachusetts Institute of Technology Press, 1964.

Gross, Feliks, *Foreign Policy Analysis*. New York: Philosophical Library, Inc., 1954.

Halle, Louis J., *Civilization and Foreign Policy*. New York: Harper & Row, Publishers, 1955.

Halperin, Morton H., *Limited War in the Nuclear Age*. New York: John Wiley & Sons, Inc., 1963.

Haviland, H. Field, Jr., *et al.*, *The Formulation and Administration of United States Foreign Policy*. Washington, D.C.: The Brookings Institution, 1960.

Heilbroner, Robert L., *The Great Ascent*. New York: Harper & Row, Publishers, 1963.

Herz, John, *International Politics in the Atomic Age*. New York: Columbia University Press, 1959.

Hull, Cordell, *The Memoirs of Cordell Hull*, 2 vols. New York: The Macmillan Company, 1948.

Huntington, Samuel P., *Changing Patterns of Military Politics*. New York: Free Press of Glencoe, Inc., 1962.

———, *The Common Defense: Strategic Programs in National Politics*. New York: Columbia University Press, 1961.

Irish, Marian D., ed., *World Pressures on American Foreign Policy*. Englewood Cliffs, N.J.: Prentice-Hall, Inc., 1964.

Jackson, Henry M., ed., *The Secretary of State and the Ambassador*. New York: Frederick A. Praeger, Inc., 1964.

Kahn, Herman, *On Escalation: Metaphors and Scenarios*. New York: Frederick A. Praeger, Inc., 1965.

———, *On Thermonuclear War*. Princeton, N.J.: Princeton University Press, 1960.

Kaplan, Morton, *System and Process in International Politics*. New York: John Wiley & Sons, Inc., 1957.

Kautsky, John H., ed., *Political Change in the Underdeveloped Countries: Nationalism and Communism*. New York: John Wiley & Sons, Inc., 1962.

Kennan, George F., *American Diplomacy, 1900–1950*. Chicago: University of Chicago Press, 1951.

———, *Realities of American Foreign Policy*. Princeton, N.J.: Princeton University Press, 1955.

————, *Russia and the West Under Lenin and Stalin.* New York: New American Library of World Literature, Inc., 1961.

————, *Russia, the Atom and the West.* London: Oxford University Press, 1958.

Kissinger, Henry A., *The Necessity for Choice.* New York: Harper & Row, Publishers, 1961.

————, *Nuclear Weapons and Foreign Policy.* New York: Harper & Row, Publishers, 1957.

————, *The Troubled Partnership.* New York: McGraw-Hill Book Company, 1965.

Knorr, Klaus, *Limited Strategic War.* New York: Frederick A. Praeger, Inc., 1965.

————, ed., *NATO and American Security.* Princeton, N.J.: Princeton University Press, 1959.

Laqueur, Walter, and Leopold Labedz, *Polycentrism.* New York: Frederick A. Praeger, Inc., 1962.

Lefever, Ernest, ed., *Arms and Arms Control.* New York: Frederick A Praeger, Inc., 1962.

Lippmann, Walter, *The Public Philosophy.* Boston: Little, Brown and Company, 1955.

Liska, George, *The New Statecraft: Foreign Aid in American Foreign Policy.* Chicago: University of Chicago Press, 1960.

Marshall, Charles B., *The Limits of Foreign Policy.* New York: Holt, Rinehart & Winston, Inc., 1954.

Morgenstern, Oskar, *The Question of National Defense.* New York: Random House, Inc., 1959.

Morgenthau, Hans J., *In Defense of the National Interest.* New York: Alfred A. Knopf, Inc., 1951.

————, *The Purpose of American Politics.* New York: Alfred A. Knopf, Inc., 1960.

Newman, James R., *The Rule of Folly.* New York: Simon and Schuster, Inc., 1962.

Nicholas, Herbert G., *The United Nations as a Political Institution.* London: Oxford University Press, 1963.

Osgood, Robert E., *Ideals and Self-Interest in America's Foreign Relations.* Chicago: University of Chicago Press, 1952.

Padelford, Norman J., and Leland M. Goodrich, eds., *The United Nations in the Balance.* New York: Frederick A. Praeger, Inc., 1965.

Perkins, Dexter, *The American Approach to Foreign Policy.* Cambridge, Mass.: Harvard University Press, 1952.

Price, Don K., ed., *The Secretary of State.* Englewood Cliffs, N.J.: Prentice-Hall, Inc., 1960.

Robinson, James A., *Congress and Foreign Policy-Making.* Homewood, Ill.: Richard D. Irwin, Inc., 1962.

Rosenau, James, *Public Opinion and Foreign Policy.* New York: Random House, Inc., 1961.

Rostow, Walt W., *The United States in the World Arena.* New York: Harper & Row, Publishers, 1960.

————, *View from the Seventh Floor.* New York: Harper & Row, Publishers, 1964.

Scalapino, Robert A., *The Communist Revolution in Asia.* Englewood Cliffs, N.J.: Prentice-Hall, Inc., 1965.

Seton-Watson, Hugh, *From Lenin to Khrushchev: The History of World Communism.* New York: Frederick A. Praeger, Inc., 1960.

Snyder, Louis L., ed., *The Dynamics of Nationalism.* Princeton, N.J.: D. Van Nostrand Co., Inc., 1964.

Snyder, Richard C., H. W. Bruck, and Burton M. Sapin, eds., *Foreign Policy Decision-Making.* New York: Free Press of Glencoe, Inc., 1962.

Sorenson, Theodore A., *Decision-Making in the White House.* New York: Columbia University Press, 1963.

Spanier, John W., *American Foreign Policy Since World War II.* New York: Frederick A. Praeger, Inc., 1965.

————, and Joseph L. Nogee, *The Politics of Disarmament.* New York: Frederick A. Praeger, Inc., 1962.

Staley, Eugene, *The Future of Underdeveloped Countries: Political Implications of Economic Development.* New York: Harper & Row, Publishers, 1961.

Steel, Ronald, *The End of Alliance.* New York: The Viking Press, Inc., 1964.

Truman, Harry S., *Year of Decisions.* Garden City, N.Y.: Doubleday & Company, Inc., 1955.

Turner, Gordon, and Richard Challener, eds., *American Strategy in the Nuclear Age.* New York: Frederick A. Praeger, Inc., 1960.

Vandenburg, Arthur W., Jr., ed., *The Private Papers of Senator Vandenburg.* Boston: Houghton Mifflin Company, 1952.

Villard, Henry S., *Affairs at State.* New York: Thomas Y. Crowell Company, 1965.

Ward, Barbara, *Policy for the West.* New York: W.W. Norton & Company, Inc., 1951.

————, *The Interplay of East and West.* New York: W. W. Norton & Company, Inc., 1957.

Wolfers, Arnold, ed., *Alliance Policy in the Cold War.* Baltimore: Johns Hopkins University Press, 1959.

Zagoria, Donald S., *The Sino-Soviet Conflict, 1956–1961.* Princeton, N.J.: Princeton University Press, 1962.

Index

371